BY CARLOS BAKER

HEMINGWAY

THE WRITER AS ARTIST

PRINCETON, NEW JERSEY

PRINCETON UNIVERSITY PRESS

1952

TO ARTHUR AND EDNA BAKER

On a Matter of Indebtedness

It would not have been possible to write this book in its present form without the kindly cooperation of a number of people. Through its president, the late Charles Scribner, the firm of Charles Scribner's Sons, Hemingway's American publishers, graciously permitted me to quote as was necessary from Mr. Hemingway's works. I owe special thanks to Mr. Scribner also for permission to examine those records which he was good enough to place at my disposal. My personal debt to Mr. Hemingway is likewise great. He patiently and generously answered certain leading questions relating to his past work while he was intensely preoccupied with the writing of a future one.

Some parts of this book were done on a grant from the Princeton University Research Committee, here very gratefully acknowledged.

For taking time from busy lives to supply certain necessary information, I have to thank Mr. Malcolm Cowley, the late Dean Christian Gauss, Mr. Archibald MacLeish, Mr. Donald Ogden Stewart, Mr. C. G. Wellington, Mr. Glenway Wescott, and Miss Ella Winter. Mr. W. L. McGeary of the *Toronto Star* performed a research job of formidable dimensions out of the goodness of his heart; I am very grateful indeed for his expenditure of time and energy, as well as for his permission to use the bibliographical materials compiled by him which appear at the end of this book. I owe also a special debt to Professor Vicente Llorens, who gave me valuable advice in connection with the chapter on *For Whom the Bell Tolls*. Mr. Stephen Parker provided welcome assistance in the preparation of the bibliography.

The staffs of the Princeton University Library, the New York Public Library, and the University of Arizona Library have been unfailingly courteous and helpful. In particular I wish to thank Mr. Frederick Cromwell, Librarian, and Mr. Jackson Carty, formerly Research Librarian, of the University of Arizona, and Messrs. Alexander Wainwright and Alexander Clark of Firestone Library, Princeton. Among many others I owe debts of gratitude to the following people for help of various kinds: Mr. Rowan Boone, Mr. and Mrs. Homer Bundy, Dr. Lyman Butterfield, Professor R. L. Cook, Mr. J. H. Cranston, Mr. F. G. Fellowes, Dr. Frank Fischer, Mrs. Kenneth Mainland, Professor Allan Macdonald, Mr. Wallace Meyer, and Mr. Lee Samuels. I have also to thank Mr. MacLeish and his publishers for permission to quote from *Actfive and other poems,* New York, Random House, 1943. Parts of chapters four and five have been published in the *Virginia Quarterly Review* and the *New York Times Book Review*. I am grateful for the courtesies extended by the editors of these publications. Finally, and for many reasons, I am indebted to my wife.

ON THE FOOTNOTES

Full citation, with place and date of publication, is usually given only in the first reference to each book. Further references use the short title, or (rarely) an abbreviation in the form of initials. Thus Gertrude Stein's *Autobiography of Alice B. Toklas*, after its first appearance, is regularly abbreviated to *ABT*.

Hemingway's letters to the author are indicated by the abbreviation *EH to CB*, with date. His letters to or from Maxwell Perkins and Fitzgerald are indicated by *EH to MP* and *EH to FSF*, or the reverse, with date or approximate date. Other letters employed are cited and dated for the record.

Full titles are used for a few of Hemingway's books. As a space-saving device, the following abbreviations have been generally used:

> *ARIT*: Across the River and Into the Trees
> *DIA*: Death in the Afternoon
> *FTA*: A Farewell to Arms
> *FWBT*: For Whom the Bell Tolls
> *GHOA*: Green Hills of Africa
> *SAR*: The Sun Also Rises
> *THAHN*: To Have and Have Not
> *FIRST 49*: The Fifth Column and the First
> Forty-Nine Stories

The last of these items, the collected short stories, has been preferred to the separate editions of the short stories for purposes of page-reference. Other references, unless otherwise indicated, are to the first American editions of Hemingway's books.

Contents

Introduction

"If I desire to pass over a part in silence," wrote Claudian in his account of Stilicho the consul, "whatever I omit will seem the most worthy to have been recorded. Shall I pursue his old exploits and early youth? His recent merits recall the mind to themselves. Shall I dwell on his justice? The glory of the warrior rises before me resplendent. Shall I relate his strength in arms? He performed yet greater things unarmed." [1]

Because this is a book about Hemingway as an artist, it contains next to nothing about his old exploits and his early youth. His strong sense of justice, like his pugnaciousness, receives only incidental consideration. There is little about his prowess as hunter or fisherman, as boxer, bullfighter, or soldier. This is not the history of his private battles or his public wars. Taken together and truly related, these would make a proper story, and in some respects a heroic one. But the time to tell that one has not yet come. It can wait.

These pages tell, instead, another story of at least equal interest to any who are seriously concerned about the course of modern literature, or about the relation, in our generation, of the artist to society. This is the story of what Hemingway has been able to perform—unarmed but for the good writer's indispensable weapons of brain and heart—during the first thirty years of his life as an artist. The dates are 1920–1952.

The first two chapters offer an account of his expatriate beginnings on the continent of Europe during the period 1920–1925. The emphasis here is on his literary activities, and it is hard to overstate the importance of the European experience in Hemingway's development as an artist. Here in 1918 he had passed through an ordeal by mortar-burst which struck him with the force of revelation. Here he returned in the post-war years to complete the first phases of his adult education. Here he

[1] *De Laud. Stilic.*, i, 13.

taught himself to write, supporting himself by work for newspaper syndicates, exploring the continent as far east as Asia Minor, and joining (chiefly for economic reasons) that band of serious British and American artists which had then gathered on the Left Bank of the Seine. Within this particular framework his early publications are discussed and evaluated.

The heart of the book is an attempt to examine Hemingway's mature work in detail, as a whole, and outside the critical stereotype of that work which has grown up in the past twenty-five years. Chapter three provides an outline of the practical esthetic assumptions with which Hemingway began and from which, with various additions and modifications, he has ever since proceeded. Chapters four and five analyze the two remarkable novels, *The Sun Also Rises* and *A Farewell to Arms*. By means of these books Hemingway's reputation as a serious writer of fiction was established and consolidated. But their chief importance is other than historical: it is moral and esthetic. They reveal, upon close analysis, a whole side to Hemingway's art which could be called "new" if it had not been there all the time—a substructure of symbolic meanings which has gone unrecorded, and for the most part unobserved, by a majority of those who have written about Hemingway.

The first forty-five stories, representing his parallel achievement in short fiction through the year 1932, provide the substance of chapter six. Although these vary in content and in quality (I dislike, for example, such pieces as "Today Is Friday" and "One Reader Writes"), the best of them provide important additional evidence that Hemingway's contribution to American writing has been unique. They develop a complexity of symbolic action and a structural sturdiness which it is the task of this chapter to demonstrate.

Chapters seven through nine cover the experimental work in fiction and non-fiction from 1932 through 1937. It is a commonplace of Hemingway criticism to say that during these five years Hemingway retrogressed as an artist. This period was ushered in by *Death in the Afternoon,* the somewhat discursive non-fictional bible of the bullfight. Critics who are committed to the notion that Hemingway's descent began after *A Farewell to*

Arms have sometimes cited the bullfight book in evidence. The period in question was brought to a close by *The Fifth Column,* Hemingway's unsuccessful invasion of the dramatic medium. Between these two dates came *The Green Hills of Africa,* a second experiment in non-fiction which is often (and I think erroneously) described as a failure, and *To Have and Have Not,* which Hemingway himself regards, though with some reservations, as a procedural error—an attempt, that is, to make a novel out of what ought to have remained a novelette about a Key West soldier of fortune named Harry Morgan. As none of Hemingway's previous work in fiction had done, this book showed a tendency to split down the middle, and certain of its seams were noticeably ragged. It not only lacked the intricate and emotionated substructure by which *The Sun Also Rises, A Farewell to Arms,* and even *The Green Hills of Africa* were sustained, but it was also written (unlike his other fiction) at disparate intervals over a three- or four-year period.

What these five years prove, however, is that between the times of his greatest achievements the true artist does not die out. Nor does he necessarily retrogress, though at the time, and in the light of the books that have preceded any new effort, there may be an *appearance* of retrogression. Nor does the artist necessarily progress, either, though everything a good artist does experimentally in such times as these is likely to serve him, either positively or negatively (as something, say, that he discovers will or will not work), in coming to his future writing. If the artist neither dies out, nor retrogresses, nor progresses, during such a period, what does he do? The answer might well be that he consolidates his holdings. Or that he seeks to strengthen or enlarge his esthetic grasp. Or that he undertakes to increase his dexterity with the instruments of his trade. Or that he tries new subjects— always experimentally—or tries for new effects to see if now he can bring them off. In such a time he prepares, though not always consciously, for a future time when all his powers, and all that he has learned of pros and cons, will collaborate to some greater end, as happened with Hemingway during the writing of *For Whom the Bell Tolls* in 1939–1940.

The discussion of these interim books, in chapters seven,

eight, and nine, has tacitly assumed that the job of the critic, appraising such work, is first of all to understand, as well as he can, the artist's situation. It is not to hold the artist up to scorn or to accuse him of meretriciousness, unless of course he has been demonstrably guilty of selling out to the writer's perennial foes. The job is rather to separate out the elements of success and the elements of failure, to account as well as possible for the existence of both, and to take note of any technical (or other) experiments which such an interim period may have produced. It is finally to recognize, what is not always immediately apparent, that each individual writer has his individual law of progress, and must be allowed to move in his own way in the performance of whatever wonders it is given him to perform— a point especially applicable to Hemingway.

If he honestly sets himself this kind of job, the student of Hemingway's work during the period 1932–1937 will find much to interest and instruct him, and much on which it is possible to set a high (if not the highest) value. This time was not for Hemingway a *belle époque* in the field of full-length fiction. It may well be significant that in 1932 Hemingway's belief in the short-story form underwent a marked revival. He so wrote Maxwell Perkins, his editor at Scribner's, on February 24 of that year, and the interest was still visible several years later. Until he got far enough into it to see the possibilities for more extended development, *The Green Hills of Africa* took in his mind the shape of a long short story. The Morgan episodes which form the real groundwork (and the only firm part) of *To Have and Have Not* were first conceived and first written as three short stories. If the critic approaches the interim period as preeminently a time when Hemingway was experimenting with the short-story form, he may come to recognize a steady series of excellent works in this genre, culminating in the spring of 1936 with the composition of "The Short Happy Life of Francis Macomber" and "The Snows of Kilimanjaro."

The author of such stories as these can hardly be said to have been in a state of decay. Instead, he had shifted his perspectives from longer to shorter fictional forms, while on two occasions he undertook to explore the possibilities of non-fiction. From

Hemingway's point of view, at any rate, *Death in the Afternoon* was not so much the beginning of his artistic decline as the fulfillment of a plan of seven years' standing. He wished to write a book on the bullfight which might help to "educate" non-aficionados into the intricacies of Spain's national spectacle. The result may well be what Malcolm Cowley calls it: the best book on the subject in any language. Hemingway himself was rather more modest in his claims for the volume. For the student of Hemingway, however, the book has the special value of shedding light down into the deeper reaches of his esthetic theory, and in particular on that conception of tragedy (neither Greek nor Elizabethan) which stands at the center of his art. The book also throws light on his conception of the nature of the hero.

If one looks at his second experiment in non-fiction, it might be argued that the technical brilliance of *The Green Hills of Africa* can not compensate for the fact that its subject-matter— a hunting expedition in Tanganyika—lacks the seriousness and the magnitude which Aristotle prescribes. Yet even if one ignores the difficulty of the technical problems there faced and smoothly overcome, he ought probably to recognize that few writers have been able to match the graphic vitality of Hemingway's presentation of the land, the natives, and the animals. Taken in these terms, and on its own experimental grounds, *The Green Hills* is not a very good example of retrogression, though one may very much prefer to read *The Sun Also Rises* and *A Farewell to Arms*.

Ten years after his completion of *A Farewell to Arms* in January, 1929, Hemingway was ready again for a major effort in the field of long fiction. What he had learned in the interim period of experimentation with short fiction and non-fiction now stood him in good stead. The result of the new effort was *For Whom the Bell Tolls*. The tenth chapter of this present work attempts to make a double explication—of the texture and structure of this novel, and of the situation of mind and heart from which it grew. If it is not a perfect novel, and this point is open to argument, *For Whom the Bell Tolls* is something better, a genuinely great novel. The aim of chapter ten is to show on what grounds this is so.

The eleventh chapter comes round, at the end of a thirty-year revolution, to the mid-century novel, *Across the River and Into the Trees.* Begun, like *The Green Hills of Africa,* as a long short story, the book gradually developed into a short novel. The fact that it was his next published book after *For Whom the Bell Tolls* placed it in the strategically vulnerable position which always results when a lesser novel follows a greater one. Moreover, it was built upon a conception quite different from that which had informed the novel of the Spanish war. It occupied a different genre within the broad range of possibilities which fiction may legitimately invoke. If *For Whom the Bell Tolls* moved in the direction of the epic, *Across the River and Into the Trees* moved in the direction of the lyric. As had happened with Hemingway throughout the 1930's, this book was a new experiment. It was not designed to resemble *For Whom the Bell Tolls* any more than, say, *To Have and Have Not* was designed as a recapitulation in different language of the themes of *A Farewell to Arms.* It was meant to say something new and different from what had been said in any of the preceding books. Also, and the point was worth noticing, it was a kind of preliminary precipitation of materials with which Hemingway would be dealing in various ways in the large novel which he interrupted in order to complete *Across the River.* This had happened once before in his career: *Death in the Afternoon* was a preliminary treatment of some of the materials which would enter into the composition of *For Whom the Bell Tolls.* The translation of Spain and the Spanish into an art form could not come all at once; it needed to pass through several stages of formulation. Similarly, Hemingway could not translate some of the experiences of World War II directly into an art form without certain intermediate steps. *Across the River* was in this sense an interim experiment looking towards the larger work that was still to come. But in another sense it was a backward look through two world wars and thirty years of experience, and an attempt to pull together in the form of a lyrical utterance the spiritual essence of those years.

Although the novel shows serious faults of communication, and although it apparently was unable to overcome by itself the prejudices it evidently aroused, it is nonetheless a more serious, substantial, and complicated piece of work than seems to have been generally recognized. It is a rough and tender fable of an earthly purgatory, and a kind of earthly paradise, with some few inscapes of an earthly inferno along the way. If the idiom is Hemingway's, the mood is Dantesque. So regarding it, and always admitting the book's tentative and preliminary nature, as well as its reminiscential nature, one may come to think of the book as a lesser completing agency in a long cycle of Hemingway's work. The eleventh chapter attempts an exposition of these points.

At the present time it is happily impossible to complete the portrait of Hemingway as artist. He has still, one hopes, a good while to live and write in. But the figure in the canvas, though not yet filled out, is by now sufficiently defined to be at least provisionally evaluated. Briefly, this is what the twelfth and closing chapter is meant to do. Like the other eleven, it is focussed on Hemingway, the writer as artist. If the reader wishes any further orientation in the critical position which the following book adopts and generally follows, Pater's definition of the "esthetic critic" may be useful: "The function of the esthetic critic is to distinguish, to analyse, and separate from its adjuncts, the virtue by which a picture, a landscape, a fair personality in life or in a book, produces this special impression of beauty or pleasure, to indicate what the source of that impression is, and under what conditions it is experienced. His end is reached when he has disengaged that virtue, and noted it, as a chemist notes some natural element, for himself and others." [2] In Pater's sense, this is a book about the special—and multiple—virtues of the work of Ernest Hemingway.

[2] Walter Pater, preface to *The Renaissance,* 1873.

HEMINGWAY
The Writer as Artist

I · The Slopes of Montparnasse

> "This is to tell you about a young writer named Ernest Hemingway, who lives in Paris . . . writes for the *transatlantic review*, and has a brilliant future. I'd look him up right away. He's the real thing."—Fitzgerald to Perkins, 1924 [1]

I. MECCA

Herman Melville called the sea his Harvard and his Yale. Ernest Hemingway's college and *gradus ad Parnassum* was the continent of Europe. Besides the electives in art and literature, there were required courses in languages, people, statecraftiness, power politics, peace conferences, and war. In the order of things, war came first, and Hemingway's freshman year was, as they say, one to remember. On a July night in northern Italy two weeks before his nineteenth birthday, an Austrian trench-mortar and a heavy machine gun wounded him so severely that his education was nearly concluded before it had well begun. At the age of twenty, with a foreign uniform, a bad limp, and a necessary cane, he returned to his native town of Oak Park, in the environs of Chicago.[2] But his stay at home was relatively brief: he had to get back to the slopes of Parnassus.

[1] Quoted by R. Burlingame, *Of Making Many Books,* New York, 1946, p. 47.

[2] Hemingway's recollection of the conglomerate uniform is that it consisted of a tunic which he "had traded someone out of," a pair of boots and a shirt bought in Gibraltar, and a black leather Italian coat with sheepskin lining which had belonged to a friend of his who had been killed. EH to CB, 10/7/51. Hemingway had himself been face to face with death, and, as Malcolm Cowley notes, his being wounded had important effects on his subsequent work. A number of the short stories reflect the shattering depth of his reaction to it. The experiences of Frederick Henry and Richard Cantwell are in part based on Hemingway's knowledge of "how it was" to be severely wounded. The date was July 8, 1918, and the place was the Italian side of the Piave near the village of Fossalta. Hemingway's birthday, contrary to the information in various reference books, was July 21, 1899—not 1898. An early and revealing comment

As the midwestern center of the promised land, Chicago might have tempted a lesser man to stay. "It was the time," wrote Sherwood Anderson, "of a kind of renaissance in the arts, in literature, a Robin's Egg Renaissance. . . . It had perhaps a pale blue tinge. It fell out of the nest. It may be that we should all have stayed in Chicago." Anderson, the arch-rebel from Elyria, Ohio, was then sitting squarely in the middle of the nest. His *Winesburg, Ohio* stories, published in 1919, had brought him both fame and a degree of notoriety, and he was seeing a novel, *Poor White,* through the press. The New York critics ("O Mecca!" cried Anderson) were hailing him as one of the fearless group who were freeing American literature from the fetters of Victorianism.[3]

But Chicago held few of them long. Besides the Mecca of Manhattan there was that paradise of expatriates, Paris, where, as Gertrude Stein said, the old prewar crowd was disappearing and a new international group, attracted in part by a happy rate of monetary exchange, was beginning to assemble. When Anderson won the *Dial* prize in 1921, he left the Chicago robin's nest, on the generous invitation of Paul Rosenfeld, to take a European holiday. They sailed in May and Anderson, always an emotional man, wept with joy when he first saw the gray old city of Paris through the haze of early summer. Sylvia Beach, the brisk and energetic little proprietress of the Shakespeare and Company bookshop in the rue de l'Odéon, soon took him to meet Gertrude Stein. They were friends from the start. Gertrude was disturbed over her growing pile of unpublished manuscripts, seeing little hope of "publication or serious recognition." Anderson was prepared to be generous. He told her how much he liked her work and what it had meant to his own development. What was more,

---

on the big wound appears in one of Hemingway's letters to Maxwell Perkins, dated December 21, 1926. It came at a time when the word "hardboiled" had begun to be generally applied to his work. "I have not been at all hardboiled," wrote Hemingway, "since July 8, 1918—on the night of which I discovered that that also was vanity." The literary allusion here is to Ecclesiastes, from which Hemingway took one of the epigraphs for *The Sun Also Rises.* On Hemingway's brief career with the Italian infantry, see Maxwell Perkins, *Current History* 52 (November 7, 1940), pp. 27–28.

[3] *The Memoirs of Sherwood Anderson,* New York, 1942, p. 199 and passim. (Hereafter abbreviated: Anderson, *Memoirs*)

he said it out loud in print soon afterwards. Paris was the place to be discovered. O Paris! O Montparnasse! [4]

When Sherwood Anderson returned to Chicago, he renewed acquaintance with a young war veteran who had been hard at work for two years as an apprentice to the art of writing, in part supporting himself during that time as a reporter and feature writer for the *Daily Star* and the *Star Weekly* of Toronto.[5] By the end of August, 1921, Hemingway had persuaded his paper that he could be trusted to serve as a foreign correspondent, with headquarters in Paris. As a former cub on the *Kansas City Star* [6] he had had little trouble in securing employment with the Toronto paper. J. H. Cranston, then managing editor, was much taken with the tall, slender, carelessly dressed young man whose account of Mayor Thomas L. Church at a local prizefight struck him as a superior piece of humorous reporting.[7]

Anderson was equally impressed, but with a side of Hemingway's writing which Cranston never saw. Anderson knew, as Cranston did not, how Hemingway had labored a whole winter in Petoskey, Michigan, and later, in the time he could spare from reporting in Toronto, over a series of short stories and the beginning of a novel.[8] Now the time had come to try his skills in another climate. Anderson later recalled the evening in Chicago when his new friend came to say goodbye: "a magnificent broad-shouldered man" climbing the stairs and shouting as he came. On his back was a large haversack filled with all the canned goods from the Hemingway shelves. "That was a nice idea," thought Anderson, "bringing thus to a fellow-scribbler the food he had to

[4] *The Autobiography of Alice B. Toklas*, 1938, pp. 240–242. (Hereafter abbreviated: *ABT*)

[5] Information furnished through the kindness of Malcolm Cowley, who states that Hemingway and Anderson met at Y. K. Smith's apartment, in the Chicago Near North Side during the winter of 1920–1921.

[6] Hemingway served as cub reporter on this paper in the winter of 1917–1918. The present managing editor, Mr. C. G. Wellington, then assistant city editor, says that Hemingway's chief assignment was to the General Hospital, and he frequently rode the ambulances with the doctors on duty. CGW to CB, 12/20/50. Cf. Julian Capers on the period, *Scribner's Magazine* 86 (September 1929), pp. 52–53.

[7] Information from W. L. McGeary, book editor of the *Toronto Daily Star*.

[8] EH to CB, 4/1/51.

abandon." Hemingway must be sure to look up Gertrude Stein when he reached Paris; Anderson wrote a letter of introduction.[9]

Unlike Anderson, who had wept with sentimental joy over Paris, Hemingway found that his first encounter with the Latin Quarter made him itch. The slopes of Montparnasse were crawling with fakes and pretenders, the vanguard of a hegira from Greenwich Village and points west.

"It is a strange-acting and strange-looking breed [wrote Hemingway to his paper] that crowd the tables of the Café Rotonde. . . . You can find anything you are looking for at the Rotonde—except serious artists."

One trouble was that tourists in the Latin Quarter, gazing raptly into the Rotonde in search of atmosphere, naturally supposed that what they saw were real Parisian artists. The real artists of Paris, Hemingway said, both hated and resented the congregation of poseurs at the corner of the Boulevard Montparnasse and the Boulevard Raspail.

"They are nearly all loafers expending the energy that an artist puts into his creative work in talking about what they are going to do and condemning the work of all artists who have gained any degree of recognition. By talking about art they obtain the same satisfaction that the real artist does in his work." [10]

On these and all their kind Tenente Hemingway declared a silent war. The pretentious clamor of the pseudo-intellectual, whether in Paris or elsewhere, was never anything it gave him joy to hear.

II. THE CONTINENTAL

Luckily for the continuing reputation of the Latin Quarter, plenty of serious young artists lived quietly and worked hard in the bystreets. There was also a select company of older expatriates who could be counted on to aid and abet promising journeymen. Soon after his arrival in Paris, Hemingway met Ger-

[9] Anderson, *Memoirs*, p. 473.
[10] Hemingway's "Paris Letter," *Toronto Star Weekly,* March 25, 1922, p. 15. According to Malcolm Cowley, Hemingway overstated his case. "You met lots of serious artists," writes Mr. Cowley, "at the Dôme, the Rotonde, and the Select."

trude Stein and, only a little later, Ezra Pound. To Miss Stein he seemed an extraordinarily handsome young man, with an air more continental than American, and she liked the way he sat in her living-room in the rue de Fleurus, looking intently at her collection of pictures, and listening quietly to the Stein monologue.[11]

Presently she went with her companion Alice Toklas to spend a literary soirée with the Hemingways at their apartment near the Place du Tertre. The poems she saw were direct and "Kiplingesque"—a kind of free verse barrack-room poetry of statement. There was also part of a novel which she disliked, and a new story called "Up in Michigan" which she said no one would ever publish because it was too frank. According to her own bland report of the encounter, she advised the young man to begin over again and concentrate. The advice was certainly sound. Nearly any 23-year-old author could profit by it, and it was approximately what Hemingway did whenever he sat down at the typewriter. For an example of Hemingway old-style one could examine the two-page fable called "A Divine Gesture," which appeared in the *New Orleans Double-Dealer* that May.[12] Long before its publication he was off on a new calendar.

Ezra Pound was among the first to see the distinctive values in Hemingway new-style. Pound had been living for about a year in a small studio in the rue de Notre Dame des Champs. The London period was behind him and he had not yet settled permanently at Rapallo. During this Parisian interlude he was doing his bustling and profane best to goad the Left Bank into significant literary

[11] *ABT,* pp. 260–263.

[12] This New Orleans periodical was the first in America to publish work by Hemingway, unless one counts the *Star Weekly* of Toronto. The two-page "Divine Gesture" fable appears on pp. 267–268 of the *Double-Dealer* for May 1922. The June number contained a four-line free-verse poem of Hemingway's entitled "Ultimately." During the winter of 1921–1922, Hemingway's recent acquaintance Sherwood Anderson was in New Orleans. There he met Julius Friend, James Feibleman, and Basil Thompson, who ran the magazine, as well as William Faulkner, an early contributor. Anderson may have served as Hemingway's unbidden agent in placing the fable and the poem with the magazine. Hemingway is unable to recall the circumstances. The fable has not been reprinted. The poem reappears on the back outside cover of Faulkner's *Salmagundi,* Milwaukee, Casanova Press, 1932.

activity. His most recent task, in which he took a justifiable pride, had been the attentive editorial reading and heavy cutting of the manuscript of Eliot's *Waste Land*. The poet later wished that Pound's skill with the blue pencil could have been preserved as "irrefutable evidence" of his critical genius.

Unlike Eliot, Hemingway felt that Pound was of greater consequence to him as a friend and companion than as an editor. The tall and somewhat shy man with the patchy red beard, fine eyes, and irrepressible hair talked away half-jokingly and half-seriously in his characteristic pidgin-slang. When he made suggestions about Hemingway's stories, the young man accepted gladly, though seldom without an argument, as many as he felt to be useful. He would not join those who turned against Pound or spoke of him as an old-fashioned and somewhat obtrusive pretender, and their association continued until Pound's economic and political obsessions made a close relationship impossible. The mark of this poet in his Paris days, as in the early period at Rapallo, was that he devoted only a fifth of his energy to his own work.

"With the rest of his time [Hemingway wrote] he tries to advance the fortunes, both material and artistic, of his friends. He defends them when they are attacked, he gets them into magazines and out of jail. He loans them money. He sells their pictures. He arranges concerts for them. He writes articles about them. He introduces them to wealthy women. He gets publishers to take their books. He sits up all night with them when they claim to be dying and he witnesses their wills. He advances them hospital expenses and dissuades them from suicide. And in the end a few of them refrain from knifing him at the first opportunity." [13]

It was a tribute to Pound's capacity for recognizing ability that he could admire talents as diverse as those of Eliot and Hemingway. When John Peale Bishop reached Paris that summer of 1922, he asked Pound who were the ablest American expatriates then in residence. For an answer, Pound took him to see Hemingway. Bishop was impressed. He found a young writer "instinctively intelligent, disinterested, and not given to talking nonsense." He seemed humble towards his craft—a good sign. More important,

[13] Peter Russell, ed., *An Examination of Ezra Pound*, New York, 1950, pp. 28 (Eliot) and 74 (Hemingway).

he reflected that "innate and genial honesty which is the very chastity of talent." His integrity could be trusted completely. "He could not be bought," said Bishop, which was a tribute in an area where bargain-counter price-tags fluttered prominently from many a lapel.[14]

To labor honestly for an honest newspaper was not, however, to be bought. Hemingway looked on his foreign correspondence quite frankly as a means of keeping alive while he taught himself to write. "The only reason for writing journalism," he said two years later, is to be well paid. "And when you destroy the valuable things you have by writing about them, you want to get big money for it." [15]

Yet he liked the job of reporting, worked hard in it, and was good at it. The stories he sent back to Canada showed a steady increase in continental *savoir-faire* and in the ability to separate political thoroughbreds from upstart statesmen. One of his personal heroes at this time was Tiger Clemenceau, the gray-gloved, hard-shelled old realist who had recently retired from public life. When Hemingway sent the *Star* an account of his interview with Clemenceau, the editor found the Tiger's opinions too rough to print. Benito Mussolini belonged to a different order of beings and a different circle of the European Inferno. Like most other foreign correspondents, Hemingway took an instant dislike to the posturing little journalist from the *Popolo d'Italia*. For all his fierceness, Clemenceau was a grand old seigneur. Mussolini, as Hemingway frankly said from the first, was a "bad character." [16]

Without losing sight of his basic job of serious writing, Hemingway devoted the greater part of 1922 to several stiff courses in political science. In Genoa during late March and early April he saw backstreet guerrilla fighting among radical groups whose self-liquidating anarchy was soon to make all Italy the prey of Mus-

[14] John Peale Bishop, "Homage to Hemingway," *New Republic* 89 (November 11, 1936), pp. 39–42.

[15] Hemingway, "Pamplona Letter," *transatlantic review* 2 (October 1924), pp. 300–302.

[16] Hemingway's poem, "They All Want Peace. What Is Peace?" so describes Il Duce. The poem was first published in the *Little Review* for April, 1923. It was later reprinted in an article by Louis Zukofsky, *Poetry* 37 (February 1931), pp. 270–271.

solini's blackshirts.[17] He interviewed George Tchitcherin, Russia's representative to the congress of nations, and later witnessed the sabotaging effect of the Soviet-German "treaty of Rapallo," an example of the kind of backstairs machination which diplomats might have remembered after the World War which was yet to come. In the fall of that year Hemingway watched the Turks prosecuting their real-estate war against the Greeks. The flight of the Greek Christian refugees through eastern Thrace was an impressive sight. Political science was here at its worst, seeming to call for another Goya and another series, though this time in prose, like *Los Desastres de la Guerra.*

"Minarets stuck up in the rain out of Adrianople across the mud flats," wrote Hemingway. "The carts were jammed for thirty miles along the Karagatch road. Water buffalo and cattle were hauling carts through the mud. No end and no beginning. Just carts loaded with everything they owned. The old men and women, soaked through, walked along keeping the cattle moving. The Maritza was running yellow almost up to the bridge. . . . It rained all through the evacuation." [18] Out of such memories may have come the association between rain and disaster of which so much is made in *A Farewell to Arms.* The refugees on the quai at Smyrna were equally pitiable, with the brown-uniformed Turks ruthlessly hastening their departure from the captured city. Nor could Hemingway soon forget how the Greeks horribly disposed of their baggage animals—breaking their forelegs with clubs and dumping them into shallow water.[19]

Covering the Lausanne conference in November, 1922, was a further educational experience. Among his associates there was William Bolitho Ryall, a brilliant and sardonic young South African who had been gravely wounded as an infantry officer in France. Ryall, better known under his later pseudonym of William Bolitho, was then serving as European correspondent for the *Manchester Guardian.* He freely discussed with Hemingway his knowledge of backstage politics. It required little urging to start him

[17] Hemingway's despatches to *Toronto Daily Star,* April 10, 13, and 18, 1922. (W. L. McGeary)

[18] *First 49,* p. 195.

[19] *ibid.,* pp. 185–186.

into a long and bitter lecture on the malady of political power and what it can do to even the best-intentioned of statesmen. There was at least a touch of "Ryallism" in Hemingway's free-verse satire on the Lausanne conference. The title sounded like a quotation from Tiger Clemenceau: "They All Want Peace. What Is Peace?" [20] Peace, one guessed, was no more than an interlude between wars which were brought on through the interaction of greed, guile, and stupidity among statesmen like those who had assembled at Lausanne.

III. CORONA

Although his free-verse satires did not necessarily prove the point, Hemingway's work for the newspapers was teaching him certain lessons in verbal economy. Lincoln Steffens, who had come up from Rome with Richard Washburn Child, the American ambassador, to "observe" the Lausanne conference, was much struck by one of Hemingway's war-cables, the short, angry description of the flight of the Greek refugees. Steffens thought that it pictured with memorable force, yet with a fitting restraint, "that miserable stream of hungry, frightened, uprooted people." But Hemingway was shy of praise. He wanted Steffens to examine the cabelese in which the story was presented. "Only the cabelese. Isn't it a great language?" Later he told Steffens that he had to quit being a foreign correspondent and compressing his observations into such economical form. He was becoming too happily fascinated with the highly compressed "lingo" of the transatlantic cable.[21]

It was well that he had kept copies of his most recent despatches. When his wife reached Lausanne to join him just before Christmas, she carried news that was almost unendurable. Nearly everything Hemingway had written during a winter in Petoskey and a summer and fall in Toronto, as well as almost all the stories and poems composed since his arrival in Paris, had been carefully copied, classified in dossiers, and put into a suitcase. At the Gare de Lyon

[20] Hemingway, "The Malady of Power," *Esquire* 4 (November 1935), pp. 31 and 198.
[21] Lincoln Steffens, *Autobiography*, New York, 1931, p. 834.

in Paris, while Mrs. Hemingway was briefly absent, the suitcase was stolen from her train compartment and never recovered. Hemingway felt so badly about the loss that he would almost have resorted to surgery in order to forget it.[22]

A few items were saved. Harriet Monroe's *Poetry* had previously accepted for publication half a dozen of the "Kiplingesque" poems. Two short stories also remained. Both, as it happened, were noticeably if not markedly Andersonian. One was the seduction story, "Up in Michigan." The story was gathering dust somewhere in a drawer. The other remaining story was "My Old Man," which would later appear as the thirteenth chapter in the American edition of *In Our Time*. Lincoln Steffens had sent it to Ray Long at *Cosmopolitan,* and it was in the mail back to Hemingway at the time the suitcase was stolen. But the survival of these items was little recompense for the loss of so many stories and poems, as well as the partly completed manuscript of what was to have been Hemingway's first novel.[23]

Early in 1923, while the Lausanne conference moved slowly towards an inconclusive conclusion, Hemingway set to work to replace what he had lost. Besides a couple of longer stories, the first result was a series of intense bitter paragraphs, brief as nightletters, in which he tried to eliminate all the words and ideas except those absolutely essential to the desired effect. Some arrested memories of his experiences on the Italian-Austrian front in 1918. Two were cameos of the war near Mons in France, done in a highly successful imitation of a British officer's narrative manner. They were directly based, in fact, on conversations between Hemingway and his good friend Captain E. E. Dorman-Smith of His Majesty's Fifth Fusiliers. (*It was a frightfully hot day. We'd jammed an absolutely perfect barricade across the bridge. It was simply priceless.*) Two others had the flavor of American and Canadian police-court experiences. Several were very recent memories of Greek refugees in Thrace and Anatolia. One was a factual account of the execution of the six Greek cabinet ministers

[22] EH to CB, 4/1/51. Cf. EH's preface to Lee Samuels, *A Hemingway Check List,* New York, 1951.
[23] EH to CB, 4/1/51.

on November 28, 1922. Hemingway was then in Switzerland and did not personally watch the shooting; an eye-witness told him about it. Still another described a garden interview with King Constantine. (*Like all Greeks he wanted to go to America.*) A few more of the miniatures, to be added somewhat later, would operate similarly with the horses and men of the Spanish bullrings. All were writer's exercises. Unlike the exercises of most writers, they were fit to print, and they helped as much as any of the early work to suggest that this was a man to watch.

The six poems in the January issue of *Poetry* were direct statements in the transitional poetic idiom of the period.[24] A modern reader who looks them up and finds that he does not like them would do well to read extensively among other published verse in the little magazines of those years: there is much more of the same. One of his, called "Oily Weather," spoke of ships ploughing the sea in an obvious sexual image. "Roosevelt" might have served Dos Passos as a sketch for *The Forty-Second Parallel;* it pointed up the contrast between TR the legendary trust-buster and Teddy Roosevelt the political fact. There were two sharp war-poems: "Riparto d'Assolto," on a group of Arditi riding camions to their death on the Italian front, and "Champs d'Honneur," an early excursion into the natural history of the dying soldier. A fifth, called "Chapter Heading," said that this generation had danced to devils' tunes and now had come shivering home to pray, a kind of premonition of the attitudes in *The Sun Also Rises.* And in another, called "Mitrailliatrice," the young poet addressed his typewriter:

> The mills of the gods grind slowly;
> But this mill
> Chatters in mechanical staccato.
> Ugly short infantry of the mind,
> Advancing over difficult terrain
> Make this Corona
> Their mitrailleuse.

[24] Published under the title of "Wanderings" in *Poetry* 21 (January 1923), pp. 193–195.

The themes in these poems were characteristic, even if the language did not always seem so. The war in Italy, a suggestion of religious feeling, a sexual image, a hatred of sham and posturing, and a conscious acceptance of the difficulty of the terrain over which the mind's infantry must advance, with only a Corona machinegun for support. If the military image was the most arresting of any in the group, Hemingway's current concern was to assault those mills of the gods, the publishers. At that date, they not only ground slowly but seemed relatively impervious to the siege of Hemingway's infantry.

The little magazines were usually glad to publish experimental writing which got nowhere in New York. The six poems of January were followed not long afterwards by six short stories—the brief, highly intense narratives with which Hemingway had been experimenting at Rapallo. When Margaret Anderson and Jane Heap made up the "Exiles" number of their *Little Review,* which appeared in April, 1923, Hemingway was among the expatriates who were welcomed to its pages. The six stories were to reappear in both the lower-case and the capitalized editions of *In Our Time,* both of which had in a sense entered their incubation period in the *Little Review*. Along with the stories, as if Hemingway might still make his way as a poet, was "They All Want Peace," the reporter's-eye-view of the Lausanne conference.

As the spring moved on, the prospect of a book of his own began to look brighter. William Bird, a newspaper man and a good friend of Hemingway's, was the proprietor of the Three Mountains Press company, which consisted of much patience, a supply of fine rag paper, and an ancient seventeenth-century hand press in a domed wine-vault on the Île St. Louis. Since the summer of 1922 he and Ezra Pound had talked of bringing out some of Hemingway's short stories, perhaps a little book, well-printed on good paper and wearing boards against the weather. But the ancient hand press ground slowly, too. William Bird was doing a series of modern writers; there were some previous commitments and he was not to be rushed.

It was different with Robert McAlmon, the "nine hundred horse power linotype-publisher" who ran the Contact Publishing Company and had his books cheaply printed for him at Dijon. By his own account he had met Hemingway at Rapallo early in the year.[25] Before you could say "In Our Time," McAlmon came out with *Three Stories and Ten Poems*. The edition ran to three hundred copies and had gray-blue paper wrappers boldly lettered in black capitals. The stories were "Up in Michigan" and "My Old Man," the survivors of the Gare de Lyon thievery, together with "Out of Season," a new and remarkable piece of work which had been written during the spring of 1923 in the mountains of northern Italy. The poems included the six from *Poetry* and four others: "Oklahoma," "Captives," "Montparnasse," and "Along with Youth." Along with youth and a burgeoning talent, that summer of 1923, Hemingway also had a first book to his credit.

Three Stories and Ten Poems marked, in a number of ways, an end and a beginning. Hemingway published little more poetry of a serious kind after this date. Nor did he do many more stories in the general category of "My Old Man," which he liked as a narrative, though he later admitted to Fitzgerald that it was the kind of story he found easiest to write.[26] The forward-looking item in the first book was "Out of Season," a remarkably subtle blend of statement and implication, and probably (if one takes the trouble to read its competitors) the best short story in English to be published during 1923. About the time of his twenty-fourth birthday there were signs of a new departure in Hemingway's work.

But there were complications, chiefly financial. In the fullness of her wisdom, Gertrude Stein had been lecturing Hemingway on the dangers of writing for newspapers if one intended to be known as a serious writer.[27] The lectures ironically summarized Hemingway's dilemma at this period. He was writing seriously, none more than he. His problem was always to get a little ahead financially so that he could spend more time on the serious writing and less on journalism. Miss Stein did not seem to realize the ever-present necessity of making limited means serve the larger ends. She advised him to resign from his newspaper work, live as simply as she

[25] Robert McAlmon, *Being Geniuses Together,* London, 1938, p. 156. Mr. Hemingway is unable to recall this meeting.
[26] EH to FSF, *ca.* Christmas, 1925.
[27] *ABT,* pp. 260–263.

and Alice B. Toklas did, and concentrate on serious authorship. The advice had the flatness of an empty purse. Soon after the appearance of *Three Stories and Ten Poems,* Hemingway returned to Toronto, in an attempt to save some money by working as a reporter for the *Star.*[28]

IV. CARPENTER'S LOFT

If Hemingway had been distinctly uncomplimentary to the grubby esthetes whom he had found on the Left Bank in 1922, the confusion must have seemed thrice confounded when he returned from Toronto to Paris at the beginning of 1924. As was proved by the subsequent careers of such unfortunates as Hart Crane, Harry Crosby, William Seabrook, and the incredible Linkey Gillespie, Montparnasse at this time offered the kind of environment which could make or mar Americans, and did both. For every serious and determined writer who came to live and work under the benison of twelve francs to the dollar, there were a dozen eccentrics, cut-ups, professional or amateur Bohemians, roisterers, playboys, and playgirls. These cluttered the cafés, cadged drinks, fought with bartenders, and slept where they fell. The general comportment reflected no credit on the narrow American main streets from which the gifted and the almost gifted had fled to the new freedom of the Montparnasse Quarter, which Ford Madox Ford once called "the latest of all Cloud-Cuckoo Lands." [29]

They were very numerous. They came from everywhere, though as often as not from the American midwest. "Young America from the limitless prairies leapt, released, on Paris," wrote Ford in a Paul-Bunyan-like overstatement. "They stampeded with the madness of colts when you let down the sliprails between dried pasture and green. The noise of their advancing drowned all sounds. Their innumerable forms hid the very trees on the boulevards. Their perpetual motion made you dizzy." [30]

[28] A somewhat garbled account of this period appears in Gregory Clark, "Hemingway Slept Here," *Montreal Standard,* November 4, 1950, pp. 13–14.

[29] F. M. Ford, *A Mirror to France,* New York, 1926, p. 105.

[30] F. M. Ford, introduction to *FTA,* Modern Library edition, p. xii.

For those who wanted it and could afford it, the life of a sybarite was available, though not without gargantuan mornings-after. Florence Martin, unofficial Duchess of Montmartre and Dowager of the Dôme, loudly proclaimed her right and exercised her privilege to live as she pleased. Mary Butts, who seemed to Douglas Goldring "a living embodiment of surrealism," devoted much of her enormous energy to the formation and development of evening parties which moved restlessly from café to café.[31] Around her chattering head, crowned with surrealist hair the color of red ink, admirers clustered like bees. A perfect foil for Mary Butts was Lady Duff Twysden, a tall, dark, slant-eyed English-woman of thirty, with a storied past, a notable capacity for drink, and a string of admirers which included Pat Guthrie, one of the Quarter's celebrated playboys. Robert McAlmon later complained of *The Sun Also Rises* for having ignored the "quantity of work-ing, producing, alert and competent people" who were then in Paris.[32] Yet his own account of a Bastille Day celebration in the Quarter, which Ezra Pound later published in his short-lived *Exile* magazine, reads something like a version of Spenser's Bower of Bliss as it might have been written by a less gifted James M. Cain. It manages to suggest that the café crowd of 1924–1925 were leading a life calculated to arouse envy in many a frustrated American breast.

The serious author, like Hemingway, could find some of his materials among those who drank and played along the Boulevard Montparnasse. But the real importance of Paris in the middle twenties was quite unconnected, as Douglas Goldring succinctly pointed out, "with the notoriety it acquired as an international pleasure resort." Few serious writers could afford to join the mad-ding crowd, even if they had wanted to do so. "The harassing nature of their work, and the physical and mental toil it involves, discourage disorderly living and prolonged over-indulgence in alcohol," [33]—though a reasonable amount of alcohol was con-sumed.

Hemingway did not, of course, live a monastic life. The passing

[31] Douglas Goldring, *South Lodge*, London, 1943, pp. 147–164.
[32] McAlmon, *op.cit.*, p. 230.
[33] Goldring, *op.cit.*, pp. 136–137.

show eddied beneath the window, and the life of the cafés could be investigated at the close of a working day. Sometimes, in quiet seasons, he began the day in a café. He took the short cut through the Luxembourg Gardens past the bust of Flaubert which seemed both a symbol and a goal. Breakfast coffee and a brioche came to a franc or less at any of the places along the rue Soufflot, and he could write all morning at a back corner table without expectation of prolonged disturbance. Afterwards he could rest strained eyes on the bronze-green of the fountains in the Place de l'Observatoire, where the water flowed thinly over the sculptured manes and shoulders of the horses. With Dos Passos in the winter afternoons he drank hot kirsch, flavored like cherry-pits. He mixed work and play at the six-day bike races. He argued the merits of race-horses with Harold Stearns and Evan Shipman, or went to the prize-fights with Sisley Huddleston and Bill Bird. When the fights were poor, Bird used to remember the brave colored fighters of the past. He had a line modified from Villon which went, "Où sont les négres d'antan?" When the fights were good, like the Mascart-Ledoux battle at the Cirque de Paris, one yelled himself hoarse and stopped in at Lipp's for a midnight beer on the way home.

Or if the news front was slack and he had recently earned some money, he hurried east towards Schruns in the Vorarlberg, as soon as the snow was right, for a few weeks of serious writing and skiing. In the spring he fished the Stockalper and hiked or bicycled back across the Rhone Valley to stop, dry and famished, for a cool beer at the wooden tables under the wisteria vines at Aigle. With the soldier, Captain Dorman-Smith, he had long and wonderful literary arguments. With the literary man, Ezra Pound, he did a kind of military tour to Piombino and Orbetello, the subject of investigation being the campaigns of the fifteenth-century Italian despot-general, Sigismondo Malatesta, patron of artists and writers, and indomitable soldier of fortune. The pair walked over the ancient battlefields and Hemingway tried to explain to Pound how the campaigns would probably have been fought.[34]

[34] *GHOA*, p. 71, and EH to CB, 4/1/51. Cf. Sisley Huddleston, *Paris Salons, Cafés, Studios*, New York, 1928, pp. 121–123.

But these days in the sun or nights in the smoky dark of the Cirque de Paris were interludes, now frequent, now widely spaced, between bouts with the heavy-duty Corona. The young couple were now renting the upper floor of a pavilion under a chestnut tree in the rue de Notre Dame des Champs. One heard from the courtyard the whine of the buzz-saw at work, smelt the sweet-sour smell of the sawdust, and disappointedly picked up the rejected stories which dropped with the rest of the mail "through a slit in the sawmill door." The serious stories still earned nothing, or at most a little. To Hemingway's desperate annoyance, the letters of rejection would never call them stories, but always anecdotes, sketches, or contes. "They did not want them," he said later on, "and we lived on poireaux and drank cahors and water." [35]

Through all the incidental hubbub of home, newspaper office, and Montparnasse, the young father kept "very earnestly at work making himself a writer." So testified Gertrude Stein, who once thought she heard him murmuring under his breath something about "the career." Whether or not he thought of it as a career, he was determined to write well whatever he wanted to write in the way he thought it must be written. The career could take care of itself, though it would still take a little longer for it to build up the necessary momentum. Fame, the by-product of the real effort, might be "flushed like quail" from the morning thickets if you worked hard enough and were lucky. So Hemingway's good friend, Archibald MacLeish, summed it up years afterwards:

> The lad in the Rue de Notre Dame des Champs
> At the carpenter's loft on the left-hand side going down—
> The lad with the supple look like a sleepy panther—
> And what became of him? Fame became of him.
> Veteran out of the wars before he was twenty:
> Famous at twenty-five: thirty a master—
> Whittled a style for his time from a walnut stick
> In a carpenter's loft in a street of that April city. [36]

[35] *GHOA*, p. 70.
[36] "Years of the Dog," in *Act five and other poems*, New York, 1943, p. 53. Quoted by permission.

In attempting to draw a contrast between the group of serious artists who were attracted to the Left Bank largely for economic reasons and, on the other hand, the wastrels and adventurers whose escapades are described in so many recent memoirs relating to the period, it is perhaps necessary to add that there was a considerable mingling of both camps in the cafés of the Latin quarter. Memories differ on the period and its emphases. What impresses Malcolm Cowley in retrospect is not so much "the affectations and dissipations as the amount of serious, even self-sacrificing ambition that was wasted, and how few survived the struggle for artistic life." The secret of Hemingway's power of survival was the time he spent alone, sharpening the English language into a precision instrument, a scalpel for the vivisection of café, and other, society.[37]

V. CAPTAIN'S CORVÉE

The beginning of the *transatlantic review* in January, 1924, under the editorship of Ford Madox Ford, was of further consequence in the continental education of Hemingway. Through the inveterate introducer Pound and William Bird the publisher, he now met the 51-year-old editor, an Englishman he could take to without difficulty. In Ford's eyes Hemingway had "rather the aspect of an Eton-Oxford husky-ish young captain from an English midland regiment"—something after the manner of Captain Dorman-Smith of the Fusiliers.[38] Young Captain Hemingway, aged twenty-four, was shortly a regular member of that inner circle who raptly heard or raucously interrupted General Ford's vast store of asthmatic reminiscences, on Conrad, Hardy, Henry James, and Sir Edmund Gosse. The Gosse and James anecdotes were among the best. Some of them would appear in Hemingway's *Torrents of Spring*.[39]

[37] Malcolm Cowley to CB, 10/20/51.

[38] A veteran of World War I in France, Captain Dorman-Smith later became a General Officer in the British Regular Army. During World War II he served as Auchinleck's Chief of Staff in the desert. Since his retirement from active duty, he has changed his name to Dorman-O'Gowan.

[39] EH to CB, 4/1/51, recalls that the meeting with Ford took place at

Ford later pretended, jocularly no doubt, that he could not recall Hemingway's exact function on the *transatlantic*. In fact, he was an associate editor who also served as a manuscript scout from time to time. According to Robert McAlmon, there were periods when Hemingway and Ivan Beede, another gifted expatriate, did most of the work of putting out the magazine, which occupied cramped editorial quarters in the little gallery above Bird's printing press at Number 29, Quai d'Anjou.

Hemingway calls his post on the *transatlantic* a real *corvée*. It was indeed a hard job without visible recompense. Perhaps modern French military usage best sums up Hemingway's sense of the term—that is, work done by soldiers on a turn-about basis "pour satisfaire aux besoins généraux de l'éxistence militaire." Here, however, one should read *littéraire* for *militaire*. "I used to go down there," writes Hemingway, "and take a batch of [manuscripts] out on the Quai and read them. [I] would make an annotation of what Ford was to say in refusal." A typical editorial note might read: "This stinks but he might write a story if he keeps trying." Then Ford, without reading the stories himself, but bringing into play his most diplomatic powers of expression, would write beautiful letters of encouragement to the aspirants. For fun and practice, Hemingway would sometimes try his hand at rewriting the submitted stories. To say nothing of the incidental amusement, Hemingway thus earned intangible profits from his position with the *transatlantic*.[40]

In his capacity as scout, Hemingway was able to do Gertrude Stein so good a turn with her unpublished book, *The Making of Americans,* that she continued to be grateful to him even after a perceptible rift had developed between them. Sooner or later, whether through ambition or some other motive, Gertrude Stein quarreled with practically all her former associates: McAlmon, Jolas, Pound, and Hemingway were only four of the number. But she could not forget that Hemingway appeared in a great hurry one February day in 1924 at her monastic, Picasso-banked quarters in the rue de Fleurus. They wanted, he said, to run her

---

Pound's studio. Cf. Ford's introduction to *FTA,* Modern Library edition, pp. xiii–xiv.

[40] EH to CB, 4/1/51. Cf. McAlmon, *op.cit.,* p. 245.

book serially in the *transatlantic,* and the first installment of fifty pages was needed immediately. Since the only available manuscript had been sewn and bound, and even wanted dusting, Hemingway helped copy out a sizable portion, performed what was needed in the way of editing, and saw it through galley-proof. Gertrude Stein was naturally delighted. The manuscript had been lying on her shelves, by her account, since its completion a dozen years before.[41]

Meanwhile, William Bird, sweating over the hand-press downstairs, was moving slowly forward with the uncapitalized (or Paris) edition of *in our time*. Only six of the fierce and obliquely tender miniatures had been printed in the *Little Review*. To these had now been added twelve more, including Hemingway's reminiscences of two of his favorite matadors, Manuel Garcia, called Maera, and the incomparable Nicanor Villalta. The whole made an extremely handsome little book on handmade Rives paper in an edition of 170 copies—a genuine collector's item as soon as the making of this particular American could be assured.

It was the sixth and last of a series printed by Bird and "edited" by Pound as "an inquest into the state of contemporary English prose." From the author's point of view, this phase of the inquest had been unconscionably slow in bringing the corpus to light. Bird was properly fussy about the design of the boards (a montage of headlines from the world press), and about the looks of the woodcut, made from a portrait of Hemingway by his friend Henry Strater, which was being used as a frontispiece. One cause of delay was the binder, who kept the sheets two full months. At last, in the spring of 1924, bound copies came through.[42]

[41] *ABT,* pp. 264–265. Cf. D. C. Gallup, "The Making of *The Making of Americans," The New Colophon,* New York, 1950, pp. 58–63.

[42] The six works in the series were Pound's *Indiscretions,* Ford's *Women and Men,* B. C. Windeler's *Elimus,* William Carlos Williams's *The Great American Novel,* B. M. G. Adams's *England,* and Hemingway's *in our time.* On the "inquest," see *Letters of Ezra Pound,* ed. D. D. Paige, New York, 1950, pp. 183–184. "It's hell," Pound wrote to Dr. Williams (from Paris, August 1, 1922), "the way I always seem to get sucked into editing something or other." Yet he threw himself into the work with much good will and devotion. Authors in the series received a fifty-dollar downpayment on delivery of the MS, with an expectation of another fifty dollars later.

A review of the little 32-page book was written in time to meet the March first deadline for the April issue of the *transatlantic*. What struck the reviewer most forcibly was the brevity of the stories. The author seized, the review said, those "moments when life is condensed and clean-cut and significant, presenting them in minute narratives that eliminate every useless word. Each tale is much longer than the measure of its lines." Hemingway had come thus far since the days of the rejection notes that would not call his stories stories, but only anecdotes, contes, and sketches. Here were the terms "narrative" and "tale"—a clear and notable gain, though Hemingway's acceptance by American magazines was still far off.[43]

The April *transatlantic* was satisfactory to Hemingway in two other respects. It contained an installment from *The Making of Americans,* which he could take pleasure in having garnered and "edited," and the literary supplement included selections from three "Works in Progress." One was by the monocled experimentalist Tristan Tzara, founder of Dada. The second choice was a piece of the huge successor to *Ulysses* by Hemingway's good friend James Joyce. The third item, by Hemingway himself, was the short story later to be called "Indian Camp." Along with two of the stories from the McAlmon edition of *Three Stories and Ten Poems,* "Indian Camp" formed the nucleus around which Hemingway was building his own work in progress.

Through the fall and early winter of 1924–1925 Captain Hemingway continued his part-time labors for General Ford. During Ford's absence on a speaking tour in the United States (which included a visit to Hemingway's home town of Oak Park), he edited the August and September issues of the magazine. An amusing aspect of the undertaking was that the new editor used the occasion to print the work of a number of his closest friends, including the young foreign correspondent, Guy Hickok. The September number contained Ford's mildly ironic comment on the work of his subordinate:

"During our absence on those other pavements this review has been ably edited by Mr. Ernest Hemingway, the admirable Young

[43] *transatlantic review* 1 (April 1924), pp. 247–248. The review is signed *M. R.*

American prose writer. [Except for two pieces] the present number is entirely of Mr. Hemingway's getting together. . . . It provides [the reader] with an unusually large sample of the work of the Young American whose claims we have so insistently—but not with such efficiency—forced upon our readers." [44]

After Hemingway's retirement from the *pro tem* editorship, the October number carried his "Pamplona Letter," and he joined with others in paying tribute to Joseph Conrad, recently deceased, in the October "supplement." Before this brilliant little magazine ceased publication in January, 1925, it had printed two more of the Nick Adams stories—to the very considerable enhancement of its pages.

His year with the *transatlantic,* corvée or no, probably helped as much as any of his other serious literary activities to get Hemingway's name and fame into general circulation around Paris. Among the more percipient it suggested that Captain Hemingway was about ready for promotion. It offered him a focus, a kind of responsibility, and a sounding-board such as he had not had up to that time.[45] Through it, perhaps, his continental education was capped with a master of arts degree. Without having yet arrived at the top of Mount Parnassus, he was obviously far above the crowd which milled around on the lower slopes of Montparnasse.

[44] F. M. Ford in *transatlantic review* 2 (September 1924), p. 213. Cf. Ford's introduction to *FTA,* Modern Library edition, p. xiv.

[45] Hemingway spent the early months of 1925 in the Vorarlberg. After his return to Paris in March, he expended considerable time and energy helping Ernest Walsh and Ethel Moorhead with the business, printing, and proofreading details for their little magazine, *This Quarter.* The first number appeared in May 1925. This number contained Hemingway's "Big Two-Hearted River" and his article on Ezra Pound. The latter was finished on March 9, 1925. On March 27, he mailed Walsh "The Undefeated." Walsh immediately accepted the story. It was first printed in *This Quarter,* in the number for Autumn-Winter 1925–1926.

II · The Making of Americans

> "Hemingway selected his audience. His
> rewards will be rich. But thank God he
> will never be satisfied. He is of the elect.
> He belongs. It will take time to wear him
> out. And before that he will be dead."—
> Ernest Walsh, 1925 [1]

I. ROUND THE QUARTER

One afternoon in Paris in the summer of 1925, Hemingway sat with two companions at a café luncheon table. The friends were F. Scott Fitzgerald and Christian Gauss. The topic of conversation was Robert Louis Stevenson's counsel to the young writer that he should play the sedulous ape to his elders until, in good time, he has developed a matter and a manner of his own.

Fitzgerald said that he owed some parts of his Princeton novel, *This Side of Paradise,* to the fiction of Compton Mackenzie. For some of the other scenes he was indebted to Joyce's *Portrait of the Artist as a Young Man.* Hemingway named Anderson's *Winesburg, Ohio* as his first pattern. "But both agreed," says Dean Gauss, "that you later had to pay for whatever help this sort of imitation gave you in your apprenticeship. It was like consulting a psychiatrist. If you were to go on your own, you soon had to wean yourself of such outside direction." [2]

The Stevenson discussion, though it was only one of many among the three friends that summer, has an important bearing on the question of formative influences in Hemingway's early apprenticeship. One hears repeatedly that his "onlie begetters" were Anderson, Pound, and Gertrude Stein, the literary psychiatrists of his youthful emergence. The position is justified if one is careful to make certain distinctions. Hemingway had reached Paris in December, 1921, carrying with him a number of short stories, some poems, and part of a novel. During the year 1922, he often talked

[1] Ernest Walsh in *This Quarter,* Vol. 1, number 2, pp. 319–321.
[2] Dean Christian Gauss to CB, 12/26/50.

over these early productions with both Gertrude Stein and Ezra Pound. Later on he told John Peale Bishop that Miss Stein's comments were nearly always just and right, where those of Pound, while useful on occasion, were quite as often completely unjustified.

Otherwise it appears that none of these except Anderson, and he only in the period 1921–1922, was in any sense "imitated" by Hemingway. The internal evidence of the short stories indicates that Hemingway was relatively free of the Anderson "pattern" as early as January, 1923. It is also clear that after the spring of 1923 he sought no editorial advice from either Gertrude Stein or Ezra Pound. Without demur Pound accepted the status of friend. Unlike Miss Stein, he made no attempt to claim credit for Hemingway's later success. Anderson specifically disclaimed any personal connection with the widespread tendency to call Hemingway one of his imitators. "More than one critic, in speaking of Hemingway's work, attributed his impulse to me," wrote Anderson. "They had even perhaps intimated that I was a strong influence. . . . Anyway it is sure that if others said I had shown Hemingway the way, I myself had never said so. I thought, as I did in the case of Faulkner, that he had his own gift, which had nothing particularly to do with me." [3] In short, neither Pound nor Anderson felt that he was the architect of the Hemingway style. Gertrude Stein could perhaps lay some claim to the honor, though her later statements on the subject are not trustworthy.

The fact was, as Anderson intimated, that Hemingway was temperamentally an originator rather than an imitator. His real apprenticeship to the art of writing filled the years 1920–1922. The beginning of 1923 is probably as good a date as any for the inception of the journeyman stage in his career. From about the time when his earlier manuscripts were stolen, he seems to have become as writer what he had long been in other respects, an independent spirit. He could still make mistakes; he had still much to learn. Though he naturally availed himself of any hints that came his way, he learned to write by writing. Both as a newspaper correspondent in the European capitals and as a serious imaginative writer in the privacy of various apartments and small studios, he trained him-

[3] Anderson, *Memoirs,* pp. 474–475.

self to observe accurately and to express clearly, subtly, and concisely what he saw, heard, and felt. What he produced in 1923 and afterwards had a tone and lustre of its own, a special quality not attributable to the "influence" of other contemporary writing.

To establish proper standards of performance, he gave himself an intensive course of reading in certain of the prose masters. Among these were, Turgenev, Chekhov, Tolstoi, Dostoievski, Stendhal, Balzac, Flaubert, W. H. Hudson, Mark Twain, Stephen Crane, Henry James, Thomas Mann, Joseph Conrad, and James Joyce. From all these he learned. In the strict sense he could not be said to have imitated any of them. Aside from the actual reading experience, which is something, when well done, involving all the artist's powers of observation, he seemed to be using the masters to test his own deepest critical convictions about the art of writing as it should be practiced.

In dozens of leisure-hour conversations like those with Dean Gauss and Scott Fitzgerald, he argued out the esthetic principles on which he took his stand and from which he proceeded. Archibald MacLeish particularly recalls the sturdiness, acuteness, and good sense of Hemingway's critical principles. Gertrude Stein and Ezra Pound were neither his only nor his closest friends among the serious writers and artists of the Latin Quarter. He was often in the company of John Dos Passos, Malcolm Cowley, Archibald MacLeish, James Joyce, Ivan Beede, Donald Ogden Stewart, Ford Madox Ford, Dr. William Carlos Williams, and Scott Fitzgerald. Among the artists, Henry Strater and Waldo Peirce were his particular friends. Hemingway talked the practice of writing with such able correspondents as Guy Hickok, Lincoln Steffens, William Bird, W. B. Ryall, and Sisley Huddleston, and with such good companions as Captain E. E. Dorman-Smith, Evan Shipman, and Harold Stearns.

Along with the serious talk went also, of course, much badinage and ordinary masculine camaraderie. Hemingway could be seen at various sporting-events around Paris, and he regularly "worked out" in the local gymnasiums. His closest associates all knew, however, that the apprentice and journeyman years, in and out of Paris, were producing a respectable volume of hard and careful work. As Sinclair Lewis was to emphasize in his Nobel Prize address some years later, Hemingway's self-imposed standards were high and exacting. "He was not given," says the late Christian Gauss, "to picking soft assignments for himself."

If he had wished to continue as an imitator instead of branching out on his own as an originator and a kind of classical revolutionary, he would have been foolish indeed to limit his perspective to the writings of Anderson or to the critical ideas of Gertrude Stein. The salon in the rue de Fleurus was not the only center of congregation for serious writers in the Paris of 1925. Just across the Luxembourg was Sylvia Beach's Shakespeare and Company bookshop. There one occasionally met T. S. Eliot, over from London in a neat business suit and bowler; his quarterly, *The Criterion*, was just at this time entering its third year, and the firm of Faber and Gwyer was on the point of bringing out the first volume of his collected verse covering the period 1909–1925. Wyndham Lewis, the English critic, periodically arrived to deliver truculent opinions on the low state of belles-lettres in Montparnasse. Ford would appear, his large frame draped in a "tent-like suit" and his voice honking (he had been gassed in the war) as he told his stories of eminent Georgian literary men.[4]

Greatest of them all, in Hemingway's opinion, was James Joyce, whose *Ulysses* could now be bought ("ordinary edition complete") for sixty francs from any Paris bookseller. His eyes were painful and he made them worse when he pored over the compendious notes for his *Work in Progress*. Without his glasses, they used to say, he resembled the picture of Shakespeare on Sylvia Beach's bookshop sign. Or, as George Antheil suggested, Shakespeare before he lost his hair. They all knew and whimsically respected James Joyce, paterfamilias, singer of songs, drinker of white wine, strainer of the patience of his wife Norah. "It was nice," said Hemingway, "to see a great writer in our time," and he listened with attention when Joyce read from the *Work In Progress*.[5]

He would keep up his friendship with Joyce as long as their paths could cross. Joyce was likewise a fomenter of literary revolu-

[4] George Antheil, *Bad Boy of Music*, New York, 1945, p. 146.
[5] Antheil, *op.cit.*, and *GHOA*, p. 71. McAlmon, *Being Geniuses Together*, pp. 282–283.

tion. But Hemingway felt no call to imitate any of his contemporaries. He had now outgrown Stevenson's advice to young writers. He had a proud prejudice against being a sedulous ape, yet he was undoubtedly sedulous.

II. EXPATRIATE

For all his industry, independence, and incorruptibility, the Hemingway of late 1924 still had that foreign look. He counted as one of the breed whom Ernest Boyd called the "transplanted transatlantics" and satirized in the first number of Mencken's *American Mercury* as "Esthete: Model 1924." Well enough known on the Rive Gauche, he was little heard of on the banks and braes across the Hudson from the Palisades, except, of course, as one of that wild gang in Paris.

"You're an expatriate [says Bill to Jake in *The Sun Also Rises*]. You've lost touch with the soil. You get precious. Fake European standards have ruined you. You drink yourself to death. You become obsessed with sex. You spend all your time talking, not working. You are an expatriate, see? You hang around cafés." [6]

This is simply a bout of persiflage between Bill Gorton and his good friend Barnes, the newspaper correspondent. Yet in 1924, for a writer not yet published in America, this negative stereotype, here so positively stated, was a serious matter. Hemingway had personally dissociated himself from the false esthetes and playboys of the Rotonde. To live on the Left Bank for economic reasons was not necessarily to share the mores of its more objectionable inhabitants. Yet the stereotype of the expatriate persisted in the public imagination. The uncritical tendency to superimpose it on any and all who lived in Paris worked to the detriment of serious artists who had little or nothing in common with the barflyblown bohemians except geographical situation.

Naturally enough Hemingway would have liked to be published in America. Despite its stiff covers and handsome format, Bird's edition of *in our time* was hardly longer than a chapbook: none of the miniatures exceeded two pages in length and one came to only

[6] *SAR*, p. 118.

eight lines. McAlmon's edition of *Three Stories and Ten Poems* was a bigger volume. But two of the three stories represented an approach to short fiction which Hemingway had outgrown before the book appeared. Now, by using the miniatures of *in our time* as interchapters (somewhat as Dos Passos was to do with his trilogy) and a new group of longer narratives as the larger substance, he could put together a respectable volume of two hundred or more manuscript pages. As if to encourage his westward glances, the United States began to take some notice of his work. L. A. G. Strong reprinted the poem "Chapter Heading" in the *Best Poems of 1923,* and *The Best Short Stories of 1923,* edited by Edward J. O'Brien, contained "My Old Man." But the year 1924, in which these postscript volumes appeared, produced no offers from American publishers.

While Hemingway still looked westward, George Antheil persuaded him to bow briefly in the other direction. The little pianist-composer from Trenton, New Jersey, had come to try Montparnasse for size in 1923, and had settled with his future wife in tiny quarters above Sylvia Beach's bookshop. He was then twenty-three, about the age at which Hemingway had reached Paris. They were all twenty-three, as Gertrude Stein observed with an air of profundity, and later on they were all twenty-six. Welcomed by Ezra Pound, who wrote a book about his music, Antheil was presently moving in the literary circle downstairs. By 1924 he had begun to serve as scout for a recently organized German periodical, *Der Querschnitt.* Published at Frankfurt-am-Main, it was edited by Count von Wedderkop, known among the Montparnassians as "Mr. Awfully Nice," in honor of the only two English words he customarily uttered. Antheil sent him some poems of Joyce's, and four poems and a short story by Hemingway. Beginning in the fall of 1924 and running through the summer of 1925, Wedderkop printed them all. One saw in the poems the satirical bent which would strongly emerge in *The Torrents of Spring,* and had already appeared in the bawdy verses on the Lausanne conference. The new ones bore sardonic titles: "The Soul of Spain with McAlmon and Bird the Publishers," "The Lady Poets with Foot Notes," "The Earnest Liberal's Lament," and "The Age Demanded." The story, whose German title was "Stierkampf," is now well known as "The Undefeated." [7]

The *Querschnitt* venture had an amusing epilogue. Ten years afterwards in East Africa, Hemingway met an Austrian expatriate with literary interests. "Hemingway," said Kandisky, "is a name I have heard. Where? Where have I heard it? Oh, yes. The *dichter*. You know Hemingway the poet?" Kandisky, it turned out, had formerly subscribed to *Der Querschnitt* for cultural reasons. "This is very strange," he said, when the identity had been established. The *dichter*, whose poetic skills had long since taken another direction, thought it was fantastic. [8]

Few Americans read *Der Querschnitt* or even knew much about Hemingway as "poet." His first offer from an American publisher, in March, 1925, was the result of another combination of circumstances. These included the appearance of his short stories, over a two-year period, in a half-dozen of the English-speaking little magazines; the intrinsic merits of the work itself; and the active recognition of his power by a few people who were in a position to do something about it.

When F. Scott Fitzgerald reached Paris for an eight-month stay early in May, 1925, one of his first acts was to pay a call on "Hemmingway" (whose name he continued for some time to misspell), thus beginning a friendship which lasted until Fitzgerald's death in 1940. Edmund Wilson had already introduced Scott to some of Hemingway's work. Impressed by its quality, Scott had urged Maxwell Perkins, his own editor at Scribner's, to get in touch with Hemingway immediately. Fitzgerald had just rounded out his fifth year as an extremely successful Scribner author and was anxious that such talent as Hemingway displayed should be recognized as quickly as possible.

By a quirk of fortune, in which a cable outran two exploratory letters from Maxwell Perkins, Boni and Liveright became Hemingway's first American publishers. Sherwood Anderson, who in 1925 was one of the firm's best-selling authors, later claimed

[7] Antheil, *op.cit.*, p. 147. The "Soul of Spain" poem was in two parts, printed in separate numbers.

[8] *GHOA*, p. 7.

credit for the first important American recognition of Hemingway. As an act of faith, he said, he had gone personally to Horace
Liveright to plead Hemingway's cause. "I went to bat," said Anderson, "for ability." Edward J. O'Brien, the short-story antholo-
gist, likewise interceded with Liveright. Ironically enough, Fitzgerald's urgings were heeded at about the same time. On February 21, 1925, Perkins wrote to Hemingway expressing interest
in seeing some of his work. The letter lacked a sufficient address
and evidently was lost. On February 26, Perkins obtained the
correct address from John Peale Bishop and immediately sent
out a follow-up letter, enclosing a copy of the first. At this date
Hemingway was writing and skiing at Schruns in the Austrian
Vorarlberg. The Perkins letter was held for him with other mail
by Sylvia Beach in Paris. About ten days before he called for his
mail in the rue de l'Odéon, he received a cable from one of the
Liveright editors offering an advance of two hundred dollars and
a request for acceptance by return cable. Hemingway accepted.

On April 15 he explained the situation to Perkins. By this date
he had received the contract from Boni and Liveright in the
form of a follow-up letter. It specified that in consideration of
their taking on *In Our Time,* the enlarged collection of short
stories, they were to have an option on his first three books. Failure
on their part to exercise this option within sixty days of receipt of
any future manuscript would cause the arrangement to lapse.
If they refused the second book, they forfeited rights to the third.
The provisions of this contract were to have important consequences in the history of Hemingway's publications in the United
States.[9]

To have been approached by two American publishers at the
instigation of several American friends was scarcely painful to
an author whose efforts had thus far met with profound silence
on the American side of the Atlantic. But his new connection with
the firm of Boni and Liveright was made somewhat less happy
by the fact that Anderson's quality as an artist had begun to
deteriorate so noticeably during the six years since *Winesburg,*

[9] Anderson *Memoirs,* pp. 474–477. EH to Maxwell Perkins, 8/31/27.
Perkins to EH, 2/21/25. EH to Perkins, 4/15/25. Also EH to CB, 4/1/51,
and EH to FSF, 12/31/25.

Ohio. Several of the recent books, and in particular *Many Marriages,* read as if they had been written by Windy McPherson's son at his windiest. Scott Fitzgerald's view of the matter was that *Many Marriages* and *Dark Laughter* were "cheap, faked, obscurantic, and awful." This, he reported, was also Hemingway's opinion. Hemingway agreed with him also, he said, in the belief that by such work as this Anderson had "let everybody down who believed in him." [10] The implication that Anderson had lost his integrity as an artist may or may not have been justified. On May 23, 1925, however, Hemingway wrote from Paris to thank Anderson for the assistance with Liveright, and to emphasize how much it meant to him to have the short stories accepted and out of the way so that his mind would be clear for future work.[11]

III. "IN OUR TIME"

The American *In Our Time* was published October 5, 1925, in a two-dollar edition of 1335 copies. Although it made several enterprising publishers prick up their ears, the book caused relatively little public stir. The advertising budget at Boni and Liveright was limited, and review copies were evidently rather parsimoniously distributed. In part, the quietness of the critical reception may reflect the prejudice which still existed in some quarters against the American writers who had "deserted" to Paris. Ernest Boyd, who conducted a book page in the *Independent,* later confessed to some such feeling about Hemingway's first volume.[12]

The book nevertheless received serious consideration from such occasional Montparnassians as Paul Rosenfeld, Anderson's friend and benefactor, and Allen Tate, who was very far from supposing that foreign residence necessarily corrupted American

[10] Quoted by Arthur Mizener, *The Far Side of Paradise,* Boston, 1951, p. 196.

[11] James Schevill, *Sherwood Anderson,* University of Denver (Colo.) Press, 1951, p. 207.

[12] *Independent,* 116 (June 12, 1926), p. 694. Malcolm Cowley notes further that first books by new authors did not sell, nor was there a good market for collected short stories.

talent. Though Rosenfeld professed to find signs of influence from Anderson and Gertrude Stein, his judgment was that the new voice was original. It managed to catch the epoch's "feeling of a harsh impersonal force in the universe, permanent, not to be changed, taking both destruction and construction up into itself, and set in motion by their dialectic." Tate stressed the nature-bias, praising "Big Two-Hearted River" as the "most completely realized naturalistic fiction of the age." Louis Kronenberger was one of those who discounted the Anderson-Stein influence. What struck him most forcibly was the non-derivative merit, which showed "no important affinity with any other writer." Kronenberger also read intellect, culture, humor, and sophistication between the lines of *In Our Time*. But the forte lay, he asserted, in life, conversation, and action. The term of praise was "synthetic observer" rather than analyst.[13]

Critical appreciation of Hemingway in the middle twenties was of a generally higher quality than that of the middle thirties when critical standards had in some quarters begun to wilt under the Marxist assault. One found a receptivity, a willingness to accept Hemingway's art on its own grounds, which the passage of ten years would somewhat dissipate. When Ernest Walsh reviewed *In Our Time* in the second number of his little magazine, *This Quarter,* he overstated his case. He nevertheless described exactly certain of Hemingway's distinguishing talents. The stories, said Walsh, gave the impression that they had been prepared for by "a growing process as natural as a plant getting ready to bloom." The great possessions of this author were a "clarity of heart" and at the same time a full and willing acceptance of his world. "In these days, when few know where they are going, we get a man who feels what he feels clearly enough to be guided by his convictions into a life that may be said to remember the classical manhood of this age." He had gone through his dreams like a man; a process of renunciation had occurred under the discipline of "a Spartan mind and will." What remained was an "uncanny mixture of boy-fresh perception" joined to an understand-

[13] Rosenfeld, *New Republic* 45 (November 25, 1925), pp. 22–23. Tate, *Nation* 122 (February 10, 1926), pp. 160–162. Kronenberger, *Saturday Review of Literature* 2 (February 13, 1926), p. 555.

ing and sympathy worthy of a far older artist. Hemingway was accordingly "the shyest and proudest and sweetest-smelling story-teller" of Walsh's reading. One found no odor of corruption about his work. It would take a long time to wear him out.[14]

If Hemingway's hopes were undercut by the size of the edition or the relative scarcity of the reviews, he could not (and did not) complain that his work had failed to receive adequate critical consideration from a select group of admirers. Fitzgerald, how-ever, took the matter almost as a personal affront—as if, say, his own judgment had been called in question by an act of silence. During frequent conversations in the summer of 1925 he had found in his new friend that quality of absolute integrity which three years earlier had so strongly impressed John Peale Bishop. In 1926, at a small swimming-beach on the Cap d'Antibes, he took Glenway Wescott aside to complain fiercely over the treat-ment which had so far been accorded to so good a writer. Ob-viously, he argued, Hemingway "was the one true genius of our decade . . . and yet he was neglected and misunderstood and, above all, insufficiently remunerated." Fitzgerald urged Wescott to further the cause.

Unable to share his friend's enthusiasm, Wescott even thought it bad for Fitzgerald's morale to entertain so unabashed an ad-miration for a fellow-writer. It suggested a willingness to leave "the graver responsibilities" to Hemingway while Fitzgerald went on merely to "write for profit and live for fun." Yet Fitzgerald's faith persisted as a kind of standard around which to rally his moral forces. He later called Edmund Wilson his intellectual, and Hemingway his moral conscience.[15]

As evidence of his belief that *In Our Time* was a bright entry in an otherwise "dismal record of high hope and stale failure" among the younger American writers, Fitzgerald now prepared an essay for *The Bookman*. He implied, without ever saying, that Hemingway's aloofness from America was one of his strongest defenses against infection. A visible danger in the period was the insincere compulsion to write "significantly" about something

[14] Reference as for footnote 1, above.
[15] Edmund Wilson, ed., *The Crack-Up*, New York, 1945, pp. 79 and 324–325. Also supplementary letter from Mr. Wescott to CB, 1/27/51.

called "the American scene," especially when that compulsion did not rise naturally within the writer himself. What had been forgotten in the goldrush to exploit native materials was the great truth, namely "that material . . . is as elusive as the moment in which it has its existence, unless it is purified by an incorruptible style, and by the catharsis of a passionate emotion." One found in the great welter of "American" writing neither style nor emotion, neither sensitivity of response to the materials nor any deeply grounded ideas about the nature of art itself.[16]

For the literary situation in America in 1925–1926, Fitzgerald blamed two men chiefly. They were H. L. Mencken and Sherwood Anderson. Though Mencken had "done more for American letters than any man alive," he was wedded to invective and had begot upon her a callous family of hammer-and-tongs boys, glib, "insensitive, suspicious of glamour, preoccupied exclusively with the external, the contemptible, the 'national,' and the drab." Anderson's trouble was not his ideas but the lack of them. Reviewers still spoke of him as "an inarticulate, fumbling man, bursting with ideas." This was obviously a pose. In fact he had "a brilliant and almost inimitable prose style" and "scarcely any ideas at all."

The capstone of Fitzgerald's essay was *In Our Time*. The single false note, in his view, was "My Old Man"—a seeming echo of the sentimental horse-stories which had inaugurated Anderson's "respectability and also his decline" a few years earlier. The rest of the book lay far outside the realm of Anderson. One found in it "something temperamentally new." Fitzgerald read "Big Two-Hearted River" with the "most breathless unwilling interest" since Conrad had first compelled him to look at the sea. Even in those other Nick Adams stories which used American backgrounds, the emphasis fell where it lay in the river story: on inner experience of a kind which knew no country yet seemed to know them all. One felt, under the surface, a snapping of ties, an awakening of unrest, a sharp nostalgic remembrance of things past, an intensity of passionate emotion. With these stories, said his friend, Hemingway had turned a corner into the street.

[16] "How to Waste Material: A Note on My Generation," *Bookman* 63 (May 1926), pp. 262–265.

By May, 1926, when Fitzgerald's essay appeared, Hemingway was far down the street with two new manuscripts under his arm. *In Our Time* was out and away and he had turned to other business. The great business was a tragicomedy on life among the Montparnassians. It had been complete in final draft since April first, and with it Hemingway was ready to make his strongest bid for wider recognition. The funny business was a satire on life among the litterateurs, with particular attention to Sherwood Anderson and an impolite bow in the direction of H. L. Mencken

IV. TRAVESTY

The Torrents of Spring, a satirical *jeu d'esprit* with a serious core, got its title from Turgenev, its locale from the state of Michigan, and its *raison d'être* from the writings of Anderson and (to a lesser degree) Gertrude Stein. That Hemingway was a satirist of ability came as no surprise to his closest friends. His letters of the period display a lively fancy and a gift of mimicry, but also a hatred of sham literary posturing and a capacity for rough and bear-like fooling that reminds one of Goldsmith's remark about Johnson: "When his pistol misses fire, he knocks you down with the butt end of it." [17]

Historically speaking, *The Torrents of Spring* is chiefly important as the first public notice that Hemingway is on his own. Writing in 1926 soon after the book's publication, Lawrence Morris correctly saw it as the somewhat ursine shrug with which Hemingway threw off the tutorship of Anderson and declared his literary independence.[18] Yet in agreeing to the justice of the statement it is well to remember that his private literary divorcement from the Anderson influence and the Stein editorship had preceded the appearance of the book by about three years.

The events leading up to Scribner's acceptance of *The Torrents of Spring* have never been fully described. The book was written with astonishing speed and great concentration during a little more than seven days in November, 1925. It came as a kind of

[17] Boswell, *Life of Johnson,* New York, 1933, Vol. I, p. 398.
[18] Lawrence S. Morris in *New Republic* 48 (September 15, 1926), p. 101.

interlude of "relaxation" between the completion of the first draft of *The Sun Also Rises* and the beginning of the final rewriting job. As a test of the quality of his satire and for their amusement, Hemingway read the whole book aloud to the Gerald Murphys. But he spent little time in polishing, and the manuscript was soon on its way to Horace Liveright.

Liveright's answering cable reached Hemingway on the last day of the year: "Rejecting *Torrents of Spring* patiently awaiting manuscript *Sun Also Rises* writing fully." In a long and troubled letter to Fitzgerald Hemingway explained that in having failed to take up the option to publish the Anderson satire, Liveright had forfeited the right to the first novel. It is clearly an apocryphal story that Hemingway wrote *The Torrents of Spring* as part of a plot to break his contract with Boni and Liveright. "I did not," he told Fitzgerald, "have that in mind in any way when I wrote it." On the other hand he had since had serious doubts that the firm could or would publish the book, since it satirized "their present ace and best-seller Anderson." [19]

Like many another young author at that time and afterwards, Hemingway had been impressed by what he knew of Maxwell Perkins. Fitzgerald's own recommendations, together with the letters which Perkins had written Hemingway, indicated a sympathy, an interest, and a capacity for critical discernment which suggested that the firm of Scribner would be a proper place to do business with. In answering Perkins's inquiries about the manuscript of *In Our Time,* Hemingway had promised him the first look at any new book in the event of a release from Liveright. After a series of communications between the author and his former publisher, Hemingway kept his promise. The manuscript was delivered to Scribner's, accepted almost immediately, though evidently with some misgiving, and published on May 28, 1926, a brief five months after Liveright's rejection.

In relation to Anderson's recent work, the travesty stood about as Fielding's *Shamela* did to Richardson's *Pamela.* The informed reader has little difficulty in recognizing allusions to *Dark Laughter, Many Marriages, Marching Men, Horses and Men*—and

[19] EH to CB, 4/1/51. EH to FSF, 12/15/25. EH to FSF, 12/31/25.

even *Winesburg, Ohio,* despite Hemingway's continuing admiration for this memorable collection. Anderson may be forgiven for calling *The Torrents* a "parodistic book which might have been humorous had Max Beerbohm condensed it to twelve pages." [20] The book would probably have been better if Hemingway had taken the time to make it shorter. More objective judges than Anderson, however, could see it as a prosaic descendant of Byron's *English Bards and Scotch Reviewers,* which could also have been cut to advantage.

The torrents of the title are those which flow in the veins of Scripps O'Neil, a Harvard esthete who has drifted into Petoskey, Michigan, soon after the close of World War I, and in the arteries of Yogi Johnson, a war veteran of Swedish descent who works in the local pump factory. When the chinook wind melts the snow along the Michigan lake-shore, both men begin to feel that vague unrest and sense of frustration so common among the brooding residents of Anderson's Winesburg. Like the Winesburghers also, neither of them is able to identify the origin or the meaning of his discomfort. Scripps, deserted by his first wife in Mancelona and newly married to Diana, the senior waitress in Brown's Beanery ("The Best by Test"), finds that the strongest tributary to his own torrent is the junior waitress, a girl named Mandy who collects and relays literary anecdotes. There is a particularly good one on the dying words of Henry James. In the face of such competition (the author generously credits Ford Madox Ford with the anecdotes), Diana is compelled to desperate measures. She reads *The Forum, The Mentor, The Literary Digest, The American Mercury, Harper's, The Bookman, The Saturday Review of Literature,* and the *New York Times Book Review;* and in an effort to hold her man she pays close attention to the literary opinions of William Lyon Phelps in *Scribner's.*

The experiment fails. Having tried unsuccessfully to tempt Scripps home with the promise of a new article on chiropractors by H. L. Mencken, Diana goes softly out into the night, leaving Scripps and Mandy in the midst of another anecdote. Yogi Johnson is last seen going back to nature as he walks down the G. R. & I.

[20] Anderson, *Memoirs,* p. 475.

Railroad tracks, accompanied by a naked Indian squaw and her papoose, and followed by a pair of woods Indians who pick up Yogi's garments as he drops them off, one by one.

The slightly sour bouquet of Winesburg is often happily caught in the streets of Petoskey. Here is Hemingway's parody of Anderson's interrogatory monologues:

"Scripps strode down the streets of Petoskey to the beanery. He would have liked to ask Yogi Johnson to eat with him, but he didn't dare. Not yet. That would come later. All in good time. No need to rush matters with a man like Yogi. Who was Yogi, anyway? Had he really been in the war? What had the war meant to him? Was he really the first man to enlist from Cadillac? Where was Cadillac anyway? Time would tell."

Or the sentimental simplicity of Anderson in climactic scenes:

"Scripps reached forward to take the elderly waitress's hand, and with quiet dignity she laid it within his own. 'You are my woman,' he said. Tears came into her eyes, too. 'Once again I say: you are my woman.' Scripps pronounced the words solemnly. Something had broken inside him again. He felt he could not keep from crying. 'Let this be our wedding ceremony,' the elderly waitress said. Scripps pressed her hand. 'You are my woman,' he said simply. 'You are my man and more than my man.' She looked into his eyes. 'You are all of America to me.' 'Let us go,' Scripps said."

Sometimes there is a glimpse of an Anderson character dreaming, like Yogi Johnson, of far-off climes. The following passage, however, is also a fine parody of Gertrude Stein's special form of echolalia:

"Going somewhere now. En route. Huysmans wrote that. It would be interesting to read French. He must try it sometime. There was a street in Paris named after Huysmans. Right around the corner from where Gertrude Stein lived. Ah, there was a woman! Where were her experiments in words leading her? What was at the bottom of it? All that in Paris. Ah, Paris! How far it was to Paris now. Paris in the morning. Paris in the evening. Paris at night. Paris in the morning again. Paris at noon, perhaps. Why not? Yogi Johnson striding on. His mind never still."

If the Anderson-Stein axis is the central object of the parody,

Hemingway occasionally strikes out good-humoredly in other directions. The last half of Chapter Two suggests Joyce's *Dubliners*. Sometimes, in the geographical catalogues, one catches an echo of the impressionism of Dos Passos, another good friend of Hemingway's. The shade of D. H. Lawrence stalks happily through the account of the captive bird warmed tenderly in Scripps's shirt-front, the appearance of the naked Indian squaw in the lunchroom, the "man-woman" talk of the self-married lovers, and the British-accented Indians in the Indian Club.

The satirical intent of the book reaches out to embrace the dedication. When the reader notices that the book is inscribed "in admiration," to H. L. Mencken and S. Stanwood Menken, he may wrongly conclude that the spirit of the bad boy of Baltimore is predominant, and that this essay in parody is to be accepted as a kind of tribute to America's ruling critic. "So many young men get their likes and dislikes from Mencken," reflects Jake Barnes in *The Sun Also Rises*.[21] Mencken's irrepressible devotion to the imported word, italicized for emphasis and used to spice the pages of the *American Mercury*, is reflected in some of Scripps O'Neil's talk: "No *politzei* for mine. They give me the *katzenjammers*. . . . No more *weltpolitik*. Take Doctor Coolidge away." In fact, however, the dedication was designed to enrage Mr. Mencken. According to Malcolm Cowley, S. Stanwood Menken, the wealthy vice crusader, stood for everything that H. L. Mencken hated. Coupling their names in a sardonic dedication was one way of making fun of both of them.[22] In the vigor of his youth, Hemingway lunged lustily at the opposition. He accepted without question an observation of Henry Fielding's which appears as an epigraph in *The Torrents of Spring:* "Life everywhere furnishes an accurate observer with the ridiculous." To this statement young Hemingway could add: "Particularly some phases of the literary life in Europe and America."

In spite of the raillery, the sometimes heavy-handed ridicule,

[21] *SAR*, p. 42.
[22] Malcolm Cowley to CB, 10/20/51. According to Datus C. Smith, Jr., it is possible that Hemingway was thinking of Mencken's leadership in The National Security League, which stood for 100% Americanism. DCS to CB, 12/18/51.

and the air of youthful cleverness which suffuse the book, the perforation of the Anderson windbag and the Stein balloon is frequently acute. One may regret Hemingway's involvement in the literary squabbling of the period. His bluntness made him a number of enemies and invited return attacks. Yet the results of the book were not entirely unhappy. As a means of secession from the firm of Boni and Liveright, *The Torrents of Spring* was a roaring, if unintended, success. Its broader significance is that it marked his public withdrawal from the patterns in which he had somewhat aloofly spent his apprentice years.

V. MARRING AMERICANS

American reviewers liked the book and agreed with its general purpose. Ernest Boyd, who had been doubtful about the merits of *In Our Time,* now found Hemingway's future prospects "immeasurably brighter." Some of the Chicago rebels, and (Boyd felt) Sherwood Anderson in particular, had run to verbal seed as a result of early success. The old laurels had dried out and needed watering, possibly with a fire hose. Hemingway had seized on Anderson's seedier qualities with good humor but also with an unerring eye for the ridiculous. He struck Boyd as "a genuine humorist and a critic so shrewd" that it was possible to hope he might "cure the disease he so well diagnoses." For Allen Tate, who had hailed the publication of *In Our Time, The Torrents* was "a small masterpiece." It managed to combine ribaldry, humor, and satire in a manner, Tate suggested, which made Hemingway "the best contemporary writer of eighteenth-century prose." [23]

The private results of the book's publication were less happy. In the two people who bore the brunt of the attack, some ill-humor was generated, and both were later to strike back at so "ungrateful" a former "pupil." Sherwood Anderson, who had once written a story with the pertinent title of "I Want to Know Why," could perhaps have taken the lampooning with good grace even when he found that some American reviewers enjoyed watching the

[23] Ernest Boyd, *Independent* 116 (June 12, 1926), p. 694. Allen Tate, *Nation* 123 (July 28, 1926), p. 89.

spectacle of Scripps O'Neil Anderson in love. His attitude as time went on settled into that of frank bepuzzlement. What motives could have impelled the pupil to reject his old master? Why did this young dog now bite the hand into which it had once placed a hundred pounds of canned goods? Why, in a rapid change of metaphor, did Hemingway want to deliver this "funeral oration" over the grave of a fellow-midwesterner who was still very much alive? Anderson wanted to know why.[24]

There was furthermore the letter, like a ghost in the under-blows, which Hemingway had written to Anderson shortly before *The Torrents of Spring* appeared. Anderson later described it as "probably the most completely patronizing" communication ever written; it seemed to imply that he was an aging champion knocked to the canvas and unable to rise again under the referee's inexorable count. The contents of the letter have since been made available in paraphrase by Anderson's biographer, Mr. James Schevill.[25] On May 21, 1926, Hemingway wrote from Madrid to say that in Paris the preceding November he had been discussing *Dark Laughter* with John Dos Passos and had gone directly home from the talk to write *The Torrents of Spring* in seven days. Unlike Johnson's *Rasselas,* set down in a similar length of time, this book was not meant to defray the funeral expenses of anyone. It was meant as a joke, but was also sincere. Anderson had written great things, but Hemingway felt that it was his duty to criticize any inferior work that Anderson might produce. Hemingway's own recollection of the document is that it was an "all-right letter" on a difficult subject which Anderson completely misunderstood.

For all her air of motherly solicitude, and her hospitality to young writers in Paris, Gertrude Stein could be feline when crossed. She seems to have felt, though she never publicly said, that her own writing had been one of the targets of *The Torrents of Spring*. In *The Autobiography of Alice B. Toklas,* that queer mixture of pith, tosh, and vinegar, she offered her own account of the well-spring of *The Torrents*. Hemingway's motive was professional jealousy, she had assured Anderson. Anderson had writ-

[24] Anderson, *Memoirs*, pp. 473–476.
[25] Schevill, *op.cit.*, p. 227.

ten some sporting stories when it was obvious that Hemingway had staked out the field of sport as his own domain. She recalled that she had once referred to Anderson as the only man in America who "could write a clear and passionate sentence." Hemingway had sharply disagreed, and had questioned Anderson's taste, as others had done and would do after reading through the work which followed the publication of *Poor White*.[26]

But Gertrude Stein went further into the realm of malice. All his close friends knew Hemingway's physical and moral courage, but there were many who were always ready to listen to gossip. "When Sherwood Anderson came to Paris [in January, 1927]," wrote Gertrude, "Hemingway naturally was afraid." She and Anderson agreed, she said, that he was yellow, "just like the flatboat men on the Mississippi River as described by Mark Twain." Such a charge was too clearly false to need refutation, though Anderson's own account in the *Memoirs* amply refutes Gertrude Stein. Anderson tells how Hemingway knocked on his door, suggested that they have a drink in a *bistro,* and then, after a brief conversation, departed as he had come. Still in the grip of his misunderstanding, Anderson was at least more charitable, saying merely that Hemingway's "absorption in his ideas may have affected his capacity for friendship." [27]

Gertrude Stein's animadversions went on. Everyone talked of Hemingway's genial habit of shadow-boxing, and all his close friends knew that he had learned to box in 1914 when he was a sophomore in high school. This did not deter Gertrude Stein: Sherwood Anderson was the one who had taught Hemingway to box, she said. Hemingway was very enthusiastic about the bullfight, and went to Spain at every opportunity in order to study it and follow the careers of the matadors. He had learned all about bullfighting from her, said Gertrude, and she had a photograph of herself and Miss Toklas, taken long ago in Spain, to prove

---

[26] *ABT,* pp. 265–270 et passim.

[27] Anderson, *Memoirs,* pp. 475–476. On Anderson's general reputation for truthfulness, see Stark Young in *Paul Rosenfeld: Voyager in the Arts,* ed. J. Mellquist and L. Wiese, New York, 1948, p. 195. Hemingway wrote Maxwell Perkins on January 20, 1927: "Sherwood Anderson is in Paris and we had two fine afternoons together. . . . He was not at all sore about *Torrents* and we had a fine time."

that she was his peer as an *aficionado*. Hemingway had helped her to publish *The Making of Americans,* which in Gertrude Stein's view really marked the inception of avant-garde literature in Paris. Very well, then, said Gertrude Stein: "He learned a great deal" from correcting the proofs of her work, and "he admired all that he learned." In fact one gathered from *The Autobiography of Alice B. Toklas* that Hemingway had been formed and made by Gertrude and Sherwood—lock, stock, barrel, and cleaning-rod— "and they were both a little proud and a little ashamed of the work of their minds."

All this, of course, was the most palpable tissue of lies. The *Autobiography* was so full of them that many of her former associates, particularly the *transition* group, felt that the book called for public contradiction. Hemingway's own rejoinder, in a passage of dialogue in *The Green Hills of Africa,* resented the boldfaced lie about his cowardice, and pointed out that what Gertrude Stein knew about the writing of dialogue had probably been learned from his own work, instead of the other way round. She was "damned nice before she got ambitious," but it was a shame to see "all that talent gone to malice and nonsense and self-praise." [28]

Her reiterated claims of leadership in the avant-garde writing of the twenties deceived people like Wyndham Lewis into supposing that Gertrude Stein mothered Ernest Hemingway into prominence. In 1934 Lewis publicly accused Hemingway of aping the "Stein-stutter" and even of taking over her kindergarten *Weltanschauung.* Others, like Dean Christian Gauss, who knew Hemingway better than Lewis did, were aware of the falseness of this view. "He knew Gertrude Stein well socially and dropped in at her salon," writes Dean Gauss, "but I don't believe she had any serious influence on him as a writer. Except for their common interest in writing and painting, their attitudes toward much of life and therefore of art diverged too widely." [29]

Fitzgerald used to say that no one had been more thoroughly robbed than Hemingway—of his manner, his style, and his sub-

[28] *GHOA,* pp. 65–66.
[29] Christian Gauss to CB, 12/26/50. Cf. J. P. Bishop, *New Republic* 89 (November 11, 1936), p. 40.

ject matter. "Probably of no other living man," wrote Dorothy Parker in 1929, "has so much tripe been penned or spoken." [30] In the Paris years Hemingway was an independent spirit, a sidelong observer of the vagaries of the Montparnassians, aggressively critical of poor writing and of all forms of literary pretension. It was undoubtedly a strategic error on his part to allow himself to become involved in the literary warfare of that period, and it was probably natural that the enemies he made should seize the occasion offered by their memoirs to attack Hemingway in turn. One senses the vengeance motive at work in the reminiscences by Margaret Anderson, Robert McAlmon, and Harold Acton, as well as those of Gertrude Stein and Sherwood Anderson.[31]

Others resented the falsification of the record. Malcolm Cowley, Archibald MacLeish, Donald Ogden Stewart, John Dos Passos, John Peale Bishop, Scott Fitzgerald, and Ford Madox Ford were among the group of loyalists. Elliot Paul recorded his view that Hemingway was in fact a "shy and diffident man, eager for appreciation and constructive criticism, not at all sure of himself, a gay companion, and a loyal friend." [32] Dean Gauss shared the opinion that Hemingway's habits and motives have been misrepresented. "His dominant interest," writes Mr. Gauss of the period of 1925, "was . . . in learning the craft of the writer. . . . Fitzgerald too was, and remained, an earnest and competent student of the art of writing, and this was one of the bonds between Scott and Hemingway. In other respects they were worlds apart. Hemingway was not interested in the Ritz or playboys. His special interest lay in the more exacting forms of physical proficiency and courage. He himself did some boxing and practiced enough self-control to keep himself in reasonable trim. There was nothing Latin-Quarterish, intellectually or esthetically pretentious about him. He had the clear eye, even temper, and easy bearing of an athlete in condition." [33]

[30] *New Yorker* 5 (November 30, 1929), pp. 28–31.
[31] See, for example, Margaret Anderson, *My Thirty Years' War,* New York, 1930; Alfred Kreymborg, *The Little World: 1914 and After,* New York, 1932, p. 142; and Harold Acton, *Memoirs of an Aesthete,* London, 1948.
[32] *Saturday Review of Literature* 17 (November 6, 1937), pp. 3–4.
[33] Christian Gauss to CB, 12/26/50.

By the spring of 1926, however, the making of Hemingway had not yet been accomplished, nor had the marring yet begun. The memoirists were still living, rather than writing, their experiences. Hemingway's writing had twice cracked, without breaking open, the American market. For those who were interested, *In Our Time* gave ample promise of an original new talent. *The Torrents of Spring* showed a temperamental opposition to the sometimes maudlin posturings, and the somewhat muddled explorations of id and ego with which Anderson and others had made their literary reputations. But if Hemingway was to achieve a revolution, one could not yet define its shape. Among his associates in the expatriate colony many shared Fitzgerald's belief that this writer was "the real thing." The reality of the thing remained to be proved, and the faith to be justified. The next three books—*The Sun Also Rises, Men Without Women,* and *A Farewell to Arms*—accomplished the revolution. Then the counter-revolution began to make itself felt.

III · The Way It Was

> "The job of the last twenty-five years was
> for the writer or artist to get what there
> was to be got (artistically) out of the
> world extant."—Ezra Pound [1]

I. PLACE, FACT, SCENE

"A writer's job is to tell the truth," said Hemingway in
1942.[2] He had believed it for twenty years and he would continue
to believe it as long as he lived. No other writer of our time
has so fiercely asserted, so pugnaciously defended, or so consistently exemplified the writer's obligation to speak truly. His standard of truth-telling has been, moreover, so high and so rigorous
that he has very rarely been willing to admit secondary evidence, whether literary evidence or evidence picked up from other
sources than his own experience. "I only know what I have seen,"
is a statement which comes often to his lips and pen. What he
has personally done, or what he knows unforgettably by having
gone through one version of it, is what he is interested in telling
about. This is not to say that he has refused to invent freely. But
he has always made it a sacrosanct point to invent in terms of
what he actually knows from having been there.

The primary intent of his writing, from first to last, has been
to seize and project for the reader what he has often called "the
way it was." This is a characteristically simple phrase for a concept of extraordinary complexity, and Hemingway's conception
of its meaning has subtly changed several times in the course of
his career—always in the direction of greater complexity. At the
core of the concept, however, one can invariably discern the
operation of three esthetic instruments: the sense of place, the
sense of fact, and the sense of scene.

The first of these, which is clearly a passion with Hemingway,

[1] Ezra Pound, quoted in Samuel Putnam, *Paris Was Our Mistress*, New
York, 1947, p. 154.
[2] *Men at War*, New York, 1942, introduction, p. xv.

is the sense of place. "Unless you have geography, background," he once told George Antheil, "you have nothing." [3] You have, that is to say, a dramatic vacuum. Few writers have been more place-conscious. Few have so carefully charted out the geographical groundwork of their novels while managing to keep background so conspicuously unobtrusive. Few, accordingly, have been able to record more economically and graphically the way it is when you walk through the streets of Paris in search of breakfast at a corner café. Or when your footfalls echo among surrounding walls on the ancient cobblestones of early morning Venice, heading for the market-place beside the Adriatic. Or when, at around six o'clock of a Spanish dawn, you watch the bulls running from the corrals at the Puerta Rochapea through the streets of Pamplona towards the bullring.

"When I woke it was the sound of the rocket exploding that announced the release of the bulls from the corrals at the edge of town. . . . Down below the narrow street was empty. All the balconies were crowded with people. Suddenly a crowd came down the street. They were all running, packed close together. They passed along and up the street toward the bullring and behind them came more men running faster, and then some stragglers who were really running. Behind them was a little bare space, and then the bulls, galloping, tossing their heads up and down. It all went out of sight around the corner. One man fell, rolled to the gutter, and lay quiet. But the bulls went right on and did not notice him. They were all running together." [4]

This scene is as morning-fresh as a design in India ink on clean white paper. First is the bare white street, seen from above, quiet and empty. Then one sees the first packed clot of runners. Behind these are the thinner ranks of those who move faster because closer to the bulls. Then the almost comic stragglers, who are "really running." Brilliantly behind these shines the "little bare space," a desperate margin for error. Then the clot of running bulls— closing the design, except of course for the man in the gutter making himself, like the designer's initials, as inconspicuous as possible.

[3] George Antheil, *Bad Boy of Music,* p. 278.
[4] *SAR,* pp. 165–166.

The continuing freshness of such occasions as this might be associated with Hemingway's lifelong habit of early waking. More likely, the freshness arises because Hemingway loves continental cities, makes it almost a fetish to know them with an artist's eye, and has trained himself rigorously to see and retain those aspects of a place that make it *that place,* even though, with an odd skill, he manages at the same time to render these aspects generically.

As with the cities—and Hemingway's preference is for the Latin cities—so with the marshes, rivers, lakes, troutstreams, gulf-streams, groves, forests, hills, and gullies, from Wyoming to Tanganyika, from the Tagliamento to the Irati, and from Key West to the Golden Horn. "None can care for literature itself," said Stevenson, somewhere, "who do not take a special pleasure in the sound of names." Hemingway's love of names is obvious. It belongs to his sense of place. But like the rest of his language, it is under strict control. One never finds, as so often happens in the novels of Thomas Wolfe or the poetry of Carl Sandburg, the mere riot and revel of place-names, played upon like guitar-strings for the music they contain. Hemingway likes the words *country* and *land.* It is astonishing how often they recur in his work without being obtrusive. He likes to move from place to place, and to be firmly grounded, for the time being, in whatever place he has chosen. It may be the banks of the Big Two-Hearted River of Northern Michigan or its Spanish equivalent above Burguete. It may be the Guadarrama hilltop where El Sordo died, or the Veneto marshes where Colonel Cantwell shot his last mallards from a duckblind. Wherever it is, it is solid and permanent, both in itself and in the books.

The earliest of his published work, descriptively speaking, shows an almost neoclassical restraint. Take a sample passage from *The Sun Also Rises,* not his earliest but fairly representative. This one concerns the Irati Valley fishing-trip of Jake Barnes and Bill Gorton.

"It was a beech wood and the trees were very old. Their roots bulked above the ground and the branches were twisted. We walked on the road between the thick trunks of the old beeches and the sunlight came through the leaves in light patches on the grass. The trees were big, and the foliage was thick but it was not gloomy. There was no undergrowth, only the smooth grass, very green and fresh, and the big gray trees were well spaced as though it were a park. 'This is country,' Bill said." [5]

It is such country as an impressionist might paint almost exactly in the terms, and the subdued colors, which Hemingway employs. More than this, however, is the fact that in such a paragraph Dr. Samuel Johnson's Imlac could find little to criticize. Even the arrangement of the beech trees themselves, like the choice of the words, is clean and classical. The foliage is thick, but there is no gloom. Here is neither teeming undergrowth nor its verbal equivalent. The sage of Johnson's *Rasselas* advises all aspirant poets against numbering the streaks of the tulip or describing in detail the different shades of the verdure of the forest. Young Hemingway, still an aspirant poet, follows the advice. When he has finished, it is possible to say (and we supply our own inflection for Bill Gorton's words): "This is country."

For all the restraint, the avoidance of color-flaunting adjectives, and the plainsong sentences (five compound to one complex), the paragraph is loaded with precisely observed fact: beech wood, old trees, exposed roots, twisted branches, thick trunks, sun-patches, smooth green grass, foliage which casts a shade without excluding light. One cannot say that he has been given a generalized landscape—there are too many exact factual observations. On the other hand, the uniquenesses of the place receive no special emphasis. One recognizes easily the generic type of the clean and orderly grove, where weeds and brush do not flourish because of the shade, and the grass gets only enough light to rise to carpet-level. Undoubtedly, as in the neoclassical esthetic, the intent is to provide a generic frame within which the reader is at liberty to insert his own uniquenesses—as many or as few as his imagination may supply.

Along with the sense of place, and as a part of it, is the sense of fact. Facts march through all his pages in a stream as continuous as the refugee wagons in Thrace or the military camions on the road from the Isonzo. Speculation, whether by the author or by the characters, is ordinarily kept to a minimum. But facts,

[5] *SAR,* p. 120.

visible or audible or tangible facts, facts baldly stated, facts without verbal paraphernalia to inhibit their striking power, are the stuff of Hemingway's prose.

Sometimes, especially in the early work, the facts seem too many for the effect apparently intended, though even here the reader should be on guard against misconstruing the intention of a given passage. It is hard to discover, nevertheless, what purpose beyond the establishment of the sense of place is served by Barnes's complete itinerary of his walk with Bill Gorton through the streets of Paris.[6] The direction is from Madame Lecomte's restaurant on the Île St. Louis across to the left bank of the Seine, and eventually up the Boulevard du Port Royal to the Café Select. The walk fills only two pages. Yet it seems much longer and does not further the action appreciably except to provide Jake and Bill with healthy after-dinner exercise. At Madame Lecomte's (the facts again), they have eaten "a roast chicken, new green beans, mashed potatoes, a salad, and some apple pie and cheese." To the native Parisian, or a foreigner who knows the city, the pleasure in the after-dinner itinerary would consist in the happy shock of recognition. For others, the inclusion of so many of the facts of municipal or gastronomic geography—so many more than are justified by their dramatic purpose—may seem excessive.

Still, this is the way it was that time in Paris. Here lay the bridges and the streets, the squares and the cafés. If you followed them in the prescribed order, you came to the café where Lady Brett Ashley sat on a high stool at the bar, her crossed legs stockingless, her eyes crinkling at the corners.

If an imaginative fusion of the sense of place and the sense of fact is to occur, and if, out of the fusing process, dramatic life is to arise, a third element is required. This may be called the sense of scene. Places are less than geography, facts lie inert and uncoordinated, unless the imagination runs through them like a vitalizing current and the total picture moves and quickens. How was it, for example, that second day of the San Fermin fiesta in the Pamplona bullring after Romero had killed the first bull?

"They had hitched the mules to the dead bull and then the whips cracked, the men ran, and the mules, straining forward,

[6] *SAR,* pp. 79–80.

their legs pushing, broke into a gallop, and the bull, one horn up, his head on its side, swept a swath smoothly across the sand and out the red gate." [7]

Here are a dead bull, men, mules, whips, sand, and a red gate like a closing curtain—the place and the facts. But here also, in this remarkably graphic sentence, are the seven verbs, the two adverbs, and the five adverbial phrases which fuse and coordinate the diverse facts of place and thing and set them in rapid motion. If one feels that the sentence is very satisfying as a scene, and wishes to know why, the answer might well lie where it so often lies in a successful lyric poem—that is, in our sense of difficulty overcome. Between the inertness of the dead bull when he is merely *hitched* (a placid verb) and the smooth speed with which the body finally *sweeps* across the sand and out of sight, come the verbs of sweating effort: *crack, run, strain,* and *break.* It is precisely at the verb *broke* that the sentence stops straining and moves into the smooth glide of its close. The massing, in that section of the sentence, of a half-dozen *s*'s, compounded with the *th* sounds of *swath* and *smoothly,* can hardly have been inadvertent. They ease (or grease) the path of the bull's departure.

The pattern in the quoted passage is that of a task undertaken, striven through, and smoothly completed: order and success. For another graphic sentence, so arranged as to show the precise opposites—total disorder and total failure—one might take the following example from *Death in the Afternoon.* The protagonist is a "phenomenon," a bullfighter who has lost his nerve.

"In your mind you see the phenomenon, sweating, white-faced, and sick with fear, unable to look at the horn or go near it, a couple of swords on the ground, capes all around him, running in at an angle on the bull hoping the sword will strike a vital spot, cushions sailing down into the ring and the steers ready to come in." [8]

In this passage, place has become predicament. The facts, thrown in almost helter-skelter, imply the desperate inward fear which is responsible for the creation of the outward disorder. Verbs are held to a minimum, and their natural naked power is

[7] *SAR,* p. 175.
[8] *DIA,* p. 226.

limited with qualifications. The phenomenon is *unable to look,* and *hoping to strike,* not *looking* and *striking.* He runs, but it is at a bad angle. The disorder of the swords on the ground and the capes all around is increased by the scaling-in of seat-cushions from the benches, the audience's insult to gross cowardice. The author-spectator's crowning insult is the allusion to the steers, who by comparison with the enraged bull are bovine, old-womanly creatures. On being admitted to the ring, they will quiet and lead away the bull the phenomenon could not kill.

The sense of place and the sense of fact are indispensable to Hemingway's art. But the true craft, by which diversities are unified and compelled into graphic collaboration, comes about through the operation of the sense of scene. Often, moving through the Latin language countries, watching the crowd from a café table or a barrera bench, Hemingway seems like a lineal descendant of Browning's observer in *How It Strikes a Contemporary.*

> You saw go up and down Valladolid
> A man of mark, to know next time you saw . . .
> Scenting the world, looking it full in face.

II. WHAT HAPPENED

Although they are clearly fundamental to any consideration of Hemingway's esthetic aims, place, fact, and scene are together no more than one phase of a more complex observational interest. The skillful writer can make them work in harmony, with place and fact like teamed horses under the dominance of the sense of scene. The result is often as striking and satisfactory to watch as a good chariot race. But the event is, after all, mainly an extrinsic matter. These are not Plato's horses of the soul.

The complementary phase is inward: a state of mind causally related to the extrinsic events and accurately presented in direct relation to those events. When Samuel Putnam asked Hemingway in the late twenties for a definition of his aims, the answer was: "Put down what I see and what I feel in the best and simplest way I can tell it." [9] Taken as absolute standards, of course, best-

[9] Samuel Putnam, *op.cit.,* pp. 128–129.

ness and simplicity will often be at variance, a fact of which Hemingway at that date was apparently becoming more and more conscious. But his aim from the beginning had been to show, if he could, the precise relationship between what he saw and what he felt.

It is characteristic of Hemingway, with his genuine scorn for overintellectualized criticism, that he has himself refused to employ critical jargon in the presentation of his esthetic ideas. It is also evident, however, that early in his career, probably about 1922, he had evolved an esthetic principle which might be called "the discipline of double perception." The term is not quite exact, since the aim of double perception is ultimately a singleness of vision. This is the kind of vision everyone experiences when his two eyes, though each sees the same set of objects from slightly disparate angles, work together to produce a unified picture with a sense of depth to it. According to Hemingway, he was trying very hard for this double perception about the time of his return from the Near East in the fall of 1922. Aside from knowing "truly" what he "really" felt in the presence of any given piece of action, he found that his greatest difficulty lay in putting down on paper "what really happened in action; what the actual things were which produced the emotion" felt by the observer. No wonder that he was finding it hard to get "the real thing, the sequence of motion and fact which made the emotion." Whatever that real thing was, if you stated it "purely" enough and were likewise lucky, there was a chance that your statement of it would be valid, esthetically and emotionally valid, forever.[10]

Fundamental to the task is the deletion of one's own preconceptions. Such and such was the way it *ought* to be, the way you *assumed* it was. But "oughts" and "assumptions" are dangerous ground for a man to stand on who wishes to take the word of no one else, and to achieve in esthetics what René Descartes thought he had achieved in philosophy, namely, a start at the start. The hope was that the genuinely serious and determined writer-observer might be able in time to penetrate behind the illusions which all our preconceptions play upon the act of clear seeing.

[10] *DIA,* p. 2.

It would then become his task to perfect himself in the discipline of double perception. To make something so humanly true that it will outlast the vagaries of time and change, yet will still speak directly to one's own changing time, he must somehow reach a state of objective awareness between two poles, one inward-outward and the other outward-inward. The first need (though not always first in order of time) is the ability to look within and to describe that complex of mixed emotions which a given set of circumstances has produced in the observer's mind. The other necessity is to locate and to state factually and exactly that outer complex of motion and fact which produced the emotional reaction.

This second class of things and circumstances, considered in their relations to the emotional complexes of the first class, would be precisely what T. S. Eliot called "objective correlatives." [11] His statement calls them variously "a set of objects, a situation, a chain of events which shall be the formula of that particular emotion; such that when the external facts, which must terminate in sensory experience, are given, the emotion is immediately evoked." He states further that the idea of artistic "inevitability" consists in the "complete adequacy of the external to the emotion." Mr. Eliot's generic description fits Hemingway's customary performance. Yet it may be noticed that Eliot's most frequent practice, as distinguished from his theoretical formulation, is to fashion his objective correlatives into a series of complex *literary* symbols. These are designed to elicit a more or less controlled emotional response from the reader (like the Wagnerian passage in *The Waste Land*), depending to some degree on the extent of his cultural holdings. With Hemingway, on the other hand, the objective correlatives are not so much inserted and adapted as observed and encompassed. They are to be traced back, not to anterior literature and art objects, but to things actually seen and known by direct experience of the world.

Hemingway's method has this special advantage over Eliot's —that one's ability to grasp the emotional suggestions embodied in an objective correlative depends almost solely on two factors: the reader's sensitivity to emotional suggestion, and the degree

[11] T. S. Eliot, *The Sacred Wood*, London, 1920, pp. 92–93.

of his imaginative and sympathetic involvement in the story which is being told. With Eliot these two factors are likewise emphatically present, but a third is added. This third, which in a measure controls and delimits the first two, is the factor of "literary" experience. One's emotional response to the Wagnerian passage cannot be really full unless he knows its origin, can see it in both its original and its new and secondary context, and can make certain quick comparisons between the two. Some, though not all, of Eliot's correlatives accordingly show a "twice-removed" quality which in a measure pales and rarefies them. They cannot always achieve the full-bloodedness and immediacy of correlatives taken directly from the actual set of empirical circumstances which produced in the author the emotion which he is seeking to convey to the reader.

The objective correlatives in Hemingway appear to be of two main types, arbitrarily separable though always working together in a variety of ways. The first may be called *things-in-context:* that particular arrangement of facts in their relations to one another which constitutes a static field of perception. The second type may be called *things-in-motion,* since the arrangement of facts in their relations one to another is almost never wholly static. One might call any combination of the two types by the generic term of *what happened,* where the idea of happening implies a sequence of events in a certain order in time, though any event in the sequence can be arrested to form a static field of observation. If you have *what happened* in this special sense, you will have a chance of reproducing, in a perspective with depth, "the way it was."

To write for permanence, therefore, is to find and set down those things-in-context and things-in-motion which evoked a reaction in the writer as observer. Yet even the presence of both of these correlatives will not suffice to produce the total effect unless one also knows and says what he "really felt" in their presence. The important corollary idea of selection, meaning the elimination of the irrelevant and the unimportant at both poles, is clearly implied in Hemingway's phrase, "stated purely enough." During the five years of his early apprenticeship and the next five in which he developed his skills with such remarkable rapidity, the discipline of double perception was for Hemingway the leading esthetic principle. It is hard to imagine a better—or more difficult—task for the young writer to attempt. Although other principles and other skills have since arisen to complement and supplement this first one, it still occupies one whole side of his attention as an artist.

III. TRUTH AND FALLACY

The basis of Hemingway's continuing power, and the real backbone of his eminence, is in practical esthetics. "Pure" or theoretical esthetics, of that special bloodless order which can argue to all hours without a glance at concretions, holds little interest for an artist of so pragmatic and empirical a cast of mind. One might even doubt that theoretical esthetics is of real interest to any genuine artist, unless in his alter ego he happens also to be a philosophical critic. If that is true, his artistic life is always in some danger, as Hemingway's is not. In esthetics as in his personal philosophy, he has labored hard to stay free of the wrong kind of illusion, and out from under the control of any cut-and-dried system, always trying instead to keep his eye trained on the thing in itself and the effect of the thing in himself. The actual, he wrote in 1949, is "made of knowledge, experience, wine, bread, oil, salt, vinegar, bed, early mornings, nights, days, the sea, men, women, dogs, beloved motor cars, bicycles, hills and valleys, the appearance and disappearance of trains on straight and curved tracks . . . cock grouse drumming on a basswood log, the smell of sweetgrass and fresh-smoked leather and Sicily." [12] Given the knowledge and experience of these and their unnamed equivalents, the artist can be at home in the world. If he is a practical esthetician whose aim is to "invent truly," he is on firm ground. By experience he knows what will do. By observation he knows what will go—like the eminently practical Aristotle of the *Poetics*.

It was once remarked, though not by Aristotle, that the province of esthetics is the true and the beautiful, the province of morality the good. Of Hemingway as a moral writer there will be much to say. It is clear that the strongest conviction in Heming-

[12] Introd. to Elio Vittorini's novel, *In Sicily*, New York, 1949.

way the esthetician—the principle underlying his sense of place and fact and scene, the principle supporting his "discipline of double perception"—is the importance of telling truth.

To get at the truth of anything is hard enough. For the young artist the task is complicated by the fact that he must steer his way with the utmost care among a set of fallacies, placed like sand-bunkers around a green, or concealed traps around desirable bait. Three of these fallacies stand out: the pathetic, the apathetic, and what may be called the kinetographic.

Ruskin named the first.[13] It is *pathetic* because it comes about through excess of emotion. It is fallacious because, when we are really dominated by an emotion, it is extremely difficult to see things as they are. The curious may read Hemingway's own half-serious opinions on the subject in a disquisition on "erectile writing," which was written to satirize Waldo Frank's *Virgin Spain* in *Death in the Afternoon.*[14] Fundamentally, as that essay makes plain, the pathetic fallacy is an error in perception. But secondarily and by a logical sequence, it is an error of expression, since what has been wrongly seen cannot be rightly described. The intensity of the emotion felt by the writer, if let go on its own, will determine his choice of words. In Charles Kingsley's *Alton Locke,* Ruskin finds an example in which the writing has been made irrational by the author's failure to control the intensity of his emotion. A girl has died in the surf and the seamen bring her body in.

> They rowed her in across the rolling foam—
> The cruel, crawling foam.

"The foam is not cruel," says Ruskin, "neither does it crawl. The state of mind which attributes to it these characters of a living creature is one in which the reason is unhinged by grief. All violent feelings have the same effect. They produce in us a falseness in all our impressions of external things, which I would generally characterize as the pathetic fallacy."

Ruskin goes on to say that the greatest artists do not often admit this kind of falseness of impression and expression. It is only the second or third rankers who much delight in it. It is a

[13] John Ruskin, *Modern Painters,* New York, 1865, Vol. 3, pp. 156–172.
[14] *DIA,* p. 53.

form of self-deception, one of the orders of sentimentality. The
good writers are not the creatures of their emotions; theirs is a
sanity which helps them to see the world clearly and to see it
whole.

Beginning with a standard of performance which rigorously excluded the pathetic fallacy, Hemingway adhered to it with a faith
just short of fanatical. He still does. Emotion was of course both
permissible and, under proper control, necessary. Excess of emotion, however, was never to be allowed. It would falsify both impression and expression. So many of our habits of seeing and
saying take their origin from recollected emotion gone stale. If
one could cut loose from these habits, three immediate results
might be expected. First, you could see what you really saw rather
than what you thought you saw. Second, you could know what
you felt rather than "what you were supposed to feel." Third,
you could say outright what you really saw and felt instead of
setting down a false (and, in the bad sense, a literary) version
of it.

Hemingway's earliest plan, therefore, was to start cleanly and
all afresh to see what effects could be achieved by straight observation of action, set forth in unadorned prose. The immediate
upshot of the effort was the kind of writing presented in the
Paris edition of *in our time*. This, for example, on part of Act
One at a bullfight:

"They whack-whacked the white horse on the legs and he
kneed himself up. The picador twisted the stirrups straight and
pulled and hauled up into the saddle. The horse's entrails hung
down in a blue bunch and swung backward and forward as he
began to canter, the monos whacking him on the back of his legs
with the rods. He cantered jerkily along the barrera. He stopped
stiff and one of the monos held his bridle and walked him forward.
The picador kicked in his spurs, leaned forward and shook his
lance at the bull. Blood pumped regularly from between the
horse's front legs. He was nervously unsteady. The bull could
not make up his mind to charge." [15]

This 120-word miniature is a writer's apprentice-exercise, a
minute of a Spanish committee meeting. Without ignoring the be-

[15] *First 49*, p. 262.

ginning (a horse has been gored by a bull) or the end (the horse
will be gored again and will die), the young writer is concentrating on the middle of an action. He puts down what he sees, exactly as he sees it. He eliminates from his view the panorama,
the weather, the crowd, the waiting matadors, the price of the
seats, the hardness of the bench on which he sits, the odor of his
neighbor, the color of the sky, the degree of the temperature.
Instead he watches the horse, and what takes place immediately
around the horse, with a tremendous intensity of concentration.
He is not guessing, even when he speaks of the horse's nervous
unsteadiness or the bull's indecision. These are immediately visible qualities, shown by the animals through their actions. The
prose is as clean as the observation. Nothing is ornamental. None
but essential modifiers are called, and only a few are chosen.
No similes, no metaphors, no literary allusions, no pathetic illusions, no balanced clauses. There is only one trick, and that is a
good one: the three-time use of the word *forward,* which adds to
the intensity of the account because "forward" is where the bull
stands with one wet horn. Otherwise there is nothing in the least
fancy. There is only an ancient horse, in very bad shape, waiting
for the *coup de grâce.*

Though he never chose similar subjects himself, Ruskin might
well have admired Hemingway's "story." He could have placed it
alongside Thackeray's account of Amelia in *Vanity Fair:* that time
when she kneels in her London drawing-room to pray for the
well-being of her husband George, in ignorance of the fact that
he lies dead at Waterloo. Ruskin's term for the literature of
straight statement, without moralizing elaboration or rococo interior decorating, is the "Make-What-You-Will-Of-It" school of
fiction—a school diametrically opposed to the school of the
pathetic fallacy. Scholars at the Spartan school of "What-You-
Will" are content to let well enough alone. Like Hemingway at
the Spanish committee-meeting, they say the thing the way it was
and let the minutes stand as written.

The passage on the horse also steers clear of the apathetic fallacy, where the reason is so cold and tight that the matter of emotion is squeezed out entirely. At first glance, it is true, one might
suppose that Hemingway had ignored both his own and the read-

er's emotions. The account includes no overt allusion to how the observer felt in the presence of Rosinante Agonistes. There is no evident plucking of the heart-strings, no visible pump inserted into the springs of human sympathy.

Yet the close reader can entertain no real doubt. The passage is neither cold, austere, nor cruel. Pity for the horse (if you are a member of that sector of mankind which pities wounded horses) is revealed by the artist's selection of details: the horse's awkward struggle to a standing position, the swinging of the exposed entrails, the jerkiness of the canter, the bite of the spurs, and the awful regularity of the pumping of the blood. A kind of implicit enmity towards the picador and the ring-servants comes out in verbs like *whack-whacked, pulled and hauled,* the second *whacking,* and the *kicking-in* of the spurs. The pity and the enmity are so firmly in check that at first—to use Aristotle's ethical terms—we suppose a *defect* of sympathy. By the same token, the *extreme* of excessive pathos is carefully avoided. What remains is the *mean,* the province of the writer who seeks to avoid both the apathetic and the pathetic fallacies.

Such an esthetic theory of the "emotive mean" leaves the practitioner open to certain criticisms. What about scope, it is asked, and what about depth? Where is the rest of the act? Who were the parents of the horse that we may establish some sort of sympathetic rapport with him? "Hemingway's art," wrote Wyndham Lewis in 1934, "is an art of the surface—and, as I look at it, none the worse for that." [16] Lewis failed, like many of his contemporaries, to look at this particular art long enough. Had he done so, he might have seen what Hemingway was doing with images and with suggestion far below the surfaces of his better stories —though not too far to be overlooked by the close and sympathetic reader. He also ignored Henry James' observation, which applies to all of Hemingway's miniatures: "an exemplary anecdote" may be also "a little rounded drama." [17] Many of our best critics have consistently underrated Hemingway's esthetic intelligence.

If his chosen approach led to pejorative judgments, or even to

[16] *Men Without Art,* London, 1934, p. 19.
[17] *Works,* New York edition, vol. 13, preface, p. v.

the suggested kind of limitation on depth and scope, Hemingway
as an apprentice craftsman was temporarily prepared to accept
them. He began, as he knew he must, by centering attention on
action, and on what he felt to be the simpler modes of action. "I
was trying to learn to write, commencing with the simplest things,"
he said in 1932, speaking of his program in 1922.[18] As in the
laboratory study of biology, one works up only very gradually
to more complex organisms. If he were to begin on the human
instead of the frog, the young biologist's ignorance might betray
him into the most unscientific (which is to say, untrue) conceptions, and he would have the further hazard of getting lost among
the ganglia. Hemingway's writing since 1922 has certainly been
none the worse for his rigorous self-imposed apprentice training.
He has gone well beyond the early state without ever losing sight
of its importance. He has continued to employ what he learned
there at the same time that he has continued to learn.

The most dangerous pitfall for the young Hemingway was what
may be called the kinetographic fallacy. This consists in the supposition that we can get the best art by an absolutely true description of what takes place in observed action. It will be kinetic
because it must move by definition. It will be graphic because it
is a picture. We write down what we see men doing, what they
say, what they look like to us. We hold a mirror and a micro-
phone up to life, and report, with absolute though selective precision, the reflections and the noises.

The dangers of such a program, if it is rigorously followed, are
clear. The absolutist desire to see and say the truth and nothing
but the truth may keep the best-intentioned writer from doing
both. No artist who reports the action of men and animals, merely
as such, will record things as they are, or really grasp and project
"the way it was." He will record actions from the outside, only as
they *look* to be. Facts will be distorted in the very attempt to avoid
distortion.

The account of the wounded horse cannot be called distortion.
But it does nevertheless consist in a concentration so intense that
the miniature itself can be appreciated without remembering the
larger context of the bullfight, the arena, the town, and the nation

[18] *DIA*, p. 2.

in which the described events took place. The spreading context can, of course, be supplied by the reader's imagination. But one could probably argue that the artist is not justified in overworking his reader's imagination to quite this extent.

Between the "defect" of too little detail and the "excess" of the sand-pile technique (where everything is put in, whether it is relevant or not, until we have a bulk on the horizon too considerable to ignore), there is a mean. By the time Hemingway wrote *The Sun Also Rises,* he was rounding out his writing by allowing the possible to enter his picture of the actual. He was beginning to admit guesses, fictions, motivations, imaginations in far greater profusion than he had done in 1922. He felt justified in doing so because he had so firmly avoided guessing throughout his apprenticeship. Now he had had sufficient experience of the kinetographic reporting of the actual so that he could trust himself to invent, though never to invent except in terms of carefully observed experience. Hemingway, therefore, did not so much avoid as transcend the kinetographic fallacy. His own summary of the "mean position" continues, of course, to stress the importance of truth-telling: "A writer's job is to tell the truth." Then he goes on. "His standard of fidelity to the truth must be so high that his invention" which comes always and invariably "out of his experience, should produce a truer account than anything factual can be." [19] This remark, set down in 1942, is the essence of twenty years of experience. It runs very close to a pronouncement by Coleridge, who also based his views on common sense and long experience: "A poet ought not to pick nature's pocket: let him borrow, and so borrow as to repay by the very act of borrowing. Examine nature accurately, but write from recollection; and trust more to your imagination than your memory." [20]

Hemingway's nearly absolute devotion to what is true, coming in an age when absolute devotions are so rare, is not only the dominant drive in his whole esthetic life, but also the firmest guarantee that his works will survive. He has continued to entertain a healthy and essentially humble conviction that the truth

[19] *Men at War,* introd., p. xv.
[20] *Table Talk* in *Works,* ed. Shedd, New York, 1853, Vol. 6, pp. 345–346.

is difficult to come by, though sometimes it may drop by chance into a writer's lap. The good parts of a book, as he told Fitzgerald in 1929, may be only something a writer is lucky enough to over-hear, or they may be the wreck of his "whole damned life." [21] But if both partake of the nature of truth, one is as good as the other, though their scope will naturally differ. Any form of truth, however, if it is put into an art form, will help the writing to survive the erosions of time. For the truth is a sturdy core, impervious to the winds of faddist doctrine and the temporary weather of an age.

IV. THE BEAUTIFUL

From truth it is only a step to beauty and *aisthetes*—"one who perceives"—is ordinarily associated with the perception of the beautiful. Although Hemingway the esthetician has spoken much of truth, he has had little to say about what constitutes for him the nature of the beautiful. In the fiction itself there is scarcely any overt emphasis on beauty for its own sake. Remembering Ruskin, one might call Hemingway's the "make-what-you-will-of-it" approach to the perception of the beautiful. It is as if Hemingway tacitly agreed with the dictum of Herbert Read: "To live according to natural law, this is also the release of the imagination. In discovering truth, we create beauty." [22]

With respect to the beautiful it appears to be a basic assumption in Hemingway's esthetic that what is true, in the sense of being natural and untinkered-with, is also beautiful. Ugliness in Hemingway is almost invariably associated with the abnormal and the unnatural: the unwomanly woman, for example, or the unmanly man. The unclean, the furtive, the cowardly, the enslaved all show an aspect of the sinister. Beauty in Hemingway is the beauty of land, of men and women, of the nobler animals, of the clean, the honest, the well-lighted, the nonconcealing, the brave.

One version of the alliance between the natural and the beautiful was very well summarized by the Emperor Marcus Aurelius.

[21] EH to FSF, from Madrid, 9/4/29.
[22] Quoted by Kenneth Rexroth in review of Read's *Collected Poems*, *New York Times Book Review*, June 17, 1951, p. 5.

"The hanging-down of grapes, the brow of the lion, the froth of a foaming wild boar, though by themselves considered they are far from beauty, yet because they happen naturally, they are both comely and beautiful." [23]

The comely is the becoming, the fitting, that which is felt to be naturally right. Whenever in the reading of Hemingway one finds himself arrested by the beauty of a passage, he may discover also that its essential naturalness, in the moral dimension of stoic esthetics, helps to explain its essential beauty.

Following the lead of the Emperor, one might turn to the examples of the rhinoceros and the kudu bull in the *The Green Hills of Africa,* one of Hemingway's least appreciated books. [24] About the rhino:

"There he was, long-hulked, heavy-sided, prehistoric-looking, the hide like vulcanized rubber and faintly transparent looking, scarred with a badly healed horn wound that the birds had pecked at, his tail thick, round, and pointed, flat many-legged ticks crawling on him, his ears fringed with hair, tiny pig eyes, moss growing on the base of his horn that grew forward from his nose. M'Cola looked at him and shook his head. I agreed with him. This was the hell of an animal."

Confronted by this passage, the naturalist might well argue that this is the way a dead rhinoceros looks. This is the nature of the beast, and if we follow Marcus Aurelius it would be necessary to conclude that the rhinoceros, since he happens naturally, is a thing of beauty and a joy forever. Yet to argue thus he would have to ignore the very careful accumulation of points in Hemingway's description which suggest the unnatural and the abnormal. The prehistoric look, for example, is not of this present world; the vulcanized-rubber appearance of the skin, though very distinctly of this world, is somehow artificial and ugly on an animal. The horn wound, badly healed and pecked at by the tick birds, has the force of an abnormality. So does the allusion to the verminous ticks, comparable to the horror of flies around a horse's crupper mentioned elsewhere in the same book. The eyes are out of proportion, and the moss at the base of the horn seems an unnatural

---

[23] *Meditations,* Book III, section ii.
[24] *GHOA,* pp. 79 and 231.

growth, like festoons of mildew on a neglected book. This is an offensive animal, disproportioned in its long hulk, abnormal in its appurtenances, a kind of mistaken hybrid, not what you would expect an animal to look like—esthetically wrong, in short, and generally objectionable.

Against such disproportion, abnormality, and unnatural naturalness, one might place the unposed portrait of the kudu bull, killed at long last after many days of unsuccessful hunting.

"It was a huge, beautiful kudu bull, stone-dead, on his side, his horns in great dark spirals, widespread and unbelievable as he lay dead five yards from where we stood. . . . I looked at him, big, long-legged, a smooth gray with the white stripes and the great curling, sweeping horns, brown as walnut meats, and ivory-pointed, at the big ears and the great, lovely, heavy-maned neck, the white chevron between his eyes and the white of his muzzle and I stooped over and touched him to try to believe it. He was lying on the side where the bullet had gone in and there was not a mark on him and he smelled sweet and lovely like the breath of cattle and the odor of thyme after rain."

This is the true hunter's esthetic appreciation. Even the non-hunter, whose conscientious or temperamental objection to killing would not permit him to write in just this way, can share the hunter's admiration for the graceful, strong, handsomely proportioned animal. The size, the clean natural colors, the wholeness ("there was not a mark on him"), and the sweet natural smell which distinguishes the grazing animals from the meat-eaters, are all factors in the kudu's esthetic attractiveness. "Beautiful . . . lovely . . . lovely." Words like these, in the context of the weary hunt now successfully crowned with antlers, are used without apology. Here is the hunter's and the esthetician's dream of an animal, as the rhinoceros was a kind of tickridden nightmare.

The quality of beauty in Hemingway's work seems to come as naturally as the leaves to a tree. Yet the carefully ordered accounts of natural scenery in his pages reveal, on close examination, a deliberate and intelligent artifice. The description is nearly always directly functional within an action. The beauty—or ugliness—of the land is made to belong to the ugliness—or beauty—

of the human events which occur in its midst. Sometimes, as in
Frank Norris, natural beauty stands in quiet contrast to whatever
it is that men and women are doing in its presence. Hemingway
uses this old trick of the naturalistic writers charily and rarely;
it is never emphasized in the black-jack manner of, say, Norris
in *The Octopus,* or Steinbeck in *The Wayward Bus.* What we
tend to get in Hemingway is a subtle interweaving of the natural
conditions in the background and the human conditions in the
foreground or the middle-distance.

When he looks at portrait-studies by the Italian masters, Hemingway is always careful to examine the backgrounds, as if to find
corroboration in another art for his ideas about the importance of
natural settings in prose fiction. He well knows the total effect
depends upon placing figures in a context—verbal, schematic,
and scenic—and in this respect he is as good a "contextualist" as
T. S. Eliot, who adopted if he did not invent this special application of the term. Although Hemingway has rigorously trained
himself in the accurate observation of natural objects, his precision of rendering does not prevent these objects from being put
to symbolic use. The discipline of double perception requires an
ability to penetrate both to the essential qualities of a natural scene
and to the essential qualities of a subjective reaction to the scene.
These, working together in a dozen ways, produce the total effect.

Hemingway's sense of beauty is stirred, his heart is moved, as
much by human beings as by landscapes or the more handsome
animals. Here again the normative judgment comes into operation. He scorns perversions of any kind. Whatever is abnormal
or unnatural according to his measurement is ugly according to
his conclusion. People about their normal business, or people who
are able under abnormal circumstances to behave like normal human beings, ordinarily strike him with the impact of the beautiful,
though he may not use the word in that connection.

The point may be illustrated by choosing an example of a set
of human beings of no extrinsic beauty at all, but modern, un-
lovely, dirty, urban, and tough. This is a group portrait of the
matadors' representatives, the trusted banderilleros who have
gathered to appraise the bulls the morning before a *corrida.*

"The representatives, usually short men in caps, not yet shaven for the day, with a great variety of accents, but all with the same hard eyes, argue and discuss." [25]

Goya would have fancied these people; Browning's poet-observer could have met them in Valladolid. Though by themselves considered they are far from beauty, yet because they happen naturally, in the morning chiaroscuro of the plaza corrals, they are both comely and beautiful to the eye of a true esthetician.

Anyone so minded could object to the foregoing position on the grounds that the natural is not by any means always to be equated with the moral. The neohumanists habitually opposed the moral to the natural; they argued that only through the operation of the inner check could the natural be housebroken into conformity with acceptable social standards. Dozens of examples could be assembled to show how anti-social and either amoral or immoral the natural man can be when he really lets himself go.

If such objections were not merely captious, they would be simply irrelevant. The neohumanists, great though their gifts were, could most of them lay no just claim to an understanding of practical esthetics.[26] For the first requirement of esthetics, at least in the area where Hemingway works, is that it shall be based on a moral view of the world. With Anton Chekhov's moral statement that "the aim of fiction is absolute and honest truth," he would agree entirely. He would also agree with Marcus Aurelius that the natural is comely and beautiful, though Hemingway offers evidence throughout his work that the natural must be defined within certain normative and essentially moral limits. Working with the concepts of truth and beauty, it thus becomes possible to see "the way it was" as an idea of empirical truth, taking due account of ugliness and deformity, but warmed and illuminated from within by the strong love of natural beauty.

V. THE SABIDURÍAN

To complete the portrait of Hemingway as esthetician, it is necessary to look at what may be called the underside of the paint-

[25] *DIA*, p. 27.
[26] For Hemingway's humorous comment on this group, see *DIA*, p. 139.

ing. The upper side is of course that whole face of his effort as artist which has as its purpose the seeing and saying of truth and "natural" beauty. Truth-telling (whether the "objective" portrayal of things and events in the phenomenal world, or the "subjective" representation of mental-emotional responses to these things and events) is one great criterion by which the worth of writing may be judged. For the upper side of Hemingway's esthetic there is perhaps no better general statement than that of Conrad in his celebrated preface to *The Nigger of the Narcissus.*

"The artist . . . like the thinker or the scientist, seeks the truth. . . . And art itself may be defined as a single-minded attempt to render the highest kind of justice to the visible universe. . . . It is an attempt to find in its forms, in its colours, in its light, in its shadows, in the aspects of matter and in the facts of life what of each is fundamental, what is enduring and essential. . . ."

Although Hemingway's admiration for Conrad is now perhaps less intense than formerly, his evident agreement with such statements as the one just quoted gave him, in the years 1923–1924, good reason to defend Conrad against his fashionable detractors, and to refuse to share in the disparagement which was at its height about the time of Conrad's death. When Ford issued the Conrad memorial supplement in the *transatlantic* for October, 1924, Hemingway made his own position clear.[27]

"The second book of Conrad's that I read was *Lord Jim* [said Hemingway]. I was unable to finish it. It is therefore all I have left of him. For I cannot reread them. That may be what my friends mean by saying he is a bad writer. But from nothing else that I have ever read have I gotten what every book of Conrad has given me."

Knowing that he could not reread them, he had saved up four of the novels to be used as a combination anodyne and stimulant whenever his disgust "with writing, writers, and everything written of and to write would be too much." In Toronto the preceding autumn he had used up three, one after the other, borrowing them from a friend who owned a uniform set. When his newspaper sent him to cover the attempt to locate anthracite coal in the Sudbury

[27] *transatlantic review* 2 (October 1924), pp. 341–342. Information in part from W. L. McGeary.

Basin mining district north of Georgian Bay in Ontario, he bought three back numbers of the *Pictorial Review* and read *The Rover,* "sitting up in bed in the Nickle Range Hotel."

"When morning came [he continued] I had used up all my Conrad like a drunkard. I had hoped it would last me the trip, and felt like a young man who has blown his patrimony. But, I thought, he will write more stories. He has lots of time."

The later reviews had all superciliously agreed that *The Rover* was a bad book. But now Conrad was dead, and "I wish to God," said Hemingway, "they would have taken some great acknowledged technician of a literary figure and left [Conrad] to write his bad stories."

The fashionable derogation of Conrad was often accompanied by the praise of T. S. Eliot as a "good writer." As for Hemingway:

"If I knew that by grinding Mr. Eliot into a fine dry powder and sprinkling that powder over Mr. Conrad's grave, Mr. Conrad would shortly reappear, looking very annoyed at the forced return, and commence writing, I would leave for London early tomorrow morning with a sausage-grinder."

Hemingway neither ground in London nor sprinkled in Canterbury. Had he done so, the topic of conversation between exhumed and exhumer might well have been Conrad's preface. In that very eloquent defence of fiction, Conrad makes three other memorable points besides insisting that the artist must seek truth.

The first is on the language of prose. The phrases "like pebbles fresh from a brook" which Ford Madox Ford admired in the early work of Hemingway were not achieved without the most careful attention to the act of verbal selection. Hemingway told Samuel Putnam in 1926 that "easy writing makes hard reading," and that he wished, if he could, to "strip language clean, to lay it bare down to the bone." [28] In practice this meant the studied deletion of all words and phrases which were in any way false. One of the difficulties with language, as many good writers have felt and as Hemingway said, is that "all our words from loose using have lost their edge." [29] Recognizing this fact, Hemingway always wrote slowly and revised carefully, cutting, eliding, substituting, experi-

[28] Samuel Putnam, *op.cit.,* p. 128.
[29] *DIA,* p. 71.

menting with syntax to see what a sentence could most economically carry, and then throwing out all words that could be
spared.

Such an artist would be obliged to agree with Conrad: "It is
only through an unremitting never-discouraged care for the shape
and ring of sentences . . . that the light of magic suggestiveness
may be brought to play for an evanescent instant over the commonplace surface of words: of the old, old words, worn thin, defaced
by ages of careless usage." Magic suggestiveness is a phrase not
to be found anywhere in the published writings of Hemingway;
yet everywhere in his language the magic of suggestion is at work
among the old, old words. If their surfaces are commonplace,
their interiors bear the imaginative supercharging which only the
true artist can bring to them. And this positive charge, which on
being released plays not over but beneath the verbal surfaces, is
one phase of the underside of Hemingway's distinguished achievement in prose.

The second phase is what Conrad calls "communication
through temperament." The Spanish word *sabiduría* comes very
close to the context of this idea. It may be defined as a kind of
natural knowledge, nothing like the "wisdom" of professional
philosophers, but a knowledge available under the surface of their
lives to all responsive human beings. According to Conrad, "the
artist appeals to that part of our being which is not dependent
on wisdom: to that in us which is a gift and not an acquisition—
and therefore more permanently enduring. . . . Fiction, if it
at all aspires to be art, appeals to temperament. And in truth it
must be . . . the appeal of one temperament to all the other
innumerable temperaments whose subtle and resistless power en-
dows passing events with their true meaning, and creates the
moral, the emotional atmosphere of the place and time." One may
remark in passing that the closing phrase, "the emotional atmosphere of the place and time," is a very concise description for a part
of what Hemingway means by "the way it was." Conrad goes on
to say that the artist's appeal must be realized through the senses
—provided of course that it is the artist's high desire to reach
the secret spring of responsive emotions.

This is also the theory and practice of Hemingway. As one

watches the establishment and development of the sabidurian images in his novels or the more ambitious short stories, one comes to see, as Mr. Theodore Bardacke has recently noticed, "this underlying use of associations and emotional suggestion," visible and even audible through the "objectively reported details." It is precisely this power which enables Mr. Malcolm Cowley to say that "Hemingway's prose at its best gives a sense of depth and of moving forward on different levels that is lacking in even the best of his imitators." Hemingway's own term for it is "the kind of writing that can be done . . . if anyone is serious enough and has luck. There is a fourth and fifth dimension that can be gotten." [30]

In a number of his works, seriously charging and recharging the old, old words and the natural, non-literary temperamental images, Hemingway the sabidurían has already done the job. We respond to it naturally as savages to thunder, or as Dr. Jung's patients to the recurrent opposed symbols of the "Wise Old Man" and "the Shadow." Whether we accept Jung's hypothesis of inherited patterns in the cells of the brain, or try to explain our responses by modern versions of Bentham's psychological hedonism, need not concern us here. However we explain the fact, it operates all through Hemingway's prose.

The total entity we respond to in a work of art is what Conrad's preface calls "the presented vision." It may be a vision of "regret or pity, of terror or mirth." The point is that in its presence no reasonably sensitive human being is an island; he is a part of the mainland. For the presented vision arouses "in the hearts of the beholders that feeling of unavoidable solidarity; of the solidarity in mysterious origin, in toil, in joy, in hope, in uncertain fate, which binds men to each other and all mankind to the visible world."

Hemingway is very clear on this matter of the presented vision. "All good books," he wrote in 1933, "are alike in that they are truer than if they had really happened and after you are finished

---

[30] Theodore Bardacke, "Hemingway's Women," in J. K. M. McCaffery, ed., *Ernest Hemingway: The Man and His Work,* New York, 1950, p. 341; see also Malcolm Cowley, *The Portable Hemingway,* introd., p. xviii. Cf. Hemingway, *GHOA,* pp. 26–27.

reading one you will feel that all that happened to you and afterwards it all belongs to you; the good and the bad, the ecstasy, the remorse and sorrow, the people and the places and how the weather was. If you can get so that you can give that to people, then you are a writer."

No two individualist authors will perfectly agree in generals or in particulars. In every author, esthetically and culturally speaking, one finds a muted echo of Blake's "I must create my own system or be enslaved by another man's." Hemingway would never write the matter of Conrad's preface in the manner of Conrad. Yet he would wholly agree with Conrad in saying to all who demand other things of the artist: "My task which I am trying to achieve is, by the power of the written word to make you hear, to make you feel—it is, before all, to make you *see*. That—and no more, and it is everything." It is everything because it encompasses both the upper- and the underside of all we know as human beings. If the artist achieves his task, it will mean that by all the means at his disposal he has transferred to his reader the true essence of "the way it was."

IV · The Wastelanders

> "It is the mark of the true novelist that in searching the meaning of his own unsought experience, he comes on the moral history of his time."—John Peale Bishop [1]

I. BEAT-UP, NOT LOST

"Hemingway's first novel might rock the country," wrote Alfred Harcourt to Louis Bromfield one day in 1925.[2] The prediction was sound. A year had not gone by before Hemingway awoke one autumn morning in Paris to find that the sun had also risen.

He had labored long and hard to give his first novel (really his third if you counted the one that was stolen and *The Torrents of Spring*) the solid structure and the freshness of texture which have since sustained it. "I started *The Sun Also Rises* on the 21st of July, my [26th] birthday, in Valencia," he writes. Work on the first draft was continued through the last ten days of July and the month of August in Valencia, Madrid, St. Sebastian, and Hendaye, and the complete run-through was finished in Paris on September 6, 1925.[3]

"There is only one thing to do with a novel," he once told Fitzgerald, "and that is to go straight on through to the end of the damned thing." [4] The remark was perhaps designed as an exhortation to Fitzgerald, whose dilatory habits in the completion of novels occasioned some pain to a friend who wished him well. The first draft of *The Sun Also Rises* was set down in approximately forty-eight writing days, but Hemingway nearly killed himself in the process. "I knew nothing about writing a novel when I started it," he recalled in 1948, "and so wrote too fast and

---

[1] John Peale Bishop, "The Missing All," *Virginia Quarterly Review* 13 (Winter 1937), p. 118. Also in McCaffery, *op.cit.*, pp. 292–307.
[2] Quoted in EH to FSF, 12/31/25.
[3] EH to CB, 4/1/51.
[4] EH to FSF, 9/13/29. Also EH to FSF, 5/4/26.

each day to the point of complete exhaustion. So the first draft was very bad . . . I had to rewrite it completely. But in the rewriting I learned much." [5]

Following a rest period during which he produced *The Torrents of Spring* and gave his first draft a chance to settle and objectify itself, he went down to Schruns in the Vorarlberg late in November. Here he spent the month before Christmas in skiing and revising his book. A trip to New York in mid-February provided a brief interlude in the concentrated labors of rewriting. These filled January, part of February, and the month of March. By April first the book was ready for the typist. Heavy cuts in the original opening and elsewhere had now reduced a much longer novel to about 90,000 words. The completed typescript was mailed to Maxwell Perkins on April 24, 1926. The total operation had covered nine months of extremely hard work.[6]

The result justified the effort. If there had been any suspicion that Hemingway's skills were limited to short fiction, the publication of the first novel on October 22, 1926, dispelled it. The book showed, said a pleased reviewer, that he could state a theme dramatically and develop it to book length, a problem not previously attacked except for purposes of travesty in the book on Anderson. Three years later, on September 27, 1929, Hemingway proved with *A Farewell to Arms* that he could do it again. The interim publication of *Men Without Women* (October 14, 1927) indicated that the novelist had not killed the short-story writer. But the books which elevated him to fame, and established him firmly on that eminence, were a pair of remarkable novels.

"Famous at twenty-five; thirty a master" was MacLeish's summary of the record. In their respective ways *The Sun Also Rises* and *A Farewell to Arms* also summarized a record. In reverse chronological order, they represented the essence of that densely packed period in Hemingway's life between 1918 and 1925. They struck a total for the meaning of his own experience, both sought

[5] *FTA,* illustrated edition of 1948, introd., p. viii.

[6] EH to CB, 4/1/51. This paragraph is based on the following additional letters: MP to EH, 2/15/26, 3/15/26; EH to MP, 3/10/26, 4/1/26, 4/19/26, 4/24/26. According to a letter from EH to MP, 11/19/26, he cut 40,000 words from the original first draft.

and unsought, and became in effect two long chapters in the moral history of the nineteen-twenties.

No book is inevitable, though every good book comes out of a strong internal compulsion. Given a man of Hemingway's talents and experience, both books happened naturally. They were done not only for reasons of normal artistic compulsion but also as a means of trying-out the moral essence of seven years. If *The Torrents of Spring* was a declaration of esthetic independence, *The Sun Also Rises* was the means Hemingway chose to declare himself out of the alleged "lostness" of a generation whose vagaries he chronicled. In 1922 he had recorded his humorous scorn for the artistic scum of Montparnasse. Now, through Jake Barnes, he withdrew to the position of a detached observer looking on at aimless revels which at once amused him and left him sick at heart. For it is one view of Jake that he is an imperturbable and damaged Hamlet. By talking thus and thus at the court of the Duchess of the Dôme, he rids himself of a deep-seated disgust for the oppressions of his environment and the people who make it oppressive. In somewhat the same fashion, *A Farewell to Arms* meant the shunting-off of the old war, writing it out, getting rid of it by setting it down in all its true intermixture of humor and horror—until, thirty years after, the rude ceremonial of Colonel Cantwell on a grassed-over Italian battleground could bury it forever.

There was much more to these first two novels, of course, than an act of personal exorcism, however complicated. For to destroy by embodying is also to create by arranging. The artist's special blessing exists in the impulse to destroy an aspect of the thing he creates, and to render permanent what for him, in another and internal dimension, must be permanently destroyed. By 1929, Hemingway had done both tasks. With the attainment, at age thirty, of his majority as a writer, he became what he had not been so completely before—the free man who has served his apprenticeship to an art and fulfilled (in quite another way) his obligations to society. From that date on he moves off on another tack, and one begins to catch echoes of one of his favored maxims: "Don't do anything too bloody long."

Of *The Sun Also Rises*, Robert Littell brightly remarked that it "won the *succès de scandale* of a *roman à clef* floated on *vin ordinaire."* [7] One immediate cause of its success was that if you knew something about the Montparnassians who frequented the Dôme, the Rotonde, the Select, the Deux Magots, the Napolitain, the Dingo Bar, or Zelli's during the period 1923–1925, you were alleged to own a key which would admit the bearer to the "real" identities of the fictional people. As Model-T jokes helped early Fords to fame, so the international guessing-game of who was who in *The Sun Also Rises* assisted with the word-of-mouth promotion of the book. The prototypes of Robert Cohn, Lady Brett Ashley, and Mike Campbell were said to be well known in the Latin Quarter. Though Pedro Romero bore the name of an eighteenth-century matador, he was clearly a fictional projection of Niño de la Palma in his great period before a series of bad horn-wounds damaged his nerve. Wielders of the key could presumably unlock the identities of Bill Gorton, Mr. and Mrs. Braddocks, Count Mippipopoulos, Wilson-Harris the Englishman at Burguete, or Robert Prentiss, the American novelist with the cultivated Oxford accent. For a time after the book was published, Paris gossip asserted that its title should have been *Six Characters in Search of an Author—With a Gun Apiece*. Still, as Hemingway pointed out to Fitzgerald, "no bullets whistled." [8] When the *scandale* had run its course, the wise ones turned to a new topic of absorbing interest: Which author had Hemingway imitated when he wrote *The Sun Also Rises,* Fitzgerald in *This Side of Paradise* or Michael Arlen in *The Green Hat?*

Littell had observed that many of the people had been "practically kidnapped" into Hemingway's novel. Such kidnapping, if that was what had taken place here, was hardly a new experiment. Sherwood Anderson, starting with the actual residents of his Chicago boarding-house and allowing his mind to play freely over their supposed frustrations, had evolved a population for his *Winesburg, Ohio.* [9] Lewis' *Main Street,* Fitzgerald's *This Side of*

[7] *New Republic* 51 (August 10, 1927), pp. 303–306.

[8] J. Charters, "The White Winers," *Esquire* 2 (August 1934), pp. 42–43 and 146. Also EH to FSF, 3/31/27.

[9] So, at any rate, Anderson once told the present writer in conversation. For a more objective account, see W. L. Phillips, "How Sherwood Anderson Wrote *Winesburg, Ohio,*" *American Literature,* 23 (March 1951), pp. 7–30.

Paradise, or a little later Bravig Imbs' *The Professor's Wife* all had recognizable real-life sources. Among the poets, Frost, Robinson, and Masters invented in terms of people they knew. Yeats in the holy land of Ireland praised Maud Gonne into public property. People knew the background of Douglas' *South Wind,* Huxley's *Antic Hay,* and Joyce's *Portrait of the Artist as a Young Man.* It was, in fact, an age of indirect or direct "transcription," when the perfectly sound esthetic theory was that the author must invent out of his own experience or run the risk of making hollow men of his characters. Hemingway shared in the belief (which has been called behaviorist) that any group of living people, placed under the microscope and candidly watched for typical or idiosyncratic conduct, can be made to provide the groundwork of a novel.

The question with any such novel is always whether it has the power to survive the immediate moment when its possible real-life origins are being gossiped about. Unless the *clef* of a *roman à clef* is finally irrelevant, the novel can have no more just claim on the interest of posterity than the society pages or racing forms from last year's newspaper. The *succès de scandale* of 1926 could not possibly explain the rapidity and assurance with which *The Sun Also Rises* became, as it has remained, one of the genuine classics of modern American fiction.

Hemingway did not at all intend to have his novel construed as a text-book of lost-generationism. But the "Lost Generation" catch-phrase, facing the title page, seemed to sum up for many people an aspect of the social history of the nineteen-twenties. Ernest Boyd said that Hemingway had triumphantly added a new chapter to the story Fitzgerald began in *This Side of Paradise.*[10] The feeling was that both books, though in far different ways, helped to anatomize the desperate gaiety with which the Jazz Age covered its melancholia. And there can be no doubt that, with his brilliant dramatization of the moral predicament of a small group of Jazz Age D. P.'s, Hemingway offered a "myth" whose extension in social space far outreached the novel's na-

[10] *Independent* 117 (November 20, 1926), p. 594. About this date Hemingway was writing to Perkins (11/16/26): "It's funny to write a book that seems as tragic as that and have them take it for a jazz superficial story."

tional boundaries of France and Spain. What he had done could be regarded as dramatized social history. But it was not intended to be the social history of a lost generation.

Towards the materials of his book Hemingway's attitude was more complex than has since been generally understood. Because he quite properly refused to explain his position in other than dramatic terms, and because, in his dramatization, he would not consent to oversimplify, he was often taken for the sentimental and mournful singer of an empty day, or, quite as erroneously, as the hardshelled and disillusioned chronicler of social disintegration.

One illustration of the extent of the misunderstanding is the contrast which Hemingway intended to draw by giving the book its two epigraphs, one from Gertrude Stein and the other from Ecclesiastes. The remark there attributed to "Gertrude Stein in conversation" did not represent the position of Hemingway. According to his testimony, she said it in French, and it was supposed to have been said to her by "a garage-keeper in the Midi describing his mechanics, the young ones: *une génération perdue.*" Gertrude Stein sought to extend the application of the remark from the young French mechanics (with their marked ineptitudes in the proper use of screwdrivers) to all the sad young men whom the late war and the high cost of living had cast up on the shores of France.[11]

As Hemingway explained to Perkins on November 19, 1926, he regarded the "lost generation" comment as a piece of "splendid bombast" and was very skeptical of "Gertrude's assumption of prophetic roles." [12] He could not agree with her at all. He himself did not feel lost. His reason for adding the quotation from Ecclesiastes was to indicate his own belief that "there was no such thing as a lost generation."

"I thought [he said in 1951] beat-up, maybe, [deleted] in many ways. But damned if we were lost except for deads, *gueules cassées,* and certified crazies. Lost, no. And Criqui, who was a real *gueule cassée,* won the featherweight championship of the world.

[11] EH to CB, Easter Sunday, 1951.
[12] EH to MP, 11/19/26.

We were a very solid generation though without education (some of us). But you could always get it." [13]

In order to write his book it had been necessary for Hemingway to dissociate himself in a moral sense from the very idea of lostness. He might tell Fitzgerald that *The Sun Also Rises* was "a hell of a sad story" whose only instruction was "how people go to hell." [14] But the point of the book for him, as he wrote Perkins, was "that the earth abideth forever." He had "a great deal of fondness and admiration for the earth, and not a hell of a lot for my generation," and he cared "little about vanities." The book was not meant to be "a hollow or bitter satire, but a damn tragedy with the earth abiding forever as the hero." [15]

The reading public in general did not appear to understand the point or the degree of dissociation between the artist and his characters. One heard that Jake Barnes was a modified self-portrait of Hemingway, dripping with self-pity, when in fact Hemingway was facing the hazards of *la vie humaine* with courage and a reasonably light heart, as, for that matter, was Jake Barnes. "There really is, to me anyway, very great glamour in life—and places and all sorts of things and I would like sometime to get it into the stuff," he wrote to Maxwell Perkins. "I've known some very wonderful people who even though they were going directly to the grave (which is what makes any story a tragedy if carried out until the end) managed to put up a very fine performance en route." [16] It ought to have been plain to discerning readers that Jake Barnes, Bill Gorton, and Pedro Romero were solid—if slightly beat-up—citizens of the republic. They were not lost. They refused to surrender to neuroses like those which beset Robert Cohn, Brett Ashley, and Mike Campbell. And three lost neurotics do not make a lost generation.

It was one of the ironies that Hemingway, having rejected the lost-generation tag both for himself and for his generation, should

[13] EH to CB, Easter Sunday, 1951.
[14] EH to FSF, [probably summer], 1926.
[15] EH to MP, 11/19/26.
[16] EH to MP, 12/7/26. A part of this letter was published by Perkins in a short commentary on Hemingway in *Scribner's Magazine* 81 (March 1927), p. 4.

find his first book widely accepted as Exhibit A of "lost-generation-ism." Another conspicuous irony was that most readers found Brett and her little circle of drinking-companions so fascinating as to overshadow the idea of the abiding earth as the true hero of the book. Hemingway's love and admiration for the natural earth was certainly quite clearly projected. Any beat-up Antaeus who could gain strength and sanity from contact with the earth was a kind of hero in his eyes, as one saw in the portraits of Barnes and Gorton and Romero. Yet all eyes were drawn towards Brett—possibly by the odd mixture of irony and pity, of condemnation and admiration, with which she was treated.

II. COUNTERPOINT

here

Hemingway had told Perkins that he cared little about the vanities. *The Sun Also Rises* was one of the proofs of that statement. The title comes from the first chapter of Ecclesiastes. It is useful to recognize the strong probability that the moral of the novel is derived from the same book: "All is vanity and vexation of spirit." All is vanity, at any rate, along the Vanity Fair of the Boulevard Montparnasse where the novelist introduces his people and completes his preliminary exposition. "Everybody's sick," says Jake's little *poule* in the Parisian horsecab. The novel goes on to prove that if you concentrate on a certain segment of expatriated society, she is very nearly right. All is vanity at the Pamplona fiesta when Cohn and Campbell, moody and sullen among the empty bottles, bicker over Brett while she makes off with the matador. All is vanity when Jake concludes this little chapter of social history in a taxi on the Gran Via of Madrid. "Oh, Jake," cries Brett, "we could have had such a damned good time together." "Yes," Jake answers, closing the volume. "Isn't it pretty to think so?"

The novel contains, however, enough bright metal to bring out by contrast the special darkness of the sullen ground. We are meant to understand that all is vanity—except the things that are not vain. The moral norm of the book is a healthy and almost boyish innocence of spirit, and it is carried by Jake Barnes, Bill Gorton, and Pedro Romero. Against this norm, in the central antithesis of the novel, is ranged the sick abnormal "vanity" of the Ashley-Campbell-Cohn triangle.

Long before the middle of the book, a reader who is reasonably sensitive to changes in tone may discover that he has been silently forced into a choice between two sets of moral and emotional atmospheres. Something tarnished is opposed to something bright; vanity is challenged by sanity; a world of mean and snarled disorder is set off against a world clear of entangling alliances. The whole mood of the novel brightens, for example, when the men-without-women, Jake Barnes and Bill Gorton, climb to the roof of the bus which will take them to Burguete in the Pyrenees. This bright mood has passed through certain preliminary stages. One is the pleasant dinner which the two friends have shared at Madame Lecomte's in Paris. Another comes when Bill and Jake entrain at the Gare d'Orsay for Bayonne. Almost immediately they are in the well-known eighteenth-century situation where every prospect pleases and only man is vile. Vile is hardly the word, of course, for all the people they meet. Certain fellow-travelers on the train, and later on the bus, admirably sustain their holiday mood. But their delight in "the country" and its quiet beauties, as seen from the train-windows, anticipates the Burguete experience.

If the reader performs the experiment of watching the country over the shoulders of the travelers, he is likely to be struck by the way in which the references to natural beauty are used to document the feeling of holiday (a holiday from the company of Brett and her friends) which Jake and Bill share. An otherwise unforgivable compression of the train-ride chapter will illustrate the point.[17]

"It was a lovely day, not too hot, and the country was beautiful from the start. We went back to the diner and had breakfast. . . . [Later] we ate the sandwiches and drank the Chablis and watched the country out of the window. The grain was just beginning to ripen and the fields were full of poppies. The pastureland was green, and there were fine trees, and sometimes big rivers and chateaux off in the trees. . . . About seven-thirty we had dinner and watched the country through the open window of the

[17] SAR, Chapter Nine.

diner. . . . It got dark and we could feel the country hot and sandy and dark outside of the window, and about nine o'clock we got into Bayonne. . . . It was a nice hotel, and the people at the desk were very cheerful, and we each had a good small room. . . . Bayonne is a nice town. It is like a very clean Spanish town and it is on a big river. . . ."

The chapter carefully establishes the beauty of the countryside and the healthy male companionship between Jake and Bill. What makes them happiest, though they do not say so, is their freedom from the petty and noxious tribulations of Robert Cohn and company.

Although they meet Cohn in Bayonne and drive with him to Pamplona, Bill and Jake have already established between them an unspoken camaraderie into which Cohn and his troubles do not greatly intrude. Across the Spanish frontier, for example, they come upon a handsome vista. "The road went on, very white and straight ahead, and then lifted to a little rise, and off on the left was a hill with an old castle, with buildings close around it and a field of grain going right up to the walls and shifting in the wind." Jake, who is riding in the front seat with the driver, turns around as if to comment on the scene. "Robert Cohn was asleep, but Bill looked and nodded his head." No word is spoken, but the friendly shared reaction of Jake and Bill is silently and strongly affirmed. Cohn is asleep and out of it.

Being so much involved in his dream of Brett, Robert Cohn, the man not free of woman, refuses to take the Burguete bus with the good companions. Instead, by way of preparation for Brett's imminent arrival, he bathes carefully, gets a shave and haircut, has a shampoo and an application of pomade, fumes petulantly over Brett's failure to reach Pamplona on schedule (she has drunk too much somewhere to the north), and watches Bill and Jake depart for their fishing-trip without the pleasure of his company.

In Burguete, for five memorable days, all is gold. At that elevation the air is cool and bracing. The good companions walk happily over the uplands among the sturdy beech-trees, fish the clear brown streams, and recline in the lap of real country. This is what they were admiring, and silently longing for, during the train-trip from Paris to Bayonne. Jake digs for worms in the grassy bank;

they catch trout; they eat rustic lunches of wine and sandwiches in the good air. At night they play three-handed bridge with the English sportsman Wilson-Harris. There is much playful and boy-like badinage. The landscape smiles, as healthful and vitalizing as ever the English Lake-district was in Wordsworth. Somewhere in the remote background, out of sight and as far out of mind as possible, is the Ashley-Campbell-Cohn triangle. The comrades are not troubled. For a brief but golden age there is "no word from Robert Cohn nor from Brett and Mike." [18]

Hemingway's careful contrast of emotional and social climates makes the prefatory quotation from Ecclesiastes directly relevant. "One generation passeth away," says the preacher, "and another generation cometh; but the earth abideth for ever." Wherever they go, Brett and her little coterie (the truly "lost" part of that otherwise unlost generation) carry along with them the neuroses of Montparnasse. But the earth fortunately abides. The sun rises and sets over the fields and woods of France and Spain. The fresh winds blow; the rivers run in the valleys; the white roads ascend the mountains. For those who will look at it, all this is available. But the wastelanders pass away and out of the picture, and there is no health in them.

This pleasurable contrapuntal method, with its subtly marked contrast of emotional and moral climates, continues into the climactic phase of the novel. Now, however, there is a new image to take the place of Burguete. When the Pamplona fiesta begins, the light (and the lightheartedness) which the fishermen have known in the Pyrenees grows dim and comes very near to going out. All the sullen jealousies and cross-purposes which Brett's presence causes are released among the vacationers. Outward signs of the venom which works within are Jake's obvious disgust at Cohn's fawning over Brett; Mike's relentless verbal bludgeon-ing of Cohn; and Cohn's physical bludgeoning of Mike and Jake. As if Brett's own neurosis were somehow communicable, her semi-voluntary victims writhe and snarl. All is vanity at Pamplona as it was in the Montparnasse cafés before the trip was under-taken.

For the Pamplona episodes the contrasting bright metal is not

[18] *SAR,* p. 129.

nature but rather a natural man, the brave matador Romero. He is used as a force of antithesis, manly, incorruptible, healthy, courageous, of complete integrity and self-possession. Beside him Mike seems a poor player indeed, and he conspicuously embodies the qualities which Cohn lacks. His control accents Cohn's emotionalism; his courage, Cohn's essential cowardice; his self-reliance, Cohn's miserable fawning dependence; his dignity, Cohn's self-pity; his natural courtesy, Cohn's basic rudeness and egotism.

The enmity between the bullfighter and the boxer—for the very nature of Romero abhors the moral vacuum in Cohn—reaches its climax when Cohn invades Romero's room and finds Brett there. In a bedroom fist-fight the boxer has every advantage over the bullfighter except in those internal qualities which fists cannot touch. Though he is knocked down fifteen times, Romero will not lose consciousness, give up, shake hands, or stop trying to hit Cohn for as long as he can see him. Afterwards, like a Greek chorus, Bill and Mike close the chronicle-history of Robert Cohn, the pomaded sulker in the tent, and Romero, the manly and unspoiled warrior.[19] "That's quite a kid," says Bill. "He ruined Cohn," says Mike. Cohn presently leaves Pamplona under the cloud of his own ruination. Romero's face may be cut up, but his moral qualities have triumphed, as they do again in the bullring the day following the brawl. He has been "beat-up" like many other members of his generation. But not "lost."

Maxwell Perkins, a good and perceptive editor, understood the intent of the novel perfectly. He admiringly called it "a healthy book, with marked satirical implications upon novels which are not—sentimentalized, subjective novels, marked by sloppy hazy thought." [20] Its morality, like its esthetics, was notably healthy. Against the background of international self-seekers like Cohn, the true moral norm of the book (Bill and Jake at Burguete, Romero at Pamplona) stood out in high and shining relief.

[19] *SAR*, pp. 210–211.
[20] Quoted in R. Burlingame, *Of Making Many Books,* p. 87.

III. CIRCE AND COMPANY

Hemingway's first novel provides an important insight into the special "mythological" methods which he was to employ with increasing assurance and success in the rest of his major writing. It is necessary to distinguish Hemingway's method from such "mythologizing" as that of Joyce in *Ulysses,* or Eliot in *The Waste Land.* For Hemingway early devised and subsequently developed a mythologizing tendency of his own which does not depend on antecedent literatures, learned footnotes, or the recognition of spot passages. *The Sun Also Rises* is a first case in point.

It might be jocularly argued, for example, that there is much more to the portrait of Lady Brett Ashley than meets the non-Homeric eye. It is very pleasant to think of the Pallas Athene, sitting among the statuary in one of her temples like Gertrude Stein among the Picassos in the rue de Fleurus, and murmuring to the Achaeans, homeward bound from the battle of Troy: "You are all a lost generation." As for Brett, Robert Cohn calls her Circe. "He claims she turns men into swine," says Mike Campbell. "Damn good. I wish I were one of these literary chaps." [21] If Hemingway had been writing about brilliant literary chaps in the manner, say, of Aldous Huxley in *Chrome Yellow,* he might have undertaken to develop Cohn's parallel. It would not have been farther-fetched than Joyce's use of the Daedalus legend in *A Portrait of the Artist* or Eliot's kidnapping of Homeric Tiresias to watch over the mean little seductions of *The Waste Land.*

Was not Brett Ashley, on her low-lying island in the Seine, just such a fascinating peril as Circe on Aeaea? Did she not open her doors to all the modern Achaean chaps? When they drank her special potion of French applejack or Spanish wine, did they not become as swine, or in the modern idiom, wolves? Did not Jake Barnes, that wily Odysseus, resist the shameful doom which befell certain of his less wary comrades who became snarling beasts?

There are even parallel passages. Says Jake Barnes, thinking of Brett: "I lay awake thinking and my mind jumping around. . . . Then all of a sudden I started to cry. Then after a while it was

[21] *SAR,* p. 149. For *Odyssey* parallels, cf. *SAR,* p. 32 and *Odyssey* x, 490–500; and cf. *SAR,* p. 164 and *Odyssey* x, 552–560.

better . . . and then I went to sleep." Says Ulysses on Aeaea:
"My spirit was broken within me and I wept as I sat on the bed.
. . . But when I had my fill of weeping and writhing, I made answer." Or what shall be made of Robert Cohn, quietly and classically asleep on the winecasks in the back room of a Pamplona
tavern, wreathed with twisted garlics and dead to the world while
Brett and the others carouse in the room beyond? "There was one
named Elpenor," says the *Odyssey,* "the youngest of all; not very
valiant in war nor sound of understanding, who had laid him down
apart from his comrades in the sacred house of Circe, seeking the
cool air, for he was heavy with wine. He heard the noise and bustle
of his comrades as they moved about."

If he had wished to follow the mythological method of Eliot's
Waste Land or Joyce's *Ulysses,* Hemingway could obviously have
done so. But his own esthetic opinions carried him away from the
literary kind of myth-adaptation and over into that deeper area of
psychological symbol-building which does not require special
literary equipment to be interpreted. One needs only sympathy and
a few degrees of heightened emotional awareness. The special
virtue of this approach to the problem of literary communication
is that it can be grasped by all men and women because they are
human beings. None of the best writers are without it. It might
even be described as the residuum of "natural knowledge" and
belief, visible in every artist after the traditional elements have
been siphoned off. This is perhaps roughly what Keats meant by
saying that Shakespeare led a life of allegory, his works being the
comments on it. Thoreau's phrase for the same thing, as R. L.
Cook has pointed out, is "dusky knowledge." Pilar, the Cumaean
sybil of *For Whom the Bell Tolls,* moves regularly in this half-
subliminal area. She inherits her skill and discernment from
Hemingway.

Under the matter-of-factness of the account of the feria of San
Fermin a sabidurían symbolism is at work. It does not become
formally apparent until the party has assembled to prepare for the
festival. Then, in several ways, it develops as a dialectical struggle
between paganism and Christian orthodoxy—a natural and brilliant use of the fact that the fiesta is both secular and religious, and

that the *riau-riau* dancers unabashedly follow the procession which bears the patron saint through the streets of Pamplona.

The contrast is admirably dramatized through Jake and Brett. Without apology or explanation, Jake Barnes is a religious man. As a professing Catholic, he attends masses at the cathedral before and during fiesta week. On the Saturday before the festival opens, Brett accompanies him. "She said she wanted to hear me go to confession," says Jake, "but I told her that not only was it impossible but it was not as interesting as it sounded, and, besides, it would be in a language she did not know." Jake's remark can be taken doubly. The language Brett does not know is Latin; it is also Spanish; but it is especially the language of the Christian religion. When she goes soon afterwards to have her fortune told at a gypsy camp, Brett presumably hears language that she *can* understand.[22]

Her true symbolic colors are broken out on Sunday afternoon. She is in the streets with Jake watching the religious procession in which the image of San Fermin is translated from one church to another. Ahead of the formal procession and behind it are the *riau-riau* dancers. When Jake and Brett try to enter the chapel they are stopped at the door, ostensibly because she has no hat. But for one sufficiently awake to the ulterior meaning of the incident it strikingly resembles the attempt of a witch to gain entry into a Christian sanctum. Brett's witch-hood is immediately underscored. Back in the street she is encircled by the chanting pagan dancers who prevent her from joining their figure: "They wanted her as an image to dance around." When the song ends, she is rushed to a wineshop and seated on an up-ended wine-cask. The shop is dark and full of men singing,—"hard-voiced singing." [23]

The intent of this episode is quite plain. Brett would not understand the language used in Christian confessional. She is forbidden to follow the religious procession into the chapel. The dancers adopt her as a pagan image. She is perfectly at home on the wine-cask amidst the hard-voiced singing of the non-religious celebrants. Later in fiesta week the point is reemphasized. Jake and Brett enter the San Fermin chapel so that Brett can pray for

[22] *SAR*, p. 156.
[23] *SAR*, p. 160.

Romero's success in the final bullfight of the celebration. "After a little," says Jake, "I felt Brett stiffen beside me, and saw she was looking straight ahead." Outside the chapel Brett explains what Jake has already guessed: "I'm damned bad for a religious atmosphere. I've got the wrong type of face." [24]

She has, indeed. Her face belongs in wide-eyed concentration over the Tarot pack of Madame Sosostris, or any equivalent soothsayer in the gypsy camp outside Pamplona. It is perfectly at home in the center of the knot of dancers in the street or in the tavern gloom above the wine-cask. For Brett in her own way is a lamia with a British accent, a Morgan le Fay of Paris and Pamplona, the reigning queen of a paganized wasteland with a wounded fisherking as her half-cynical squire. She is, rolled into one, the *femme fatale de trente ans damnée*. Yet she is always and conspicuously herself. The other designations are purely arbitrary labels which could be multiplied as long as one's list of enchantresses could be made to last. They are not necessary to the full symbolic meaning which Brett has in her own right and by virtue (if that is the word) of what she is made to do in the book.

Although Hemingway carefully skirts the moralistic, as his artistic beliefs require, the moral drift of the symbolic story is unmistakable. Shortly after *The Sun Also Rises* appeared, he remarked, as he had never overtly done in the book, that "people aren't all as bad as some writers find them or as hollowed out and exhausted emotionally as some of the *Sun* generation." [25] The restriction was conspicuous. He did not say, "the lost generation." He said rather, "some of the *Sun* generation." His indictment, put into dramatic terms, was directed against those who allowed themselves to flounder in an emulsion of ennui and alcohol when there was so much else to be done, whether one was a championship-winning *gueule cassée* like Criqui or an ordinary citizen like Jake, engaged in readjusting himself to peace-time living. In contrast to the "hollow men" who went off the stage with something resembling a whimper, Hemingway presented another set of men who kept their mouths shut and took life as it came.

[24] *SAR*, p. 216.
[25] EH to MP, 12/7/26.

The emotional exhaustion of "some of the *Sun* generation" is accentuated by the oppositions Hemingway provides. Obviously no accidental intruder in the book is Romero, standing out in youthful dignity and strength against the background of displaced wastrels among whom Jake moves. The same is true of the interlude at Burguete, with Jake and Bill happily disentangled from the wastelanders, as if in wordless echo of Eliot's line: "In the mountains there you feel free." However fascinating Brett and Cohn and Mike may be as free-wheeling international adventurers, the book's implicit attitude is one of quizzical condemnation towards these and all their kind.

Despite this fact, one finds in the presentation of Brett Ashley an almost Jamesian ambiguity. It is as if the objective view of Brett were intentionally relieved by that kind of chivalry which is never wholly missing from the work of Hemingway. On the straight narrative plane the book appears to offer a study of a war-frustrated love affair between Brett and Jake. Brett's Circean characteristics are only partly responsible for the sympathy with which she is treated, though all enchantresses from Spenser's Acrasia to Coleridge's Geraldine are literally fascinating and Brett is no exception. Whenever Jake takes a long objective view of Lady Ashley, however, he is too honest not to see her for what she objectively is, an alcoholic nymphomaniac. To Cohn's prying questions about her, early in the book, Jake flatly answers: "She's a drunk." [26]

There is, nevertheless, a short history behind her alcoholism and her constant restless shifting from male to male. During the war she was an assistant nurse; her own true love died; she married a psychotic British baronet who maltreated her; and at the time of the book she is waiting for a divorce decree in order to marry the playboy Mike Campbell. Furthermore—and this fact calls forth whatever chivalry one finds—she is in love with Jake, though both of them realize the hopelessness of the situation. She has not, as her fiancé observes, had an absolutely happy life, and Jake is prepared to take this into account when he judges her character. "Don't you know about Irony and Pity?" asks Bill

[26] *SAR*, p. 39. Cf. also pp. 211–212.

Gordon during a verbal bout at Burguete. Jake knows all about them. They are the combination he uses whenever he thinks about Brett.[27]

One of the ironies in the portrait of Brett is her ability to appreciate quality in the circle of her admirers. After the trip to San Sebastian with Robert Cohn she quickly rejects him. She does not do so sluttishly, merely in order to take up with another man, but rather for what to her is the moral reason that he is unmanly. Towards her fiancé Mike Campbell the attitude is somewhere in the middle ground of amused acceptance. He is Brett's sort, a good drinking companion living on an income nearly sufficient to allow him a perpetual holiday. "He's so damned nice and he's so awful," says Brett. "He's my sort of thing." Even though Brett can be both nice and awful with her special brand of ambiguity, she does save her unambiguous reverence for two men. One is the truly masculine Jake, whose total sexual disability has not destroyed his manhood. The other is Romero, whose sexual ability is obviously a recommendation but is by no means his only claim to admiration. It is finally to Brett's credit, and the measure of her appreciation of quality, that she sends Romero back to the bullring instead of destroying him as she might have done. This is no *belle dame sans merci*. She shows mercy both to her victim and to the remaining shreds of her self-respect.

The Heloisa-Abelard relationship of Brett and Jake is Hemingway's earliest engagement of an ancient formula—the sacrifice of Venus on the altar of Mars. In one way or another, the tragic fact of war or the after-effects of social disruption tend to inhibit and betray the normal course of love, not only in *The Sun Also Rises* but also in *A Farewell to Arms, To Have and Have Not, The Fifth Column, For Whom the Bell Tolls,* and *Across the River and Into the Trees*. Brett, the first of the victims, is a kind of dark Venus. If she had not lost her "true love" in the late war, or if Jake's wound had not permanently destroyed his ability to replace the lost lover, Brett's progressive self-destruction would not have become the inevitable course it now appears to be.

Much of the continuing power of *The Sun Also Rises* comes from its sturdy moral backbone. The portraits of Brett Ashley and

[27] *SAR*, p. 117.

Robert Cohn, like that of their antithesis Romero, are fully and memorably drawn. A further and deep-lying cause of the novel's solidity is the subtle operative contrast between vanity and sanity, between paganism and orthodoxy, between the health and humor of Burguete and the sick neuroses of the Montparnassian ne'er-do-wells. Other readers can value the book for the still-fresh representation of "the way it was" in Paris and Pamplona, Bayonne and Burguete, during the now nostalgically remembered middle Twenties. Yet much of the final strength of *The Sun Also Rises* may be attributed to the complicated interplay between the two points of view which it embodies. According to one of them, the novel is a romantic study in sexual and ultimately in spiritual frustration. Beside this more or less orthodox view, however, must be placed the idea that it is a qualitative study of varying degrees of physical and spiritual manhood, projected against a background of ennui and emotional exhaustion which is everywhere implicitly condemned.

V · The Mountain and the Plain

> "Learn about the human heart and the
> human mind in war from this book."—
> Hemingway, in another connection.[1]

I. LANDSCAPE IN GORIZIA

The opening chapter of Hemingway's second novel, *A Farewell to Arms,* is a generically rendered landscape with thousands of moving figures. It does much more than start the book. It helps to establish the dominant mood (which is one of doom), plants a series of important images for future symbolic cultivation, and subtly compels the reader into the position of detached observer.

"In the late summer of that year we lived in a house in a village that looked across the river and the plain to the mountains. In the bed of the river there were pebbles and boulders, dry and white in the sun, and the water was clear and swiftly moving and blue in the channels. Troops went by the house and down the road and the dust they raised powdered the leaves of the trees. The trunks of the trees too were dusty and the leaves fell early that year and we saw the troops marching along the road and the dust rising and leaves, stirred by the breeze, falling and the soldiers marching and afterward the road bare and white, except for the leaves."

The first sentence here fixes the reader in a house in the village where he can take a long view across the river and the plain to the distant mountains. Although he does not realize it yet, the plain and the mountains (not to mention the river and the trees, the dust and the leaves) have a fundamental value as symbols. The autumnal tone of the language is important in establishing the autumnal mood of the chapter. The landscape itself has the further importance of serving as a general setting for the whole first part of the novel. Under these values, and of basic structural importance, are the elemental images which compose this remarkable introductory chapter.

The second sentence, which draws attention from the moun-

[1] Hemingway, *Men at War,* introd., p. xx.

tainous background to the bed of the river in the middle distance, produces a sense of clearness, dryness, whiteness, and sunniness which is to grow very subtly under the artist's hands until it merges with one of the novel's two dominant symbols, the mountain-image. The other major symbol is the plain. Throughout the sub-structure of the book it is opposed to the mountain-image. Down this plain the river flows. Across it, on the dusty road among the trees, pass the men-at-war, faceless and voiceless and unidentified against the background of the spreading plain.

In the third and fourth sentences of this beautifully managed paragraph the march-past of troops and vehicles begins. From the reader's elevated vantage-point, looking down on the plain, the river, and the road, the continuously parading men are reduced in size and scale—made to seem smaller, more pitiful, more pathetic, more like wraiths blown down the wind, than would be true if the reader were brought close enough to overhear their conversation or see them as individualized personalities.

Between the first and fourth sentences, moreover, Hemingway accomplishes the transition from late summer to autumn—an in-exorability of seasonal change which prepares the way for the study in doom on which he is embarked. Here again the natural elements take on a symbolic function. In the late summer we have the dust; in the early autumn the dust and the leaves falling; and through them both the marching troops impersonally seen. The reminder, through the dust, of the words of the funeral service in the prayer-book is fortified by the second natural symbol, the falling leaves. They dry out, fall, decay, and become part of the dust. Into the dust is where the troops are going—some of them soon, all of them eventually.

The short first chapter closes with winter, and the establish-ment of rain as a symbol of disaster. "At the start of the winter came the permanent rain and with the rain came the cholera. But it was checked and in the end only seven thousand died of it in the army." Already, now in the winter, seven thousand of the wraiths have vanished underground. The permanent rain lays the dust and rots the leaves as if they had never existed. There is no excellent beauty, even in the country around Gorizia, that has not some sadness to it. And there is hardly a natural beauty in the whole first chapter of *A Farewell to Arms* which has not some symbolic function in Hemingway's first study in doom.

II. NOT IN OUR STARS

To call *A Farewell to Arms* a "first" study in doom might seem unfair to *The Sun Also Rises*. But the total effect of the first novel, whatever its author's intention, is closer to that of tragicomedy than of tragedy. The tragic sense of life exists in the undertones of *The Sun Also Rises*. Its surface tone is, however, somewhere within the broad range of the comic. Reading it, one is oftener reminded of the tragi-comic irony of a work like Chaucer's *Troilus and Criseyde* than, say, the tragic irony of the Greeks and the Elizabethans. The operation of pity—again as in Chaucer— is carefully equivocal, somehow in itself a phase of irony, and under a restraint so nearly complete that it can scarcely move. Possibly because of the nature of the material, possibly because of the cultivated habit of understatement, one does not find in *The Sun Also Rises* the degree of emotional commitment which becomes visible in *A Farewell to Arms*.

After the experience of writing and revising his first novel, Hemingway worked more wisely and more slowly on his second. The preparation of the first draft took six months instead of six weeks. It was begun in Paris about the first of March, 1928. Through the spring and summer the work went on in Key West, where Hemingway made himself relax by deep-sea fishing while writing some 40,000 words. He continued the draft in Piggott, Arkansas, and Kansas City, Missouri, where he ran the total number of words to something like 87,000. The book was completed in preliminary form near Big Horn, in Sheridan County, Wyoming, about the end of August, 1928.

Following a brief interlude, he began revision, an extremely painstaking job of cutting and rewriting which filled another five months. On January 22, 1929, he wrote Perkins that the final draft stood complete in typescript, and by mid-February it had been decided to serialize the book in *Scribner's Magazine,* beginning with the number of May, 1929. Still Hemingway was dissatisfied. In Paris during the spring he continued to labor over the galley-proofs of the magazine version, rewriting some portions and keeping them by him until the last possible moment. Book-proof reached him in Paris on June 5, 1929.[2] By the twenty-fourth, when he had finally satisfied himself that everything possible had been done, he was able to report to Perkins that he had at last achieved a "new and much better ending" for his novel. There is a persistent tradition that the present ending was rewritten seventeen times before Hemingway got the corrected galley-proof aboard the boat-train.

In the midst of life, runs the Book of Common Prayer, we are in death. "During the time I was writing the first draft," said Hemingway in 1948, "my second son Patrick was delivered in Kansas City by Caesarean section, and while I was rewriting my father killed himself in Oak Park, Illinois. . . . I remember all these things happening and all the places we lived in and the fine times and the bad times we had in that year. But much more vividly I remember living in the book and making up what happened in it every day. Making the country and the people and the things that happened I was happier than I had ever been. Each day I read the book through from the beginning to the point where I went on writing and each day I stopped when I was still going good and when I knew what would happen next. The fact that the book was a tragic one did not make me unhappy since I believed that life was a tragedy and knew it could only have one end. But finding you were able to make something up; to create truly enough so that it made you happy to read it; and to do this every day you worked was something that gave a greater pleasure

---

[2] Details on the composition are drawn from the following letters: *EH to MP*, 3/17/28, 3/21/28, 6/7/28, *ca.* 9/5/28, 9/28/28, 1/8/29, 1/10/29, 1/22/29, 6/7/29, 6/24/29. Also EH to Bridges, 5/18/29; and *MP to EH*, 5/24/29, and 7/12/29. At the time he began *FTA*, Hemingway had been for some time at work on another novel—"a sort of modern *Tom Jones*," which was up to nearly 60,000 words when he dropped it in favor of the story of Frederick Henry and Catherine Barkley. On Thanksgiving Day, 1927, he told Perkins that he had completed 17 chapters of the *Tom Jones* work and was only a third through. He had decided to change the narrative method to the third person, having "got tired of the limitations" imposed by first-person narrative. But *FTA*, like *SAR*, used the first-person method. Hemingway did not begin to employ the third person consistently until the middle 1930's.

than any I had ever known. Beside it nothing else mattered." [3]

The appearance of *A Farewell to Arms* in book form on September 27, 1929, marked the inception of Hemingway's still lengthening career as one of the very few great tragic writers in twentieth-century fiction. His next book, *Death in the Afternoon,* furthered his exploration into the esthetics of tragedy. Through the 1930's he continued at intervals to wrestle with the problem. *To Have and Have Not* (though with limited success) examined the tragic implications of social and political decay. *For Whom the Bell Tolls* attacked a similar problem on an epic and international scale. Ten years after that, at the age of fifty, Hemingway rounded out a full twenty years of work in tragedy with his character-study of Colonel Richard Cantwell.

The position occupied by *A Farewell to Arms* among Hemingway's tragic writings may be suggested by the fact that he once referred to the story of Lieutenant Frederick Henry and Catherine Barkley as his *Romeo and Juliet.*[4] The most obvious parallel is

[3] See Hemingway's introduction, dated June 30, 1948, to the illustrated edition of *FTA,* New York, Scribner's, 1948, pp. vii–viii. Hemingway seems to be in error when he gives the impression that the original publication date was "the day the stock market crashed"—that is, October 30, 1929. The book had been published September 27th. For an excellent review of *FTA* following publication, see Malcolm Cowley, *New York Herald Tribune Books,* October 6, 1929, pp. 1 and 6.

[4] The *Romeo and Juliet* comment is quoted by Edmund Wilson in "Ernest Hemingway: Bourdon Gauge of Morale," which first appeared in the *Atlantic Monthly* 164 (July 1939), pp. 36–46. The essay was collected in *The Wound and the Bow,* New York, 1941, and reprinted by J. K. M. McCaffery, ed., *Ernest Hemingway, The Man and His Work,* New York, 1950, pp. 236–257. Further page-references to this essay will be to the McCaffery reprint only.

It is of some interest to notice that Bertrand Russell on an American lecture tour denounced the novel as a piece of Victorianism. See Irene and Allen Cleaton, *Books and Battles,* New York, 1937. Compare further the opinion of Oliver Allston (Van Wyck Brooks) that *FTA* is another version of the Evangeline story. See *The Opinions of Oliver Allston,* New York, 1941, p. 173.

Boston and Italy had other opinions. The serialization of the novel began in *Scribner's Magazine* in May 1929 (Vol. 85, pp. 493 ff.) and ran to October (Vol. 86, pp. 20 ff.). One startling event of the summer was the banning of the June and July issues from public sale on the orders of Chief of Police Michael H. Crowley of Boston. The result, however unhappy that Henry and Catherine, like their Elizabethan prototypes, might be seen as star-crossed lovers. Hemingway might also have been thinking of how rapidly Romeo and Juliet, whose affair has begun as a mere flirtation, pass over into the status of relatively mature lovers. In the third place, he may have meant to imply that his own lovers, caught in the tragic pattern of the war on the Austrian-Italian front, are not far different from the young victims of the Montague-Capulet family feud.

Neither in *Romeo and Juliet* nor in *A Farewell to Arms* is the catastrophe a direct and logical result of the immoral social situation. Catherine's bodily structure, which precludes a normal delivery for her baby, is an unfortunate biological accident. The death of Shakespeare's lovers is also precipitated by an accident— the detention of the message-bearing friar. The student of esthetics, recognizing another kind of logic in art than that of mathematical cause-and-effect, may however conclude that Catherine's death, like that of Juliet, shows a kind of artistic inevitability. Except by a large indirection, the war does not kill Catherine any more than the Veronese feud kills Juliet. But in the emotional experience of the novel, Catherine's dying is directly associated and interwoven with the whole tragic pattern of fatigue and suffering, loneliness, defeat and doom, of which the war is itself the broad social manifestation. And one might make a similar argument about *Romeo and Juliet*.

In application to Frederick and Catherine, the phrase "star-

---

for censorship, was increased sales for the book. A poet in *The Daily Oklahoman* felt that

> *Scribner's* may have larger circulation
> Since Boston with its codfish and its beans
> Deems Hemingway a menace to the nation.

Both the novel and the film were banned in Italy by Mussolini's government. It was felt that they showed Italian military valor in an ugly light. The film, which Hemingway resented as a falsification of his intention, was released in December 1932. Samuel Putnam notes that up to 1947 Hemingway was still popular with Italian anti-fascists. (*Paris Was Our Mistress*, p. 132.)

FTA is the only one of Hemingway's works to appear in three media. The novel was successfully dramatized by Lawrence Stallings, and presented at the National Theatre, September 22, 1930. See *New Republic* 64 (October 8, 1930), pp. 208–209.

crossed lovers" needs some qualification. It does not mean that they are the victims of an actual malevolent metaphysical power. All their crises are caused by forces which human beings have set in motion. During Frederick's understandably bitter ruminations while Catherine lies dying in the Lausanne hospital, fatalistic thoughts do, quite naturally, cross his mind. But he does not, in the end, blame anything called "Fate" for Catherine's death. The pain of her labor reminds him that her pregnancy has been comfortable and apparently normal; the present biological struggle is perhaps a way of evening things up. "So now they got her in the end. You never got away with anything." But he immediately rejects his own inference: that is, that her sufferings in labor are a punishment for sinful pleasures. Scientifically considered, the child is simply a by-product of good nights in Milan —and there is never a pretence that they were not good. The parents do not happen to be formally married; still, the pain of the child-bearing would have been just as it is even if they had been married fifty times. In short, the pain is natural, inevitable, and without either moral or metaphysical significance. The anonymous "they" is nothing but a name for the way things are.

A little later Frederick Henry bitterly compares the human predicament first to a game and then to a swarm of ants on a log in a campfire. Both are homely and unbookish metaphors such as would naturally occur to any young American male at a comparable time. Living now seems to be a war-like game, played "for keeps," where to be tagged out is to die. Here again, there is a moral implication in the idea of being caught off base— trying to steal third, say, when the infield situation and the number of outs make it wiser to stay on second. "They threw you in and told you the rules and the first time they caught you off base they killed you." One trouble, of course, is that the player rarely has time enough to learn by long experience; his fatal error may come in the second half of the first inning, which is about as far as Catherine seems likely to go. Even those who survive long enough to learn the rules may be killed through the operation of chance or the accidents of the game. Death may, in short, come "gratuitously" without the slightest reference to "the rules."

It is plainly a gratuitous death which comes to the ants on the

burning log in Frederick's remembered campfire. Some immediately die in flame, as Catherine is now dying. Others, like Lieutenant Henry, who has survived a trench-mortar explosion, will
manage to get away, their bodies permanently scarred, their future
course uncertain—except that they will die in the end. Still others,
unharmed, will swarm on the still cool end of the log until the
fire at last reaches them. If a Hardyan President of the Immortals
takes any notice of them, He does little enough for their relief.
He is like Frederick Henry pouring water on the burning campfire log—not to save the ants but only to empty a cup.

Catherine's suffering and death prove nothing except that she
should not have become pregnant. But she had to become pregnant in order to find out that becoming pregnant was unwise.
Death is a penalty for ignorance of "the rules": it is also a fact
which has nothing to do with rule or reason. Death is the fire
which, in conclusion, burns us all, and it may singe us along the
way. Frederick Henry's ruminations simply go to show that if
he and Catherine seem star-crossed, it is only because Catherine
is biologically double-crossed, Europe is war-crossed, and life is
death-crossed.[5]

III. HOME AND NOT-HOME

As its first chapter suggests, the natural-mythological structure
which informs *A Farewell to Arms* is in some ways comparable
to the Burguete-Montparnasse, Catholic-Pagan, and Romero-
Cohn contrasts of *The Sun Also Rises*. One has the impression,
however, of greater assurance, subtlety, and complexity in the
second novel, as if the writing of the first had strengthened and
consolidated Hemingway's powers and given him new insights
into this method for controlling materials from below.

Despite the insistent, denotative matter-of-factness at the surface of the presentation, the subsurface activity of *A Farewell to
Arms* is organized connotatively around two poles. By a process
of accrual and coagulation, the images tend to build round the
opposed concepts of Home and Not-Home. Neither, of course, is
truly conceptualistic; each is a kind of poetic intuition, charged

[5] On Catherine's bad luck, see *FTA*, pp. 342, 350.

with emotional values and woven, like a cable, of many strands. The Home-concept, for example, is associated with the mountains; with dry-cold weather; with peace and quiet; with love, dignity, health, happiness, and the good life; and with worship or at least the consciousness of God. The Not-Home concept is associated with low-lying plains; with rain and fog; with obscenity, indignity, disease, suffering, nervousness, war and death; and with irreligion.

The motto of William Bird's Three Mountains Press in Paris, which printed Hemingway's *in our time,* was "Levavi oculos meos in montes." The line might also have served as an epigraph for *A Farewell to Arms.* Merely introduced in the first sentence of the first chapter, the mountain-image begins to develop important associations as early as Chapter Two. Learning that Frederick Henry is to go on leave, the young priest urges him to visit Capracotta in the Abruzzi. "There," he says, "is good hunting. You would like the people and though it is cold, it is clear and dry. You could stay with my family. My father is a famous hunter." But the lowlander infantry captain interrupts: "Come on," he says in pidgin Italian to Frederick Henry. "We go whorehouse before it shuts." [6]

After Henry's return from the leave, during which he has been almost everywhere else on the Italian peninsula *except* Abruzzi, the mountain-image gets further backing from another low-land contrast. "I had wanted," says he, "to go to Abruzzi. I had gone to no place where the roads were frozen and hard as iron, where it was clear cold and dry and the snow was dry and powdery and haretracks in the snow and the peasants took off their hats and called you Lord and there was good hunting. I had gone to no such place but to the smoke of cafés and nights when the room whirled and you needed to look at the wall to make it stop, nights in bed, drunk, when you knew that that was all there was."

Throughout Book I, Hemingway quietly consolidates the mountain-image. On the way up towards the Isonzo from Gorizia, Frederick looks across the river and the plain to the Julian and Carnic Alps. "I looked to the north at the two ranges of moun-

[6] *FTA,* pp. 9, 13.

tains, green and dark to the snow-line and then white and lovely
in the sun. Then, as the road mounted along the ridge, I saw a
third range of mountains, higher snow mountains, that looked
chalky white and furrowed, with strange planes, and then there
were mountains far beyond all these that you could hardly tell
if you really saw." [7] Like Pope in the celebrated "Alps on Alps
arise" passage, Hemingway is using the mountains symbolically.
Years later, in "The Snows of Kilimanjaro," he would use the
mighty peak of East Africa as a natural image of immortality,
just as in *The Green Hills of Africa* he would build his narrative
in part upon a contrast between the hill-country and the Serengetti Plain. When Frederick Henry lowers his eyes from the far-
off ranges, he sees the plain and the river, the war-making equipment, and "the broken houses of the little town" which is to be
occupied, if anything is left of it to occupy, during the coming
attack. Already now, a few dozen pages into the book, the
mountain-image has developed associations; with the man of
God and his homeland, with clear dry cold and snow, with polite
and kindly people, with hospitality, and with natural beauty.
Already it has its oppositions; the lowland obscenities of the
priest-baiting captain, cheap cafés, one-night prostitutes, drunk-
enness, destruction, and the war.

When the trench-mortar explosion nearly kills Henry, the
priest comes to visit him in the field-hospital, and the Abruzzi
homeland acquires a religious association. "There in my country,"
says the priest, "it is understood that a man may love God. It is
not a dirty joke." Repeating, for emphasis, the effect of the
priest's first account of the highland country, Hemingway allows
Frederick to develop in his mind's eye an idyllic picture of the
priest's home-ground.

"At Capracotta, he had told me, there were trout in the stream
below the town. It was forbidden to play the flute at night . . .
because it was bad for the girls to hear. . . . Aquila was a fine
town. It was cool in the summer at night and the spring in Abruzzi
was the most beautiful in Italy. But what was lovely was the fall
to go hunting through the chestnut woods. The birds were all good

[7] *FTA,* p. 48.

because they fed on grapes, and you never took a lunch because the peasants were always honored if you would eat with them in their houses. . . ." [8]

By the close of Book I, largely through the agency of the priest, a complex connection has come clear between the idea of Home and the combination of high ground, cold weather, love, and the love of God. Throughout, Hemingway has worked solely by suggestion, implication, and quiet repetition, putting the reader into potential awareness, readying him for what is to come.

The next step is to bring Catherine Barkley by degrees into the center of the image. Her love affair with Henry begins as a "rotten game" of war-time seduction. Still emotionally unstable and at loose nervous ends from her fiancé's death, Catherine is a comparatively easy conquest. But in the American hospital at Milan, following Henry's ordeal by fire at the front not far from the Isonzo, the casual affair becomes an honorable though unpriested marriage. Because she can make a "home" of any room she occupies—and Henry several times alludes to this power of hers—Catherine naturally moves into association with ideas of home, love, and happiness. She does not really reach the center of the mountain-image until, on the heels of Frederick's harrowing lowland experiences during the retreat from Caporetto, the lovers move to Switzerland. Catherine is the first to go, and Henry follows her there as if she were the genius of the mountains, beckoning him on. Soon they are settled into a supremely happy life in the winterland on the mountainside above Montreux. Catherine's death occurs at Lausanne, after the March rains and the approaching need for a good lying-in hospital have driven the young couple down from their magic mountain—the closest approximation to the priest's fair homeland in the Abruzzi that they are ever to know.

The total structure of the novel is developed, in fact, around the series of contrasting situations already outlined. To Gorizia, the Not-Home of war, succeeds the Home which Catherine and Frederick make together in the Milan Hospital. The Not-Home of the grim retreat from the Isonzo is followed by the quiet and happy retreat which the lovers share above Montreux. Home ends

[8] *FTA*, p. 78.

for Frederick Henry when he leaves Catherine dead in the Lausanne Hospital.

Developed for an esthetic purpose, Hemingway's contrasting images have also a moral value. Although he has nothing to say about the images themselves, Mr. Ludwig Lewisohn is undoubtedly correct in saying that *A Farewell to Arms* "proves once again the ultimate identity of the moral and the esthetic." In this critic's view, Hemingway "transcended the moral nihilism of the school he had himself helped to form" by the very intensity of his feelings for the contrast of love and war. "The simply wrought fable," Lewisohn continues, ignoring all the symbolic complexities yet still making a just appraisal, "has two culminations—the laconic and terrible one in which the activity of the battle police brings to an end the epically delineated retreat of the Italian army with its classically curbed rage and pity . . . and that other and final culmination in Switzerland with its blending in so simple and moving a fashion of the eternal notes of love and death." The operation of the underlying imagery, once its purposes are understood, doubly underscores Mr. Lewisohn's point that there is no moral nihilism in the central story of *A Farewell to Arms*.[9]

The use of rain as a kind of symbolic obligato in the novel has been widely and properly admired. Less apparent to the cursory reader is the way in which the whole idea of climate is related to the natural-mythological structure. (Hemingway's clusters of associated images produce emotional "climates" also, but they are better experienced than reduced by critical descriptions.) The rains begin in Italy during October, just before Henry's return to Gorizia after his recovery from his wounds. The rains continue, at first steadily, then intermittently, throughout the disastrous retreat, Henry's flight to Stresa, and the time of his reunion with Catherine. When they awaken the morning after their reunion night, the rain has stopped, light floods the window, and Henry, looking out in the fresh early morning, can see Lake Maggiore in the sun "with the mountains beyond." Towards these mountains the lovers now depart.

Not until they are settled in idyllic hibernation in their rented chalet above Montreux are they really out of the rain. As if to

[9] *Expression in America,* New York, 1932, p. 519.

emphasize by climatic accompaniment their "confused alarums of struggle and flight," the rain has swept over them during their escape up the lake in an open boat. Once in the mountains, however, they are out of the lowlands, out of danger, out of the huge, tired debacle of the war. Above Montreux, as in the priest's homeland of Abruzzi, the ridges are "iron-hard with the frost." The deep snow isolates them, and gives them a feeling of domestic safety, tranquillity, and invulnerability.

For several months the rainless idyll continues. "We lived through the months of January and February and the winter was very fine and we were very happy. There had been short thaws when the wind blew warm and the snow softened and the air felt like spring, but always the clear, hard cold had come again and the winter had returned. In March came the first break in the winter. In the night it started raining."

The reader has been prepared to recognize some kind of disaster-symbol in the return of the rains. Much as in *Romeo and Juliet,* several earlier premonitions of doom have been inserted at intervals. "I'm afraid of the rain," says Catherine in the Milan Hospital one summer night, "because sometimes I see me dead in it." In the fall, just before Henry returns to the front, they are in a Milan hotel. During a break in the conversation the sound of falling rain comes in. A motor car klaxons, and Henry quotes Marvell: "At my back I always hear Time's wingèd chariot hurrying near." He must soon take a cab to catch the train that will project him, though he does not know it yet, into the disaster of the great retreat. Months later, in Lausanne, the Marvell lines echo hollowly: "We knew the baby was very close now and it gave us both a feeling *as though something were hurrying us and we could not lose any time together.*" (Italics added.) The sound of the rain continues like an undersong until, with Catherine dead in the hospital room (not unlike that other happy one where their child was conceived), Henry walks back to the hotel in the rain.[10]

[10] *FTA,* pp. 135, 165, 267, 326, and 332 show, in order, the various premonitions and the obligato use of rain. Malcolm Cowley was one of the first of Hemingway's critics to point to his symbolic use of weather. See *The Portable Hemingway,* New York, 1944, introd., p. xvi.

One further reinforcement of the central symbolic structure is provided by the contrast between the priest and the doctor, the man of God and the man without God. In line with the reminiscence of *Romeo and Juliet,* it may not be fantastic to see them respectively as the Friar Lawrence and the Mercutio of Hemingway's novel. The marked contrast between the two men becomes especially apparent when Henry returns to the Gorizia area following his discharge from the hospital.

The return to Gorizia is a sharp come-down. After the "home-feeling" of the hospital and the hotel in Milan, the old army post seems less like home than ever. The tenor of life there has noticeably changed. A kind of damp-rot afflicts morale. The major, bringing Henry up to date on the state of affairs, plays dismally on the word *bad.* It has been a "bad summer." It was "very bad" on the Bainsizzá plateau: "We lost three cars. . . . You wouldn't believe how bad it's been. . . . You were lucky to be hit when you were. . . . Next year will be worse. . . ." As if he were not fully convinced by the Major's despair, Henry picks up the word: "Is it so bad?" The answer is yes. "It is so bad and worse. Go get cleaned up and find your friend Rinaldi."

With Rinaldi the doctor, things also are bad, a fact which has been borne in upon the major so strongly that he thinks of Rinaldi when he mentions the word *bad.* Things are not bad for Rinaldi from a professional point of view, for he has operated on so many casualties that he has become "a lovely surgeon." Still, he is not the old Mercutio-like and mercurial Rinaldi. If mercury enters into his picture at all it is because he has syphilis, or thinks he has. He is treating himself for it and is beginning to entertain certain delusions of persecution. Except for his work, and the temporary opiates of drink and prostitutes, both of which interfere with his work, Rinaldi, the man of the plain, the man without God, is a man without resources.

With the priest, the man from the Abruzzi highlands, tacitly reintroduced as a contrast for Rinaldi, things are not so bad. "He was the same as ever," says Henry at their meeting, "small and brown and compact-looking." He is much more sure of himself than formerly, though in a modest way. When Rinaldi, in the absence of the foul-mouthed captain, takes up the former indoor game of priest-baiting, the priest is not perturbed. "I could see," says Henry, "that the baiting did not touch him now."

Out of the evils of the past summer the priest has even contrived to gather a nascent hope. Officers and men, he thinks, are gentling down because they "realize the war" as never before. When this happens, the fighting cannot continue for very much longer. Henry, playing half-heartedly the *advocatus diaboli,* argues that what the priest calls "gentling down" is really nothing but the feeling of defeat: "It is in defeat that we become Christian . . . like Our Lord." Henry is maintaining that after the fearless courage of His ministry, Our Lord's gentleness and His refusal to fight against the full brunt of the experience on Calvary became the ideal of Christian meekness. If Peter had rescued Christ Jesus from the Garden, suggests Henry, Christian ethics might be something different. But the priest, who is as compact as he looks, knows otherwise. Our Lord would not have changed in any way. From that knowledge and belief comes the priest's own strength. He has resources which Dr. Rinaldi, the man without God, does not possess.[11]

The priest-doctor contrast is carried out in the sacred-versus-profane-love antithesis which is quietly emphasized in the novel. Through the agency of Rinaldi the love affair begins at a fairly low level. The doctor introduces Frederick to Catherine, and takes a jocularly profane view of the early infatuation, seeming to doubt that it can ever be anything but an unvarnished war-time seduction. On the other hand, the background symbols of home and true love and high ground suggest that the lovers' idyllic life in Switzerland is carried on under the spiritual aegis of the priest. Neither Rinaldi nor the priest appears in the latter part of the book. But when, having been driven to the lowlands by the rains of spring, Catherine enters the hospital, it is naturally enough a doctor who takes over. And though this doctor does all he can to save her life, Catherine dies.

Projected in actualistic terms and a matter-of-fact tone, telling the truth about the effects of war in human life, *A Farewell to Arms* is entirely and even exclusively acceptable as a naturalistic

---

[11] On the low morale among the Italian troops, see *FTA,* pp. 174–175. On Rinaldi's affliction, see p. 181. On the priest's firmness, see pp. 183–184.

narrative of what happened. To read it only as such, however, is to miss the controlling symbolism: the deep central antithesis between the image of life and home (the mountain) and the image of war and death (the plain).

IV. THE FEMALE OF THE SPECIES

Coleridge once made the questionable remark that in Shakespeare "it is the perfection of woman to be characterless. Every one wishes a Desdemona or Ophelia for a wife—creatures who, though they may not always understand you, do always feel [for] you and feel with you." [12] To make so inordinate a generalization, Coleridge was obliged to ignore the better than half of Shakespeare's "perfect" women who are anything but characterless.

The modern reader, brought up on similar generalizations about the heroines of Hemingway, may wish to reconsider the problem. The most frequent adverse comment on Hemingway's fictional heroines is that they tend to embody two extremes, ignoring the middle ground. This fact is taken to be a kind of sin of omission, the belief being that most of their real-life sisters congregate and operate precisely in the area which Hemingway chooses not to invade at all.

The strictures of Mr. Edmund Wilson may be taken as typical of a recurrent critical position. He puts the argument in terms of a still-to-be-written chapter on the resemblances between Hemingway and Kipling. The two writers seem to him to share in "certain assumptions about society" with particular reference to the position of women. Kipling and Hemingway show, says Mr. Wilson, "much the same split attitude toward women. Kipling anticipates Hemingway in his beliefs that 'he travels fastest who travels alone' and that 'the female of the species is more deadly than the male'; and Hemingway seems to reflect Kipling in the submissive infra-Anglo-Saxon women that make his heroes such perfect mistresses. The most striking example of this is the amoeba-like little Spanish girl, Maria, in *For Whom the Bell Tolls*. Like the docile native 'wives' of English officials in the early stories of

[12] Coleridge, *Table Talk,* in *Works,* ed. Shedd, vol. 6, p. 349.

Kipling, she lives only to serve her lord and to merge her identity with his; and this love affair with a woman in a sleeping-bag, lacking completely the kind of give and take that goes on between real men and women, has the all-too-perfect felicity of a youthful erotic dream." [13]

The relevance of this commentary is that it underscores the idea of the two extremes in Hemingway's fictional treatment of women. In one group are the "deadly" females. Their best-realized (because most sympathetically presented and most roundly characterized) representative is Brett Ashley. The horrible example would presumably be someone like Margot Macomber, who is really and literally deadly. In varying degrees—and the fact that it is a matter of degree ought to be noticed—these women are selfish, corrupt, and predatory. They are "bad" for the men with whom they are involved. At the other extreme would stand the allegedly docile and submissive mistress-types, of whom Catherine Barkley and Maria are the conspicuous examples. These, for Mr. Wilson, are incredible wish-projections, youthfully erotic dream-girls, or impossibly romantic ideals of wife-hood. They bear, it seems, little resemblance to the women with whom one is acquainted. Where now, Mr. Wilson seems to be asking, are the day-by-day vagaries, the captious bickerings, the charming or enraging anfractuosities which combine to produce the "normal" or "real" married state? The greater number of the female kind obviously occupy some realm intermediate between the Becky Sharps and the Amelia Sedleys, between the pole of Goneril and Regan and the pole of Ophelia and Desdemona. By his failure, or his tacit refusal, to depict realistically the occupants of this realm and to use them as the heroines of his fiction, Hemingway has somehow failed in his obligation to present things as they are.

This point of view naturally affects Mr. Wilson's judgment of *A Farewell to Arms*. On the whole he finds the novel to be "a less serious affair" than Hemingway's previous work. Catherine Barkley and Frederick Henry, at least during the period of their Swiss idyll, strike him as "not in themselves convincing as human personalities." For him their relationship is merely an

[13] McCaffery, *op.cit.*, p. 254, note.

idealization, "the abstraction of a lyric emotion." [14] Mr. Cowley evidently shares this view. "To me," writes Mr. Cowley, "[Catherine] is only a woman at the beginning of the book, in her near madness"—as if, perhaps, some degree of emotional instability were a criterion of credibility in the portrait of a fictional heroine.[15]

For those who find it hard to accept Mr. Wilson's view of Catherine as an abstraction and of Maria as an amoeba, four practical points might well be made. The first has to do with the relation of Brett Ashley and Catherine Barkley to what Mr. Wilson might call the Great Infra-Anglo-Saxon tradition of fictional heroines. It is of some interest to observe that Mr. Wilson's strictures on the heroines of Hemingway could be applied with equal justice, not only to the heroines of Kipling but also to a considerable number of other heroines throughout the history of English and American fiction. Hemingway shares with many predecessors an outlook indubitably masculine, a certain chivalric attitude not without ironic overtones, and a disinclination to interest himself in what may be called the prosaisms of the female world.

The second point is that through a method of comparative portraiture, Hemingway carefully establishes a moral norm of womanly behavior. Then, whether by ethical intent or by temperamental attitude, he uses the established norm as a means of computing various degrees of departure f om it. Depending on their own views in this area, readers may find Hemingway's "norm-women" less interesting and less credible than their "abnormal" cousins. For the inveterate reader of fiction and narrative poetry it is perhaps a psychological truism that the *femme fatale,* the general type of the temptress, seems more "interesting" than the stable heroine.

In the early work of Hemingway the point is well illustrated by the contrast between Brett and Catherine. There are, to begin with, certain resemblances. Like Brett, Catherine is an Englishwoman; like Brett, she is beautiful, tall, and blonde. She talks as Brett does, stressing certain words which in print are italicized.

[14] *ibid.,* p. 242.
[15] Malcolm Cowley to CB, 10/20/51.

Like Brett, she has lost her own true love early in the war, and her emotions, like her way of life, have become confused as a result of the bereavement. But here the resemblances stop.

Brett's neurosis drives her from bar to bar, from man to man, and from city to city. None of it is any good: her polygamy, with or without benefit of justices of the peace, leads only to more of the same, as one drink leads to another in the endless round. Brett is not "good" for the men she knows. Romero wants her to let her hair grow out, to become more feminine, to marry and live with him. The basic abnormality at work in Brett opposes such feminization. She is the short-haired companion of men, wearing a man's felt hat, calling herself a "chap." She does not really like other women, and neither has nor wishes to have any real friends among them. She is never happier than in the Pamplona wine-shop, the center of raucous masculine singing, as if she were a half-woman half in love with damnation.

Catherine Barkley, on the other hand, is all woman. At once dependent and independent, she half-mothers, half-mistresses Frederick Henry. She wants no other life than with him, no other man than he. She drinks little and displays none of Brett's geographical restlessness. She is temperamentally monogamous. Where she is, home is. Even the red-plush hotel room in Milan (which for several minutes makes her feel like a whore) is changed by her presence until she herself can feel at home in it. "In a little while," says her lover, "the room felt like our own home. My room at the hospital had been our own home and this room was our home too in the same way." Trying at first to help her out of the harlot-feeling, Henry kisses her and assures her, "You're my good girl." "I'm certainly yours," says Catherine, wryly. But she is also, and preeminently, a "good girl"—even more so, for example, than Hardy's Tess, who was so designated on the title page.[16] As if Hemingway were looking back for contrast to the Circean figure of his first novel, Rinaldi refers to Catherine as "your lovely cool . . . English goddess." But she is a woman, not a goddess. She rescues, pities, comforts, companions, and sustains, just as she in turn is rescued from the "craziness" induced

[16] On Catherine's connection with the "home-feeling," see *FTA,* p. 163. Rinaldi's remark on her goddess-like qualities is on p. 71.

by her lover's death when she has finally involved herself sufficiently in Henry's growing love. Her hair is long; she dresses like a woman and gets on well with other women like her friend Ferguson. Yet she is evidently happiest alone with her husband. She would be unhappy and possibly frightened on the wine-cask in Pamplona. She is at ease in Milan in the midst of a war because she is a young woman in the midst of love. Like Maria, she is a completing agent for the hero, and is in turn completed by her association with him. But Brett, on the other hand, is an agent of depletion, as she herself realizes, and as her unselfish renunciation of Romero is presumably meant to show.[17]

The third point to be made about Hemingway's heroines is that they are, on the whole, an aspect of the poetry of things. It is perhaps a sign of an attitude innately chivalric that they are never written off, as sometimes happened in Kipling, as mere bundles of rags, bones, and hanks of hair. Even Margot Macomber, in the bottomless slough of her bitch-hood, is seen to be "damned beautiful." The treatment of Catherine, like that of Brett, shows in Hemingway a fundamental indisposition to render his heroines "reductively." And if one argues that he nowhere seems to commit himself to the emancipation of women, or to become in the usual sense of the term an ardent feminist, the answer would be, perhaps, that his women are truly emancipated only through an idea or ideal of service. His heroines, to make the statement exactly, are meant to show a symbolic or ritualistic function in the service of the artist and the service of man.

The final point grows naturally out of the preceding ones. It is, in brief, that all of Hemingway's heroines, like all of his heroes, are placed in a special kind of accelerated world. We do not see them puttering in their kitchens, but only dreaming of that as a desirable possibility. They are never presented as harassed mothers; their entire orientation tends to be, in this connection,

[17] Mr. Theodore Bardacke has an interesting essay on "Hemingway's Women" in McCaffery, op.cit., pp. 340–351. Among its contributions is a discussion of Hemingway's "symbolic" use of long and short hair as a mark of femininity or the relative lack of it. The point is of special interest in connection with Maria, who has been raped and shorn by the fascists. The growing-out of her hair is a reminder of her gradual return to mental and physical health under the double tutelage of Pilar and Roberto.

premarital. Wars and revolutions, the inevitable enemies of peace and domesticity, set them adrift or destroy their lives. Yet they contrive to embody the image of home, the idea if not the actuality of the married state, and where they are, whatever the outward threats, home is.

Mr. Wilson's feeling that Catherine is not convincing as a human personality, his belief that her love affair with Frederick Henry is an "abstraction of lyric emotion," may be partly explained by the fact that a majority of the characters in the first two novels are oddly rootless. With a few notable exceptions like Robert Cohn, Brett Ashley, or the priest from Abruzzi, they seem on the whole to possess no genealogies or previous biographies. We know nothing about Henry's background, and next to nothing about Catherine Barkley's. Like Jake Barnes, Bill Gorton, and Dr. Rinaldi, they seem to come from nowhere, move into the now and here, and depart again for nowhere after the elapsed time of the novels. They have substance and cast shadows, but they lack the full perspective and chiaroscuro that one finds among most of the people in *For Whom the Bell Tolls*. We are seldom permitted to know them in depth. The inclination is to accept them for what they do more than for what they are. They are the men and women of action, the meaning of whose lives must be sought in the kind of actions in which they are involved, very much, again, as in *Romeo and Juliet*.

This feeling about the characters can be accounted for in two different ways. One has to do with Hemingway's esthetic assumptions as of 1928–1929; the other is a natural consequence of the kind of stories he chose to tell. His working assumption that character is revealed through action will, if rigorously adhered to, produce the kind of fiction in which characterization-in-depth is in a measure sacrificed to the exigencies of narrative movement. Even there, however, it is advisable to notice that a close reading of any of the early books reveals far more in the way of nuances of light and shade, or in subtle shifts of motivation, than one at first imagined was there. This half-concealed power is easily explained by what is now acknowledged in all quarters: Hemingway's carefully controlled habit of understatement. As for the second explanation, it might be pointed out that nearly all the important characters in the first two novels are "displaced persons" —either men fighting a war far from their former home-environments, or aliens in foreign lands whose ties with nearly everything they have known before are now severed—for better or for worse, but severed.

These two explanations, the esthetic and the "geographical," may throw some further light into the reasons behind Mr. Wilson's strictures. If Hemingway had not yet met head-on the problem of characterization-in-depth, perhaps it was unfair to ask a writer who had done so much so brilliantly that he should do so much more. He had developed a memorably individualized style— whittled it, as MacLeish said, from the hard wood of a walnut stick. He showed an unerring ability to keep his narratives in motion. Finally, he had achieved mastery of that special combination of naturalistic and symbolic truth-telling which was the despair of those who could (and so frequently did) imitate his style and his narrative manner.

In the absence of other evidence, it is probably wisest to assume that Hemingway knew what he was doing. That he could draw a character fully, roundedly, and quickly is proved by a dozen minor portraits in the first two books—Cohn's acidulous mistress, for example, or Brett's friend Mippipopoulos, or the wonderful old Count Greffi, with whom Henry plays at billiards and philosophy in the hotel at Stresa, or the Milanese surgeon who does the operation on Henry's leg after the affair of the trench mortar, a surgeon who seems, and is, four times as good as the three old-maiden doctors who have wisely wagged their heads an hour before and advised Henry to wait six months for the operation. These are only four examples, but they are enough to show that the ability to draw character was by no means lacking in the Hemingway of 1929. If he went no deeper into the backgrounds of his displaced persons, he went as deeply as he needed to do for the purposes of his narrative. And the paring-out of the superfluous had always been one of his special addictions.

There is, finally, a *tendenz* in *A Farewell to Arms* which helps to account for the opinion that Hemingway has somehow failed in his attempt to present Catherine as a credible characterization. In a large and general way, the whole movement of the novel is from concretion towards abstraction. This became apparent in our consideration of the wonderfully complex opening chapter, and the importance of the observation is enhanced by what happens in the closing chapters of the book. The fact that the whole story is projected in actualistic terms ought not finally to obscure the symbolic mythos on which it is built and from which a great part of its emotional power derives. Catherine may be taken as an English girl who has a Juliet-like liaison with a young American officer. Similarly, one may read the novel as a naturalistic narrative of what happened to a small group of people on the Italian front during the years 1917–1918.

In the central antithesis between the image of life, love, and home (the mountain), and the image of war and death (the plain), Catherine however has a symbolic part to play. It is indeed required of her that she should become, as the novel moves on towards its dénouement, more of an abstraction of love than a down-to-earth portrait of an actual woman in love and in pain. The truly sympathetic reader may feel that she is a woman, too. But if she does move in the direction of abstraction, one might argue that the *tendenz* of the novel is in this respect symbolically and emotionally justified. For when Frederick Henry has closed the door of the hospital room in order to be alone with his dead wife Catherine, he learns at once, as if by that act, the finality and totality of his loss. It is the loss of a life, of a love, of a home. Saying good bye is "like saying good bye to a statue." The loved woman has become in death an abstract unvital image of her living self, a marble memorial to all that has gone without hope of recovery. Her death exactly completes the symbolic structure, the edifice of tragedy so carefully erected. This structure is essentially poetic in conception and execution. It is achieved without obvious insistence or belaboring of the point, but it is indubitably achieved for any reader who has found his way into the true heart of the book. And it is this achievement which enables Hemingway's first study in doom to succeed as something far more than an exercise in romantic naturalism. Next to *For Whom the Bell Tolls,* it is his best novel.

VI · The First Forty-five Stories

"A man should find things he cannot lose."—A major in Milan [1]

I. UNDER THE ICEBERG

"The dignity of movement of an iceberg," Hemingway once said, "is due to only one-eighth of it being above water." His short stories are deceptive somewhat in the manner of an iceberg. The visible areas glint with the hard factual lights of the naturalist. The supporting structure, submerged and mostly invisible except to the patient explorer, is built with a different kind of precision— that of the poet-symbolist. Once the reader has become aware of what Hemingway is doing in those parts of his work which lie below the surface, he is likely to find symbols operating every- where, and in a series of beautiful crystallizations, compact and buoyant enough to carry considerable weight.

Hemingway entered serious fiction by way of the short story. It was a natural way to begin. His esthetic aims called for a rigorous self-discipline in the presentation of episodes drawn, though always made over, from life. Because he believed, firmly as his own Abruz- zian priest, that "you cannot know about it unless you have it," [2] a number of the stories were based on personal experience, though here again invention of a symbolic kind nearly always entered into the act of composition.

The early discipline in the short story, and it was rarely any- thing but the hardest kind of discipline, taught Hemingway his craft. He learned how to get the most from the least, how to prune language and avoid waste motion, how to multiply intensities, and how to tell nothing but the truth in a way that always allowed for telling more than the truth. From the short story he learned wonderfully precise lessons in the use of dialogue for the purposes of exposition. Even the simpler stories showed this power. In the struggle with his materials he learned to keep the poker face of

[1] *First 49,* p. 369.
[2] *FTA,* p. 77.

the true artist. Or, if you changed the image to another game, he learned the art of relaying important hints to his partner the reader without revealing all at once the full content of his holdings. From the short story he gained a skill in the economical transfer of impressions—without special rhetoric or apparent trickery. His deepest trust was placed in the cumulative effect of ostensibly simple, carefully selective statement, with occasional reiteration of key phrases for thematic emphasis.

Like James, he has been rightly called an architect rather than a manipulator, and he himself has said that prose is architecture rather than interior decoration—an esthetic fact which the short story taught him.[3] The writing and rewriting of the stories gave him invaluable experience in the "hows" of fiction, and suggested almost endless possibilities for future development. When he was ready to launch out into the novel, he might have said, as Henry James did about *Roderick Hudson:* "I had but hugged the shore on sundry previous small occasions; bumping about, to acquire skill, in the shallow waters and sandy coves of the short story." [4] The difference was that on occasion, though not invariably, Hemingway's cove dropped off quickly into waters that were deep enough to float an iceberg.

Through the year 1939, he had published fifty-five short stories.[5] This count does not include all the sixteen short miniatures of *In Our Time* or several others which appear as interludes among the technical expositions of *Death in the Afternoon.* Most of the fifty-five were collected in 1938 in *The Fifth Column and the First Forty-nine Stories.* There omitted was "The Man with the Tyrolese Hat" from *Der Querschnitt* (1936). Also still unreprinted in 1951 were three stories, first printed in *Esquire Magazine,* about Chicote's Madrid bar during the Spanish Civil War, as well as two others first published in *Cosmopolitan* in 1939. The volume of 1938 contained four stories not previously brought together: "Old Man at the Bridge," cabled from Barcelona in April,

[3] *DIA,* p. 191.
[4] Henry James, *Works,* New York edition, Vol. 1, preface, p. vi.
[5] For titles and publication dates of these short stories, see bibliography. "The Man with the Tyrolese Hat" is actually an extract from *The Green Hills of Africa* about the Austrian trader Kandisky.

1938; "The Capital of the World," a fine story on the "athlete-dying-young" theme, with a setting in Madrid and, as leading character, a boy from Estremadura; and the two long stories which grew out of Hemingway's hunting-trip in Africa, "The Short Happy Life of Francis Macomber" and "The Snows of Kiliman-jaro." But the first forty-five stories may be conveniently taken as a kind of unit, since they were all written within ten years, and since they represent what Hemingway thought worthy of includ-ing in his first three collections: *In Our Time* (1925), *Men With-out Women* (1927), and *Winner Take Nothing* (1933). Taken together or separately, they are among the great short stories of modern literature.

Their range of symbolic effects is even greater than the variety of subjects and themes employed. The subjects and themes, in turn, are far more various than has been commonly supposed. Like any writer with a passion for craftsmanship, Hemingway not only accepts but also sets himself the most difficult experimental problems. Few writers of the past fifty years, and no American writers of the same period except James and Faulkner, have grap-pled so manfully with extremely difficult problems in communi-cation. One cannot be aware of the real extent of this experimenta-tion (much of it highly successful, though there are some lapses) until he has read through the first three collections attempting to watch both the surfaces and the real inward content. Even that task, though pleasurable as a voyage of discovery, is harder than it sounds. For it is much the same with the short stories as with *The Sun Also Rises* and *A Farewell to Arms:* they are so readable as straight narratives that one is prepared to accept them at face-value—to admire the sharp lines and clean curves of the eighth of the iceberg above the surface, and to ignore the real causes of the dignity or worth of the movement.

With perhaps half a dozen exceptions, each of the short stories doubly repays the closest reading. The point could be illustrated as many times as there are stories to serve as illustrations. As one example, there is the Chekhov-like "Alpine Idyll," an apparently simple tale in which two American sportsmen have gone skiing in Switzerland. On the way to a village inn in a Swiss valley, the Americans pass a cemetery where a burial has just taken place.

When they reach the inn, they drink at one table; at another table, the village sexton splits a bottle of wine with a Swiss peasant from the lonely mountain-country up above. When the peasant leaves to go to another tavern down the street, the Americans hear the story behind the burial.

In the winter the peasant's wife died. Since he could not bury her, he placed the body in his woodshed. There it froze stiff in the intense mountain cold. Whenever the peasant went to get wood to keep himself warm, he found that the body was in his way. So he stood it up against the wall. Later, since he often went for wood at night, carrying a lantern, and since the open jaws of the corpse provided a convenient high place, he took to hanging his lantern in his dead wife's mouth. Evidently he thought nothing of it at the time. By spring, when he was able to bring the body to the valley for burial, the mouth had become noticeably ragged. This is the shocking anecdote under which the story is built.

Actually, however, the story is not "about" the peasant. Its subject, several times emphasized early in the narrative, is "not ever doing anything too long." The Americans have been trying some spring skiing high in the Silvretta. Much as they love the sport, they have found it a queerly unpleasant experience. May is too late in the season to be up there. "I was a little tired of skiing," says one. "We had stayed too long. . . . I was glad to be down, away from the unnatural high mountain spring, into this May morning in the valley." When the story of the peasant and his wife is told, the idea of the "unnatural" and the idea of "not ever doing anything too long" are both driven home with a special twist of the knife. For the peasant has lived too long in an unnatural situation; his sense of human dignity and decency has temporarily atrophied. When he gets down into the valley, where it is spring and people are living naturally and wholesomely, he sees how far he has strayed from the natural and the wholesome, and he is then deeply ashamed of himself. For spring in the valley has been established by the skier's internal monologue as the "natural" place. In the carefully wrought terms of the story, the valley stands in opposition to the unnatural high mountain spring. The arrival of this season in the area near his lonely hut has activated the peasant to bring his wife's body down to the valley for burial.

But for him the descent has been especially meaningful—nothing less, in short, than a coming to judgment before the priest and the sexton. Here again, the point is made possible by careful previous preparation. One of the skiers has commented on the oppressiveness of the spring sun in the high Silvretta. "You could not get away from the sun." It is a factual and true statement of the skier's feeling of acute discomfort when the open staring eye of the sun overheated him and spoiled the snow he wished to ski on. But it is also a crafty symbolic statement which can later be brought to bear on the unspoken shame of the peasant, who could not get away from the open staring eye of the "natural" people who in a sense brought him to judgment. Like "Alpine Idyll," many of the stories deserve to be read with as much awareness, and as closely, as one would read a good modern poem.

The consideration of "Alpine Idyll" makes another point relevant: the frequent implication that Hemingway is a sports-writer. In some of the hop-skip-and-jump critiques of Hemingway, the reader is likely to find "Alpine Idyll" classified as a skiing story. But to say that Hemingway sometimes deals with sports like horse-racing, boxing, bullfighting, fishing, and skiing really tells very little even about the "sports-stories." None of them is primarily "about" a sport; and only ten of the first forty-five make special or incidental use of any sport at all. The point of "Cross-Country Snow," which opens with a breathlessly described skiing episode, is something quite different from the statement that skiing is fun. The true function of the opening is to summarize, dramatize, and establish firmly a phase of masculine living (men-without-women) which is being justly challenged by another phase of living—and in such a way that a state of tension is set up between the two. When a choice is compelled, Nick Adams, one of the skiers, readily accepts the second phase. Similarly, although one might classify "Out of Season" as a fishing story, the point of the story is that nothing (including fishing) is done. The strength of the story is the portrayal of the officious guide Peduzzi, a fine characterization. He serves to focus sharply the "out-of-season" theme, which relates both to the young man's relations with his wife Tiny, and to the proposal (by Peduzzi) that the young man fish out of season in evasion of the local game laws.

If one turns from these to the two long stories, "Fifty Grand" and "The Undefeated," both of which devote considerable space to the close descriptions of athletic events, it might be argued that here, anyhow, Hemingway's real interest is in the athletic events.[6] Not so. His interest is in the athletes, and not so much because they are athletes as because they are people. The two stories may be seen as complementary studies in superannuation. Jack Brennan, the aging welterweight fighting his last fight in Madison Square Garden, is a rough American equivalent to the veteran Manolo Garcia, meeting his last bull under the arclights of the bullring in Madrid.

Both men show, in crucial situations, the courage which has sustained them through their earlier careers. Both are finished. Jack earns his fifty thousand both by standing up under the intentional low blow of his opponent and by thinking fast enough under conditions of extreme pain to return the low blow, lose the fight, and win the money he has bet on his opponent. Manolo earns the right to keep his *coleta,* the badge of the professional matador, by a courage that is much greater than his aging skill, or, for that matter, his luck. The stories are as different in conception and execution as the Spanish temperament is from the Irish-American, or the bullfight from the prizefight. The sign at the center of the Brennan story is a certified check for fifty thousand dollars; a bullfighter's pigtail is the sign at the center of the other. One could almost believe that the stories were meant to point up some kind of international contrast.

Yet the atmosphere in which both stories transpire is one of admirable courage. The aging athletes Brennan and Garcia stand in marked opposition to another pair who are united by their too early acceptance of defeat. These are the half-symbolic Ole Andreson, the intended victim of Al and Max in "The Killers"—

----

[6] Hemingway grouped these two stories with "My Old Man" as belonging to another category than stories like "Out of Season." These three were "the kind that are easy for me to write." His own preferences among the early stories were for "Big Two-Hearted River," "Indian Camp," "Soldier's Home," and the first and last paragraphs of "Out of Season." EH to FSF, from the Vorarlberg, *ca.* 12/20/25.

the only real classic to emerge from the American gangwars of the prohibition era except W. R. Burnett's *Little Caesar*—and the half-symbolic figure of William Campbell, the man under the half-symbolic sheet in the story half-symbolically called "A Pursuit Race."

"Half-symbolic" is an awkward term. What makes it necessary in talking about stories like "A Pursuit Race" and "The Killers" is that both Andreson and Campbell are real enough to be accepted in non-symbolic terms. They are dressed in the sharp vocabulary of the naturalistic writer. We are given (almost coldly) the place, the facts, the scene, out of which grows, however, an awful climate of hopelessness and despair. It is impossible to escape the conviction that the function of these two is to stand for something much larger than themselves—a whole, widespread human predicament, deep in the grain of human affairs—with Andreson and Campbell as the indexes.

The Chesterfield-coated killers, Al and Max, are likewise the indexes of a wider horror than their cheap and ugly hoodlumism could ever be in itself. Nowadays the generic term for that horror is fascism, and it may not be stretching a point to suggest that, with "The Killers," Hemingway solidly dramatized the point of view towards human life which makes fascism possible. If that is so, then the figures of Andreson and even Campbell take on a meaning wide as all the modern world. They are the victims, the men who have given up the fight for life and liberty. Nothing can rouse them any more.

Whatever it is that William Campbell seeks to escape by remaining in bed, the ultimate horror gets its most searching treatment in "A Clean Well-Lighted Place," a superb story and quite properly one of Hemingway's favorites. It shows once again that remarkable union of the naturalistic and the symbolic which is possibly his central triumph in the realm of practical esthetics. The "place" of the title is a Spanish café. Before the story is over, this place has come to stand as an image of light, cleanness, and order against the dark chaos of its counter-symbol in the story: the idea of *nada*, or nothingness. The *nada*-concept is located and pinned to the map by a kind of triangulation-process. The three elements consist in the respective relationships of an old waiter and a young waiter to an elderly man who sits drinking brandy every night in their clean, well-lighted café.

The old waiter and the young waiter are in opposition. They stand (by knowledge, temperament, experience, and insight) on either side of one of the great fences which exist in the world for the purpose of dividing sheep from goats. The young waiter would like to go home to bed, and is impatient with the old drinker of brandy. The old waiter, on the other hand, knows very well why the old patron comes often, gets drunk, stays late, and leaves only when he must. For the old waiter, like the old patron, belongs to the great brotherhood: all those "who like to stay late at the café . . . all those who do not want to go to bed . . . all those who need a light for the night." He is reluctant to see his own café close—both because he can sympathize with all the benighted brethren, and for the very personal reason that he, too, needs the cleanness, the light, and the order of the place as an insulation against the dark.

The unspoken brotherly relationship between the old waiter and the old patron is dramatized in the opening dialogue, where the two waiters discuss the drinker of brandy as he sits quietly at one of the tables. The key notion here is that the young and rather stupid waiter has not the slightest conception of the special significance which the old waiter attaches to his young confrère's careless and unspecialized use of the word *nothing*.

Young Waiter: Last week he tried to commit suicide.
Old Waiter: Why?
Young Waiter: He was in despair.
Old Waiter: What about?
Young Waiter: Nothing.
Old Waiter: How do you know it was nothing?
Young Waiter: He has plenty of money.

They are speaking in Spanish. For the old waiter, the word *nothing* (or *nada*) contains huge actuality. The great skill displayed in the story is the development, through the most carefully controlled understatement, of the young waiter's mere *nothing* into the old waiter's Something—a Something called Nothing which is so huge, terrible, overbearing, inevitable, and omnipresent that, once experienced, it can never be forgotten. Sometimes in the day, or for a time at night in a clean, well-lighted place, it can be held temporarily at bay. What links the old waiter and the old patron most profoundly is their brotherhood in arms against this beast in the jungle.

Several other stories among the first forty-five—perhaps most notably the one called "A Way You'll Never Be"—engage the *nada*-concept. And whoever tries the experiment of reading "Big Two-Hearted River" immediately after "A Clean Well-Lighted Place" may discover, perhaps to his astonishment, that the *nada*-concept really serves as a frame for what is ostensibly one of Hemingway's happiest stories.

If we read the river-story singly, looking merely at what it says, there is probably no more effective account of euphoria in the language, even when one takes comparative account of *The Compleat Angler,* Hazlitt on the pleasures of hiking, Keats on the autumn harvest, Thoreau on the Merrimac, Belloc on "The Mowing of a Field," or Frost on "Hyla Brook." It tells with great simplicity of a lone fisherman's expedition after trout. He gets a sandwich and coffee in the railway station at St. Ignace, Michigan, and then rides the train northwest to the town of Seney, which has been destroyed by fire. From there he hikes under a heavy pack over the burned ground until he reaches a rolling pine-plain. After a nap in a grove of trees, he moves on to his campsite near the Two-Hearted River. There he makes camp, eats, and sleeps. Finally, as sum and crown of the expedition, there is the detailed story of a morning's fishing downstream from the camp. At the surface of the story one finds an absolute and very satisfying reportorial accuracy. The journey can even be followed on a survey-map.

During one of the colloquies of Dean Gauss, Fitzgerald, and Hemingway in the summer of 1925, "Big Two-Hearted River" came up for consideration. Both of Hemingway's friends had read it in the spring number of Ernest Walsh's little magazine, *This Quarter.* Half in fun, half in seriousness, they now accused him of "having written a story in which nothing happened," with the result that it was "lacking in human interest." Hemingway, Dean Gauss continues, "countered by insisting that we were just ordinary book reviewers and hadn't even taken the trouble to find out what he had been trying to do." This anecdote is a typical instance of the unfortunately widespread assumption that Hemingway's hand can be read at a glance. Dean Gauss remarks that his own return to the story was profitable. There was much more there than had first met his eye.[7]

For here, as elsewhere in Hemingway, something is going on down under. One might echo Hamlet's words to the ghost of his father: "Well said, old mole, canst work i' the earth so fast?"— and with just Hamlet's mixture of admiration and excitement. Malcolm Cowley, one of the few genuinely sympathetic critics of Hemingway, has suggested that "the whole fishing expedition . . . might be regarded as an incantation, a spell to banish evil spirits."[8] The story is full of rituals. There is, for example, the long hike across the country—a ritual of endurance, for Nick does not stop to eat until he has made camp and can feel that he has earned the right to supper. There is the ritual of home-making, the raising-up of a wall against the dark; the ritual of food-preparation and thoughtful, grateful eating; of bedmaking and deep untroubled sleep. Next morning comes the ritual of bait-catching, intelligently done and timed rightly before the sun has warmed and dried the grasshoppers. When Nick threads one on his hook, the grasshopper holds the hook with his front feet and spits tobacco-juice on it—as if for fisherman's luck. "The grasshopper," as Mr. Cowley says, "is playing its own part in a ritual." The whole of the fishing is conducted according to the ritualistic codes of fair play. When Nick catches a trout too small to keep, he carefully wets his hands before touching the fish so as not to disturb the mucous coating on the scales and thus destroy the fish he is trying to save. Down under, in short, the close reader finds a carefully determined order of virtue and simplicity which goes far towards explaining from below the oddly satisfying effect of the surface story.

Still, there is more to the symbolism of the story than a ritual of self-disciplined moral conduct. Two very carefully prepared atmospheric symbols begin and end the account. One is the burned ground near the town of Seney. The other is the swamp which lies farther down the Big Two-Hearted River than Nick yet wishes

---

[7] Christian Gauss to CB, 12/26/50.
[8] Malcolm Cowley, introd., *The Portable Hemingway,* p. xix.

to go. Both are somehow sinister. One probably legitimate guess on the background of the first is that Nick, who is said to have been away for a long time, is in fact a returned war-veteran, going fishing both for fun and for therapeutic purposes. In some special way, the destroyed town of Seney and the scorched earth around it carry the hint of war—the area of destruction Nick must pass through in order to reach the high rolling pine plain where the exorcism is to take place. In much the same way, the swamp symbolizes an area of the sinister which Nick wishes to avoid, at least for the time being.

The pine plain, the quiet grove where he naps, the security of the camp, the pleasures of the open river are, all together, Nick's "clean, well-lighted place." In the afternoon grove, carefully described as an "island" of pine trees, Nick does not have to turn on any light or exert any vigilance while he peacefully slumbers. The same kind of feeling returns that night at the camp after he has rigged his shelter-half and crawled inside. "It smelled pleasantly of canvas. Already there was something mysterious and home-like. . . . He was settled. Nothing could touch him. . . . He was there, in the good place. He was in his home where he had made it." Back in the low country around Seney, even the grasshoppers had turned dark from living in the burned-over ground. Up ahead in the swamp "the big cedars came together overhead, the sun did not come through, except in patches; in the fast deep water, in the half light, the fishing would be tragic. . . . Nick did not want it." For now, on his island between sinister and sinister, Nick wants to keep his fishing tender and if possible comic.

II. THE EDUCATION OF NICHOLAS ADAMS

"Big Two-Hearted River" was based on an expedition which Hemingway once made to Michigan's northern peninsula. His determination to write only those aspects of experience with which he was personally acquainted gave a number of the first forty-five stories the flavor of fictionalized personal history. He was always prepared to invent people and circumstances, to choose backgrounds which would throw his people into three-dimensional re-

lief, and to employ as symbols those elements of the physical setting which could be psychologically justified by the time and
place he was writing about. But during the decade when the first
forty-five stories were written, he was unwilling to stray very far
from the life he knew by direct personal contact, or to do any more
guessing than was absolutely necessary.

The recurrent figure of Nicholas Adams is not of course Hemingway, though the places Nick goes and the events he watches
are ordinarily places Hemingway had visited or events about
which he had heard on good authority and could assimilate to his
own experience of comparable ones. Future biographers will have
to proceed warily to separate autobiographical elements from the
nexus of invented circumstances in which they may be lodged.
For present purposes it is enough to notice that well over half of
the first forty-five stories center on Nick Adams, or other young
men who could easily be mistaken for him.

They might be arranged under some such title as "The Education of Nicholas Adams." It could even be said that when placed
end to end they do for the twentieth century roughly what Henry
Adams did for the nineteenth, though with obvious differences
in formality of approach. The education of Henry Adams in
Boston, Quincy, Berlin, London, and Washington presented an
informative contrast with the education of Nicholas Adams in
Chicago, northern Michigan, Italy, and Switzerland. Nick's life in
the twentieth century was on the whole considerably more spectacular than Henry's in the nineteenth; it was franker, less polite,
less diplomatic. Chicago, where Nick was born just before the
turn of the century, was a rougher climate than Henry's mid-
Victorian Boston, just as Nick's Ojibway Indians were far more
primitive than Henry's Boston Irish. Partly because of the times
he lived in and partly, no doubt, because he was of a more ad-
venturous temperament, Nick came more easily on examples
of barbarism than Henry was to know until his visit to the South
Seas. In place of the Great Exposition of 1900 which so stimu-
lated Henry's imagination, Nick was involved in the World's Fair
of 1914–1918. But in retrospect one parallelism stood out mo-
mentously: both Henry and Nicholas had occasion to marvel bitterly at how badly their respective worlds were governed.

Nick's father, Dr. Henry Adams, played a notable part in Nick's early education. He was a busy and kindly physician whose chief avocations were hunting and fishing. There was opportunity for both in the Michigan wood and lake country where the Adams family regularly summered. Mrs. Adams was a Christian Scientist; her temperament was as artistic as that of her husband was scientific. After the death of Nick's grandfather she designed a new house for the family. But Nick was his father's son, loving his father "very much and for a long time." From the son's fictional reminiscences a memorable portrait of Dr. Henry Adams is made to emerge. He was a large-framed man with a full dark beard, a hawklike nose, striking deepset eyes, and an almost telescopic power of far-sightedness. Though they gradually grew apart, they were the best of companions during Nick's boyhood. In middle life Dr. Adams died by his own hand for reasons that Nick sorrowfully hints at but does not reveal.

Ten of the stories record Nick's growing-up. He recalls the move from one house to another and the accidental burning of Dr. Adams's collection of Indian arrowheads and preserved snakes. One Fourth of July, he remembers (and it is one of the century's best stories of the growing-up of puppy-love) there was a ride in a neighbor's wagon back from town past nine drunken Indians, while bad news of his girl, Indian number ten in the story called "Ten Indians," was relayed to him by his father on his return home. Nick had already had his adolescent sex-initiation with the same girl, a half-breed named Trudy. He watched a very humiliating argument between his father and a crew of sawyers, and a terrifying Caesarean birth and suicide (addition and subtraction simultaneously achieved) at the Indian settlement. Nick's best friend in Michigan was a boy named Bill who could talk baseball, fishing, and reading with equal ease. Both in Michigan and in Illinois Nick encountered the underworld. It was part of his informal education to be manhandled by two gangsters in a Chicago lunchroom, and to share supper with two tramps, one of them a dangerously punch-drunk ex-prizefighter, in the woods near Mancelona, Michigan.

Like Hemingway, Nick Adams went to war. The earliest glimpses of his career as soldier come in the sixth and seventh miniatures of *In Our Time*. One shows Nick fiercely praying while Austrian artillery pounds the Italian trenches near Fossalta di Piave. In the other, he has been hit in the spine by an Austrian bullet and is leaning back with paralyzed legs against the wall of an Italian church. "Now I Lay Me," one of the longer stories, shows Nick as twice-wounded Tenente Adams, troubled by insomnia and talking out the night with his Italian orderly, a fellow-Chicagoan. "In Another Country" does not name its narrator, but it could well be the same young Tenente in conversation with an Italian major, a fellow-patient in the base hospital at Milan. In "A Way You'll Never Be," Nick is reporting back to battalion headquarters in American uniform. Though he is still recuperating from a severe wound and battle-shock, he is supposed to help build morale among Italian troops by means of the uniform. It is meant as a sign that the A. E. F. will shortly come to their support.

There are no Nick Adams stories of the homecoming, the process which Henry Adams found so instructive after his service abroad. The fate of the male character in "A Very Short Story" might, however, be thought of as one episode in the postwar adventures of Nick Adams. In a base-hospital at Padua, he falls in love with a nurse named Luz—an idea much expanded and altered in *A Farewell to Arms*. But when the young man returns to Chicago to get a good job so that he can marry Luz, he soon receives a letter saying that she has fallen in love with a major in the Arditi. The protagonist in "Soldier's Home" is called Harold Krebs, and he is a native of Oklahoma rather than Illinois. But once again the story might have had Nick Adams as its central character. Like Nick's mother, Mrs. Krebs is a sentimental woman who shows an indisposition to face reality and is unable to understand what has happened to her boy in the war.

Nick Adams returned to Europe not long after the armistice. "Cross-Country Snow" reveals that he is married to a girl named Helen who is expecting a baby. "Out of Season" and "Alpine Idyll" could easily be associated with Nick's life on the continent, while the very moving "Fathers and Sons," which stands as the concluding story in Hemingway's collected short fiction, shows Nick on one of his return trips to the United States, driving his own son through familiar country and thinking back to the life and the too early death of the boy's grandfather, Dr. Henry Adams.

The story of Nick's education, so far as we have it, differs in no essential way from that of almost any middleclass American male who started life at the beginning of the present century or even with the generation of 1920. After the comparatively happy boyhood and the experimental adolescence, the young males went off to war; and after the war, in a time of parlous peace, they set out to marry and build themselves families and get their work done. The story of Adams is a presented vision of our time. There is every reason why it should arouse in us, to use the phrase of Conrad, "that feeling of unavoidable solidarity" which "binds men to each other and all mankind to the visible world."

Future biographers, able to examine the Nick Adams stories against the full and detailed background of Hemingway's life from his birth on July 21, 1899, until, say, his thirty-first birthday in 1930, should uncover some valuable data on the methods by which he refashions the actual into the shape of a short story. What they may fail to see—and what a contemporary evaluator is justified in pointing out—is that Hemingway's aim in the Nick Adams stories is always the aim of an artist. He is deeply interested in the communication of an effect, or several effects together, in such a way as to evoke the deep response of shared human experience. To record for posterity another chapter in his own fictional autobiography does not interest him at all.

III. MANY CIRCLES

"Really, universally, relations stop nowhere," said Henry James in one of his prefaces, "and the exquisite problem of the artist is externally but to draw, by a geometry of his own, the circle within which they shall happily *appear* to do so." [9] The first forty-five stories of Hemingway draw many such circles—concentric, tangential, or overlapping—in which to contain the great variety of human relations which interest him. Two of the circles, and they might be seen as tangential, are those called Home and Not-Home.

[9] *Works*, New York edition, Vol. 1, p. vii.

Nick Adams is perfectly at home in his tent in the Michigan wilderness, but the institution that is supposed to be home for the returned veteran Krebs merely causes him acute discomfort. Bed is home to William Campbell. The sheet drawn up over his face is a protection against the Not-Home of the active world, though it is also, in movies and in morgues, the accepted ritualistic sign that the person underneath is dead. The clean, well-lighted café is much more home than his actual home to the old Spaniard who comes there nightly to stay until the place closes.

The Not-Home is another of the names of *nada,* which Carlyle once rhetorically defined as the vast circumambient realm of nothingness and night. It was perhaps never more sharply drawn than by Goya in the horrific etching which he calls "Nada." An arc of the *nada*-circle runs all the way through Hemingway's work from the night-fears of Jake Barnes to the "horrorous" of Philip Rawlings and the ingrowing remorse of Richard Cantwell. Malcolm Cowley has well described him as one of "the haunted and nocturnal writers," akin, in his deeper reaches, to Melville and Hawthorne.[10] Another way of defining *nada* might be to say, indeed, that it falls about midway between the "Black Man" of Hawthorne and the "White Whale" of Melville. In the first forty-five stories, this besieging horror of the limitless, the hallucinatory, the heartland of darkness, bulks like a Jungian Shadow behind the lives of many of the protagonists. Outside the circle which Hemingway has drawn by the special magic of his geometry, man's relations to the shadow stop nowhere.

But the Home-circle has another alternate than that of *nada.* This is the idea of male companionship, rough and friendly camaraderie, an informal brotherhood with by-laws which are not written down but are perfectly understood and rigidly adhered to by the contracting parties. Hemingway summed up the matter in his title *Men Without Women.* For woman, closely associated with the Home-symbol, stands in opposition, perhaps even in a kind of enmity, to that wholly happy and normal condition which two men, hiking or drinking or talking together, can build like a world of their own. One sees this world in the Burguete of Jake Barnes and Bill Gorton, in the Gorizia of Lieutenant Henry and

[10] *The Portable Hemingway,* introd., p. vii.

Doctor Rinaldi, in the Guadarrama hide-out of Robert Jordan and Anselmo, and in the Gritti Palace Hotel dining-room where Colonel Cantwell and the Gran Maestro (with their unspoken loyalties, their completely shared ethical code, and their rough and friendly badinage) discuss together the latest affairs of *El Ordine Militar, Nobile y Espirituoso de los Caballeros de Brusadelli.*

"Dramatize it, dramatize it," cried Henry James. "Then, and not sooner, would one see." [11] The most direct dramatization of the men-without-women theme occurs in "Cross-Country Snow." Here Nick Adams and his friend George, between whom there is something of a father-and-son relationship, are skiing near Montreux. When they stop for wine at the inn, the obvious pregnancy of their waitress reminds George that Nick's wife Helen is expecting a child. Both men know that the birth of the child will certainly interrupt and probably destroy their comradeship. "Maybe we'll never go skiing again," says George. "We've got to," Nick answers. "It isn't worth while if you can't." George wishes, boy-like, that they could make some kind of promise about it. "There isn't any good in promising," says young Nick Adams. "It's hell, isn't it?" says George. "No, not exactly," says Nick.

Nick and George are as free and happy as Jake and Bill at Burguete. On the other side, for Nick, is all that involvement with woman, all the approaching domestication, all that half-ruefully, uncomplainingly accepted responsibility which will arrive at the moment Nick's fatherhood begins. It is not exactly hell. That is the province of *nada*. Nick recognizes, without complaint, that domestic responsibility presents a powerful case. It could, conceivably, cancel out those things in his life that are symbolized by the skiing with a good companion. And really, universally, the opposed relations of Men-without-women and Men-with-women stop nowhere. The conversational episode in the inn near Montreux is simply the little circle in which they *appear* to do so.

Closely related to the Men-without-women theme is that of fathers and sons. In the early Nick Adams stories Nick is seen as the son of a father; in the latest, he is the father of a son. Some half-dozen of the first forty-five stories draw circles around the

[11] Henry James, *Works,* New York edition, Vol. 17, p. xxvii.

father-son relationship. It is movingly dramatized, for example, through Nick's sympathy with his father's shame and anger after the encounter with the sawyers, in which Dr. Adams has been insultingly bested. The following conversation closes "The Doctor and the Doctor's Wife":

"Your mother wants you to come and see her," the doctor said.

"I want to go with you," Nick said.

"All right. Come on, then," his father said. . . .

"I know where there's black squirrels, Daddy," Nick said.

"All right," said his father. "Let's go there."

At the other end of the line there is Nick's unspoken sympathy for his own son "Schatz" in the little story called "A Day's Wait." Not knowing the difference between Fahrenheit and centigrade thermometers, the boy (who had gone to school in France) naturally supposes that with a temperature of 102 degrees he will certainly die. It was common talk among his French schoolmates that you could not live with a temperature of 44 degrees, normal being 37 degrees. During the day's wait, he manages to keep a firm and stoical grip on himself. When he learns the truth, which is also the time when Nick first understands what is troubling the boy, the hold gradually relaxes. "The next day," says Nick, with a laconic quality that nearly conceals his own emotion, the boy's hold on himself "was very slack and he cried very easily at little things that were of no importance."

A third aspect of the father-and-son theme is the inevitable and paradoxical gulf between generations. It shows very clearly in the early story, "My Old Man," with its contrast between Joe's adoring innocence and his father's vicious world of thrown horse-races. But the paradox of togetherness and separateness is nowhere more poignantly dramatized than in the Nick Adams story called "Fathers and Sons." One great skill of the story is its compression of the generations of men, until the whole Adams clan of grandfather, father, son, and son's son are seen in a line, each visible over his son's shoulder. Each father is near his son, each son near his father. Yet between each generation comes the wall which neither side can fully cross—or would want to if it were possible.

IV. MANY MARRIAGES

Paradox is also at work in what may be called Hemingway's "marriage-group," that very considerable number of the first forty-five stories where the subject is some form of male-female relationship. Like Chaucer or Shakespeare or Keats or Browning, he watches with fascination the odd wave-like operation of attraction and repulsion between the two sexes. In his poems "Meeting at Night" and "Parting at Morning," Browning dramatizes the magnetic attraction of a tryst, and the "need for a world of men" which afterwards draws the lover away as rapidly as he came. Hemingway's stories often engage this paradox.

The women in Hemingway nearly always fail to understand fully the strength and extent of the attraction-repulsion phenomenon. Often, however, they are compelled—and it is on the whole an unhappy experience for them—to recognize its existence. One example will serve. "Up in Michigan," the earliest story in the collection, written in Paris in December, 1921, is one of the very few which Hemingway chooses to tell from the woman's point of view. Here a fine, neat country girl named Liz Coates worships a fine handsome blacksmith named Jim Gilmore from a respectful distance. One foggy evening, after a hunting trip, a good dinner, some whiskey, and exposure to the heat of an open fire, Jim rudely, painfully, and crudely seduces Liz on a cold boat-dock. Afterwards, being unable to talk to or even to wake her importunate lover, Liz covers him with her coat and walks home. This story is the first in a long line of similar instances where male virility, though often rough and wayward in its manifestations, seems to be the axis on which the world of womankind revolves.

"Cat in the Rain," another story taken in part from the woman's point of view, presents a corner of the female world in which the male is only tangentially involved. It was written at Rapallo in May, 1923. From the window of a hotel room where her husband is reading and she is fidgeting, a young wife sees a cat outside in the rain. When she goes to get it, the animal (which somehow stands in her mind for comfortable bourgeois domesticity) has disappeared. This fact is very close to tragic because of the cat's association in her mind with many other things she longs for:

long hair that she can do in a knot at the back of her neck; a candle-lighted dining-table where her own silver gleams; the season of spring and nice weather; and, of course, some new clothes. But when she puts these wishes into words, her husband mildly advises her to shut up and find something to read. "Anyway," says the young wife, "I want a cat. I want a cat. I want a cat now. If I can't have long hair or any fun, I can have a cat." The poor girl is the referee in a face-off between the actual and the possible. The actual is made of rain, boredom, a preoccupied husband, and irrational yearnings. The possible is made of silver, spring, fun, a new coiffure, and new dresses. Between actual and possible stands the cat. It is finally sent up to her by the kindly old inn-keeper, whose sympathetic deference is greater than that of the young husband.

In "The Kreutzer Sonata," Tolstoi presents an extreme example of the mild schizophrenia where a desired involvement and a desired freedom co-exist in the mind of the male. Two of Hemingway's stories approach the same problem in a comic spirit. In "The End of Something," Nick bluntly concludes his serious love affair with Marjorie, evidently by previous agreement with his friend Bill. In "The Three-Day Blow," while the wind of autumn rises in background accompaniment, Nick and Bill converse on the mature wisdom they showed in having stopped the love affair before it went too far. Despite this wisdom, Nick cannot help feeling uncomfortable about the finality of the termination. Thus when Bill rather cynically guesses that it might not be so final after all, Nick is wonderfully relieved. He can always go into town where Marjorie lives on the coming Saturday night. It is "a good thing to have in reserve."

Despite the need for detachment after involvement, Hemingway's work always stresses the essential normality and rightness of the male-female relationship.[12] Anything which distorts it, any-

[12] A passage of dialogue between Hemingway and the Old Lady (*DIA*, 179–180) bears on this point. "Do you know any true stories about those unfortunate people?" says the Old Lady, meaning by unfortunate the sexually abnormal. "A few," answers Hemingway, "but in general they lack drama, as do all tales of abnormality, since no one can predict what will happen in the normal while all tales of the abnormal end much the same."

thing which brings it to an unhappy conclusion, is basically a kind
of tragedy. In 1918, for example, there was a major in a Milan
hospital whose wounded right hand had shrunk until it was no
bigger than a baby's. Before the war he had been the best fencer
in Italy. He was now using an exercise machine which was supposed to strengthen and enlarge the withered hand. Beside him
at these sessions was a young American, taking similar treatments
for a wounded leg, but more hopeful of its restoration. One day
the major asked the American if he were married, and the American replied that he would like to be.

"The more of a fool you are," the major said. He seemed very
angry. "A man must not marry."

"Why, Signor Maggiore?"

"Don't call me 'Signor Maggiore.' "

"Why must not a man marry?"

"He cannot marry. He cannot marry," he said angrily. "If he
is to lose everything, he should not place himself in a position to
lose that. He should not place himself in a position to lose. He
should find things he cannot lose."

The major's wife had just died of pneumonia. Death is the absolute distortion, the unequivocal conclusion. The story, and there
is much more to it, is called "In Another Country." The country
is Italy; but it is also another country still, a country (it is just
possible) where a man can find things he cannot lose.

Divorce or separation is a form of death in Hemingway's
marriage-group. In the ironic story called "A Canary for One,"
the narrative turns upon a point of information not revealed until
the final sentence: "We were returning to Paris to set up separate
residences." Hemingway's strategy here is to establish through
dialogue a parallel between the about-to-separate husband and
wife and an enforced separation about which they hear on the
train-ride between Cannes and the Gare de Lyon in Paris. They

---

It might be added that Hemingway everywhere celebrates the normal
values of sexual intercourse between a man and a woman who are in love.
It is probable that he agrees with the opinion of Remy de Gourmont: "Il
y aurait peut-être une certaine corrélation entre la copulation complète et
profonde et le développement cérébral." See Ezra Pound's postscript to
his translation of de Gourmont's *Natural Philosophy of Love,* published
by Boni and Liveright, New York, 1922.

share a compartment with a deaf American lady who is taking home to her daughter a canary which she has picked up during a Cook's Tour. The lady's conviction that "American men make the best husbands" embroils the reader in a double irony. Two years before, she has broken up a match between her daughter and a Swiss engineering student on the grounds that "I couldn't have her marrying a foreigner." The daughter's reaction has not been favorable. "She doesn't seem to take an interest in anything. She doesn't care about things." The canary is a consolation prize, a substitute interest which will obviously fail. But the lady will not give up her belief that Americans make the best husbands, even though she is in the same compartment with an American couple whose marriage has failed.

The canary (if the lady would face it) and the couple (if the lady knew about them) might together penetrate the lady's rock-ribbed assurance that she is in the right. Both the married people must henceforth content themselves with those forlorn substitutes for each other of which, in another domestic situation, the canary is the epitome. But the lady's deafness is itself a symbol of her impenetrability to suggestion; and she will never know how much the canary will mean to the about-to-separate American couple as a symbol of distortion.

Other stories explore the predicament of divorce. Mr. Johnson, a writer waiting for his train in the station café at Vevey, desperately supposes that he can blunt the edge of the shame he feels by talking over his imminent divorce with three dignified Swiss porters. Though he buys them wine, and curiously raises what for him is the central question, he is met by that sympathetic but somewhat enigmatic politeness which was to be expected.

"You say you have never been divorced?"

"No," says one porter. "It would be too expensive. Besides, I have never married."

"Ah," says Johnson. "And these other gentlemen?"

"They are married."

"You like the married state?" says Johnson to one of them.

"Oui. C'est normal."

"Exactly," says Johnson. "Et vous, monsieur?"

"Ça va," says the third porter.

"Pour moi," says Johnson, "ça ne va pas."

Seeing then, after a futile attempt to change the subject, that his bull-blundering investigation has come to nothing, Johnson excuses himself and goes outside. "It had only made him feel nasty"—because he has possibly embarrassed the porters while certainly embarrassing himself, but mainly because he has recognized, with more shame and discomfort than ever, the normality of the married state, the "abnormality" of his own, and, finally and acutely, that whole nexus of half-humorous shrugging acceptance which is summed up in the second porter's "Ça va." Pour Monsieur Johnson, ça ne va pas.

If the healthy married state, or its approximate equivalent, is strongly recommended in these stories as the normal situation for men and women, one finds also the occasional recognition of other forms of abnormality than divorce. There is, for example, the extreme travesty of the relationship between "Mr. and Mrs. Elliot," who at last settle into an old-maid marriage, all calm and acceptable superficially, all in jagged remnants underneath. Another story, "The Sea Change," examines at its crux the problem of an otherwise satisfactory liaison. The girl faces the pull of an unnatural attraction, and the lover sees that he has no choice but to let her go. Except for one pronoun, and a noun which the girl rejects as too ugly to apply to her own situation, the story might be that of an ordinary lovers' triangle, with the girl leaving one man for another. The pronoun appears in the man's fierce threat towards the third corner of the triangle: "I'll kill her," he cries.

V. MANY MUST HAVE IT

To say that Hemingway is preoccupied with such subjects would be wrong. His preoccupation is rather with the healthy norm of ordinary sexual behavior. He merely sees that the normality of the norm is sometimes most effectively measured in terms of departures from it. Furthermore, a writer dedicated, like Hemingway, to the rendering of things as they are soon recognizes that departures from the usual are numerous enough to make ignoring them a fault of seeing. His personal views, which can be determined inductively, seem to range from the artist's simple acceptance of the fact that abnormality exists up to an outright scorn full of moral echoes of disgust and disapproval, or over into an amused raillery at the expense of the afflicted. Somewhere near the area of simple acceptance would be the story called "A Simple Enquiry," in which an Italian major asks his youthful orderly certain guarded but leading questions. These are familiar enough in an amusing way to all who have ever been through the stock interview with the army psychiatrist at an induction center. Before this particular interview is over, the reader is aware that the major's interests are not, on the whole, scientific.

Among the humorous stories is one called "The Light of the World." Hemingway includes it among the six or seven which he likes best, though he says that "nobody else ever liked" it.[13] One need not like the substance of the story, or the people, or the language. But even with these reservations, one can still enjoy the story's triumph, which is that it adds up to a very complicated defense of the normal against the abnormal. The scene is a provincial railroad depot in northern Michigan at an autumn nightfall. Two tough youngsters, coming in, find themselves in the midst of ten men and five women. The group conversation, conducted in roaring comic terms, establishes the homosexuality of one of the men to serve as contrast to the loudmouthed lying sentimentality of one of the five prostitutes. She says that she was once the true love of Steve Ketchel, a prizefighter. Her forthright contradicter, an even fatter professional tart named Alice, stands (at least in context) for the normal, the honest, and the sound. The raucous play of human emotion, bald as a turkey-egg, loud as a brawl, sets up an effective contrast to the furtive yearnings of the homosexual cook. In an odd way, and not without some strain on the moral judgment, the huge Alice in her iridescent silk dress comes to be the true heroine of the comedy. Love may be, as the sentimental blonde asserts, the light of the world. But an even stronger light may be cast by the honest common sense of people like Alice, the Michigan Wife of Bath.

Hemingway's skills as a comic writer are probably not enough

[13] One of Hemingway's letters to Perkins suggests that this story has some points in common with Maupassant's *La Maison Tellier*. EH to MP, 7/31/33.

appreciated. "The Gambler, the Nun, and the Radio," for example, is a fine and subtle study, depending to a great degree on
the humor of character, and setting up a memorable contrast
among three levels of the apprehension of reality.[14] So is the portrait of the old French couple in "Wine of Wyoming." Here as
elsewhere in the first forty-five stories, it is his championship of
the normal and the natural which runs like a backbone down
through the substance of the tales he elects to tell.[15] His devotion
to the honest and the actual is a moral decision which also happens to coincide with his esthetic views.

The record, if it is examined justly and with detachment, simply
does not bear out the frequent critical implication that he in-
vokes the spectacular or leans on the unusual to carry the burden
of his stories. If "Hills Like White Elephants" throws light into
the nether regions of selfish human abnormality—which is one
way of looking at the matter of abortion—one can balance it with
such insights into the normal married state as "Cat in the Rain."
The raving sentimentality of the peroxide blonde in "The Light
of the World" is neatly deflated by the solid honesty of Alice, who
has long since left (if she was ever inside) her friend's cheap and
banal wonderland. Even the nightly excursions of the old Spanish
waiter into that vast *nada* which lies outside the normal world of
everyday affairs are wrenched back by a final twist into the realm
of the recognizable. "After all," he says to himself, "it is probably only insomnia. Many must have it." The world of Hemingway's short stories is above all the world we know. Many of us
have it—or at least enough of it so that we easily recognize its
outlines in his pages.

His oddly continuing reputation as an "archpriest of violence"
really finds little support in the first forty-five stories. The over-
whelming majority are extremely non-athletic. Their points are
carried by talk far more often than by action. Outwardly, at least,
nothing much happens, even though several kinds of burning

---

[14] This story evidently grew out of Hemingway's hospitalization in Bill-
ings, Montana, following an automobile accident in November 1930. The
story was finished early in February 1933.

[15] "Wine of Wyoming" is apparently related to Hemingway's sojourn in
the Sheridan area during the summer of 1928. The story contains topical
allusions to the presidential candidacy of Governor Alfred E. Smith.

emotion are implied and at intervals may erupt into the briefest violence of language. Otherwise there is seldom more movement than such as is necessary to raise a glass to the lips, row a boat across an inlet, cast a fly into a troutstream, or ski down a snowy slope into the true center of a story.

At café tables, in quiet rooms, or in the compartments of trains, men and women talk together with a concentrated diffidence which almost conceals the intensity of their feelings. Upon examination, it turns out to be this very intensity, this intensity very close to the intensity of poetry, which has deceived some of his critics into supposing that Hemingway is an exponent of violence for its own sake. Even in the relatively rare athletic stories, this is never so. He is after intensity, and his brand of intensity is to be achieved not by physical exercise but only through the exercise of the utmost restraint.[16]

[16] The origin of the titles *Men Without Women* and *Winner Take Nothing* may be noted for the record. The first was evidently a twist on the title of a novel by Ford, *Women and Men*. Hemingway's title was given in turn a twist by Wyndham Lewis for his critical book, *Men Without Art*. Hemingway's jocular explanation of his choice of the title was that he hoped the book would have a big sale among graduates of Vassar and homosexuals. EH to FSF, *ca.* late September 1927. But he had already given Perkins a serious explanation: "In all of these [stories], almost, the softening feminine influence [is] absent," whether as a result of "training, discipline, death, or other causes." EH to MP, 2/14/27. Hemingway had decided on the *Winner Take Nothing* title by 6/11/33. The title derives from the epigraph of the book. This epigraph, ostensibly drawn from an antique book of rules for gaming, was actually written by Hemingway himself. EH to CB, 11/22/51.

VII · The Spanish Earth

> "Like a bistro to which you can take your own food on condition that you wash it down with a bottle of the host's unpredictable wine, Spain is the traditional ruminating ground."—Geoffrey Brereton [1]

I. TAUROMAQUIA

After the land of his birth and boyhood, Italy was Hemingway's first love, and France his second. But of all the nations of Europe, Spain in the period before Franco stood out most strongly in his affections. There was even a time, in Burguete in 1925, when he told his new friend Fitzgerald that his idea of heaven would be a big bullring in which he owned two barrera seats, with a troutstream outside that no one else was allowed to fish. [2] Almost from the beginning of his career he had been writing about Spain and the people of Spain. There were, however, two more or less distinct periods of interest. The first, 1922–1932, used Spanish backgrounds for six of the miniatures of *In Our Time*, as well as for five of the longer stories. All but the introductory section of *The Sun Also Rises* was laid in Spanish towns (Burguete, Pamplona, and Madrid). The terminal book for this period was *Death in the Afternoon*, completed in 1931–1932, though begun much earlier and sporadically worked on through most of the time between the fall of 1929 and its publication in the fall of 1932. It was primarily a Baedeker of the bullfight, and it sought to do in graphic prose something like what Goya's "Tauromaquia" had achieved on canvas. But it was undertaken also as a preliminary summing up of ten years of intermittent experience with the Spanish earth and the people who lived on it.

The second period, culminating in *For Whom the Bell Tolls*, ran from 1936 to 1940. The Spanish Civil War—a tragedy

[1] *New Statesman and Nation* 39 (June 24, 1950), p. 716.
[2] EH to FSF, from Burguete, July 1, 1925.

enacted on a far greater scale and with far greater suffering and bloodshed than the weekly tragedies of the *corridas de toros*—was a strong catalyst to Hemingway's imagination. His interest in war as a subject, and his love of first-hand experience as an object, made it almost obligatory that he should watch over the Spanish tragedy until the final curtain fell. In 1937 he worked with Joris Ivens on a war-documentary film, *The Spanish Earth,* in which his friends MacLeish and Dos Passos had an equal interest. Hemingway not only accompanied Ivens and his cameraman, John Ferno, but also provided the commentary and the sound-track narration. In the fall of the same year he drafted his only full-length play, *The Fifth Column.* It showed that Hemingway's capabilities as playwright were strictly limited. Its subject was that of espionage and counter-espionage in the besieged city of Madrid.

Seventeen months after Madrid fell to the fascists on March 28, 1939, he completed *For Whom the Bell Tolls.* It is still, and may well continue to be, the one indubitable classic among the accounts, both fictional and non-fictional, which took Spain's civil tragedy as subject matter. Although the author's sympathies are clearly on the people's side, the book is in no sense a propagandist tract. Its depth and its lucidity arise from its summing up of Hemingway's long and devoted (but also artistically detached) affection for the land and the people—including his sensitive appreciation of the way these were changed, and yet not changed, by the tragic fact of civil war.

The end-product of the first ten years in Spain, *Death in the Afternoon,* has been called the best work on bullfighting in English. It is quite likely the best of its kind in any language and Hemingway worked long and hard to make it so. It is a serious attempt to write a technical handbook of *toreros,* memorable (and not so memorable) *corridas,* and the noble animals, in such a way as to interest and instruct the lay reader. For his amusement, it is diversified with narratives and sketches, often prejudiced commentaries on the arts, satire of *The Torrents of Spring* variety, characterizations, word-pictures, and observations of a social and ethnological nature. It also contains a glossary of Spanish terms; several appendices including an estimate of the author's good friend,

Sidney Franklin, the bullfighter from Brooklyn, New York; and a careful selection of photographs which Hemingway gathered and winnowed during a stay in Spain in May, June, and July, 1931.

Some such book as *Death in the Afternoon* had been on Hemingway's mind for more than seven years before the final version appeared. His first letter to Maxwell Perkins on April 15, 1925, said that he hoped sometime to write a sort of Doughty's *Arabia Deserta* of the bullring, a large book full of wonderful pictures.[3] But the project was sidetracked while Hemingway prepared *In Our Time* for publication by Liveright, composed *The Torrents of Spring,* and finally established his reputation as an artist with *The Sun Also Rises, Men Without Women,* and *A Farewell to Arms.*

He continued his studies of the bullfight in Spain during the summer of 1926, and in December of that year indicated once more to Perkins how close to his heart the bullfight book still was. It must be not merely a textbook history or an apologia for bull-fighting, but, if possible, "the bullfight itself." Except for church ritual, it was the one thing that had come down intact from the old days in Spain. It was of great tragic interest, being literally a matter of life and death. Few people outside Spain knew much about the real art of the *torero.* Finally, bullfighting was a profession in which a young peasant or bootblack could make eighty thousand a year before the age of twenty-three. Such a combination of interests, said Hemingway, must inevitably "do something" to people. But his book would take a long time to finish.[4]

It did. He returned to Spain in the summer of 1929 and made further notes on the status of the sport. But it was not until the fall of 1930 that he was able to report to Maxwell Perkins that the still untitled bullfight book was nearly finished. Two chapters, four appendices, and the glossary then remained to be done. But the work was again interrupted, this time by a serious automobile

---

[3] EH to MP, 4/15/25. Mr. Hemingway denies the recurrent rumor that *Death in the Afternoon* was originally planned in collaboration with Picasso about 1925, with Hemingway doing the text and Picasso the pictures, the whole to be published in a deluxe German edition. EH to CB, 4/1/51.

[4] EH to MP, 12/6/26.

accident and a long period of recuperation. Further observations were added in Spain in the summer of 1931. The glossary was completed in Paris during August. During the last two weeks of November the final chapter was written. After six weeks of revision, the manuscript was completed on January 13, 1932. It was at last published on the 26th of September.[5]

It was the large handsome book with wonderful pictures which Hemingway had looked forward to writing seven years earlier. It was a history, a guide, a report, and a descriptive analysis bound into one. Yet it cannot be too strongly emphasized that the initial impulse behind the book was esthetic. Hemingway was drawn to the bullfight in the early twenties because it seemed to promise an opportunity to study a simple, cruel, and barbaric sport, showing a definite three-act pattern ending in death. Of all the legitimate "subjects that a man may write of," death was one of the simplest, apparently, and one of the most fundamental.[6] By watching it enacted, thought Hemingway, he might get the "feeling of life and death"—the deep contiguity—which he always wanted in his writing. *Death in the Afternoon* shows how the idea grew.

As he watched, time after time, the killing of bulls and the goring of horses and men, he learned more than he had first bargained for about the nature of tragedy, tragic catharsis, the tragic sense of life, and the feeling of doom. Having come only to observe, he remained as an *aficionado*. His presence during the destruction of 1500 bulls, over a ten-year period, convinced him that the bullfight was neither simple, barbaric, cruel, nor really a sport. It was complex in the extreme, ritualized and stylized nearly to the point of decadence.

Though ostensibly an athletic contest between a wild animal and a dismounted man, it differed from other sports in being played "for keeps" at the highest possible stakes. Very early he came to believe that it was "not a sport but a tragedy." [7] He developed the true *aficionado*'s appreciation of bravery, dignity, passion, and *pundonor,* as well as the opposites and the sundry shad-

---

[5] EH to MP, 10/28/30, 8/1/31, 12/9/31, 1/14/32.

[6] *DIA,* pp. 2–3.

[7] *DIA,* p. 16. Hemingway had said the same thing much earlier in one of his despatches to the *Toronto Star Weekly.*

ings of these qualities. He learned many lessons in how to tell the false from the real, the pose from the risk, the decadent from the healthy. Also useful to a foreigner (who was likewise a novelist) was what one learned about the inside of the Spanish temperament. The initial esthetic impulse grew outwards, without losing its esthetic significance, to suggest the outlines of a whole culture.

A very careful and sometimes labored distillation of all the years during and after his nominal residence in Paris, when Hemingway was nearly as often in Spain as out of it, *Death in the Afternoon* was not to be confused with the "one-visit books." [8] These impressionistic tours, written by observant travelers who saw the sights by day and kept diaries by night, required quick publication before the complications set in. According to Hemingway, two good examples of the "one-visit" books would be Julius Meier-Graefe's *The Spanish Journey* and Waldo Frank's *Virgin Spain*. He wished his own book, like that of Professor Robert Jordan, to contain "what he had discovered about Spain in ten years of travelling in it, on foot, in third-class carriages, by bus, on horse- and mule-back, and in trucks." [9] Hemingway could hardly have written a one-visit book even if he had wanted to do so. He had been in Spain so often that the country was a part of him.

Because *Death in the Afternoon* is primarily a handbook of tauromaquia, other aspects of Spanish life gain only incidental admittance. Yet Hemingway's account (in the novel) of Jordan's knowledge of Spain is a sincerely modest understatement of his own: "He knew the Basque country, Navarre, Aragon, Galicia, the two Castiles, and Estremadura well." An attentive and sympathetic reader should be able to gain from the bullfight handbook a vicarious knowledge of "the way it was" for the devoted traveler in Spain in the last years of the monarchy and the first of the People's Republic. Hemingway is invariably trustworthy, for example, on the atmosphere of the cities and towns; the raw ugliness of Bilbao, the tawdry cheapness of Santander, the green oasis of Aranjuez on the brown plain among dirt-colored and stone-green hills. Or the precipitous picturesqueness of Ronda where, if your

[8] *DIA,* p. 52.
[9] *FWBT,* p. 248.

honeymoon or elopement could not succeed in such an environment, "it would be as well to start for Paris and both commence
making your own friends." He recalls the Senegal heat of Cordoba
in summer, the semi-tropical freshness of Valencia (so well remembered by Pilar), the swimming by night off the beach at Grau,
the high cloudless Spanish sky arching over the mountain city
of Madrid, Hemingway's favorite of them all. The sense of place is
strong in the book.

For the sense of the past, so important in *For Whom the Bell
Tolls,* there were the villages with bells, the squares with standing
horses—"the small, careful stepping horses"—the ancient, eroded,
baked-clay hills, or the powdery, hub-deep dust of the dipping
country roads. One got the sense of the past from the crowding,
various smells: leather, road-dust, olive-oil, tarry wineskins, loops
of twisted garlics. Or from the rope-soled shoes, the natural
wooden pitchforks with branches for tines, or the fine old castle
at the head of the valley near Aoiz.

If one comes fresh to a reading of *For Whom the Bell Tolls*
after having laid down *Death in the Afternoon,* he will see how
much of the old Spain has been transferred out of the manual
and into the novel, always with a noticeable gain in dramatic intensity. For, in the novel, what was formerly only a piece of direct
personal observation has very often taken on a functional significance. One of the uses of *Death in the Afternoon,* both for Hemingway and for the serious student of his work, is that it serves as
a kind of sourcebook for *For Whom the Bell Tolls.* In the mob-
murder of the fascists by Pablo and his associates, for example,
the wooden pitchforks are put to a use for which they were never
meant by their rural manufacturers. The welcome sense of abun-
dance in that semi-arid land is not lost on the guerrillas in their
necessarily somewhat austere mountain fastness. They can recall
such delicacies as the fresh strawberries packed on damp green
leaves in wicker baskets, asparagus as thick as thumbs, Valencia
melons, the cider of Bombilla, prawns sprinkled with lime juice,
and the delectable sea-food *paellas.* The sense of place and fact
and scene are strong in the novel not only because Hemingway
knows the country, but also because, in a preliminary way, he had
seized on and arranged them in the earlier book.

Despite romantic overtones (the natural consequence of writing about a country one loves and has been happy in), *Death in the Afternoon* is about an actual Spain. It is honest and realistic. It is even, in certain respects, straightforwardly reportorial, a fact which tells somewhat against it when it is compared with works of fictional art. *For Whom the Bell Tolls* combines a similar tough-minded sense of the actual with similar romantic overtones. Unlike *Death in the Afternoon*, however, the novel has completely assimilated the reportorial element to the needs of art. In the novel, that is to say, we are not told: we learn by experience so sharp that it hardly seems vicarious.

To attempt to compare *Death in the Afternoon* with *For Whom the Bell Tolls* is of course to understand that no genuine comparison is possible. One is intended, as Hemingway reminds us in his "Bibliographical Note" at the end of the book, "as an introduction to the modern Spanish bullfight," where the attempt has been to "explain that spectacle both emotionally and practically." It was written for that purpose because there was no other book in Spanish or English which did precisely that kind of job. The novel, on the other hand, is not a handbook of anything, but an art work of a very high imaginative order. The motivations of the two books are accordingly quite different.

For the student of Hemingway who is seriously interested in the developmental aspects of his fiction, a reading of *Death in the Afternoon* is indispensable. In the same way, one's appreciation of the imaginative stature of *Huckleberry Finn* as a work of art is considerably enhanced by a reading of *Life on the Mississippi*. *Life on the Mississippi* is obviously not in the same class with *Huckleberry Finn*. The laws which govern the composition of such diverse books cannot be the same. But this is hardly to say that the study of *Death in the Afternoon* will not, in various ways, illuminate the study of *For Whom the Bell Tolls*. One of the values of the bullfight book is the light it throws on the esthetics of tragedy in Hemingway.

II. THE ESTHETICS OF TRAGEDY

Nowhere in either of Hemingway's Spanish books could one find the "bedside mysticism" of Waldo Frank's *Virgin Spain*. A comparison between *Death in the Afternoon* and Frank's travelogue emphasizes the great differences between the two men in point of esthetic view. Frank was sometimes excellent as when, describing a dance, he heard "the castanets click their dry commentary," or when he caught some Aragonese peasants as "small weazened men, with heads like nuts and eyes like iron." But Frank loved pseudo-poetry. The girls of Cordoba struck him as "sinuous walking lilies," promising a "snare of momentary passion." [10] When he really set forth in pursuit of an *O Altitudo,* he was capable of flights like the following, on Saragossa's cathedral, *Nuestra Senora del Pilar:*

"From its mournful mass rise suddenly, inappositely, the huge *azulejo* domes, their hypertrophic rhetoric gleaming of Andalusia and Morocco."

In something like the railing manner of *The Torrents of Spring,* Hemingway called this "erectile writing," or the unavoidable mysticism of one who "writes a language so badly he cannot make a clear statement." [11] To account for the unrelieved turgidness of the prose in *Virgin Spain,* he developed a bawdy hypothesis like one of Swift's in *A Tale of a Tub*. Hemingway's own problem in *Death in the Afternoon* was of a different kind. "Madame," he asks the old lady who winningly serves as his tuning fork, "does all this writing of the bullfights bore you?" The old lady says that her patience is a little limited. "I understand," says the author. "A technical explanation is hard reading. It is like the simple directions which accompany any mechanical toy and which are incomprehensible." [12] Whatever the limitations of his own expository writing might be, and they might be many, Hemingway did not take refuge in pseudo-poetry. His prose contained nothing

[10] *Virgin Spain:* Castanets (p. 84), peasants (p. 92), Cordoban girls (p. 60). With Frank's picture of Spanish women contrast Hemingway's (*DIA,* pp. 41–42).

[11] On *erectile writing* see *DIA,* pp. 53–54. See Dos Passos's review of *Virgin Spain* in *New Masses* 1 (July 1926), p. 27, for a similar position.

[12] *DIA,* p. 179.

turgid or intentionally obscure. The reader found no hypertrophic rhetoric gleaming through the pages of *Death in the Afternoon*. Its essential down-to-Spanish-earthness was one of its values.

Frank and Hemingway are in agreement on the larger three-act outline of the typical Spanish bullfight. "The horse," says Frank, "is the comedian of the drama." What happens to the horse is farce, though it involves also a "sense of the imminence of danger." For what has happened to the horse may happen to a man. Hemingway likewise observes that "in the tragedy of the bullfight the horse is the comic character." Frank's account of the second act shows the banderilleros enraging and sobering the bull to make him realize "that the holiday of the horse is no more." By the end of the act the bull is chastened, "cleansed for the tragedy." For Hemingway, the bull in Act Two has lost the free wild quality he began with, gone on the defensive, and become more dangerous in that now, sobered and serious, "he aims every horn stroke," concentrating his hatred on an individual object. One finds nothing in Hemingway about the bull's being cleansed for the tragedy, however, and it is apparent that he has kept his writer's eye more steadily fixed on the animal than has Frank.

At the climactic moment of the killing in Act Three, both writers agree that a profundity of feeling is transferred to the spectator. Frank says that the torero is enacting "the ultimate rite of life" by assuming proprietorship of "the ultimate gift of the gods," which is death. Hemingway's view is again similar: "When a man is still in rebellion against death he has pleasure in taking to himself one of the Godlike attributes, that of giving it." This gift is given in pride—"a Christian sin and a pagan virtue. But it is pride which makes the bullfight, and true enjoyment of killing which makes the great matador." [13]

So far Hemingway will go in Frank's company. But in his down-to-earthness he is never tricked into the pseudo-poetic erotic symbolism of a passage like this of Frank's: "And now another change in the beauty of their locked encounter. The man becomes the woman. This dance of human will and brutish power is the

[13] Cf. *Virgin Spain*, pp. 232–233 and *DIA*, p. 6. On the sobered bull see *DIA*, p. 98. On the killing of Act III, compare *Virgin Spain*, p. 234, and *DIA*, p. 233.

dance of death no longer. It is the dance of life. It is a seaching symbol of the sexual act. The bull is male; the exquisite torero, stirring and unstirred, with hidden ecstasy controlling the plunges of the bull, is female." This is erectile writing with a vengeance. Frank, says Hemingway, discovered some "wonderful stuff about Spain during his short stay there preparatory to writing of the soul of the country, but it is often nonsense." At least it is the kind of writing against which Hemingway had been in very open rebellion since the beginning of his career. *Death in the Afternoon* proceeds sensitively but also with sanity. "The beauty of the moment of killing is that flash when man and bull form one figure as the sword goes all the way in, the man leaning after it, death uniting the two figures in the emotional, esthetic, and artistic climax of the fight. That flash never comes in the skillful administering of half a blade to the bull." The reader will see how simple it would have been to write these sentences in the erotic manner. Knowing truth from falsehood, however, Hemingway does not confuse the torero with a woman, the uniting of the two figures with the sexual act, or the thrust of the blade with the thrust of anything else. His habitual devotion to the truth of the matter may not always save him from self-deception. But he is never guilty of Freudian fiddle-faddle.[14]

He well knows, nevertheless, what emotional and spiritual intensity a genuine fight can produce. The effect can be "as profound as any religious ecstasy"—an experience ordered, formalized, passionate, and with a mounting disregard for death which leaves the spectator "as empty, as changed, and as sad" as any other tragic catharsis.[15]

Death is for Hemingway somewhere near the center of life. Some of his critics have not seen that after the tragi-comedy of *The Sun Also Rises,* all of Hemingway's novels have been tragedies. Nor have they usually understood that such a tragedian must employ his interest in death at the center of the art form he uses. As soon as Hemingway abandoned his early misconception of the bullfight, he immediately saw it as an art form of great com-

[14] Cf. *Virgin Spain*, p. 235, and *DIA*, pp. 53 and 247.
[15] *DIA*, pp. 206–207.

plexity, always producing, when it was well done, tragic emotions and effects. If falsified or weakly performed, it could of course fall as flat as an amateur production of *Hamlet*. Without death at the end of it, further, it would be anticlimactic and unfulfilled, as if one were to tack a happy ending to *King Lear*. The proximity of death gave meaning to all parts of the *corrida*. But the torero alone performed a special work of art in bringing death extremely close, by enthralling it in an art form in such a way as to transmit to the observer the feeling of his own immortality. When the feeling stretched between spectator and actor, the torero cut it with his sword, as a taut wire is cut, relieving the tension and allowing the spectator to relax back into the ultimate emotional situation which Aristotle called catharsis.[16]

The Castilian attitude towards death is evidently very close to Hemingway's own. Unlike the Galicians and the Catalans, who have very little feeling for death, the Castilians "have great common sense. . . . They know death is the unescapable reality, the one thing any man may be sure of. . . . They think a great deal about death and when they have a religion they have one which believes that life is much shorter than death." Since by going to the bullring they have a chance of seeing death "given, avoided, refused, and accepted," they pay their money and go.[17] Such a healthy attitude towards death is one way of overcoming the usual sentimental taboos. To face the fact of death is as necessary to the writer of tragedy as a healthy facing of the other facts of life. If it is a general attribute of the English, the French, and the Americans to "live for life" and to avoid discussion or thought of death, their chances of writing good tragedy are so much the worse.

Hemingway's first visits to the bullfights were made for "the feeling of life and death" which he thought might be gained there. *Death in the Afternoon* shows what happened when Hemingway had learned his way into the esthetics of tragedy which govern the bullfight. It also helps to explain his sense of belonging among the people of the two Castiles, his special love for the people of

[16] *DIA*, pp. 213.
[17] *DIA*, pp. 265–266.

Madrid and the country round it. This locale, this people, and this sense of belonging were important factors in the development of *For Whom the Bell Tolls*.

III. THE HERO AS PRAGMATIST

If Spain taught Hemingway something about the tragic facts of life, it likewise contributed to his conception of the nature of heroism. His earliest and most revealing statements on the qualities of the hero come in *Death in the Afternoon*. Evidently his standard of selection falls somewhere between the hero as man of action and the hero as artist. For the first of these one need look no further than the indomitable figure of Manuel Garcia, called Maera.

"Era muy hombre," says Hemingway of Maera, who for a number of seasons served Belmonte as banderillero and then went on to be a brilliant matador. "Tall, dark, thin-hipped, gaunt-eyed, his face blue-black even after a close shave, arrogant, slouching, and sombre," Maera became one of the "best and most satisfying" fighters in Hemingway's lengthy experience as a spectator. The story of his encounter with the cement-shouldered bull at the close of the eighth chapter of *Death in the Afternoon* documents Hemingway's admiration, with reasons. As his qualities are summed up there, Maera was "generous, humorous, proud, bitter, foul-mouthed, and a great drinker. He neither sucked after intellectuals nor married money. He loved to kill bulls and lived with much passion and enjoyment although the last six months of his life he was very bitter. He knew he had tuberculosis and took absolutely no care of himself; having no fear of death, he preferred to burn out, not as an act of bravado, but from choice." [18] The reader of *Across the River and Into the Trees* will find a number of these qualities translated to fictional form in the person of the professional soldier, Colonel Cantwell.

Goya, the hero as artist, had certain characteristics in common with the hero as man of action. These showed most graphically in the kind of painting he chose to do. According to Hemingway, who contrasts Goya with Velásquez and especially with El Greco,

[18] *DIA*, pp. 77, 80–83.

Goya's painting was the direct outcome of his hard-won empirical convictions. He believed in "blacks and grays, in dust and in light, in high places rising from plains, in the country around Madrid, in movement, in his own cojones, in painting, in etching, and in what he had seen, felt, touched, handled, smelled, enjoyed, drunk, mounted, suffered, spewed-up, lain-with, suspected, observed, loved, hated, lusted, feared, detested, admired, loathed, and destroyed. Naturally no painter has been able to paint all that but he tried." [19] No student of Hemingway can fail to see how exactly this description of Goya's beliefs summarizes the attitudes of all the fictional heroes from Lieutenant Henry to Colonel Cantwell.

The realm in which these heroes move is extraordinary in two important particulars. First, it is a world in a state of flux, like Goya's revolutionary Spain or like the tense microcosm of the various bullrings in which Maera so brilliantly fought his battles. This world requires constant activity of its inhabitants. Second, it is a world screened, as it were, at both ends. One finds that the hero's experiential heritage from the past has little direct bearing on his decisions, though occasionally, as in the case of Robert Jordan's warrior-grandfather, a heroic action in the past may serve as a model for the hero in a present-day predicament. With this kind of exception, however, the Hemingway hero must work out his values for himself almost, if not quite, on the spot. Nor does he incline to take count of the future, the long future after death. He finds his way of life through action, and he acts in the way of the world.

"Perhaps as you went along," Jake Barnes once ruminated, "you did learn something. I did not care what it was all about. All I wanted to know was how to live in it. Maybe if you found out how to live in it you learned from that what it was all about." [20] How to live in it. How to live. The Hemingway hero is always a pragmatist. The function of his thought is, in the end, to serve as a guide for action. The abstraction has little meaning for him until it is particularized in a specific situation. Like Keats, to be convinced of the truth of a thing, he must have tried it on his own pulses. Indeed, much that Hemingway wrote of Goya could also

[19] *DIA,* p. 205.
[20] *SAR,* p. 153.

apply to Keats. The hero tests "truth" by observing the practical consequences of belief. His cast of mind is towards the integration of what is workable. But his vision is usually narrowed to the problems of immediate need. He is at some pains to keep his values from hardening into a final scheme. By preference and predetermination they are held in a more or less fluid state.

One naturally thinks of William James's formulation: pragmatism is "the attitude of looking away from first things, principles, 'categories,' supposed necessities, and of looking towards last things, fruits, consequences, facts." Although the statement summarizes with some precision the attitude of Hemingway's heroes, it is only partly applicable to Hemingway himself. For, as artist and esthetician, he must be and indubitably is concerned with first things and principles as well as the last things—consequences and facts.

His abnegation of his inheritance from the past means that the Hemingway hero must learn his own way to a great extent independently of every other man. In one way this fits the facts of living as we know them. The full significance of a piece of inherited folk-wisdom, say a proverb, never comes really home to us until we have the experience that proves it true. At another and higher point, however, the process of independent discovery, if insisted on exclusively, is a kind of willful evasion of a great part of what we need to know. It is probably fair to say that Hemingway's heroes are anti-intellectuals and even behaviorist anarchists to the extent that each of them must work out his code for himself, without taking full cognizance of the accumulated experience of other men. Yet this is true, to a more limited extent, of most people. At their own dramatic level of working matters out in action, Hemingway's heroes belong among the normal males of our time.

"I did not care what it was all about" is Jake Barnes's way of saying that he has not found any world view which will entirely account for and contain the facts of the world as he has garnered them through youth, war, demobilization, frustrated love, and work for the newspapers. In one of Albert Schweitzer's studies of Goethe, the position is admirably expanded. "Because he knows this one thing," says Schweitzer, "that he belongs to nature and to God, Goethe needs no artistically constructed world view complete to the last detail, but is satisfied to live with a world view which is not complete and cannot be completed. He does not want to be richer than he can be through the absolutely honest acquisition of truth. With that he is confident that he can live." [21] One might not entirely agree with Schweitzer on the question of Goethe's attitude towards a *Weltanschauung*. But Jake Barnes almost takes the words out of Schweitzer's typewriter. "It seemed like a fine philosophy," says Jake about one of his attempts to account for the human predicament. "In five years, I thought, it will seem just as silly as all the other fine philosophies I've had." No ethical or metaphysical speculation can adequately represent the world as it is, unless, of course, it is a scheme to avoid the schematic.

Although the Hemingway hero is not a reasoner in the abstract, and therefore not a builder of world-views, he is an extraordinarily careful planner on the practical plane. It is presumed to be the intelligent man's duty and responsibility to use his powers of planning to the utmost. Leaving as few unknowns as can be, he must organize the known, predict possible variables, estimate the probabilities, decide on a mode of action, and act. If his advance preparation has been good, his results have a chance of being good—up to a point. Beyond that point luck takes over, luck being the unpredictable contingency, present in the unknowns and the possible variables, which may go for or against the best of planners.

Even luck, however, may be controlled in a negative way if one takes the further commonsense precaution of following the rules. Knowledge of the rules of living is perhaps the hardest of the lessons man must learn because there is really no short cut to it. Yet one measure of man's ability to live successfully in the world is clearly his ability to assimilate and then to follow the rules. Matthew Arnold's generic term for this ability was the "sense for conduct." But whatever Arnold may have believed, the sense for conduct is not an innate characteristic. It must be learned empirically. As for the rules, when one gets to know them they are seen to conform rather closely to what would result if the Decalogue were intelligently revamped to present-day usage with-

[21] Albert Schweitzer, *Goethe: Four Studies,* Boston, 1949, p. 49.

out recourse to any form of legalism. One does not commit adultery, bear false witness, steal, or covet—at least not often. He honors his father and mother if they are worth admiration. If not, he can always go back to his grandfather or grandmother, or adopt someone to honor. The matter of conduct demands concentration. "We are mathematicians only by chance," said Dr. Johnson, "but we are perpetual moralists." Simple, unthinking loyalty to another man's code of behavior will not suffice. One must sensibly and consciously choose an ethical pattern whose virtues have been pragmatically proved by one's own experience, including one's experience of watching the conduct of his living companions.

If varying degrees of rationalism, pragmatism, and empiricism meet and merge in the working philosophy of the Hemingway hero, one finds also a suggestion of psychological hedonism. Man's natural tendency, according to the formula promulgated by Benthamist ethics and adapted into a new context by Freudian psychology, is to seek pleasure and avoid pain. Jake Barnes and Brett Ashley, evaluating their past actions and seeking moral guidance for future conduct by discovering which make them feel good and which bad, are perfectly practical Benthamites, whatever their Freudian frustrations. In the world of action, of Lockean empiricism, Jamesian pragmatism, and perhaps even Deweyan instrumentalism, it is hardly surprising to find a Benthamist idea. The falsehood, of course, is to insist that these heroes are merely psychological or ethical hedonists. The rules in Hemingway are far more extensive and complex than that.

The sturdiness of Hemingway's position from an empirical point of view is that the meaning of conceptions must be sought in their practical consequences. This hardly makes him the atavistic man over whom some critics have crowed. (Wyndham Lewis refers, for example, to his "penetrating quality, like an animal speaking.") [22] But it does raise the question, so often raised and answered in the affirmative, of whether or not Hemingway is a "primitivist." To an extent he seems to be. His truth and his beauty are generally to be found in the natural rather than the artificial. In further support of the idea, one could point to his evident admiration of active virtues like courage or what the Spanish call

[22] Wyndham Lewis, *Men Without Art,* London, 1934, p. 17.

pundonor, which "means honor, probity, courage, self-respect and pride in one word." [23] Or his praise of man's ability to handle the instruments of sport or warfare or love-making—the clubs, rods, guns, swords, or other equipment with which he works. If, like the historical primitivist, he seems often to portray a state of society in which such active virtues and skills are necessary for survival, he does not follow the historical primitivist in idealizing that state of society. Unlike the nineteenth-century romantic primitivists, he does not lose himself in a golden age of the remote past or in a future and roseate Utopia. He finds the skills and virtues here and now on the battlefronts and in the bullrings of the world. And there are many bullrings besides those ordinarily so designated, just as there are many battlefronts. The manly virtues, at any rate, are as whole and real now as they were in Sparta, and as useful to man at play or at work. All of this would suggest that the loose term primitivist is a misnomer for Hemingway. Call him a utilitarian, one who realizes that (especially in the present state of the world) such skills and virtues are indispensable, and indeed are constantly in use whether or not a war is on.

If he agrees with Tolstoy that western society is decadent and immoral (and there is plenty of evidence in Hemingway to support the view), he would not, like Tolstoy, seek to impose a primitivistic social idea on the modern world. For he is the pragmatist rather than the idealist. By definition and temperament, he does not in his fiction go beyond a series of individual performances which are too limited in actual scope, even when placed end to end, to constitute a complete social ideal or form the basis for an ideal society. At the same time, no social ideal or ideal society would succeed unless it took account of such virtues and skills as Hemingway celebrates.

This is not to say, of course, that some of the individual performances (for example, Robert Jordan's) will not serve to suggest symbolically a larger social ideal out of which might grow, in the course of time and with luck, a better society. There is an ethical content in Hemingway which transcends the pleasure-pain strategy, a content not less useful because of the author's refusal to state it in other than dramatic terms, worked out in action.

[23] *DIA,* p. 91.

But here again, his perennial distrust of the abstract blue-print, as well as the whole slant of his esthetic conviction, gives him pause and makes him stop short of using his fiction for the purposes of social programming.

One conspicuous virtue of *Death in the Afternoon,* and it is always a virtue in an artist or an art, is the temperamental rejection of the bloodless abstraction. The heroes Hemingway chooses, Goya on canvas and Maera on the bloody sand, are *aficionados* of the actual, believing in what they empirically know, facing the facts of life, one of which is the fact of death, in full consciousness of the inter-relations and the psychological interdependence of the two. The same sturdy quality of belief runs like a thick red line through the whole gallery of Hemingway heroes, and evidently through the consciousness of the artist to whom they owe their origin.

Death in the Afternoon has not yet converted the Anglo-Saxon world to a love of the bullfight, nor is it likely to do so. The author of such a book must expect to find a considerable degree of resistance among those who do not wholly share his interests and his experience. Hemingway admits in the course of the book that some of the technical descriptions may be incomprehensible, which is another way of saying that to the uninitiated or the unsympathetic or the uninterested, parts of the book will seem dull. Other readers, for sundry reasons, may be disgruntled by the tabulation, in one of the appendixes, of "Some Reactions of A Few Individuals to the Integral Spanish Bullfight." Some of Hemingway's critics have even professed to find evidence of a kind of hectic hysteria within the book itself, a point for which the objective reader is likely to discover little support.

Whatever its limitations—and one may doubt that Hemingway finally achieved his aim of writing an *Arabia Deserta* of the bullfight—much of the book remains sound and true. Reviewing a British reissue of *Death in the Afternoon* some twenty years after its original appearance, Geoffrey Brereton attributed the book's staying qualities to "the author's obstinate devotion to the fact and its accompanying sensation." The devotion was evidently intense enough to save Hemingway from "gross errors of observation" and to minimize his "errors of judgment." [24] If one wishes to state the case somewhat more positively, there can be little doubt that Hemingway's enviable ability to stand at once inside and outside of history brings his account of bullfighting—at certain points in the handbook—close to the realm of art.

[24] Same reference as for headnote to this chapter. See above, note 1.

VIII · The Green Hills of Africa

> "I was always discovering places where I
> would like to spend my whole life."—
> W. B. Yeats, *Autobiographies* [1]

I. SAFARI

Hemingway's earliest book review, published in 1922 soon
after he reached Paris, was in praise of *Batouala,* a novel about the
life and death of a native African chieftain which had won its
Negro author, René Maran, the Goncourt Academy prize of
5000 francs for the best fiction by a young writer in 1921. What
made the book newsworthy was Maran's straightforward indictment of French colonial policy in the heart of Africa. For the
young artist Hemingway, however, it was chiefly remarkable for
its unimpassioned presentation of the way it was in an African
village from the native's point of view. "You smell the smells of
the village," wrote the reviewer, "you eat its food, you see the
white man as the black man sees him, and after you have lived
in the village you die there. That is all there is to the story, but
when you have read it, you have been Batouala [the native chief],
and that means that it is a great novel." [2]

Though it has long been forgotten, this review may well mark
the beginning of Hemingway's interest in Africa. Still, he had enjoyed shooting since boyhood, and the plains and hills of East
Africa were a logical destination for one who wanted to hunt on
a bigger scale than was common in Europe or the United States.
He wrote Maxwell Perkins from Wyoming in the fall of 1930
to say that though he had shot much game on the high slopes of
the western mountains, he was still dreaming of a trip to Africa. [3]
If he had another motive than the wish to hunt the green hills of
Tanganyika, it was that of the artist—the aim of seeing for him-

---

[1] Yeats, *Autobiographies* (new edition, New York, 1927), p. 73. Mr.
Hemingway is an avowed admirer of this book.
[2] *Toronto Star Weekly*, March 25, 1922, p. 3.
[3] EH to MP, 9/28/30.

self, perhaps, just how close to the actual René Maran's *Batouala* really was.

"What do you want?" asked a man named Kandisky not long after Hemingway reached the game country of East Africa in the winter of 1933–1934. Kandisky was an expatriate Austrian who worked as employment agent for an Indian sisal-grower in Tanganyika. He had a consuming interest in literature, and none whatsoever in big-game shooting. "To write," answered Hemingway, "as well as I can and learn as I go along. At the same time I have my life which I enjoy and which is a damned good life." Was the hunting of kudu an important part of life, Kandisky wanted to know: "You really like to do this, what you do now, this silliness of kudu?" Hemingway replied that he would as soon hunt kudu as explore the Prado. Both were necessary to a writer.[4] He did not feel apologetic for doing as he liked to do with his life, particularly if he kept his eyes and ears open.

The four-month trip had begun with embarkation from Marseilles in November, 1933, and would end April 3, 1934, when the Hemingways returned to New York on the *Paris*. By the middle of December, 1933, the motorized outfit had moved west from Mombasa, and from the first hunting headquarters at M'utu-Umbo, to an encampment on the Serenea River at the far side of the Serengetti Plain. The hunters arrived in time to watch the migration of huge herds of wildebeeste and other grazing creatures, "a plainfull of moving animals" whose numbers were officially estimated at nearly three million. Here also were the very numerous beasts of prey which followed and fed on the grazing-stock. By January the party's bag already included several kinds of gazelles, antelope, waterbuck, and impalla rams, as well as leopard and cheetah. In something over two weeks along the fringes of the plain, they saw eighty-four lions and took their quota of four. Happily also, and to the vast amusement of the gun-bearer M'Cola, they had destroyed some thirty-five hyenas.

Along with the good luck went some that was bad. Whatever happens to a writer, as Hemingway told Fitzgerald later on that spring, ought to be of some use to him. If one is hurt, the thing is not to complain about it but to find some way of putting the hurt

[4] *GHOA,* p. 25.

to work. Hemingway was speaking, as usual, from experience. Early in January he fell ill of an amoebic dysentery, probably contracted on the dirty French ship coming down through the Red Sea and the Indian Ocean. Though he continued to hunt on every day but two, his condition presently became so serious that he was advised to leave the expedition for medical treatment. In an occurrence of which he would later make fictional capital, employing it as the closing incident (much altered, of course) in "The Snows of Kilimanjaro," he was flown out from the Serengetti on January 16 in a small two-seater plane. The 400-mile dogleg route went by way of the Ngorongoro Crater and the Rift Escarpment to the pleasant town of Arusha. From there they flew past the huge elongated bulk of Mount Kilimanjaro (with the dramatically sudden rise of its main peak) and to Nairobi in Kenya.

Following a period of medical care, Hemingway grew strong enough to rejoin the expedition. It had now moved cross-country to the area south of Ngorongoro in the vicinity of the Rift Valley and Lake Manyara. As his strength slowly returned, Hemingway's delight in the country began once more to rise. Sometimes the sweep and roll of the brown land—as well as the shy herds of antelope—reminded him of the western plains of Wyoming; again, in the uplands, he thought of abandoned New England apple orchards, with ancient gnarled trees well spaced out among the flourishing grass. At other times they would come on terrain that looked for all the world like a remembered part of Aragon or Galicia. Now they shot buffalo and rhinoceros, and hunted kudu and sable until the arrival of the rains in February sent them back to the Kenya coast for a round of sailfishing. In a decrepit launch called the *Xanadu*, Ancient Mariner Hemingway and his white hunter proved to themselves that all the big game was not on shore.[5]

The Tanganyika safari could have been just another hunting-

[5] See Hemingway's articles in *Esquire*, as follows:
"a.d. in Africa," 1 (April 1934), pp. 19, 146.
"Shootism versus Sport," 2 (June 1934), pp. 19, 150.
"Notes on Dangerous Game," 2 (July 1934), pp. 19, 94.
"Sailfish off Mombasa," 3 (March 1935), pp. 21, 156.
Also EH to FSF, 5/28/34.

adventure in the life of the world-traveling Hemingway. But this
hunter was also an artist. "You ought to always write it," he remarked to his white hunter one February night in the hills above
Lake Manyara, "to try to get it stated. No matter what you do
with it." [6] Back in Key West during the summer and fall he decided what to do with it. He would write a true account, changing
some of the names but not the situations, of that last month in
Africa before the seasonal rains had worked north from Rhodesia
and the shooting was over.

After this had been set down, to be serialized first in *Scribner's
Magazine* and afterwards published (on October 25, 1935) as
The Green Hills of Africa, there would be time to invent people
and situations against the background of the Serengetti Plain and
the country just south of Mount Kilimanjaro. This he did in the
form of two remarkable short stories, both composed in the
spring of 1936: "The Snows of Kilimanjaro," published in *Esquire* for August, 1936, and "The Short Happy Life of Francis
Macomber," published in *Cosmopolitan* that September.

II. THE ESTHETICS OF PURSUIT

The Green Hills of Africa was frankly an experiment. "The
writer," says the foreword, "has attempted to write an absolutely
true book to see whether the shape of a country and the pattern
of a month's action can, if truly presented, compete with a work
of the imagination." Telling the truth was nothing new with Hemingway, though he had normally woven truth together with care-

---

[6] *GHOA,* p. 193. The composition of *GHOA* began mid-April 1934,
soon after Hemingway's return to Key West. By June 20, he had reached
p. 141 of the MS (*ca.* 20,000 words). By October 3, the word-length was
50,000, and on November 16 Hemingway wrote Perkins that he had
finished the first draft (73,000 words) that morning. He had already been
over the first half of it three times, rewriting and cutting. The completed
MS was finally sent to Scribner's on February 7, 1935. It was serialized,
with excellent decorations by Edward Shenton, in *Scribner's Magazine,*
May to October 1935. It is of interest that the book began as a short story,
growing to book-length as Hemingway's sense of the value of his subject
grew; and that Hemingway compared it in his mind to "Big Two-Hearted
River." The working title through 1934 was *The Highlands of Africa.*
Hemingway decided on the present title sometime in January 1935.

fully controlled invention. What was new here, what constituted the experiment proper, was the determination to stay absolutely with the facts as they happened in Africa—Hemingway would spare no one, including most of all himself, in the attempt to provide a straight record.

The two major aspects of the experiment are the attempt at verisimilitude ("the shape of a country") and architectonics ("the pattern of a month's action"). The first of these had the importance it had always had in Hemingway's work. Here it meant specifically the attempt to transfer to the unsafaried reader a sense of the way it was to move cross-country through the hills and plains of Tanganyika. He wished to project accurately and sharply his own apprehensions of the lie of the land, the habits of the animals, the living personalities of the natives he met, the state of the weather, the quality of the food, the methods of the camp, the procedures of the hunt, and—running through it all like elastic threads in a pattern—the emotional tensions and re- laxations which gave the events of each day their tone and mean- ing.

From this point of view, *The Green Hills of Africa* is clearly successful. "Nothing that I have ever read," said Hemingway, "has given any idea of the country or the still remaining quantity of game." The reader of Hemingway's book can have no such complaint. There is the lion, a few feet off, "looking yellow and heavy-headed and enormous against a scrubby-looking tree in a patch of orchard bush." Frightened by the explosion of the Mann- licher, he moves off "to the left on a run, a strange, heavy- shouldered, foot-swinging cat run." Or there is the hyena, "com- ing suddenly wedge-headed and stinking out of the high grass by a *donga*," or dry watercourse, to lope away across "the brown plain, looking back, mongrel-dog-smart in the face." One sees the cloud of flamingoes rising into the sun across Lake Manyara, "making the whole horizon of the lake pink." Again, an entire "sky full of locusts" passes westward, with daylight flickering through their massed moving wings "like an old cinema film." [7]

The way it was to see the animals; to sit in a twig-and-branch blind by a salt-lick at dawn; to watch the quarry, long-waited-for

[7] Lions and others: *GHOA*, pp. 40, 37–38, 133, 184.

but now scared away by some small noise or slight odor, trotting nervously out of range; to follow the "starry splatter" of blood-spoor across the rocky hills in the hot afternoon—such experiences as these are available to any reader who would like to have them. There is also much more—the look of various sections of that country, the feel of the air in sundry weathers, the manners and character of the natives, and the conduct of daily life on safari. These the author manages to transmit without recourse either to the Rider Haggard romanticizing of many travel-books or the "it-is-important-to-note" pose of the amateur ethnologist.

It is probable that this communication of the sense of place, and the sense of the immediacy and palpability of the experience in that place, is what gives *The Green Hills of Africa* its special distinction. "I loved this country," says Hemingway on one occasion, "and I felt at home, and where a man feels at home, outside of where he's born, is where he's meant to go." He had got the home-feeling also among the happy hunting-grounds of Montana and Wyoming in 1928 and 1930. One of the canyons opening into the Rift Valley reminded him strongly of the south slopes of Timber Creek in the Clark's Fork country of northwest Wyoming near the wild eastern boundary of the Yellowstone. Some of the timbered mountains he now saw might well be the American peaks, Pilot and Index, transplanted to African settings without loss of face. One who had trailed deer, moose, elk, and big-horn sheep among the American Rockies could scarcely avoid feeling at home in the mountain-terrain of Tanganyika.[8]

The necessity of achieving verisimilitude is common to both fiction and non-fiction. So is the challenge of working out a reasonably tight architectural structure. In these two respects, at any rate, *The Green Hills of Africa* rises above the status of a "noble experiment" and becomes in its own right a work of art. Yet if one compares the book with such novels as *A Farewell to Arms* and *For Whom the Bell Tolls*, the lower stature of *The Green Hills* is evident enough. For even in the hands of a skilled writer, the unvarnished truth can rarely equal in emotional intensity a

[8] *GHOA*, pp. 283–284 and 92. See also Hemingway's essay, "The Clark's Fork Valley, Wyoming," in *Vogue* 93 (February 1939), pp. 68, 157.

fictional projection of that truth. To accept in any "absolute" sense the obligation of portraying non-fictional events precisely as they happened is to fetter the imagination, to limit, perhaps fatally, the novelist's comparative freedom of movement in and through his materials. Because of these fetters and limits, however cheerfully Hemingway assumes them for experimental purposes, the non-fiction book about Africa cannot fairly stand comparison with the novel of Italy and the novel of Spain.

The other side of Hemingway's undertaking is an architectonic experiment of great interest. What he had to work with, as the foreword indicates, was a "month's action." The period to be covered was that which lay between the author's return from medical treatment at Nairobi and the party's final retreat to the coast in the face of seasonal rains—roughly January 21 to February 20, 1934. To complicate the structural problem further, Hemingway wished to deal with certain incidents from the Serengetti period of December and early January—notably the shooting of the first lion, and M'Cola's amusement over the self-eating hyena. Such incidents as these were to be inserted as flashbacks, for the purpose of the dramatic contrast, in the main course of the action.

Given that month of unprocessed raw material, the basic technical problem was to discern the action-pattern, and to select out those events which would best dramatize it. Another immediate necessity was to rearrange, not the actual order of events, but the order in which the events were to be presented to the reader. The author was not content with a simple play-by-play description of the events as they happened, in the manner of a sports reporter broadcasting a football game. Such a procedure, obviously the easiest, would not satisfy his formal architectonic requirements.

Still another aspect of the experiment was Hemingway's attempt to use the mountain-plain contrast which had informed *The Sun Also Rises* and *A Farewell to Arms*. The book makes it quite clear that he preferred the timbered hills to the plains of Tanganyika. On the Serengetti they had ridden too much in cars. Though it teemed with game, the country there stretched out flat, hot, brown, dusty, and unbroken. At that time also, Hemingway was seriously ill with one of man's most miserable and dispiriting diseases. Part of the experiment, therefore, was to project several degrees of that misery to the reader.

Among the green hills of the final month, the party could move on foot and at will over rugged, broken terrain. The recuperating patient now "had that pleasant feeling of getting stronger each day." Once, on the way east from Kandoa-Irangi and Kibaya across the flatlands and desert-country, he asked his white hunter what the continent was like further south. It was nothing, said Pop, but "a million miles of bloody Africa." [9] The phrase summed up Hemingway's own emotional attitude towards the lowlands of Tanganyika and a great part of his hunting-experience there. Up in the forested mountains again, he felt much better. This was the kind of hunting, and the rugged kind of country, to which he had always felt emotionally drawn.

The task which Hemingway undertook in writing *The Green Hills of Africa* was therefore a difficult one. He had not only assumed the obligation of verisimilitude, both as to the country and to the residents of that country whether human or animal. He had also faced up to a fairly complicated structural problem, and rendered even this more difficult by his attempt to deal with contrasting emotional atmospheres.

As this was a hunting expedition its fundamental form was obviously pursuit. The book is accordingly divided into four parts: "Pursuit and Conversation" (two chapters); "Pursuit Remembered" (chapters iii–ix inclusive); "Pursuit and Failure" (two chapters); and, with a serious pun on the Declaration of Independence, "Pursuit as Happiness" (the closing chapters xii–xiii). The form of the book is so devised as always to point to the climactic account of the kudu-hunt in the twelfth chapter. To achieve this pointing, the opening chapters deal with the early phases of the kudu sequence. They have been after kudu ten days and the oncoming rains will allow them only three days more. The seven intervening chapters—"Pursuit Remembered"—double back in time to the relatively unsatisfactory rhinoceros and buffalo hunting before the party went after the kudu. From this

[9] *GHOA,* p. 159.

beginning the reader is gradually returned to the then present until, in the tenth chapter, the splicework is completed and one finds himself back in the time of the book's opening.

The formal advantages of such a procedure are clear. Much less obvious is the author's careful preparation of the reader for an appreciation of the natural beauties of the ultimate kudu bull. He leads up very deftly to the high-tension emotional excitements which surround that event. The whole "Pursuit Remembered" section is geared into the marked contrast which is to come. As part of the total plan of attack, Hemingway places various disappointments, dissatisfactions, and emotional confusions under the surface of the prose in the "buildup" sections of his book.

The bagging of the first lion, for example, took place back on the edge of the Serengetti Plain. Hemingway carefully reduces it to an emotionally unsatisfactory event. The party had been "prepared for a charge, for heroics, and for drama." But the lion succumbed with disappointing ease. Even while the natives shouted their victory song, with its imitation of the deep, asthmatic cough of the lion as an iterative chorus, Hemingway was feeling "more let down than pleased." This was not what they had paid to see. Of course it *was* what they had paid for, like everything else recorded in the book. But Hemingway is writing that way as a part of his plan of attack. Similarly, he tells us that he admired and respected the heavy power of the buffalo, yet felt that this truck-like, scaly-hided creature was slow and ponderous. "All the while we shot I felt it was fixed and that we had him." The buffalo had neither the speed, the grace, nor the elusiveness of the kudu.[10]

The kudu is clean and beautiful. Through the early parts of the book Hemingway subtly introduces, at strategic intervals, various images of physical disgust and loathing to point up his later contrast. The hyenas skulking along the plain are seen as foul, hermaphroditical, belly-dragging beasts. The rhinoceros, described in a detailed set-piece still pointing towards the kudu-bull, is "the hell of an animal"—hulking, malformed, anachro-

[10] One suspects that Mr. Wilson's misunderstanding of Hemingway's plan underlies his belief that *GHOA* is "one of the only books ever written which make *Africa and its animals* seem dull." (Italics mine.)

nistic, and tick-ridden. One allusion to the ever-possible snakes in the underbrush has the force of a minor horror. Even more loathsome is the incident of the baboons. While the party was in search of buffalo, they came to a part of the forest which had just been traversed by a tribe of baboons. Hemingway uses an obviously effective concentration of disgust-words when he says that the whole area was filled with "a nasty stink like the mess cats make."

From the ninth chapter onwards, through the frustrations of "Pursuit and Failure," the reader is led upwards to the quarry of the twelfth, the crown of the expedition and the artfully-prepared-for crown of the book. For "Pursuit as Happiness" is handsomely embodied in the very opposite of all preceding disgusts and disappointments: "the huge beautiful kudu bull," sweetsmelling, wholesome, perfectly formed and marked, with the walnut-meat-colored horns sweeping back from the proud head. The thirteenth chapter, closing the book, is by intent a structural anti-climax—the uncrowned (or cow-crowned) pursuit of the wounded bull-sable—bringing the reader back to solid ground after the glories he has known. The form of the book has in fact been conditioned throughout by Hemingway's "emotionated" recollection of the best and worst parts of the safari. But it is planned, and worked out as an entity, with very thoughtful attention to the esthetic principles of big-game hunting in Africa.

Other formal, and semi-formal, aspects of the book show the same kind of careful planning, designed to enable "the truth" to compete with fiction. What the trade knows as *love-interest* enters in a subdued form, and the foreword (Mark-Twain-like) directs any dissatisfied reader "to insert whatever love interest he or she may have at the time." *Suspense* is always present in the formula of pursuit as well as in the sense of urgency at the approach of the seasonal rains. Hemingway, indeed, once comments on "that most exciting perversion of life: the necessity of accomplishing something in less time than should truly be allowed for its doing." *Conflict* is established in the undeclared war between the author and his colleague Karl, a lucky hunter who consistently manages to bring in better trophies, though as a pursuer of game he is much less experienced than his grumpily loyal opposition. And for an *idyllic interlude* we have the wing-shooting on the flats of Lake Manyara, with teal, black duck, and snipe enough to satisfy the greediest consumer.

As always with Hemingway, however, form is inseparable from substance, and it is to the packed substance of the book that one can always return with profit. There are the night birds rising "in soft panic" from the sandy edges of the tracklike road as the car-lights shine into their eyes; the red-clay-colored rhino, seen clear and small through binoculars, "moving with a quick, water-bug-like motion" across the far flank of a hill; the cough of a leopard hunting baboons in the night-time forest; the "shiny dark splatter" of dried buffalo-blood on a stone, and later the sad dying bellow of the same buffalo, "like hearing a horn in the woods." [11]

There is no neglect of humankind: the ebullient Kandisky; the brave and laconic white hunter Pop; the tensely generous Karl, least obtrusive of shooting companions. Among the most substantial parts of the book are the portraits of the natives. Hemingway's fine old gun-bearer, M'Cola, plays a very winning Nigger Jim to the author's over-explosive Huckleberry Finn. An association between them which began in shared suspicion develops into one of mutual respect and genuine friendship. In the manner of true comrades, for example, they share many private jokes. One only partly shared is M'Cola's amusement over religious belief. Charo, the other gun-bearer, is a highly devout Mohammedan. "All Ramadan he never swallowed his saliva until sunset." When the sun is nearly down one evening, Hemingway sees him watching it nervously.

"Charo was deadly thirsty and truly devout and the sun set very slowly. I looked at it red over the trees, nudged him and he grinned. M'Cola offered me the water bottle solemnly. I shook my head and Charo grinned again. M'Cola looked blank. Then the sun was down and Charo had the bottle tilted up, his Adam's apple rising and falling greedily and M'Cola looking at him and then looking away."

This is close to high comedy, done without words in complete pantomime. [12]

[11] Night birds and others: *GHOA,* pp. 5, 50, 58, 114, 119.
[12] *GHOA,* pp. 38–39.

The relationship with M'Cola produces several other degrees of the comic. Often the joke is on Hemingway. From M'Cola's position, bird-shooting, whiskey-drinking, beer-bibbing, and failure to hit a large target through excitement or bull-headedness, were all good jokes. Hyenas were a farcical, low-comedy dirty joke. Between Hemingway and his wiry old companion the humor of character is tossed back and forth like a medicine ball. For the out-and-out comic, nothing could be better than the self-complacent theatrical posing of one of the native guides, an efficiently unendurable "sportsman" for whom Hemingway conceived an instant dislike. Though he is nicknamed David Garrick, out of compliment to his studied stage-presence, he is obviously the Malvolio of the piece. He is just as obviously in need of the deflation he finally gets—to M'Cola's deep amusement—at the hands of the author.

Besides these full-length portraits, there are other quick line-drawings of a variety of people. One is the matchless tracker Droopy, wearing a red fez and little else but courage and enthusiasm. Another, Droopy's antithesis, is the evil-smelling Wanderobo, solemn as a stork, "useless as a bluejay." Still another is Kamau, the Kikuyu driver, who "with an old brown tweed coat some shooter had discarded, trousers heavily patched on the knees and then ripped open again, and a very ragged shirt, managed always to give an impression of great elegance." [13] But it was an elegance backed up with a modesty, a skill, and a pleasantness of demeanor which Hemingway very much admired. One of the happiest sections of the book is the group-portrait of the merry Masai, joyously racing the car, delighting in the noise of the klaxon, and eating with relish the cold tinned mincemeat and plum pudding which the visitors hand out as largesse to good humor.

There is much more. There is the sense of home as the firelight gleams through the trees to guide the returning, dogtired hunters; the oncoming file of porters bringing back "quarters of tommy, Grant, and wildebeeste, dusty, the meat seared dry by the sun"; the smiling, bulldozing insistence of the native boys that one's canvas *bathi* of warm muddy water is ready to be entered. There

[13] *GHOA,* p. 177.

are the meals, happily detailed, like the midday dinner in the shade of a big tree under the green fly of the dining-tent: "Grant's gazelle chops, mashed potatoes, green corn, and then mixed fruit for dessert"; or the picnic lunch of cold sliced tenderloin, bread, mustard, and canned plums, eaten, with one's back against a tall tree, at the edge of shadowy woodland; or the banquet of roast teal, shot at Lake Manyara, and eaten with red wine and Pan-Yan pickles in the cold house high in the hills.[14]

There is much meat in *The Green Hills of Africa,* both the kind that walks on four hooves to be shot as food or trophy, and the less tangible kind which one is glad to have because of what it reveals about the complexities of the narrator's character, his prejudices, judgments, and reminiscences, and his ideas on life and art. René Maran, as well as some of his successors to the Goncourt Academy prize, might be glad to have written thus richly of the pursuit of the kudu in the Tanganyika bush.

III. WHAT DO YOU THINK OF RINGELNATZ?

"I knew a good country when I saw one," said Hemingway of his latest love, Africa. "Here there was game, plenty of birds, and I liked the natives. Here I could shoot and fish. That, and writing, and reading, and seeing pictures, was all I cared about doing. And I could remember all the pictures. Other things I liked to watch but they were what I liked to do."

The implications of such a statement were distressing to Herr Kandisky, the little bandy-legged, culture-hungry man in leather shorts and Tyroler hat. He could not find his way comfortably into a mind where kudu and Prado ruled as approximate co-equals. Africa's big game meant less than nothing to him; it was too familiar. But the big game of literary Europe and America— there was another matter. How could it be that this literary man, this *Dichter,* this former contributor to *Der Querschnitt,* should attach any significance to the pursuit of the kudu when it was so clearly within his power to pursue the things of the mind? Kandisky pushed down hard on the other scale in Hemingway's

[14] Wildebeeste and others: *GHOA,* pp. 74, 60, 29, 111, 134.

balance. The honor of the Prado, the world of art as opposed to the world of nature and the kudu, must somehow be upheld. What about Hemingway's reading?

Under Kandisky's persistent questioning the Prado aspect emerged. Hemingway gladly set forth his definition of good literature, and with a show of geniality allowed himself to be trapped into certain judgments of individual writers.

"Tell me," asked Kandisky, "what do you think of Ringelnatz?"

"He is splendid."

"So. You like Ringelnatz. Good. What do you think of Heinrich Mann?"

"He is no good."

"You believe it?"

"All I know is that I cannot read him?"

"He is no good at all. I see we have things in common." [15]

What Hemingway had in common with his interlocutor was a love of those books which can be read, above all, with a sense of personal participation. About a year after the interview with Kandisky, he prepared a list of the sixteen titles in fiction which he "would rather read again for the first time" than be assured of a million-dollar annual income. The million-dollar list was, one observed, predominantly continental. Only two English and two American works were included: *Wuthering Heights* and *Far Away and Long Ago*, *Huckleberry Finn* and *Winesburg, Ohio*. George Moore's *Hail and Farewell* and Joyce's *Dubliners* (along with Yeats's *Autobiographies*) represented the Irish. Mann's *Buddenbrooks* was the sole German entry. All of the others were French and Russian. Stendhal's *The Red and the Black* and *The Charterhouse of Parma*, Tolstoi's *Anna Karenina* and *War and Peace* were major items. But one also found Dumas' *Queen Margot*, Flaubert's *Madame Bovary*, Dostoievski's *Brothers Karamazov*, *The Sportsman's Sketches* of Turgenev, and Maupassant's bucolic comedy on *The House of Madame Tellier*.[16]

Later in 1935, for the benefit of an apprentice writer who asked for a reading-list, Hemingway repeated most of these titles and

[15] *GHOA*, pp. 7 and 285. The excellent humorous poet Hans Bötticher (pseud.-Joachim Ringelnatz) died the year this conversation took place.
[16] *Esquire* 3 (February 1935), p. 21.

added five more authors: two novels by his old master Henry Fielding, three by Captain Marryat, and the short stories of Kipling, Stephen Crane, and Henry James. This time also he added Joyce's *Portrait of the Artist* and *Ulysses,* Flaubert's *Sentimental Education,* "any other two" novels by Dostoievski, and "all of Turgenev." The total roster came to perhaps twenty-five titles. But the list, said Hemingway, could easily be quadrupled.[17]

Neither to Kandisky nor to the young apprentice did Hemingway explain the reasons for his preferences. Nor has he ever selected any "hundred best novels." But as a writer who has always read the work of others both hungrily and seriously, his primary aim has been to establish standards and norms for his own performance. Writing is competitive, he has said. The writer must therefore discover, by selective reading, what he has to beat or to equal.

Aside from its help in the establishment of standards, writing succeeds or fails for Hemingway according to whether or not it conveys to the reader a sense of "the way it was" at the time and place the novelist has chosen to write about. Reading Tolstoi's *Sebastapol Sketches* one February noon as he lay in the shadow of trees on a Tanganyika hillside, he found himself imaginatively sharing in the military life of Czarist Russia. This sense of participation was the standard he had used in judging René Maran's *Batoula* in 1922 and Conrad's *The Rover* in 1923. Something similar happened when he moved among the rural scenes of Turgenev, or shared the second breakfasts of the burghers in Mann's family Buddenbrooks. One walked delightedly at Sorel's side through the domestic and ecclesiastical complications of *The Red and the Black*. Because all great writers appear to share in the ability to involve the reader's imagination, "we have been there," said Hemingway, "in the books." He was thinking of his African safari, but also of his boyhood in Michigan, his education in Paris, his experiences in Madrid and Key West and Wyoming, when he added, speaking for himself and all writers, "Where we go, if we are any good, there you can go as we have been." [18] For the practical esthetician, no other standard of judg-

[17] *Esquire* 4 (October 1935), pp. 21, 174A, 174B.
[18] *GHOA,* p. 108.

ment is qualitatively preferable to this principle of the "participation index."

There are other practical standards, and it is not difficult to see them operating between the lines of Hemingway's pseudo-diffident lecture to Kandisky on the nature of literature. One is a standard of vital verisimilitude. The writing must be true to our sense of the way things happen, but also vital in the sense that nothing that is in life, whether language as it is spoken or thought as it is thought or action as it is acted, can be wholly excluded without some loss to the vital principle. In one of the letters to Maxwell Perkins, written about the time when the serialization of *A Farewell to Arms* had stirred up the censors in Boston, Hemingway says that he feels, however modest the effects may be, that he is fighting "for the return to the full use of the language." [19] This determination helps to account for his general disagreement with and opposition to the genteel tradition in American letters.

Towards writers who flourished before 1880 Hemingway is evidently little drawn. His attitude, for example, to the giants of the New England renaissance resembles the view a frequenter of orchards in apple time might later take to the fruit after it had been cut into strips, strung on strings, and hung in the rafters to dry out. For the benefit of Kandisky, Emerson is grouped with Hawthorne and Whittier, and they are characterized as "very good men with the small, dried, and excellent wisdom of Unitarians; men of letters; Quakers with a sense of humor. . . . They were all very respectable. They did not use the words that people have always used in speech, the words that survive in language. Nor would you gather that they had bodies. They had minds, yes. Nice, dry, clean minds." [20]

This is admittedly a safari's eye view of the flowering of New England, suggesting that the flower lies pressed in a book instead of nectareously blooming on the vine. And it is no more than Whitman, to take a single instance, felt about transcendentalism and certain of its habits of abstract thought. In fact Hemingway's position was at least adumbrated in some of Father Taylor's wry

[19] EH to MP, 6/7/29.
[20] *GHOA*, p. 21.

pronouncements on the course of Unitarianism in New England. Hemingway's humorous statement is obviously open to all kinds of objections. But on the score of the limitations which the genteel tradition placed upon the use of language, it is clearly justified. Even Emerson admitted to similar opinions, though he had a temperamental bias against acting on them.

Two other practical standards emerge in what Hemingway told Kandisky about Thoreau and Melville. The first is his opposition to the intrusion of the "literary" quality in "naturalistic" writing; the other is his dislike of "rhetoric." One might expect that Hemingway would be more sympathetic than he is towards Thoreau, the man of the woods, and Melville, the man of the sea. The late F. O. Matthiessen once pointed out, for example, that many of "Thoreau's convictions about the nature of art look forward to Hemingway's." Among the resemblances is Thoreau's well-developed admiration for the writer who is "satisfied with giving an exact description of things" *as they appear to him* and as they exert "their effect upon him." Thoreau liked Homer's wonderful skill in conveying the physical sensation of action: "If his messengers repair but to the tent of Achilles, we do not wonder how they got there but accompany them step by step along the shore of the resounding sea." [21]

Under the surface of both Thoreau and Hemingway one finds an operative consciousness of what Thoreau himself called "dusky knowledge," a sense of the connotations of things existing in and below their denoted shapes and colors. But Hemingway draws back from the intrusion of the "literary quality" in Thoreau. It tends to stand between his powers of apprehension and the capacity to transcribe directly "from the life." Matthiessen observes, tongue in cheek, that "Thoreau's product was ordinarily somewhat less full-bodied" than one finds in D. H. Lawrence or Hemingway.[22] And Hemingway's comment sums up the matter: "I cannot read other naturalists unless they are being extremely accurate and not literary." [23]

It is once again the intrusion of a "literary" drapery between

[21] *American Renaissance,* New York, 1941, p. 85 and note.
[22] *ibid.,* p. 165.
[23] *GHOA,* p. 21.

the artist and the actual which limits Hemingway's admiration for Melville. Considering how much he might have liked Melville if they had met, or comparing their respective obsessions, or seeing their shared respect for the man who can do things "properly," one regrets the brevity of Hemingway's characterization of Melville:

"We have had writers of rhetoric who had the good fortune to find a little, in a chronicle of another man and from voyaging, of how things, actual things can be, whales for instance, and this knowledge is wrapped in the rhetoric like plums in a pudding. Occasionally it is there, alone, unwrapped in pudding, and it is good. This is Melville." [24]

This is not Melville, of course. But it is a single point made against Melville by another writer who had sought from the first to rid his own writing of all forms of padding, all ornamental literary language, and who told Maxwell Perkins in 1926 that one of his great aims was "trying to write books without any extra words" in them.[25] Hemingway's own Ahabs and Starbucks and Billy Budds speak a stylized dialogue. Yet they talk more like people than like the devils of Milton or the supermen of Kit Marlowe. It is in great part his refusal to puddingize his plums that gives Hemingway's work its special quality of direct, undraped transcription from the life around him.

If we look, on the other hand, to American writers for whom Hemingway has expressed admiration, we find three singled out: James, Stephen Crane, and Twain. This is not a preferential order. These are "the good writers" but that is "not the order they're good in. There is no order for good writers." He likes the short stories of James, giving special mention to *Madame de Mauves* and *The Turn of the Screw,* and (among the longer works) *The American* and *The Portrait of A Lady.* From Crane he has singled out *The Red Badge of Courage* as "one of the finest books of our literature," a "boy's dream of war" that is "truer to how war is than any war the boy who wrote it would ever live to see." Of the shorter pieces, Hemingway likes both *The Open Boat* and *The Blue Hotel,* with the second the better of the two. As for

[24] *GHOA,* p. 20.
[25] EH to MP, 8/26/26.

Twain, whom Kandisky recalled only as a "humorist," Heming-way was unequivocal:

"All modern American literature comes from one book by Mark Twain called *Huckleberry Finn*. If you read it you must stop where the Nigger Jim is stolen from the boys. That is the real end. The rest is just cheating. But it's the best book we've had. All American writing comes from that. There was nothing before. There has been nothing as good since." [26]

The dogmatic tone invites rejoinder. Yet in terms of the practical esthetician, scanning the field for evidence of an indubitably "modern" note in American writing, the choice of *Huckleberry Finn* is hardly astonishing. Rereading the book with Heming-way's own work in mind one is constantly arrested by events and passages where the tone and strategy are (by anticipation) Hem-ingwayesque.

"It was a monstrous big river down there—sometimes a mile and a half wide; we run nights and laid up and hid daytimes; soon as night was most gone we stopped navigating and tied up—nearly always in the dead water under a towhead; and then cut young cottonwoods and willows, and hid the raft with them. Then we set out the lines. Next we slid into the river and had a swim . . . then we set down on the sandy bottom where the river was about knee-deep, and watched the daylight come. . . . The first thing to see, looking away over the water, was a kind of dull line—that was the woods on t'other side; you couldn't make nothing else out; then a pale place in the sky; then more paleness spreading around; then the river softened up away off and warn't black any more, but gray. . . ."

"You do not know how long you are in a river when the cur-rent moves swiftly. It seems a long time and it may be very short. The water was cold and in flood and many things passed that had been floated off the banks when the river rose. I was lucky to have a heavy timber to hold on to, and I lay in the icy water with my chin on the wood, holding as easily as I could with both hands. I was afraid of cramps and I hoped we would move toward the shore. We went down the river in a long curve. It

<hr />

[26] *GHOA*, p. 22. See also *Esquire* 4 (October 1935), p. 21 and *Men at War*, introd., p. xvii.

was beginning to be light enough so I could see the bushes along the shoreline. There was a brush island ahead and the current moved toward the shore." [27]

Huck's native idiom betrays the first passage as Twain's; the grammatical usage shows that the second is from Hemingway. Otherwise Frederick Henry's river might be the Mississippi in early spring, and Huck's (by deleting the cottonwoods) the Tagliamento in June. The shared quality—and one comes on it dozens of times in the course of Huck's journey downstream— is one of direct and "simple" transcription of things as they are, without literary interpositions, and with many similarities in the general drift of the syntax.

No influence is alleged. What Hemingway found effective in Twain was whatever corroborated his own point of view about the writer's obligation to truth. A whole chapter of comparable passages could be assembled: Huck's description of the interior of the Grangerford household, for example, with Hemingway's picture of the interior of Harry Morgan's living-room in *To Have and Have Not;* or Hemingway's characterization of the native guide Garrick (the theatrical one) with Huck's descriptions of the King and the Duke. But the chapter would merely under- score the point already made, which is that Twain's notable ability to project in ostensibly "simple" language the essence of active experience is the quality that endears *Huckleberry Finn* to Hem- ingway. "Simplicity," wrote Lytton Strachey, "is often the surest test of an artist's power. A bad artist must fail when he is simple; but whoever is simple and succeeds must be great." [28]

Their common interest in war, the sea, the American west, and the men-without-women situation would sufficiently explain Hem- ingway's neighborly feeling for Crane. But there is also in Crane what Mr. John Berryman describes as "the immense power of the tacit"—a quality which "gives his work kinship . . . with Chekhov and Maupassant." [29] A similar operative grasp on this power, and a similar kinship may be noted in the best of Heming- way's short stories. The vivid impressionism of Crane, in some

[27] *Huckleberry Finn,* opening of Ch. XIX; *FTA,* opening of Ch. XXXI.
[28] *Spectator* 101 (October 3, 1908), pp. 502–503.
[29] *Stephen Crane,* New York, 1950, pp. 291–292.

ways his most spectacular poetic skill, is present, though relatively rare, in Hemingway. Take, for example, the portrait of André Marty in *For Whom the Bell Tolls:*

"The tall, heavy old man looked at Gomez with his outthrust head and considered him carefully with his watery eyes. Even here at the front in the light of a bare electric bulb, he having just come in from driving in an open car on a brisk night, his gray face had a look of decay. His face looked as though it were modelled from the waste material you find under the claws of a very old lion." [30]

The last touch seems Cranesque without being precisely duplicable anywhere in Crane. The image is used focally because the completed portrait of Marty will fill out the thematic suggestion of senile decadence. Hemingway's usual practice is far closer to that of such post-impressionists as Cézanne, just as on the whole his imagery (like his irony) is cooler, less explosive, less tricky than Crane's. He is a neighbor rather than an occupant of Crane's house.

At first glance the connection is not apparent between the world of Henry James, society-centered, ghoul-haunted, politely agonistic, externally inactive, and that of Hemingway, sharp in definition, quick in movement, and (at least comparatively) brash in manner. The difference in idiom is also striking, though no greater than one would expect to find between a late Victorian and a leader in the twentieth-century revolt against the bourgeois norms of *politesse*. But it is a matter of at least preliminary interest that Hemingway has written on three of the topics which most engaged James's imagination: the American in Europe, the artist in society, and the buried life which rises up to obsess its unwilling recollector. The reader of James also gets a fairly constant illusion of being directly in touch with human life at an essentially non-literary level, and without the intrusion of a "literary" personality between reader and experience.

As Hemingway moved through the experimental period of the nineteen thirties, he independently faced, on a number of occasions, certain technical problems which had earlier engaged the attention of James. One noticed his deepening interest, for ex-

[30] *FWBT,* p. 417.

ample, in the establishment of various centers of revelation. Like
James, however, he tended to concentrate on the individual mind
as the instrument of revelation, and to project his stories as from
one engaged on a journey of discovery, finding out more and
more about the central situation and its implications while he
progressed through it.

There is also the matter of dialogue. No one engaged in a sys-
tematic examination of resemblances between James and Hemingway could afford to ignore similarities in the conduct of the
conversations. One need not be put off by the far greater elabo-
rateness of James's framing phrases. Hemingway tends to eliminate stage directions as far as possible, though as his work has
developed he has been more willing than formerly to make some
concessions in this matter. What we remember chiefly is "Rinaldi
said" or "she said," the bareness being with Hemingway a matter
of principle, looking to the elimination of all that is not necessary.
In James the phrases range from "I gaily confessed" through
"she rather inscrutably added" and on to "I attempted the grimace
of suggesting." Like his use of italicized words, these phrases are
meant to mark the tone and emphasis, the special ring, of a particular speech. James is in effect gesturing silently from the
prompt-box. Hemingway, on the other hand, expects the reader
to supply or discover the interpretation, always seeking to reduce
his directives to the least obtrusive of available mechanisms.

Yet if one tries the experiment of lifting a Jamesian conversation *verbatim* from its framework, substituting "he saids" and "she
saids" for James's more complicated directives, the dialogue proceeds in a manner scarcely distinguishable from Hemingway's.

"I'm afraid you don't approve of them," he said.

"They are very common," she said. "They are the sort of American that one does one's duty by not—not accepting."

"Ah, you don't accept them?"

"I can't . . . I would if I could but I can't."

"The young girl is very pretty."

"Of course she's pretty but she is very common." [31]

This is a conversation about Daisy Miller and her family—the
early James. Miles Winterbourne and his aunt Mrs. Costello are

[31] *Daisy Miller*, Part I.

the speakers. It is laconic, often stichomythic. It uses a technique familiar to readers of Hemingway in the repetition of key words and phrases. Here, for example, the key word is *common*. Mrs. Costello uses it in her opening remark about the Miller family, and in her final characterization of Daisy. This gives the quoted segment a stanzaic roundness of its own, so that one might say the colloquy transpires between *common* and *common*. Winterbourne uses the word *approve* in his first statement. In her reply, the aunt nearly echoes it. Then, catching herself, she takes refuge in the weaker word *accepting*. *Accept* is a word used of fine society, with many overtones. *Approve* implies individual character judgment. Mrs. Costello is staying carefully on the social plane, knowing quite well that what Winterbourne really has in mind is the true character of Daisy herself—not a social but an individual matter. The little conversation thus embodies the major theme of the book—the conflict between individual rights or freedoms and the arbitrary norms of society. It is also a tightly knit conversation, each sentence linked to its successor by an echoed word. Thus Winterbourne echoes his aunt's *accept*. She repeats *I can't*. He takes the new tack of Daisy's *prettiness*. She echoes the word *pretty* and returns to the opening word *common*.

In a comparable passage from *A Farewell to Arms*, the key word is *love*. Frederick and the priest are talking of the Abruzzi.

"You love the Abruzzi!"

"Yes, I love it very much."

"You ought to go there then."

"I would be too happy. If I could live there and love God and serve Him."

"And be respected," I said.

"Yes and be respected. Why not?"

"No reason not. You should be respected."

"It does not matter. But there in my country it is understood that a man may love God. It is not a dirty joke."

"I understand."

He looked at me and smiled. "You understand but you do not love God."

"No."

"You do not love Him at all?" he asked.

"I am afraid of Him in the night sometimes."

"You should love Him."

"I don't love much." [32]

Like the passage from *Daisy Miller,* this segment of dialogue embodies the theme of the novel in so far as the priest and his homeland and his love of God are the spiritual goals towards which Frederick is moving through the deepening of his love for Catherine. A linkage is carefully established between ideas of love, respect, and happiness in such a way that when these key tones are struck again at intervals throughout the book, one half-consciously recognizes them as something entered on the score of memory and now played back in a different context.

What Hemingway thinks of Ringelnatz or of the holdings of the Prado are matters of importance to any who would see his art against the background of European and American art and literature. Future investigators of Hemingway's literary background are likely to find many resemblances, both profound and superficial, between his work and that of the European masters he used to borrow from Sylvia Beach's bookshop in the rue de l'Odéon during his expatriate years. One recalls that he got the title of *The Torrents of Spring* from Turgenev; or that he tends to think of his short story, "The Light of the World," in connection with Maupassant's "Maison Tellier"; or that Bridges re-

[32] *FTA,* pp. 76–77. Another remarkable similarity in the conduct of dialogue by James and Hemingway is what may be called the hovering subject. James often establishes the subject of a conversation by hint and allusion rather than overt statement. At other times he introduces the subject briefly (often it is a single word at the end of a sentence), and then conducts the dialogue by reference to it, while it hovers, helicopter-like, over the surface of the conversation. In either instance the neuter pronoun *it,* or its unuttered equivalent, is the index to what is being talked about. *It* is the apex of a pyramid whose base is the dialogue, and the real subject is the star at which the apex points. Of many instances, one might cite the interchange between Mrs. Bread and Newman in *The American,* Chapter XIV. Of many instances in Hemingway, see the talk on food between Gino and Frederick in *FTA,* Chapter XXVII. For a discussion of the differences between Hemingway and James, the reader may consult George Hemphill's essay in McCaffery, *op.cit.,* pp. 329–339. A number of further allusions to James in later chapters of this present work will make it plain that I am unable to share Mr. Hemphill's belief: "There is a broad rift in the possibilities of fiction today. . . . Hemingway and James are representative of the factions."

jected the "Alpine Idyll" story, refusing to print it in *Scribner's Magazine* because it was "too terrible"—like something by Chekhov or Gorky.[33] But the future investigators are almost certain to discover, before they have gone very far, that Hemingway's doctrine of "imitation" is of a special kind. What he imitates is nature, the world around him, expansed before his eyes. Dante, like his renaissance audience, is dead. The modern writer writes for his own and future time. It is proper that he should know Dante, indeed that he should have a close reading acquaintance with the best that has been said, thought, and painted from Dante to Shakespeare, from Cervantes to Goya, and from Tintoretto's *Crucifixion* to Picasso's *Guernica*. But what he seeks to imitate is not the texture, it is the stature of the great books he reads and the great pictures he admires. These show what can be done with words and paint, with intellect and emotion; they also show what can be equalled if the modern writer has the time, the gifts, the devotion, and the luck: and if, chiefly, he chooses to derive his own work from the life of his time rather than from the art of former times.

IV. DANGEROUS GAME

In the other two stories which grew out of his African adventure, Hemingway abandoned his experimental attempt to see whether an "absolutely true book" like *The Green Hills of Africa* could compete on terms of equality with a work of the imagination. In "The Short Happy Life of Francis Macomber" and "The Snows of Kilimanjaro" he was still determined to tell "the truth"; but now he was ready to invent the characters, and to imagine the circumstances in which they were to be entangled. The circumstances in these two stories differ markedly. At the same time they share certain inward thematic stresses. Both deal, for example, though in varying ways, with the achievement and loss of moral manhood. Both look further into the now familiar men-without-women theme. The focal point in each is the corrupting power of women and money, two of the forces aggressively men-

[33] MP to EH, 6/14/26.

tioned in *The Green Hills of Africa* as impediments to American writing men.

Francis Macomber does not write. He is a wealthy American sportsman hunting the Tanganyika plains with his wife. But he must nevertheless wrestle with problems relating to women, money, and moral manhood. Easily the most unscrupulous of Hemingway's fictional females, Margot Macomber covets her husband's money but values even more her power over him. To Wilson, the Macombers' paid white hunter, who is drawn very reluctantly into the emotional mess of a wrecked marriage, Margot exemplifies most of the American wives he has met in the course of his professional life. Although his perspectives are limited to the international sporting set, the indictment is severe. These women, he reflects, are "the hardest in the world; the hardest, the cruelest, the most predatory, and the most attractive, and their men have softened or gone to pieces nervously as they have hardened." [34] With Margot in mind, this story might well have carried the title which Hemingway attached to one of his despatches from Tanganyika to *Esquire:* "Notes on Dangerous Game." The lion and the buffalo are vanquishable in a way that Margot is not.

Too much money and a woman also underlie the predicament of Harry, the dying author in "The Snows of Kilimanjaro." Having given up to a luxurious way of life by marrying wealth and then growing into complete dependence on it, he has died artistically long before his physical death. What harrows him more than the knowledge of approaching dissolution is the consciousness of all the literary riches, none of them committed to paper, which will go with him underground. Worst of all are the sharply etched memories of his former life—Liberty, Integrity, Opportunity—qualities which were all once joyously owned and now are all irrecoverably lost.

So both stories are moral tragedies tipped with irony. Macomber dies at the very moment he is commencing to live. Harry's death by gangrene symbolizes all spiritual suicides among American writers. "We destroy them in many ways," said Hemingway

[34] *First 49,* p. 107.

sardonically in *The Green Hills of Africa*. "First, economically. They make money . . . increase their standard of living and . . . are caught. They have to write to keep up their establishment, their wives, and so on, and they write slop . . . not on purpose, but because it is hurried. . . . Then, once they have betrayed themselves, they justify it and you get more slop." [35] Whether through women or the desire for money, self-betrayal is what kills a man before he has lived out his time. Women and money are nothing but instruments and agents: they exist, sometimes passively, sometimes aggressively, to help the individual writer in his moral self-destruction. If he surrenders, the fault is his own. The emphasis on the value of integrity in these short stories suggests that they may be thought of as two more chapters in the history of Hemingway's artistic obsessions.

The happy life of Francis Macomber begins on the plains of East Africa and lasts about thirty minutes. The tall young man has previously disgraced himself before his wife, his British white hunter, and his gun-bearers, by ignominious flight from a wounded and charging lion. Besides the loss of his own self-respect, such as it was, the extreme mental tortures of the experience include the barbed and vicious scorn of his wife, the lifted eyebrows and unspoken insults of the white hunter Wilson, and the visible disapproval of the native boys in his entourage. After a night of torment, during which he is obliged to watch his wife sleepily returning from the Englishman's tent, the party goes after buffalo. Since the wife knows her husband for a coward, she seems to have him where she wants him, which is under her thumb.

Suddenly, in the midst of the second day's shooting and with the white hunter as an aid, Macomber loses his fear. His wife at once senses and hates this change because it undermines her power. But Wilson silently welcomes Macomber into manhood, and together they enter the tall grass after one of the wounded buffalo, leaving the wife behind them in the open car.

Almost immediately the buffalo charges. Fearless and happy in its path stands Macomber, a coward no longer, reveling in his new-found self-trust, firing repeatedly until the buffalo is practically upon him. Then a bullet from his wife's Mannlicher plows

[35] *GHOA*, p. 23.

through his skull from back to front and the short happy life is over.

The great technical virtue of this story—and it is one of Hemingway's favorites possibly for this reason—is the development of an emotional intensity to a degree seldom approached in modern literature. The ragged feelings generated by the lion-incident and verbalized in a kind of noonday nightmare during the conversations in the dining-tent, are just short of unendurable to any who have entered into the spirit of the situation. Yet the tension actually mounts when, during the next day's shooting, we watch the Macombers in their contest for the possession of a soul.

Hemingway silently points up this contest by the varying positions of the central trio in their boxlike open car. On the way to the lion, Macomber sits in front, with Margot and Wilson in the back. After that day's débâcle, Macomber slumps in the back seat beside his frozen wife, Wilson staring straight ahead in the front. When Macomber has proved himself with the three buffalo, it is Margot who retreats into the far corner of the back seat, while the two men happily converse vis-à-vis before her. And finally, as Macomber kneels in the path of the buffalo, it is his wife from her commanding position in the back seat of the car who closes the contest.

Of equal interest is the skill with which Hemingway balances off the two days of hunting against each other. Part of the balance is achieved by the repetition of first effect: the buffalo, like the lion of the preceding day, is wounded, takes cover, and charges without warning. This time, however, the charge moves into a reversed moral situation. Between times, by various devices, the reader has been fully awakened to the degree of physical courage needed in facing wounded and dangerous animals. But where the lion was an instrument for the establishment and build-up of emotional tension, the oncoming horns of the buffalo are the pronged forceps for Macomber's moral birth. Two different worlds fill the two adjacent days.

The yardstick figure, Wilson, a fine characterization, is the man free of woman and of fear. He is the standard of manhood towards which Macomber rises, the cynical referee in the nasty war of man and wife, and the judge who presides, after the murder, over the further fortunes of Margot Macomber. His dominance over the lady is apparent from the moment she sees him blast the lion from which Macomber ran. But he accepts that dominance only because it is thrust upon him. The kind of dominance he really believes in, and would gladly transfer to the suffering husband, is well summarized in a passage from Shakespeare's *Henry IV* which he quotes as a kind of tribute to Macomber's own loss of fear on the second day: "By my troth, I care not; a man can die but once; we owe God a death . . . and let it go which way it will, he that dies this year is quit for the next. . . ." [36] Having brought out, almost by accident, this attitude he has lived by, Wilson is much embarrassed. "But he had seen men come of age before and it always moved him. It was not a matter of their twenty-first birthday."

Those who object that true manhood is not necessarily proved by one's ability to face a charging beast may be doing Hemingway an injustice. Dramatically speaking, physical courage is often a convenient and economical way of symbolizing moral courage. We are glad, for example, at Hamlet's skill and bravery with the foils. In this African story Hemingway is obviously dealing with both kinds of courage, though, as the situation naturally requires, it is the physical aspect which is stressed.

It would be possible to argue that Francis and Margot Macomber are more nearly caricatures than people. The probability is that the line-drawing in their portraits is the natural consequence of an approach to material chosen for its intrinsic emotional intensity rather than to provide opportunity for depth of characterization. One rightly concludes that they are as fully developed as they need to be for the purposes of the narrative. Further development might well impede the quick march of the short, happy life.

Still it is true that Hemingway's satirical steam, never far below the surface, tends to erupt whenever he deals with leisure-class wastrels. The tendency is visible, for example, in the accounts of Cohn and Campbell in *The Sun Also Rises*. In *Death in the Afternoon,* the author scornfully watches the bored, sport-shod,

[36] *First 49,* p. 131. The speech is made by one of the country soldiers, Feeble, in *II Henry IV,* iii, ii, 253–258.

ex-collegians who leave the *corrida* early. The same reaction appears in his sketches of the wealthy yachtsmen in Key West harbor in *To Have and Have Not,* part of which was written at the same time as the Francis Macomber story. It is almost as if, throughout the Depression, Hemingway had resolutely set himself to oppose F. Scott Fitzgerald's temperamental conviction that the rich are glamorous. As Hemingway's scorn rises, the satirical steam-pressure rises with it, and the result is often close to caricature.

If the story of the Macombers is judged, as it probably should be judged, in terms of an experiment in the development of emotional intensity, it is hard to match. As an instance of tragic irony, exemplified in overt action, it has its faults. But dullness is not one of them, and formally speaking the story is very nearly perfect.[37]

V. LESSON FROM THE MASTER

"The Snows of Kilimanjaro" is a tragedy of a different order.[38] Its setting is the final afternoon and evening in the second life of a writer named Harry, dying of gangrene in a camp near the edge of the Tanganyika plains country. "Francis Macomber" proceeds through and by action; "The Snows of Kilimanjaro" is an experiment in the psychology of a dying man. Like *Across the River and Into the Trees,* it contains almost no overt physical activity, though much is implied. Judged in terms of its intention, it is a triumphant piece of writing.

Hemingway's own experiences on safari help to account for the origin of the story. The undeveloped germ of "Francis Macomber" may have been the occasion when Hemingway and M'Cola entered a bush-covered area in pursuit of a lion they heard but never saw. The general outline of "The Snows" was

[37] This story was Hemingway's choice for *This Is My Best,* ed. Whit Burnett, New York, 1942. He so wrote Mr. Burnett 5/12/42. See *infra,* p. 22.

[38] Hemingway once told Roger Linscott that he regarded "The Snows" as "about as good as any" of his work in short fiction. "On the Books," *New York Herald Tribune Book Review,* December 29, 1946. The story was finished April 7, 1936. EH to MP, 4/9/36.

almost certainly suggested by Hemingway's own grave illness, the flight out of the plains country, and the distant view of the enormous, snow-capped mountain of Kilimanjaro. During the flight east, and no doubt also during the period of treatment in Nairobi—his head aching and his ears ringing from the effects of emetine [39]—Hemingway had ample time to reflect on a topic which would naturally occur to him in such a situation: the death of a writer before his work is done. As in "Francis Macomber," however, most of the other circumstances of the story were invented.

Like Hemingway, the writer Harry in the story has been "obsessed" for years with curiosity about the idea of death. Now that it is close he has lost all curiosity about it, feeling only a "great tiredness and anger" over its inexorable approach. "The hardest thing," Hemingway had written in *The Green Hills of Africa,* is for the writer "to survive and get his work done." [40] This is mainly because the time available is so short and the temptations not to work are so strong. Harry has succumbed to the temptation *not* to work at his hard trade. Now his time is over, and possessive death moves in.

The story gains further point and poignancy from another obsession of Harry's, the deep sense of his loss of artistic integrity. Despite the difference between London and Tanganyika and the lapse of time between the rule of Edward VII and that of Edward VIII, Hemingway's position is that of Henry James in "The Lesson of the Master." Harry's dying self-accusations are well summarized in the words of Henry St. George, the sold-out novelist in James's novelette. "Don't become in your old age what I have in mine," he tells his young admirer, "—the depressing, the deplorable illustration of the worship of false gods . . . the idols of the market; money and luxury . . . everything that drives one to the short and easy way." [41] The dying writer in Hemingway's story has followed that route, and his creeping gangrene is the mark he bears. He knows that he has traded his

[39] The principal alkaloid of ipecac, used as a specific in the treatment of amoebic dysentery.

[40] *GHOA*, p. 27.

[41] James, *Works,* New York edition, vol. 15, p. 36.

former integrity for "security and comfort," destroying his talent by "betrayals of himself and what he believed in." Henry or Harry, England or Africa, the lesson of the master is the same: Thou shalt not worship the graven images of false gods, or acquiesce in the "life of pleasant surrender." [42]

Although the setting of "The Snows of Kilimanjaro" is as completely un-Jamesian as one could possibly imagine, the themes which the story engages are, on the contrary, very close to those regularly employed by James. "I wonder," Hemingway once ruminated, "what Henry James would have done with the materials of our time." One answer might be that a modern James would simply have altered the costume, the idiom, and certain of the social customs which appear in his novels. The themes, which were matters of greatest interest to him, would scarcely need to be changed at all. The close reader of "The Snows of Kilimanjaro" easily recognizes and responds to its theme of confrontation. The dying writer is far different from the ghost of his former self, the young, free, unsold writer who took all Europe as his oyster and was seriously devoted to his craft. As he listens to the self-accusations with which Harry tortures himself, the reader acquainted with James may be reminded of "The Jolly Corner." In this long story, an American expatriate, returning to his old and empty house at the corner of the American city street, finds himself beleaguered by the ghost of his other self, the ravaged man he might have been had he not followed his esthetic ambitions to Europe. Although the situation is obviously quite the opposite of the one detailed by Hemingway, the strategy is exactly the same: the face-to-face confrontation of an ego by an alter ego. The corner of the tent in which Harry finally dies might well be called, in an echo of Jamesian irony, the jolly corner.

The story is technically distinguished by the operation of several natural symbols. These are non-literary images, as always in Hemingway, and they have been very carefully selected so as to be in complete psychological conformity with the locale and the dramatic situation. How would the ideas of death and of immortality present themselves in the disordered imagination of a writer dying of gangrene as he waits for the plane which is sup-

[42] *First 49*, pp. 158, 160, 162.

posed to carry him out of the wilderness to the Nairobi hospital? The death-symbols were relatively easy. Every night beasts of prey killed grazing animals and left the pickings to those scavengers of carrion, the vultures and the hyenas.

It is entirely natural that Harry, whose flesh is rotting and noisome—is, in fact, carrion already—should associate these creatures with the idea of dying. As he lies near death in the mimosa shade at the opening of the story, he watches the birds obscenely squatting in the glare of the plain. As night falls and the voice of the hyena is heard in the land, the death-image transfers itself from the vultures to this other foul devourer of the dead. With the arrival of his first strong premonition of death, which has no other form than "a sudden, evil-smelling emptiness," Harry finds without astonishment that the image of the hyena is slipping lightly along the edge of the emptiness. "Never believe any of that," he tells his wife, "about a scythe and a skull." His mind has been far away in the days of his former life in Paris, and now it has come back to Africa. "It can be two bicycle policemen as easily, or be a bird. Or it can have a wide snout like a hyena." Death has just come as if to rest its head on the foot of the cot, the direction from which the infection will rise up towards the vital center. Presently it moves in on him, crouching on his chest so that he cannot breathe.

Harry's dying directive, "Never believe any of that about a scythe and a skull," is an important commentary on Hemingway's own habitual approach to the development of natural symbols. He is prepared to use, where they conform to the requirements of an imaginary situation, any of the more ancient symbols—whether the threes and nines of numerology, or the weight of the Cross in Christian legend. But the scythe and the skull, though ancient enough, simply do not fit the pattern of Harry's death and are therefore rejected in favor of the foul and obscene creatures which have now come to dominate Harry's imagination.

Like the death-symbol, the image for immortality arises "naturally" out of the geography and psychology of the situation. When the weight leaves his chest, Harry finds that morning has brought the rescue plane to carry him to Nairobi. Helping him aboard,

Old Compton says that they will have to refuel at Arusha. Everything happens as if it were actually happening—the take-off, the long view of the plain and its moving animals, the hills and forests to the east passing in slow majesty under the belly of the plane—until it dawns on Harry that for some reason they have by-passed Arusha. At first he does not know why. But as the plane emerges from a rain-squall, he suddenly sees ahead of them the square top of Kilimanjaro, "wide as all the world," incredibly white in the sun. "Then he knew that there was where he was going."

While he was in Africa Hemingway learned that the Masai name for the western summit of Kilimanjaro is Ngàje Ngài, which means "House of God." The association between mountainous terrain and the idea of home was, however, already an old one in his mind. He had used it symbolically in the Burguete section of *The Sun Also Rises* and also, far more extensively, in the Abruzzi and the Montreux locale-images of *A Farewell to Arms*. "I will lift up mine eyes to the hills," runs the Psalm, "from whence cometh my help." But there is no psalm-quoting in the back-to-earth dénouement of Hemingway's story. There is only Harry's wife Helen, waking in the middle of the night down in the flat plains-country, far from Kilimanjaro, and calling to a husband who does not answer.[43]

[43] Psalm 121 might do as a motto for Hemingway's collected works. In this connection one might suggest the relevance of the leopard whose enigmatic history is given in the epigraph of "The Snows." "Close to the Western summit of Kilimanjaro there is the dried and frozen carcass of a leopard. No one has explained what the leopard was seeking at that altitude." Professor C. C. Walcutt (*Explicator* 7, April 1949, item 43) sees that the conflict in Harry's life is between a "fundamental moral idealism" and an "aimless materialism." When Harry looks at Kilimanjaro, he sees it as a symbol of Truth, the "undefined ideal for which he has struggled." The leopard is then a symbol for Harry's moral nature. It is not logical that Harry "should continue to believe in man and search for meanings and values"; neither is it logical that "a purely predatory leopard" should have reached that snowy height. What drove the leopard there "is the same sort of mystery as the force that keeps idealism alive in Harry. All reason, in a predatory world, is against it, but there it is." Following this line, Professor E. W. Tedlock, Jr. finds that both leopard and mountain symbolize the preservation of integrity for Harry. "In contrast to the leopard's dried and frozen carcass," writes Tedlock, "Harry lies dying of a gangrenous leg amid heat and glare." The physical infection is the re-

Anyone interested in the methods by which the patterns of experience are translated to the purposes of art should find abundant materials for study in the three stories—non-fiction and fiction—which grew out of Hemingway's African expedition. The foreword to *The Green Hills of Africa* contains an implicit question. Given a country as interesting as Africa, and given the shape of a month's hunting-action there, and given the author's determination to tell only the truth, the question then becomes this: Can such a book possibly compete on equal terms with a work of the imagination? The answer is that it certainly can *compete*, provided always that the narrative is managed by a very skilled writer who takes both truth (the truth of "the way it was") and beauty (the extremely careful formal construction) as his watchwords. Yet the experiment proved also that the narrator who takes no liberties with the actual events of his experience, who tells things exactly as they were, who invents nothing and suppresses nothing important, will place himself at a real disadvantage in the competition. He gives the opposition too large a handicap. Good as *The Green Hills of Africa* is in two respects (verisimilitude and architectonics), it lacks the intensities which Hemingway was able to pack into "The Short Happy Life of Francis Macomber," and it cannot possibly achieve anything like the genuine pathos of "The Snows of Kilimanjaro." The experience of wrestling with the African book, followed as it was with the writing of the two short stories, undoubtedly established one esthetic principle very firmly in Hemingway's mind. The highest art must take liberties, not with the truth but with the modes by which the truth is projected. This was no new discovery for Hemingway. But for any serious writer it is a useful maxim.

---

sult of carelessness—"the typical analogue of a spiritual infection also resulting from carelessness." Thus we have both physical and spiritual decay, while leopard and mountain represent those things which do not decay. Professor Tedlock calls attention to how often Harry's thoughts "revert . . . to experiences in high altitudes and snow." Physically, this can be explained as the "feverish man's desire for coolness and relief"; spiritually the reversions represent a longing for "the good life" of the past. (See *Explicator* 8, October 1949, item 7).

IX · Depression at Key West

> *"Having* is not an absolute, but a gradated power; and consists not only in the quantity or nature of the thing possessed but also (and in a greater degree) in its suitableness to the person possessing it and in his vital power to use it."—John Ruskin [1]

I. THE FASHION OF THE TIMES

Hemingway set down his convictions on the writer in politics in the fall of 1934. "A writer can make himself a nice career while he is alive," said he, "by espousing a political cause, working for it, making a profession of believing in it, and if it wins he will be very well placed. . . . A man can be a Fascist or a Communist and if his outfit gets in he can get to be an ambassador, or have a million copies of his books printed by the government, or any of the other rewards the boys dream about. . . . But none of this will help him as a writer unless he finds something new to add to human knowledge while he is writing." [2]

As for making one's latest piece of fiction into an amateur textbook of economics, Hemingway's position was clear. "Books should be about the people you know, that you love and hate, not about the people you study up about. If you write them truly they will have all the economic implications a book can hold." Once again, the artist was speaking. Those who wished to and could were welcome to write the histories, the economic treatises, the political expositions, the interpretations of current trends. The serious artist, whose task it was to write fiction that would survive, must take a different course. "A country, finally, erodes and the dust blows away," said Hemingway, "the people all die and none of them were of any importance permanently, except those

---

[1] *Unto This Last,* Essay IV, "Ad Valorem." Cf. Ruskin's definition of wealth: "The possession of the Valuable by the Valiant."

[2] "Old Newsman Writes," *Esquire* 2 (December 1934), pp. 25–26.

who practised the arts. . . . A thousand years makes economics silly and a work of art endures forever, but it is very difficult to do and now it is not fashionable." [3]

Hemingway's views on man in society were determined, in the 1930's, by three major considerations. First, he was a veteran of World War I, and he knew what war was really like. Second, he was a veteran newspaper correspondent who had watched, with increasing disgust and hatred, the postwar machinations of European diplomats and dictators in their struggles for power. "It is not enough," said he, "to have a big heart, a pretty good head, a charm of personality, baggy pants, and a facility with a typewriter to know how the world is run; and who is making the assists, the put-outs, and the errors; and who are merely the players and who are the owners." As an old newsman, he was prepared to defend the position that "no history is written honestly. You have to keep in touch with it at the time, and you can depend on just as much as you have actually seen and followed." Nor could he agree with the earnest liberals who were invoking *Das Kapital* as a political and economic bible or were beginning to write in the overblown style of the *Communist Manifesto*. "It isn't all in Marx nor in Engels," said Hemingway. "A lot of things have happened since then." [4]

Much, indeed, had happened, and in the course of his coverage of the European newsfronts or in his clinical observations of the Machado regime in Cuba, he had become familiar with the two ends of the scale: the behind-the-scenes operations of the planners and the power-mongers, and the ultimate blood-spilling among those who fought out the issues in the streets. When Clemenceau's Garde Républicaine broke up the parade of war-mutilated poilus, the results were not greatly different from those which ensued upon Hoover's dispersal of the bonus army at Anacostia Flats, whether in their effect on human relations, or in the amount of blood that flowed. Seen in the flesh and in conflict, the Cuban revolutionists were much like the Italian revolutionists he had watched in the streets of Genoa in 1922. Whether it formed

[3] *GHOA,* p. 109.
[4] "Old Newsman Writes," *loc.cit.*

a pool among the peanut shells on a Havana sidewalk or stained the front of a dirty shirt somewhere in Illinois, the blood of people looked about the same everywhere. To show that this was a fact was one prerogative of the artist.

The third factor in the development of Hemingway's views on the writer in politics was the most important. This was his belief that the novelist who pontificated on the course of contemporary history would always tend to betray his real artistic purposes. Even Tolstoi, great as he could be at his best, allowed himself ponderous commentaries which exposed the limits of his historical knowledge. "I love *War and Peace*," said Hemingway, "for the wonderful, penetrating, and true descriptions of war and of people but I have never believed in the great Count's thinking. I wish there could have been someone in his confidence with authority to remove his heaviest and worst thinking and keep him simply inventing truly. He could invent more with more insight and truth than anyone who ever lived. But his ponderous and Messianic thinking was no better than [that of] many another evangelical professor of history, and I learned from him to distrust my Thinking with a capital T and to try to write as truly, as straightly, as objectively and as humbly as possible." [5]

Thinking with a capital T (which does not rule out another hard kind of thinking which the artist must do) may be vainglory in a writer of fiction. It may well, in the end, be the greatest enemy a writer can have, though he has many, all the time, of both the inner and the outer kind. To pass off amateur "history" or political propaganda as real writing seemed to Hemingway to be an evasion of the serious writer's fundamental obligation. It went without saying that those who played the market of current public interest in a particular political or economic fad or fashion of the age were heading for a crash as writers, no matter how much money they might make in the process. "The hardest thing in the world to do," said Hemingway, "is to write straight honest prose on human beings. First you have to know the subject; then you have to know how to write. Both take a lifetime to learn, and anybody is cheating who takes politics as a

[5] *Men At War*, New York, 1942, introd., p. xviii.

way out. It is too easy. All the outs are too easy, and the thing itself is too hard to do." [6]

When the Great American Depression, which made many things possible that had not been possible before, assisted in promoting a marriage between literature and politics, Hemingway was not a member of the wedding. The vows had been spoken often enough in the literary history of the United States, though usually, one noticed, in times of moral rather than merely political crises. What made the depression marriage memorable was that the contracting parties had so recently been living in widely separated areas. Jazz Age literature, with some few exceptions, had flirted most noticeably and openly with Sigmund Freud and Tristan Tzara. In Greenwich Village and its purlieus after the war the loudest talk was likely to be about dreams and sex and psychoanalysis, or about the latest esthetic experiments of Dada. It is true that if one listened closely at a prohibition beer-party in 1925 or 1926, a persistent Marxist mutter was audible among the intelligentsia—something like bridesmaids whispering over the qualities of the groom. But the engagement was not announced or the bans called until the crash of 1929, and the real wedding had to wait for the Depression.

The hard glitter of the new European political ideologies did not cause Hemingway to mistake them for gold. As a working newspaper correspondent on the continent, he had been too intimately in touch with the political actualities for a number of years. By 1923 he was on record as anti-Mussolini, and at a time when many of his fellow Americans were still saying that Mussolini's regime was doing those lazy and shiftless Italians a lot of good. He personally dates his anti-fascism from the murder of Giacomo Matteotti in June, 1924.[7] The socialist Matteotti was virtually the only prominent outspoken Italian critic of Mussolini's *fascisti* between their seizure of power and his death. Many an earnest liberal dated his own change of heart from the kidnapping and murder of Matteotti by Mussolini's henchmen.

Throughout the Jazz Age, Hemingway continued his opposition to the spread of fascism. His short story called "Che Ti Dice

[6] "Old Newsman Writes," *loc.cit.*
[7] EH to CB, 4/1/51.

La Patria" is a true account of a motor-trip he made through Fascist Italy with his friend Guy Hickok.[8] It left no doubt in the minds of *New Republic* readers, when it first appeared there in 1927, as to where Hemingway stood on Il Duce and the political philosophy (if that was the name for it) by which he continued in power. Nor did one gather, though the evidence was sparser, that Hemingway was an avid supporter of Lenin or Trotsky or Stalin. The young and starry-eyed revolutionist is a recurrent and often a pitiable figure in his fiction. The short story called "The Revolutionist" can hardly be said to blaze with the message of the *Communist Manifesto*. As a young artist developing his art, and as a veteran who had fought and been badly wounded in the most wasteful butcher-shop of all wars, he had a right to feel sick at the mention of capitalized Great Causes. He was too busy with his serious writing, and his work for the news-services among the political entanglements of the European continent, to follow Mike Gold in anti-capitalist or anti-republican war-whoops. Though he once sent them the story "Alpine Idyll" when the editors asked him for a contribution, and twice wired them memorials on the dead, at their request, his considered opinion of *The New Masses* was that it was a puerile house-organ.[9]

As an artist, he would not have been at all surprised in the winter of 1929–1930 to hear a critic say that his first two novels showed no special political bias. Had he cared to do so, he might have pointed out that his attitude towards the wastrels of *The Sun*

[8] The new title may be translated, "What do you hear from home?" or "What is the news of the fatherland?"

[9] "Alpine Idyll" was not printed by the magazine; EH to FSF from Paris, [*ca.* September] 1926. At the time of the scandalous, and needless, drowning of the work camp veterans in September 1935, Hemingway's party was the first to visit Camp Five on Matecumbe Key. He was horrified and angry at the failure of those in charge to rescue the veterans in time, and saw more dead in one place than he had seen since the lower Piave in June 1918. On September 14, 1935, he wired a 2800-word despatch on the hurricane disaster to *The New Masses* at their request. He would take no pay, since, as he told Perkins (9/14/35), he did not believe in making money out of murder. But, as he also told Perkins, he had less respect than ever for the magazine and its policy. For the story, see *New Masses* 16 (September 17, 1935), p. 9. A somewhat similar despatch on "The American Dead in Spain" was wired to this magazine three years later. See *New Masses* 30 (February 14, 1939), p. 3.

Also Rises, though tinged with compassion, could likewise be seen as a viewing-with-alarm of one phase of capitalism's drunken hayride through the Jazz Age. Or he could have said that *A Farewell to Arms* was an anti-war novel, while the execution scene beside the Tagliamento, being an example of force exerted by legally constituted bullies, was a condemnation of what would later be known as the fascist temperament. It is clear enough that in the 1920's he read at least some of the signs of the times. Without adopting the political jargon of the period, he was sufficiently aware of the implications inherent in the growing political decadence of European society. But he had preferred to work at his art rather than to confuse his job of work with that of the propagandist.

When the Depression reaffirmed for American society the connection between literature on the one hand and politics and economics on the other, the minority fashion of the late twenties became the majority fashion of the early thirties. As often happens in such a situation, some of the true artists suffered for remaining true to their esthetic convictions. Writers began to be judged according to a politico-economic scale of values. A left-of-center man could often get an A for effort even while he committed all the literary sins known to human society. A rightist or a middle-of-the-roader, deeply committed to serious authorship, would find his best work rewarded with an E for Escapism, or possibly an F, for failure to include some account of the latest streetcar strike in Waban, Massachusetts. Reviewers had a new measuring-stick, although, happily, many of them clung to sounder standards.

To certain members of the new Marxist clan, Hemingway began to look unfashionable in the early 1930's. *Death in the Afternoon* came out in the dead vast and bottom of the Depression. And how could he have the temerity to publish a manual of the bullfight while Americans were selling apples on street-corners, fighting over restaurant garbage cans for food, or being laid off in wholesale lots? *Winner Take Nothing,* the short-story collection of 1933, did nothing to alleviate the situation. Where, in these stories, could one read about the Gastonia strike of the spring of 1929, about General Douglas MacArthur and the bonus army rout at Anacostia Flats? What about the Russian Five-Year Plan, the inside life of union organizers, the May Day celebrations in Union Square?

"It is difficult," wrote Wyndham Lewis in 1934, "to imagine a writer whose mind is more entirely closed to politics than is Hemingway's." [10] The critic went on to say that Hemingway appeared to be interested "in the sports of death, in the sad things that happen to those engaged in the sports of love . . . in war, but *not* in the things that cause war, or the people who profit by it, or in the ultimate human destinies involved in it." Where, in *A Farewell to Arms,* could one find anything about Wilson's Fourteen Points? Why didn't the Montparnassians of *The Sun Also Rises,* in some of their aimless talk, ever analyze the causes of the war? What about the arms manufacturers who had worked behind the scenes to protract the fighting and enlarge their profits? The destinies of Catherine Barkley, Frederick Henry, Dr. Rinaldi, Jake Barnes, and Brett Ashley were not ultimate enough for Mr. Lewis's requirements.

The publication of *The Green Hills of Africa* in 1935 seemed to confirm Lewis's case. Why did Hemingway waste time and talent in Tanganyika which might better have been employed in writing of the American scene, labor strife, money barons, municipal slums like those that produced Stephen Crane's *Maggie,* or the lengthening bread-lines—not to mention beautiful, full bosomed girl-agitators who looked like Sylvia Sidney?

The year in which Mr. Lewis's book appeared saw the publication of a long short story by Hemingway. It was called "One Trip Across" and would subsequently form a unit in the novel *To Have and Have Not.* Written in Madrid in September 1933, the story was included in *Cosmopolitan* for April 1934. It introduced the person of Harry Morgan, ex-policeman from Miami, charter-boat fisherman out of Key West, a proud and independent man who took to smuggling as a means of supporting his wife and daughters in lieu of letting them go on relief. The second Harry Morgan story, in which he lost his right arm by gunfire and his boat by confiscation, and in which his cargo was contraband liquor from Cuba, was written at Key West in November 1935. When it appeared in *Esquire Magazine* for February 1936, it carried the

[10] *Men Without Art,* London, 1934, pp. 17–18.

ironic title of "The Tradesman's Return." [11] This was the second unit of the budding novel.

By the middle of July 1936, Hemingway had decided (unluckily, as it turned out) to make a novel of the Morgan story. The book as he then envisioned it would draw a sharp environmental contrast between Key West and Havana. It would contain what Hemingway had learned about the mechanics of revolution, a topic in which he had taken an artist's interest since 1931, and would attempt to show how revolutionary thought and action affects those involved. Its theme would be the decline of the individual.[12] Another Morgan story, probably longer than the first two, would combine with some additional Key West material to round out Morgan's career in a short, intense, and angry novel.

Off paper, the plan seemed excellent. One difficulty about getting the rest of the novel on paper was the outbreak of the Spanish Civil War, which occurred just about the time the decision to complete the book was made. Hemingway's heart lay in Madrid, and as an artist he was still deeply interested in war. Although he was anxious to cross to the scene of the conflict, he was equally determined to finish his work before setting sail. A writer ought always to write, he had told Perkins some years before, as if he were going to die at the end of a book. There was always an off chance that he might not come back from Spain, and he did not wish to leave a partially completed work. Under these kinds of moral pressure, he bowed out of his arrangement with *Esquire,* went out to Montana for peace and quiet, and worked steadily through August and September on the third Morgan story. The typescript had grown to 354 pages by early November. Back in Key West at the beginning of the New Year he completed the first draft on January 2, 1937.

Despite multiple pressures, the Morgan story had come out well. What troubled Hemingway was the companion story on the moral misfortunes of a writer called Richard Gordon. He had invented the story as a means of throwing Harry Morgan's mas-

[11] EH to MP, 12/7/35. Hemingway also wrote "The Capital of The World" at about the same time. This was first published in *Esquire* with the title, "The Horns of the Bull."
[12] EH to MP, 7/11/36.

culine virtues into bolder relief. There was not time enough, evidently, to make the two contrasting stories combine satisfactorily. He continued to tinker the Gordon-Bradley story until he left New York for Spain on February 27, 1937. But it still did not please him. He planned to revise it further upon his return.[13]

The cause of Republican Spain made thorough revision impossible. His work on a documentary film, *The Spanish Earth,* and his speech to the Writer's Congress in June left him only a period of three or four weeks to put the manuscript in publishable shape. He told Perkins that he did not consider it "a real novel," though possibly the Morgan story alone would make a good novelette. There was evidently some thought of using the three Morgan items at the head of an omnibus collection of short stories and articles. After this idea had been abandoned as unwise, Hemingway turned to a hasty reading of the proofsheets, completing the job between July 18 and August 7. By the time *To Have and Have Not* was published (October 15, 1937), he was back in Spain.[14]

Like his play, *The Fifth Column,* which was written in Madrid that fall under conditions far from ideal, *To Have and Have Not* shows marked deficiencies as a work of art. Unlike *The Fifth Column,* however, the novel contains some of Hemingway's best writing along with much that simply does not cohere. The intrinsic values of the Morgan trilogy are esthetically undermined by the story of Richard Gordon and company, as if, say, the Gordon business were a fifth column at work within the Morgan business. What had looked in theory like a feasible scheme of moral contrast became in practice a novel divided against itself. Once such a distinction has been made, the reader is in a position to appreciate the worth of the good parts of the novel, and to understand why, considered as an artistic unit, *To Have and Have Not* is Hemingway's least satisfactory book. One may notice in passing that William Faulkner's double-focussed novel, *The Wild Palms,* published in 1939, represents a similar experiment in contrasting characters. In Faulkner, however, the story of the doctor and his

[13] EH to MP, 8/26/36, 11/8/36, 12/15/36.
[14] EH to MP, 6/10/37, 8/9/37. Two weeks after publication *THAHN* stood fourth on the national best-seller lists. By March 10, 1938, five months after publication, the book had sold 36,000 copies.

mistress does not so much undermine as serve to enhance the story of the convict. The convict is the rough moral equivalent of Harry Morgan in Hemingway.

The novel as published contains Hemingway's notes towards the definition of a decaying culture, and his disgust with the smell of death to come. Throughout the early nineteen-thirties he had been experimenting with one technical problem after another in the attempt to develop his art. He was not only seeking to advance his dexterity with a prose instrument earlier forged and tempered, but he was also beginning to attack the problem of cultural synecdoche, the means by which the novelist, presenting and evaluating the things he has known, summarizes dramatically the moral predicament of his times. One saw this tendency at work in both *Death in the Afternoon* and *The Green Hills of Africa*. The assumption in *To Have and Have Not* was that Depressed America at large could be anatomized by using a microscope on Key West in little. America at its worst was fully visible in Key West during the period 1932–1936. If, as one gathered, the whole organism was diseased, he could examine the smear on the slide to see what malignant forces were at work.

A major difference between this novel and much depression-inspired proletarian fiction was that it really embodied the diagnostic notes on decay; it did not preach them. This was a treatise in economics and revolutionary politics which chose to present its findings, not in propagandistic set speeches or in interminable discussions between a young organizer and his experienced mentor, but in straightforward, illustrative dramatic terms. For this reason, and in spite of its serious faults, *To Have and Have Not* may be said to stand as a somewhat more persuasive social documentary than a great deal of the soap-bubble proletarian literature which appeared, shone brightly, and vanished down-wind— through inherent structural weaknesses, an internal content that was mostly air, and the pressure of changing circumstances—during the period when so many blew the Marxist pipe.

Hemingway was not out to please the "recently politically enlightened critics." What he had written about "the boys" in 1934 he could still apply in 1937. "If the book is good, is about something that you know, and is truly written, and reading it over you see that this is so, you can let the boys yip." Then the noise "will have that pleasant sound coyotes make on a very cold night when they are out in the snow, and you are in your own cabin that you have built and paid for with your work." [15]

II. SOMETHING KNOWN

To Have and Have Not was "about something" Hemingway knew. By the time of the book's publication he had been living in Key West for nearly ten years, and by 1935 his stucco house on Whitehead Street was listed in the town's guide-book as one of the points of interest for visiting tourists. He knew all about charter-boat fishing, which he regularly followed as a means of relaxing from the hard trade of writing, and he had spent some time during the spring and summer of 1933 abroad the 34-foot launch *Anita,* owned and captained by Joe Russell of Key West. When Captain Russell retired ashore to take care of his profitable bar in Key West, Hemingway continued his maritime activities with his own boat, the *Pilar,* which was built for him after his return from Africa.[16]

He also had occasion to mingle with the unemployed war veterans, several hundred of whom were at this time stationed in work camps on the Upper and Lower Matecumbe Keys. They were part of a depression-inspired FERA project building roads and bridges between Miami and Key West. On pay-days they used to come down to Joe Russell's Key West bar to refresh themselves and enjoy a general rough-house. Entering the bar one day, Hemingway was hailed by one of the drunken veterans. He had a broken leg and a pair of crutches and was enthroned on a billiard table in the rear of the room. His fun for the day was to call unsuspecting visitors over for a talk and then to attempt to knock them out with a crutch. Since that morning his ruse had worked perfectly three times. Hemingway, warned by the proprietor, kept out of range. But his memory of this and other scenes of the same general character helped him to invent one of the

[15] "Old Newsman Writes," *loc.cit.* Note 2 *supra.*
[16] *Esquire* 2 (August 1934), pp. 19, 156, 158. Cf. *Esquire* 5 (April 1936), pp. 31, 184–185.

most effective episodes in *To Have and Have Not*. The semi-
comedy of the pay-dazed veterans had a tragic dénouement in
the fall of 1935. On September third, a hurricane cut a wide swath
east of Key West, destroying the Matecumbe work-camps and
drowning more than 200 of the men. While the scandal swept
across the nation and an investigation was begun in an attempt to
fix the blame, Hemingway joined the volunteer workers who
helped collect the dead from the watery débris all along the
stricken Keys.[17]

Besides the charter-boat marlin-fishing and the depressed peoples who were cast up on the Keys like economic driftwood, a
third element which was to go into *To Have and Have Not* was
now borne in upon Hemingway. As the Morgan story took shape
in his imagination, another began to rise up beside it. Morgan
was the individualist man of action, first crippled and then killed
as an indirect result of social corruption. What about that other
individualist, the artist, doing his work and earning his bread in
the midst of the same corruption? Between this Jamesian topic
and the problems which beset Harry Morgan of Key West there
appeared to be some relationship. "The Snows of Kilimanjaro,"
completed in April 1936, shortly before Hemingway began to
push the work on *To Have and Have Not,* took as its protagonist
an artist who had succumbed to the temptations of wealth and
privilege. Was it merely a coincidence that his name was Harry,
too?

Harry the artist had traded on his talent instead of using it.
He had supposed that he could write stories about the "very rich,"
as if he were a kind of "spy in their country" while still remaining
ethically separate from them. Instead, he had merely surrendered
to creature-comfort and mental laziness. Harry's friend Julian
(who was called Scott Fitzgerald in the first printed version of
"The Snows of Kilimanjaro") had been wrecked by the leisure
class in a way that was essentially different but hardly less devas-
tating.[18] He thought the rich "a special glamorous race and when

---

[17] *Esquire* 4 (August 1935), pp. 19, 182. Cf. *Esquire* 2 (October 1934),
pp. 21–22. For Hemingway's report on the disaster, see *New Masses* 16
(September 17, 1935), p. 9.
[18] *Esquire* 6 (August 1936), pp. 27, 194–201.

he found out they weren't it wrecked him just as much as any other thing that wrecked him."

Julian is obviously not to be confused with the artist Harry in the African story. He is a being of another order. Yet the whole problem of the cracked-up artist was dramatized for Hemingway in this period of the middle thirties by Scott Fitzgerald's losing fight against the furies that beset him. It came home to him in a special way. Between late 1933 and 1936, Hemingway had contributed twenty-five articles, chiefly in the form of "letters" on fishing and hunting, to the new men's magazine, *Esquire*.[19] Until the Spanish Civil War interrupted the arrangement, which gave Hemingway a completely free hand, these epistles, averaging about 1700 words each, held the lead position in almost every number. They earned Hemingway a following among fellow-sportsmen while enraging a lesser number of the avant-garde and leftist critics, who felt that in being fairly well paid for this form of journalism, Hemingway was lowering his literary standards. What gave Hemingway pause, during his tenure as chief letter-writer for the magazine, was that Scott Fitzgerald's graphic account of his own crack-up also ran in a series through the pages of *Esquire*.[20]

He did not, of course, take Fitzgerald as his subject. The "crack-up" articles, which are among the classic statements on the theme, left nothing more to be said during Fitzgerald's rapidly diminishing lifetime. Yet all through the early thirties the subject of the artist's jeopardy had been in Hemingway's mind, and it is at least a reasonable speculation that the Fitzgerald articles served as a kind of catalyst, being, as it were, too big to miss. The social aspect was important. "Writers should work alone," Hemingway had written in 1934. "They should see each other only after their work is done, and not too often then. Otherwise they become like writers in New York. All angleworms in a bottle, trying to derive knowledge and nourishment from their own contact and from the bottle. Sometimes the bottle is shaped art, sometimes economics, sometimes economics-religion. But once they are in the bottle they

---

[19] For a complete listing, including short stories, see Bibliography.

[20] *Esquire* 5 (February 1936), pp. 41, 169; (March 1936), pp. 35, 182; (April 1936), pp. 39, 202.

stay there. They are lonesome outside of the bottle. They do not want to be lonesome. They are afraid to be alone in their beliefs." Other writers tried to save their souls with what they wrote, or were ruined by "the first money, the first praise, the first attack." Sometimes they became frightened enough to join organizations that did their thinking for them.[21] Much could happen and most of it was bad. Now, because Hemingway was dramatizing a double indictment of American society for its predatory attitude towards both writers and individualistic men-of-action, he placed Harry Morgan and the wholly invented figure of the writer Richard Gordon side by side in his depression-novel of Key West. It is of interest to discover what the contiguity produced.

III. MORGAN AND GORDON

Harry Morgan was a supreme individualist, but he was also an American type. To put it another way, he was an American type because of his individualism, his cold courage, his resourcefulness, and his self-reliance. If American readers in the 1930's could not recognize in Harry Morgan a lineal descendant of the American frontiersman, the man who made his own laws and trusted in his own judgments, they were perhaps far gone in group thinking. Both in the Far West and in Key West Hemingway had met men of the frontier temperament, so that he did not lack for contemporary models. If one wanted a historical ancestor for Harry Morgan, however, he had only to look at some of the accounts of Wyatt Earp in the 1880's. Harry had been a police officer in Miami before he came to Key West. Earp had been a Kansas sheriff before he went west to Tombstone. Fraud such as the economic royalist Johnson practiced on Harry Morgan was close to the rule of life in Tombstone. The smuggling of alien Chinese from Cuba to the United States was not far different either in principle or in practice from the rustling of cattle across the Mexican border. Harry Morgan, badly wounded by Cuban customs officials as he runs out a boat-load of illicit liquor, is in effect repeating the experience of the marauding gringos who ran afoul of armed Mexicans during raids well within living memory. Plying between

[21] *GHOA*, pp. 21–22 and 24.

Cuba and Key West—a Latin country and a rough American town—Morgan is a typical nineteenth-century frontiersman in a twentieth-century frontier situation.

But the Morgan story, like *A Farewell to Arms,* is a study in doom. If one wishes to see it as an instance of "cultural synecdoche," there is no difficulty in taking Morgan as the type of the old self-reliant individualist confronted by an ever-encroaching social restraint—the civil disobedient who, like Thoreau, is opposed in principle to a corrupt federalism, but is unwilling, having never heard of Thoreau's program, to content himself with passive resistance. But Morgan has two factors to contend with which did not bother the Wyatt Earps of the old frontier. One is officious bureaucracy as dramatized in the power-proud figure of Frederick Harrison, the man who loses Harry his boat. "For your information," says Harrison, "I'm one of the three most important men in the United States today." It may not be fanciful, in view of Hemingway's long familiarity with the type, to see Harrison as a notable instance of the fascist mentality.

The second force is memorably represented by the Cuban revolutionaries, in descending order from the young idealist Emilio (who very much regrets the necessity for the terrorist phase of the revolution) down to the moon-faced Roberto who has killed so much in the time of Machado that he has come to enjoy political murder for its own sake. Emilio calls Roberto a good revolutionary but a bad man. Through this pair Hemingway summarizes the revolutionary party mentality of the Comintern, Latin style.

Morgan, who bears the name of a famous pirate, entertains equal scorn for both fascism and communism, though he is wise enough to recognize their power as adversaries long before the two groups, working in quite different ways, lose him first his boat and then his life. From the time he is defrauded of honest earnings by the unscrupulous capitalist Johnson, Harry Morgan is doomed, and the steps in his destruction are clearly marked out. A plague, he might well say, on all three such houses. His dying words on the hopeless situation of "one man alone" ring the knell of nineteenth-century frontier individualism. As long as the tactics and problems remain those of the frontier, Harry can survive. But fascism and communism, like the greed of irresponsible capital-

ism, are more formidable enemies, too powerful for one man alone
to withstand.

Hemingway made over the Morgan trilogy into a novel by two
important additions. Remembering that the book, like much of
his writing at this time, was experimental in nature, it might be
observed that both additions have the effect of enlarging Harry
Morgan's stature. The first addition is the provision of a home-life
for the hero. Harry's wife Marie is a kind of faithful Molly Bloom
whose closing soliloquy is Harry's personal epitaph. The second
addition, quantitatively much more extensive than the story of
Marie Morgan, deals with the crack-up of Richard Gordon, proletarian novelist, playboy, and sojourner in the Key West artist's
colony. This was Hemingway's strategic error.

One would scarcely need Hemingway's melancholy diatribe on
sold-out American writers in *The Green Hills of Africa* in order
to recognize Gordon as a representative figure. His character and
activities likewise serve as a foil for those of Harry Morgan.
Harry's marriage is a success, Gordon's a miserable failure. Harry
is tough, bitter, honest with himself; Gordon is a self-deceiver, a
self-apologist, a self-pitier. One is an expert strategist in all that
concerns his means of livelihood and his life as a man, while the
other is a false practitioner who manages to conceal his limitations
even from himself. Morgan can handle his own affairs; Gordon is a
kept man in a morally unkempt society.

The climactic phase of the novel centers on the doom of both
men. When Gordon enters, the time is already at hand when he
will be compelled to face the facts of his life, just as Morgan,
though in a quite different manner, must face up to the inexorable
facts by which group-man seizes dominance over the self-starting
individualist. Gordon's doom is in its way as inevitable as Morgan's. In quick succession his self-respect receives two damaging
blows. One comes when his wife leaves him with a fine Irish
tongue-lashing for his failure as a husband, the second sinks home
when a companion at the bar who happens to be familiar with
the actualities of unemployment, tells him exactly what his "proletarian" fiction is worth. The bloody figure of Richard Gordon
on his way home to an empty house in the dark is neither comic
nor tragic. It is an image of the writer irrevocably spoiled by the

smart-set lionizers, the ruthless bohemians, and the literary fad-
dists whose ways he has been following. Now he has met his moral
"comeuppance," a situation not unlike the confrontation of self
by self which occurs with another writer in "The Snows of Kilimanjaro." There are no degrees of chastity, but Gordon is considerably lower on the scale of the unchaste than the Harry who
dies of gangrene in Tanganyika.

Morgan is clearly impervious to the kind of corruption which
dooms Gordon. He pointedly rejects, for example, the yahoo-like
advances of a Key West literary slummer. "Shut up, you whore,"
says Harry Morgan, and the lady eventually obeys. Yet Gordon
allows himself to be taken up, and (what is worse) taken in, by
the wealthy Helene Bradley, a slummer on the grand scale and
the exact moral equivalent of African gangrene. Though both
Morgan and Gordon are victimized, it would be a mistake to
suppose that their adversaries are the same. Where the man-of-
action loses livelihood and life to something like fascism and something like communism, the parlor-pink novelist is a casualty to
capitalism's leisure class.

Strong esthetic grounds exist for the belief that the novel would
have been better without the figure of Gordon. For the story of
the writer suffers, perhaps unduly, when it is placed beside the
story of Morgan's downfall. Where the piratical smuggler credi-
bly epitomizes the self-reliant man, Gordon seems by contrast a
kind of caricature, somewhat as Francis Macomber suffers by his
proximity to the white hunter Wilson: on straight esthetic grounds.
If Gordon's pipsqueak misadventures help to bring out the stark,
tough actualities of Morgan's life and thus enlarge the boatman's
moral stature, the contrast backfires when it is looked at from the
other end. The nearness of Morgan dehumanizes Gordon to a
shadowy emblem. Although Hemingway, as in the Macomber
story, appears to feel some compassion, his scorn for the obvious
hollowness of the society life Gordon leads is finally uppermost,
and the writer's stature shrinks to that of a dwarf at the court of
the Duchess of Key West. On the other hand, in a queer way, the
author's scorn for Frederick Harrison (a caricature also) and
the Cuban terrorists only serves to increase his—and our—respect
for Morgan.

Two "exemplums" in *To Have and Have Not* operate, still somewhat oddly, in precisely the same way. One helps the novel forward; the other, esthetically speaking, is a backfire. The stories of Morgan and Gordon might be interpreted as instances in which the middle parts of fortune are invaded by the corrupting extremes. In order to emphasize for the reader the broad applicability of his social accusations, Hemingway provides two remarkable passages on the extremes of the economic have-and-have-not scale. Both are tours de force, but one succeeds as a version of the actual where the other fails because it seems obviously rigged.

The episode which backfires is the roll-call of the occupants of five yachts tied up at the Key West finger piers the night Harry Morgan is brought in from the Gulf. Two homosexuals, keeper and kept; one narcissistic adulteress; and one old economic royalist worrying over income-tax evasion are at least numerically balanced by one healthy, respectable upperclass family and two of the 324 intrepid Esthonians who are sailing around in different parts of the world and sending back articles to the Esthonian newspapers. The real imbalance is in the satire itself; this is an extreme overstatement on one of the social extremes. Instead of enhancing the effect, this piece of satire oddly cheapens the whole atmosphere when Morgan's bullet-riddled boat and body are towed past the silent yachts. The reader finds himself resenting the episode as gratuitous over-emphasis.

Much more effective is the remarkable sketch of the displaced veterans in their nocturnal drink-and-slugfest in Freddy's Bar. These men stand at the other extreme. They are the "desperate ones . . . the ones with nothing to lose . . . the completely brutalized ones." Hoover ran them out of Anacostia Flats; Roosevelt shipped them south "to get rid of them." [22] Coldly intelligent and well-educated communists are infiltrating their camps. They are as much the prey to these borers from within as the wealthy yachtsmen are prey to fascist-minded bureaucrats of the stamp of Frederick Harrison. The veterans' irrational and aimless brutality serves a better purpose in the novel than the roll-call of the

[22] *THAHN,* p. 206. According to a *New Masses* editorial for September 16, 1935, the Roosevelt administration was supposed in some quarters to have "drowned" the veterans.

yachts; for if Morgan was brutal and desperate, he was brutal to some end and desperate for good reason. These depressed peoples have been kicked around for so long that they now take a masochistic delight in their ability to absorb more punishment.

"Let us in," the bloody-faced one said. "Let in me and my old buddy." He whispered into Richard Gordon's ear, "I don't have to hand it out. I can take it."

"Listen," the other Vet said as they finally reached the beer-wet bar, "you ought to have seen him at noon at the Commissary at Camp Five. I had him down and I was hitting him on the head with a bottle. Just like playing on a drum. I bet I hit him fifty times."

"More," said the bloody-faced one.[23]

Malcolm Cowley once referred to this section of the book as a Walpurgisnacht, and the image is perfectly exact.[24] Hemingway does not spoil the direct impact of this wild scene with any contiguities. It is a terrible indictment made with a wry smile but also with an unmistakable sickness at the stomach, as if Key West had somehow got detached from its moorings and were pitching and wallowing in an ugly sea of social neglect. The same society has driven Harry Morgan to piracy and Richard Gordon to a kind of literary racketeering which passes in some circles of hell for art.

But the exemplums of the corrupt yachtsmen and the brutalized veterans, as well as the story of Richard Gordon's crack-up, have yet another function in the book. They suggest the possibility that *To Have and Have Not* is a title with a reciprocal action. Its economic meaning is clear and obvious. As one of the *Have-Nots,* Harry Morgan must take desperate measures for survival, and his adversaries are those who *Have* money, power, prestige, and unearned privilege. Yet this is a novel, not a treatise in economics. John Ruskin, whose approach to economic problems always emphasized morality over money, once defined *having* as a power whose importance lay "not only in the quantity or nature of the thing possessed" but also, and more significantly, "in its suitableness to the person possessing it and in his vital power to use it." [25]

[23] *THAHN,* p. 202.
[24] *New Republic* 92 (October 20, 1937), pp. 305–306.
[25] Ruskin, *Unto This Last,* Essay IV.

On these ultimately moral grounds, a reversed interpretation of the title suggests itself. Harry Morgan *has* a combination of social courage and personal integrity precisely suited to his character. The same qualities are notably absent among the leisure-class wastrels and other ne'er-do-wells by whom he is surrounded and with whom he is contrasted. He shows a "vital power" in putting his possessions to use. *To Have* what Harry has in the way of self-reliance, self-command, and self-knowledge is qualitatively superior, one would judge, to the strictly economic forms of having. Interpreted in this way, the Have-Nots of the title would embrace representatives of every class and occupation: wealthy yacht-owners, middle-class artists like Gordon, simple alcoholics like Harry's super-cargo Eddy, or the brutalized veterans who give and take their punishment in the Walpurgisnacht atmosphere of Freddy's Key West bar.

IV. THE MATTER OF TECHNIQUE

Few of Hemingway's critics, either in 1937 or since, seemed able to appreciate the difficulty of the technical experiments in *To Have and Have Not* or the skill with which some of them were overcome. For those who wished to pay attention, however, the Key West novel repaid the effort. One experiment which failed was the attempt to dove-tail and arc-weld two essentially disparate plots; another was the use of caricature, which seemed out of place in connection with the power and the fury of the Morgan story. But three other experiments—with the maintenance and release of emotional intensity, with the establishment of multiple perspectives, and with the building up of an ordinary Key West charter-boat fisherman to a figure of heroic proportions—were distinctly worth noticing.

For some readers one trouble with the Morgan story was that it was almost too intense—like the thumbing-out of Gloucester's eyes in *King Lear* or the axe-murder in *Crime and Punishment*. The incidents of the smuggled Chinese and the boat-battle with the Cuban revolutionaries seemed to be designed to give the reader a feeling something like that of walking in front of a battery of machine-guns manned by epileptics. Both developed a degree of tension just short of the unendurable. Fitzgerald wrote Hemingway a few months before he died that there were paragraphs and whole pages of *To Have and Have Not* which were "right up with Dostoievski in their undeflected intensity." [26]

It is not part of Hemingway's aim to deflect his intensities, but one can watch with interest his attempts to relieve them. Book I quickly establishes the atmosphere in which Harry moves by an account of a Havana gun-battle between two groups of Cuban revolutionists. This is followed with a full account of a day's deep-sea fishing, exciting in itself as a study in pursuit yet carried on at a pitch considerably lower than the man-hunt by land with which the book began. After Johnson runs out on Morgan without paying the bill, the episode of the smuggled Chinese begins to take shape, gather momentum, and develop a new and undeflected intensity. A brief account of the homeward cruise again provides relief and brings this phase of the story to a satisfactory and rounded conclusion.

The rum-running story, conducted throughout at a considerably lower emotional temperature, rises in mid-career to the time when Morgan and his Negro companion Wesley are nearly arrested by the officious Washington bureaucrat Harrison. Here the relief is provided by the humor of character, and the deflation of false pride, in a manner which anticipates the incident of El Sordo and the boastful fascist captain in *For Whom the Bell Tolls*. Captain Willie, a handsomely realized character-study, shouts his warning to the two wounded men in the booze boat:

"Listen. Get on into town and take it easy. Never mind the boat. They'll take the boat. Dump your load and get into town. I got a guy here on board some kind of a stool from Washington. More important than the President, he says. He wants to pinch you. He thinks you're a bootlegger. He's got the numbers of the boat. I ain't never seen you so I don't know who you are. I couldn't identify you—"

The boats had drifted apart. Captain Willie went on shouting, "I don't know where this place is where I seen you. I wouldn't know how to get back here."

[26] FSF to EH, 11/8/40. See *The Crack-Up,* ed. Edmund Wilson, New York, 1945, p. 284.

"O. K.," came a shout from the booze boat.

"I'm taking this big alphabet man fishing until dark," Captain Willie shouted.

"O. K."

"He loves to fish," Captain Willie yelled, his voice almost breaking. "But the son of a bitch claims you can't eat 'em."

"Thanks, brother," came the voice of Harry.

"That chap your brother?" asked Frederick Harrison, his face very red but his love of information still unappeased.

"No, sir," said Captain Willie. "Most everybody goes in boats calls each other brother."

"We'll go into Key West," Frederick Harrison said; but he said it without great conviction.[27]

The third story early achieves and steadily maintains an always mounting intensity up to the point of the gunfight with the Cuban revolutionists, then slowly decelerates through the account of Harry's dying and on to the moment of his death in the hospital. After this, in a manner somewhat like the Molly Bloom sequence at the close of Joyce's *Ulysses,* comes the soliloquy by Marie Morgan—a final chorus of lament for the slain. If one examines the Morgan trilogy as an experiment in the development and relief of emotional tension, he may find it easy to share Fitzgerald's enthusiasm, whether or not he is reminded of Dostoievski.

Besides the experimentation with emotional tensions, *To Have and Have Not* is distinguished by experiments with varying points of view. Since it must introduce the character and clarify the motives of Harry Morgan, the opening story is his own first-person narrative throughout. Part Two, on the rum-running episode, offers another perspective on Morgan, treating him almost as if he were a stranger, and gaining a special detachment by the use of the third-person narrative. We are made to share "the tradesman's return" as if somehow aboard the boat as a silent partner. This method is relieved by one shift in point of view midway in the story. When Captain Willie Adams and his two passengers are close enough to the booze boat so that Harrison becomes suspicious about what may be happening, we are taken aboard Captain Willie's boat for the comic interlude of his defiance. This

[27] *THAHN,* pp. 82–83.

double view of Morgan's predicament gives the story a length of perspective which it would lack if, like the first one, it were told entirely in the first person or entirely from the silent-partner position aboard Harry's boat.

Part Three carries the experiment further. It opens with a first-person narrative by Albert Tracy, Morgan's indigent colleague in the affair of the Cuban terrorists. This opening has a triple purpose. We get a picture of Morgan in action through the mind of someone other than Harry or the author. We learn also enough about Albert so that we are able to sympathize with him and therefore feel his loss the more when he is callously murdered by the Cubans. Finally, we are prepared, through this special knowledge of Albert, to accept the comic and almost farcical wailings and posturings of the shrewish Mrs. Tracy when she learns of her husband's death. Having treated him badly while he lived, she is prepared to put on a stirring show as the very recent widow who has lost her helpmate. Her obviously half-devised mourning is effective in the total structure of the book in that it provides a contrast with Marie Morgan's realistic and dignified acceptance of her own husband's death.

After Tracy's narrative, Hemingway introduces a short internal monologue by Morgan, the intent here being to establish with us a sense of his feeling of reluctant desperation. "I don't want to fool with it," Harry muses, "but what choice have I got? They don't give you any choice now. I can let it go; but what will the next thing be? I didn't ask for any of this and if you've got to do it you've got to do it." [28] In this mood he agrees to carry the Cubans across the straits to Cuba. From this point onwards, the third-person narrative begins again—chiefly objective, though occasionally dipping into Harry's thought-stream to show his reactions to each of the changing situations as they arise. Along with these semi-soliloquies, the author twice provides access to Marie Morgan's thoughts. This is done partly, as with Tracy, to confirm her in the reader's sympathies, and partly to provide yet another perspective on Harry Morgan.

Up through the fatal wounding aboard the *Queen Conch,* the story is therefore a straightforward third-person narrative, with

[28] *THAHN,* p. 105.

limited use of thought-reporting where it is required. After the shooting, however, there is one very striking camera-eye snapshot of the launch as she drifts in the Gulf Stream.

"She drifted broadside to the gentle north wind about ten miles outside of the north-bound tanker lanes, gay looking in her fresh white and green, against the dark, blue Gulf Stream water. . . . There was no sign of life on her although the body of a man showed, rather inflated looking, above the gunwale, lying on a bench over the port gasoline tank and, from the long seat alongside the starboard gunwale, a man seemed to be leaning over to dip his hand into the sea. His head and arms were in the sun and at the point where his fingers almost touched the water, there was a school of small fish . . . that had deserted the gulf weed to take shelter in the shade the bottom of the drifting launch made in the water, and each time anything dripped down into the sea, these fish rushed at the drop and pushed and milled until it was gone. . . . They had long since pulled away the ropy, carmine clots and threads that trailed in the water from the lowest splintered holes. . . . They were reluctant now to leave a place where they had fed so well and unexpectedly." [29]

The oppressive silence here, the *Queen Conch* with her quiet cargo of dead men, the one still-living occupant, and the tropical fish silently feeding in the shadow of the silently drifting launch, provides an effective contrast to the fury of the gun-battle which has taken place the night before. It likewise serves to remind the reader of Hemingway that nature's quietude, nature's continuum, nature's great age, when these are compared with the fury and the mire of human veins, and the brevity of man's time on earth, are something like an echo of the passage from Ecclesiastes which was used as one of the headnotes to *The Sun Also Rises*. The sun also ariseth in 1935, as it did in 1925 over the Pyrenees at Burguete; the Gulf Stream, like the Irati river, still runs without interruption; the fish still feed and swim while the generations of mankind pass away.

We see no more of Morgan until the Coast Guard cutter tows the launch back to Key West while the ship's officers question him,

[29] *THAHN,* pp. 178–180. The passage is too long to quote in full, and should be read in context for the total effect.

without success, on the origin of the tragedy. His career closes, as the book closes, with Marie's requiem-soliloquy. Basing his conclusion on the Morgan trilogy, the reader may well decide that the virtuosity of the narrative technique alone is enough to set the book off in a kind of lonely triumph from most of the writing of the middle thirties.

By many carefully planned devices, Harry Morgan's stature is raised to dimensions just short of heroic. Two of these—Marie's silent soliloquies and the contrast which Richard Gordon unwittingly provides—have already been mentioned. Some of the others may be quickly noticed. Harry's working associates serve, for example, to emphasize his self-command (contrast Eddy the alcoholic), his unwillingness to compromise with the truth (Beelips the lawyer is the contrasting figure here), and his tough resourcefulness (as contrasted, say, with the character of Albert Tracy, a poor hungry player who struts and frets a brief hour only to be murdered and dumped overboard by the callous Roberto). The rum-running story underscores Morgan's capacity for stoic endurance—always a trait of Hemingway's heroes. Both Harry and his assistant have been shot—he severely in the arm, Wesley in the leg. All the way across the straits, Wesley has moaned and complained. By morning Harry has tired of the noise.

"Who the hell's shot worse?" he asks. "You or me?"

"You're shot worse," Wesley admits. "But I ain't never been shot. I didn't figure to get shot. I ain't paid to be shot. I don't want to be shot."

"Take it easy, Wesley," says Harry. "It don't do any good to talk like that."

And while his companion blubbers with his face in a corner, Harry continues to lift the heavy sacks of liquor and to drop them over the side with his one good arm.[30]

When the figure of Harry Morgan is looked at phlegmatically, outside the frame of the story, he seems very much like any other tough Key West fisherman. It would be easy to write him off as a low-class murderer, a one-armed bandit, an inveterate opportunist whose complete callousness towards bloodshed is the measure of his moral standing. When Mrs. Laughton, drinking cuba

[30] *THAHN,* pp. 70 and 75.

libras at Freddy's Bar, casts sheep's-eyes at Morgan and admires his "beautiful face," Freddy believes that Mrs. Laughton has had one too many drinks. "Take it easy, lady," says Freddy. "He's got a face like a ham with a broken nose on it." [31] Freddy's physiognomic perceptions are clear and sharp.

It is, nevertheless, the task of any good story to enthrall the reader into certain illusions in terms of which his evaluation of character can take place. Within the illusion provided by *To Have and Have Not,* Harry Morgan emerges as a heroic and morally indefatigable figure, standing out like a stoic statue above the heads of his associates, gifted with qualities and abilities and determinations to which none of his companions can lay equal claim.

If one is compelled, in final judgment, to say that *To Have and Have Not* fails as a novel—and it does fail for the reasons already outlined—it is all the more important that the virtues of the Morgan trilogy should receive due recognition. In two respects, at least, the Morgan story looks forward to *For Whom the Bell Tolls.* One of these is the demonstrated skill in the development of emotional intensity—a skill visible also in "The Short Happy Life of Francis Macomber," which belongs to the same chronological period as the third Morgan story. The second is to be found in Hemingway's capacity for the enlargement of character to heroic proportions. What Hemingway learned from his experiments with Harry Morgan was put to excellent use in the portraits of Robert Jordan and the gypsy Pilar during the composition of *For Whom the Bell Tolls.*

[31] *THAHN,* p. 137.

X · The Spanish Tragedy

> "Hemingway . . . is obviously the person who can write the great book about the Spanish War."—Cyril Connolly, 1937 [1]

I. A MATTER OF CHOICE

When Hemingway spoke to the Second American Writers' Congress in Carnegie Hall, New York City, the evening of June 4, 1937, he was newly back from two months' reporting on the Spanish Civil War. It was his first public speech. Since, in the course of it, he denounced the native and foreign fascists then operating in Spain, some of his large audience supposed that they were witnessing the wonderful transformation of a non-political writer to one who was socially conscious. [2]

Two days later, in one of the closing speeches of the Congress, Joseph Freeman thought he saw an important lesson in Hemingway's "conversion." He drew his text from an anecdote about Napoleon and Goethe. When Goethe said that he was writing a play about the destiny of man, Napoleon answered that politics is destiny. In an epoch like our own, said Freeman, politics, in its broadest sense, *is* destiny. "Even if you begin as Hemingway began, with a simple emotional desire to transmit experience, to find and convey the truth, if you follow the truth to its logical conclusion, you will end where Hemingway has ended now, in the People's Front." [3]

All this about "logical conclusions" (with the implication that the logic of history eventually forces a writer to support a political party-line) was Marxist language and typical Marxist thinking. The explosion of political circumstances in Spain had presumably blasted Hemingway out of his non-political lethargy and deposited

[1] Cyril Connolly, *New Statesman and Nation* 14 (October 16, 1937), p. 606.

[2] *Writer's Congress proceedings:* published in book form with a selection of the speeches, *The Writer in a Changing World,* ed. Henry Hart, New York, Equinox Cooperative Press, 1937.

[3] *Goethe and Napoleon: ibid.,* pp. 234–235.

him safely in the camp of the Spanish Loyalists. Gone was his "simple emotional desire to transmit experience," and perhaps his wish "to find and convey the truth." At any rate, these desires were now channelized in a political direction. According to Freeman, Hemingway was espousing a Cause. The political left, though very supercilious about his former childishness, was ready to welcome this talented if prodigal son back into the state of political awareness.

The only trouble with Freeman's conclusion was that Hemingway was still of Goethe's persuasion. "A writer's problem does not change," he told his audience. "It is always how to write truly and having found out what is true to project it in such a way that it becomes a part of the experience of the person who reads it." As to forms of government, he frankly continued, really good writers seem to have been rewarded under almost any system of government which they could tolerate. "There is only one form of government," said he, "that cannot produce good writers, and that system is fascism. For fascism is a lie told by bullies. A writer who will not lie cannot live and work under fascism." [4] Although, as a friend of Spanish democracy, Hemingway believed in the Republican side, his statement did not mean that, *as an artist,* he was pro-Republican or pro-Communist. What it emphatically meant was that as artist and man, he was anti-fascist, and had been for years.

Hemingway had followed political developments in Spain from the beginning of his career. The almost medieval country he had known in the nineteen-twenties during Alfonso's eight-year dictatorship-by-royal-decree had begun to change rapidly in 1931 with the overthrow of the monarchy and the establishment of the Democratic Republic of Workers.[5] As a student of revolutions

[4] *Hemingway's speech: ibid.,* pp. 69–73.

[5] The period covered was September 16, 1923, through the election of April 12, 1931. This was roughly the period of Hemingway's closest association with Spain and the Spanish, until the Civil War. The Democratic Republic was established April 14, 1931, with a new flag of red, yellow, and purple—irreverently described by Pilar and others as "blood, pus, and permanganate" (*FWBT,* p. 66). The old flag of yellow and gold had been referred to as "pus and blood." The flag under Franco is referred to in terms not generally printable.

who had watched, with an artist's eye, the development and decline of the troubles in Cuba during the early nineteen-thirties,
he had regretted not being on hand for the events which took place
in Spain during April and May of 1931, though he was in Spain
that summer and learned from his friends what had happened. As
an American and as a Catholic convert of some years' standing,
he had in general approved the separation of the Church and the
State achieved by the Democratic Republic, though he had naturally deplored the anti-clerical riotings which preceded it.[6] He had
welcomed in principal, if not in all details, the extensive program
of long-overdue reforms, covering nearly every aspect of Spanish
civil life, which was instituted by the same government.

He was in Africa when the conservative reaction—largely the
work of the landed aristocracy, the Army, and the Church—
countermanded many of the reforms accomplished in the Cortes
between the spring of 1931 and the spring of 1933.[7] In Spain
before the African trip he had gone shooting in Estremadura with
Luis Quintanilla, an ardent Republican who was later jailed by
the conservatives for his political activities.[8] At the same time
Hemingway had been embarrassed by a newspaper article which
called him "the friend of Spain" in bold capitals. The country, he
pointed out, was split wide open, and was "inhabited by too many
politicians for any man to be a friend to all of it with impunity."
Under the Republic, he saw, the country was more prosperous;
more money was coming in from taxes. But the peasants, like
some he had recently seen in Estremadura, were still the forgotten
men. Despite the newfound evidences of prosperity it was clear to
Hemingway that much of the money was going where it had always gone—into the pockets of those in power. The aims of the
Republic were just and sound, but the "great new bureaucracy"

[6] *Anticlerical riots:* In Madrid on May 12, 1931, mobs burned churches
and convents. At this time also anticlerical activity was widespread in
other Spanish cities. Martial law was proclaimed. This is the period referred to by the guerrillas in the novel as "the start of the movement."

[7] *Conservative reaction:* General election of November 19, 1933.

[8] Quintanilla, the Republican artist (born 1905) who painted Hemingway's portrait. Dos Passos and Hemingway jointly sponsored an exhibition
of Quintanilla's excellent work in New York City, November 20 to December 4, 1934. See Hemingway's article, *Esquire* 3 (February 1935), pp.
26–27.

was not, strictly speaking, selflessly devoted to the welfare of Spain. "Politics," said Hemingway, "is still a lucrative profession." To the ironist, the rise of Spain's new bureaucracy made the spectacle of Spanish government "more comic than tragic." To the friend of Democratic Spain, however, the comedy did not seem like something that would last. "The tragedy," said Hemingway, "is very close." [9]

The first act of the Spanish tragedy was in fact only a month off when Hemingway made his prediction. The failure of Spain in 1933 to extend the revolution of 1931 came about, he afterwards observed, because "the mass of the people were not ready for it and they did not want it." As late as 1937, the leftist Joseph Freeman could corroborate Hemingway's earlier view. One must face the issue frankly, Freeman told the Writer's Congress: "The majority of the Spanish people" did not even then "want socialism." They were fighting for "a democratic republic." [10] What made the events of the autumn of 1933 tragic in their results was the degree to which socialism had infiltrated the republican bureaucracy, and fascist thinking the minds of the reactionary army officers. The tragedy was launched in Spain.

Between 1933 and 1936, while Hemingway watched with care, the second act of the tragedy built up. Conservative elements formed a strong anti-Marxist alliance. The restive reform groups, including both moderates and extremists, banded together in a Popular Front organization, precipitating the bloody and desperate general strike of October 1934, which further widened the gap between the workers and the conservative groups. But when the 1936 elections produced a decisive Republican majority, the long-frustrated reformers moved rapidly to enforce the terms of their program. Further civil disorders followed. In March, the Army threatened to seize the government if order were not restored. In April the government countered with a thorough shake-up of the Army command, including the exile of some of the more dangerous general officers who showed Hitlerite ambi-

[9] "Friend of Spain": See Hemingway's letter of that title, *Esquire* 1 (January 1934), pp. 26, 136. Cf. Hemingway's remark that "Spain is an open wound in the right arm that cannot heal because the dust gets in it." *Gattorno*, foreword, Havana, 1935, p. 12.

[10] Joseph Freeman in *The Writer in a Changing World*, p. 237.

tions. But the efforts of the Popular Front, which was torn by internal dissensions, were neither strong nor extensive enough. On July 17, 1936, insurrections of army garrisons began all over Spain. Despite reprisal action and the immediate mobilization of a Loyalist militia, Mola and Franco moved quickly and according to a carefully prepared plan. The third act of the Spanish tragedy burst out in civil war.

To Hemingway, who had watched and commented on Acts One and Two, Act Three was no surprise. He had heard talk of the next European war in the Montparnasse cafés in the fall of 1933, and had been distressed, as any old soldier must be, by the widespread assumption that it was inevitable. In the summer of 1935 he had stated forthrightly that a war was "being prepared and brought closer each day with all the premeditation of a longplanned murder." This veteran correspondent knew that Europe had always fought; the intervals of peace were only armistices. Hitler's desire for war in Europe was obvious. Although Mussolini, Hemingway's old enemy through the 1920's, was not especially anxious for a war in Europe, he was very busy making Ethiopia "fit for Fiats." The general war, said Hemingway, would not come in 1935 or 1936, but in 1937 or 1938, "they [would] fight." He did not foresee, publicly at least, that Spain would become a sort of international testing-ground for Germany, Italy, and Russia before the Spanish Civil War was a year old. Otherwise, in selecting 1937 as a possible date for the outbreak of a war involving several European nations (which of course happened in Spain) he had made a fairly sound prediction.[11]

He began the year 1936 with a condemnation of the Ethiopian campaign, calling Mussolini "the cleverest opportunist in modern history," and noting that while the sons of the dictator were aviators in action against a non-existent Ethiopian air-force, the poor men's sons of Italy were dying as foot-soldiers. When would the poor men's sons learn who their real enemy was, and why? Hemingway had always regarded Mussolini, says Dean Gauss, as "a fakir and a grandstand player." The march on Rome in 1922 had

[11] See Hemingway, "A Paris Letter," *Esquire* 1 (February 1934), pp. 72, 156; "Notes on the Next War," *Esquire* 4 (September 1935), pp. 19, 156; and "The Malady of Power," *Esquire* 4 (November 1935), pp. 31, 198.

been possible owing to the "wave of disgust," Hemingway said, which "followed the farcical failure of the Italian radicals to cooperate." [12] But for a good many years now the Italian situation had been anything but a farce, and the grandstand player, though still a fakir, was also a dangerous force. Hemingway could not foresee that within a year of his public condemnation of Mussolini's activities in Ethiopia, the opportunist Mussolini would be moving his legions into Spain. Still less could he foretell the feelings with which former Tenente Ernesto Hemingway of the Italian infantry would walk through the scrub oak woods of Brihuega in the spring of 1937, inspecting the bodies of the poor men's sons who had died in the name of their real enemy, Il Duce. [13]

Hemingway's temperamental and long-term distrust of all behind-the-scenes "deals" and "arrangements" in Europe found ample evidence to support it among the Italian dead at Brihuega. The world was not run as the statesmen said it was run; one had to be able to distinguish between the poor players and the true owners. The "starry-eyed" of all countries, not to mention the conscripted sons of the Italian poor who would never see any more stars or anything else, were more than likely to be "sucked in." Both these phrases came frequently to Hemingway's mind whenever he wrote about European politics.

Why, then, did he bother with a country which was torn with "deals" and "arrangements"? Hemingway's answer is forthright. "There were at least five parties in the Spanish Civil War on the Republic side. I tried to understand and evaluate all five (very difficult) and belonged to none. . . . I had no party but a deep interest in and love for the Republic. . . . In Spain I had, and have, many friends on the other side. I tried to write truly about them, too. Politically, I was always on the side of the Republic from the day it was declared and for a long time before." [14] When the Civil War broke out, it was necessary for him to make a choice of proper action.

[12] *Ethiopian Campaign:* See Hemingway, "Wings Always Over Africa," *Esquire* 5 (January 1936), pp. 31, 174–175. CG to CB, 12/26/50.

[13] See the reprinting of EH's NANA despatch in *New Republic* 90 (May 5, 1937), pp. 376–379. The crushing defeat of Mussolini's troops occurred in the period of March 11–23, 1937.

[14] EH to CB, 4/1/51.

II. THE BIG STAGE

He soon made up his mind, though not without some of the qualms which usually attend the realist in reaching such decisions. By the end of 1936 he had raised $40,000 on personal notes to help equip the Loyalists with ambulances and medical supplies. In January 1937 he became chairman of the Ambulance Committee, Medical Bureau, American Friends of Spanish Democracy. The name of the organization fairly described Hemingway's position and the reasons behind it.

Once you are fighting a war, as he said in 1942, you have no choice but to try to win it.[15] On this principle, he worked hard for the Loyalists, among whom were many native Spaniards who shared his interest in and love for the Republic, whatever their buried feelings about the foreign communists who were moving into Madrid to join the war against the fascist aggressors, native and foreign. From the money-raising activities of 1936 through the end of the war in 1939, he was either in Spain, or working for the Republic outside Spain, or writing about the course of the conflict. His labors took him into the heart of the war on four separate occasions.[16]

His first trip began on February 27, 1937, when he sailed on the *Paris* to report the war for the North American Newspaper Alliance. From Toulouse in mid-March he flew south to Barcelona. From there a plane carried him down the east coast, over the yellow sprawl of Valencia far below, and into the airfield at Alicante, where he found the Loyalists in a holiday mood over the recent defeat of the Italians at Brihuega.

When Hemingway reached the battlefield, getting up at dawn of a late March morning and driving up from Valencia, the Italian dead still lay where they had fallen. As an objective reporter, he was compelled to conclude that, whatever his own low opinion of Mussolini, and whatever Loyalist propaganda might say to the

[15] *Men At War,* introd., p. xi.

[16] *Four trips to Spain:* Besides the newspaper reports of Hemingway's arrivals and departures as listed in *New York Times Index* for these years, see the further reprintings of NANA despatches in the *New Republic:* Vols. 93 (January 12, 1938), pp. 273–276; 94 (April 27, 1938), pp. 350–351; and 95 (June 8, 1938), pp. 124–126.

contrary, the Italian poor men's sons had died bravely, the victims of superior fire-power, strong air attacks, and inadequate protection from the rocky terrain. These dead did not look to an objective observer like fascist devils cowering in death before the Marxist angels of destruction. They were men who had been killed. They were another example of *Los Desastres de la Guerra*. One more of Europe's intermittent periods of armistice had ended and these were among the victims.

As a friend to the Spanish Republic, Hemingway was ready to help with the development of a documentary film, *The Spanish Earth*.[17] During April and early May he joined the young Dutch director, Joris Ivens, and his cameraman, John Ferno, working in and near besieged Madrid. Wearing a Basque beret, windbreaker, and heavy field boots, the American guide made a picturesque figure. The film-makers had set up an observation post only ten minutes' walk away, and they watched Miaja's Loyalist strikes in the depression below the city, or photographed the mangled bodies of the Madrileños in the streets and squares where Rebel artillery had permanently interrupted their civilian lives. Like every other Loyalist sympathizer who saw the results, Hemingway resented the totalitarian tactics of murdering non-participant citizenry with high explosives. The Rebels, as he told the Writers' Congress in

[17] *The Spanish Earth:* 1000 copies of the sound-film text (it was exhibited in silent form, with spoken commentary by Ivens, at the Writers' Congress) were published in Cleveland, Ohio (J. B. Savage Company, June 1938). The 60-page book contains an emotional and somewhat inaccurate introduction by Jasper Wood and decorations by Frederick K. Russell. Besides the introduction, the text consists entirely of a transcript of Hemingway's sound-track commentary, and "The Heat and the Cold," a short reminiscence of experiences in Spain during the filming, written by Hemingway and reprinted from *Verve* (Spring 1938). The film was undertaken in aid of the people of Spain by an organization called *Contemporary Historians,* including John Dos Passos, Lillian Hellman, Archibald MacLeish, and Ernest Hemingway. All of these had early recognized the threat of fascism to the free world. The film itself was designed to show the efforts of the Spanish peasantry to reclaim for agricultural purposes land which had been misused and neglected for many generations. Because of the war, their efforts were defeated and they were betrayed. The film's six-reel message could be summed up in the directive: get rid of war. The film seeks dramatic focus by recounting in part the experiences of a young Spaniard named Julian who comes from the village of Fuenteduena.

June, had been beaten in every major engagement up to that date; what they could not win in the military way, they sought to win by the mass-murder of civilian populations.

Often, at considerable personal risk, Ivens, Ferno, and Hemingway moved out into the hills of Morata de Tajuña to get pictures of tanks and infantry in action. Ivens and Ferno sometimes distressed their companion by unrealistically exposing themselves to enemy fire. Hemingway cabled MacLeish that there was some doubt about Ivens' survival because he was taking the daily risks of a regular infantry officer. In his turn, Hemingway distressed his companions by carrying strong Spanish onions in the pockets of his field-jacket as a means of assuaging hunger. For battle-thirst, the trio carried a large flat silver flask of whiskey. It was always empty by four in the afternoon until they discovered the wisdom of bringing along an auxiliary bottle.

In 1940, looking back on this spring of 1937, Hemingway said that "the period of fighting when we thought that the Republic could win was the happiest period of our lives." For the duration of that war, except for writing his play, he contented himself with NANA despatches, a few short stories, and the brief script of *The Spanish Earth*.[18] He might have agreed, if confronted with it, to the sentiments of Philip Freneau's couplet:

> An age employed in edging steel
> Can no poetic raptures feel.[19]

Poetic raptures in Freneau's sense of the phrase had never much engaged Hemingway. But during the long armistice between his discharge from the Italian base-hospital and the outbreak of new hostilities in Europe, he had felt justified in learning to write and in continuing to mind it as his proper business. Having served

[18] See "The Heat and the Cold" reference in note 17, and also the remarks by A. MacLeish, *The Writer in a Changing World*, p. 206. Ivens had left the U.S. December 26, 1936, and was in and near Madrid from January 1, 1937, until early May. See also Hemingway's preface to Gustav Regler, *The Great Crusade*, New York, 1940, p. viii.

A brief glimpse of Hemingway in Spain is provided by Constancia de la Mora, *In Place of Splendor*, New York, 1939, p. 290. See also the vignette in Stephen Spender, *World Within World*, New York, 1951, pp. 229–231.

[19] Philip Freneau, "To an Author" (1788), lines 35–36.

time "for society, democracy, and the other things quite young," he had felt no compulsion to enlist in the French Foreign Legion or to aid the Chinese in throwing back the Japanese invaders. His clear responsibility, as he saw it, was to the art of writing well, and he willingly exchanged the "pleasant, comforting stench of comrades" for the job of the individualist artist who must work alone if he is to get his work done.[20]

Now, however, he reversed the procedure, declining further writing until the war could be won and the fascist menace—with its enmity towards all honest writers—could be reduced in scale. It was a reasonably happy period for him because it was something like the old times in Italy along the lower Piave where he had served nearly twenty years earlier. The stench of brave comrades was as pleasant and comforting in the spring of 1937 as it had been in the spring of 1918. The cause was at least as good and possibly better. There was also the reasonable expectation that if one survived, with all that he had learned about the art of writing during the long armistice, he had a chance of writing a book about this war which would be better than any of the earlier books.

Though politics had brought the war on, it had little to do with the comradeship among the Loyalist soldiers in whose company Hemingway now moved. They were of all political persuasions from militant Comintern communism to the point around the center where—as artist, American, semi-detached observer, student of war, and unpartied supporter of the Spanish Republic—Hemingway stood. The Eleventh and Twelfth Brigades (really the First and Second) were his chief centers of operation. The Eleventh was German. Though they were ardent anti-Nazis and had a remarkable commander named Hans, "most of them were communists" and "they were a little serious to spend much time with." Hemingway's Republican heart was with the Twelfth Brigade, a very mixed group politically, a memorably gay assemblage as comrades. One staunch friend was Werner Heilbrun, the medical officer of the outfit. He could always provide transport, good cheer, or a hot meal at night for the dusty and famished wayfarers. Heilbrun was killed in a strafing attack at Huesca soon after the Carnegie Hall speech, and Hemingway donated to his widow the

[20] *GHOA*, p. 148.

proceeds from the printed version of *The Spanish Earth*. Another friend was Gustav Regler, calm, cheerful, tough, and one of the ablest fighting officers in the brigade. His novel, *The Great Crusade*, was published in the United States in 1940, translated by Whittaker Chambers and Barrows Mussey, and with a preface by Hemingway. The commander of the Twelfth, General Lucasz, was one of Hemingway's good friends, and a good gay man at their party of May 1, playing a tune on a pencil held against his teeth. A month later, Lucasz, too, was dead.[21]

By May 19, Hemingway was back in the United States. Between this date and his departure again on August 14 he was extremely busy. He had accepted an invitation to speak before the general assembly of the forthcoming Writers' Congress. With this out of the way he prepared the sound-track for *The Spanish Earth*, working with Ivens throughout. By July 8, the film was ready and that evening, on invitation from the White House, Ivens and Hemingway showed the film to President and Mrs. Roosevelt. Later showings brought thousands of dollars in voluntary contributions to Loyalist Spain, and the public release came in New York in August. The brawl with Max Eastman on August 11 in the office of Maxwell Perkins was a comic interlude.[22] Three days later Hemingway sailed back to the tragedy.

On this second visit (August 14, 1937–January 28, 1938) he found that the third act of the tragedy had moved well along. "Où sont les amis d'antan?" he might now have asked himself, except that he already knew. Lucasz and Heilbrun were dead and buried; Regler, wounded by a pound and a half of steel which un-

[21] Hemingway's preface to Regler, *Great Crusade,* pp. vii–x.

[22] For a dispassionate account of what happened in the office of Maxwell Perkins on the fifth floor at 597 Fifth Avenue on August 11, 1937, see the *New York Times* for August 14 (p. 15), August 15 (p. 31), and August 16 (p. 21). Of comic interest is an item in the catalogue of the House of Books, Ltd., *First Editions of Modern Authors with a Notable Hemingway Collection,* New York, n.d., p. 40. A copy of Max Eastman's *Art and the Life of Action,* New York, 1934, is there offered for $75. According to the note, this damaged copy (lacking pp. 7–84) shows on p. 95 a spot caused by contact "with Mr. Eastman's nose when Mr. Hemingway struck him with it in a gesture of disapproval of the critical essay 'Bull in the Afternoon.' " In the lower right hand corner is a presentation inscription in Hemingway's hand, "For Arnold [Gingrich] from Papa [Hemingway]," witnessed by the signature of Maxwell Perkins, August 12, 1937.

covered his kidneys and exposed the spinal cord, lived to be put in a French concentration camp after the Spanish war was over. Madrid itself, "the capital of the world," was a tangle of bitter and cynical intrigue. If the winter and spring of 1937 had been the golden age of the International Brigades, now was the winter of their discontent.

This second trip produced *The Fifth Column*. Despite its historical interest, it is a bad play. Written in the Hotel Florida in a dollar-a-day room (low price: high danger) exposed to the German batteries on Garabitas Hill, the play was completed and sent out of the country late in December 1937, just before the taking of Teruel. It sought to present Hemingway's tough-minded apprehension of the state of things in Madrid that fall. Civilians were dying in the daily bombardments, food was becoming scarcer, hopes of lifting the siege were growing dim, and the malignant growth of treason operated deep in the city. By comparison and in retrospect, the spring of 1937 had been gay.

Whatever its dramatic shortcomings, *The Fifth Column* was an attempt to draw the actual Madrid of the fall of 1937 as it might have appeared in the uncensored despatches of a very objective war correspondent. Like the film, the play showed that war is hell. Unlike the film, the play showed that at some level and out of necessity, war is waged by demons. Though still nominally sympathetic to the Republic, *The Fifth Column* could hardly be described as a vehicle for Loyalist propaganda. When he published it in 1938 (before the end of the war), Hemingway answered those "fanatical defenders of the Spanish Republic" who protested that his play did not sufficiently emphasize "the nobility and dignity of the Spanish people." This was a play about the regrettable necessity of fanaticism. It was not intended to show nobility and dignity. To present any adequate idea of the complex Spanish temperament or the even more complex Spanish predicament would require many plays and many novels. *The Fifth Column*, meanwhile, was in the nature of an on-the-spot report, and a prediction of things to come. Hemingway did not pretend that it was much more than that.[23]

[23] See Hemingway's preface to *First 49*, New York, 1938, for a short account of the composition of the play and of the author's views on his

The background action of *The Fifth Column* is, in the play, what it was in the cellars of Madrid in 1937, a cloak-and-pistol, spy-and-counter-spy struggle of the most ruthless and melodramatic kind. In the foreground of the play, however, are two of Hemingway's familiar oppositions: home against war, and the lover against the lonely and essentially womanless worker. The hero is an Anglo-American soldier of fortune named Philip Rawlings. Ostensibly a blasé war-correspondent more given to playboying than to workhorsing, he is secretly a Republican agent in the fight against fascist infiltration. Though his job sometimes nauseates him, he believes that he understands its importance. He performs creditably and coldly. His human sensibilities are stirred, however, by an American named Dorothy Bridges. While she plays at being a war-correspondent, she too has secret plans: to marry Philip. One might construe her name as a pun. She bridges the gap back to the past, the years before fascism turned imperialistic, and when man's inhumanity to man was at least somewhat less spectacular than at present. "Her name," says Hemingway, "might also have been Nostalgia."

Philip's choice is between home and war—leaving Madrid with the girl or continuing to fight fascism. "If the play has a moral," writes Hemingway, "it is that people who work for certain organizations have very little time for home life." Without concurring in the politics or G.P.U. methods of the organization he serves (and he resembles Robert Jordan in that respect), Philip chooses to stay on in Madrid. In the closing scene he sums up the kind of life he might conceivably live with Dorothy Bridges:

"A thousand breakfasts . . . on trays in the thousand fine mornings of the next three years. . . . Auteuil steeplechasing . . . and nip back into the bar for a champagne cocktail and ride back in to dinner at La Rue's and weekends go to shoot pheasants in the Sologne. . . . And fly out to Nairobi and the old Ma-

---

material. "While I was writing the play," he says (p. v), "the Hotel Florida . . . was struck by more than thirty high explosive shells. So if it is not a good play perhaps that is what is the matter with it." His view of the play in November 1951 was that it is probably the most unsatisfactory thing he ever wrote. After much bad luck and several false starts, the play was adapted by Benjamin Glaser and produced by the Theatre Guild in New York in the winter of 1940.

thaiga Club . . . [or] . . . to Lamu where the long white beach is, with the dhows beached on their sides, and the wind in the palms at night. . . . Or . . . Malindi where you can surfboard on the beach . . . [or] the Sans Souci in Havana . . . to dance in the Patio. . . ."

Sans-Souci is the word for it. Dorothy wants to know why they can't visit these places together. But they are all behind Philip like a distant past. "Where I go now I go alone, or with others who go there for the same reason I go." This is the region of man at work, man without woman. Rawlings, soldier of fortune, has given up the pursuit of happiness for the pursuit of enemies of liberty. "We're in for fifty years of undeclared wars," he tells Comrade Max, "and I've signed up for the duration."

Hemingway is not, of course, to be confused with Rawlings. As an artist whose books had been banned in Fascist Italy, and as the friend of many honest Spaniards who had suffered heavily in try-ing to inaugurate and consolidate the Republic, he had personal reasons for hating fascism. Russian-style communism was scarcely better, though friends of the Spanish Republic, once the war broke out, had no choice but to work with this wing of the popular front coalition. But the writer's problem was different from that of Philip Rawlings. Whatever happened to soldiers of fortune during a half-century of undeclared wars, Hemingway's obligation was still to tell the truth as he saw it.

To learn the truth he made two more extended visits to Spain. The third trip began on March 19, 1938. When he returned for the summer on May 31, he told American reporters that the Loy-alists would win, though they were now clearly on the defensive. Privately, however, he must have known that they were doomed. Too much of Spain had fallen to Franco and company. Too many foreign powers were pouring in men and material on the wrong side. Fifth columns were at work in major cities. The Madrileños were starving. By far the gloomiest trip of all was the fourth, be-ginning September first. That winter saw the collapse. Barcelona fell late in January, and Madrid followed at the end of March.

One had no feeling of tragic catharsis when the curtain came down on Act III of Spain's tragedy. You could already hear them shifting the scenery in preparation for the gigantic epilogue.

III. PARTISAN

The publication of *For Whom the Bell Tolls* on October 21, 1940, raised again (as Freeman had raised it in 1937) the question of Hemingway's political colors. Once more, as in the 1930's, certain critics failed to take his position as artist sufficiently into account. Mr. Edmund Wilson, for example, referred (quite erroneously) to Hemingway's "Stalinism." Hemingway flatly denies the allegation: "I had no Stalinist period." To Mr. Edwin Burgum, on the other hand, *For Whom the Bell Tolls* seemed to offer evidence that Hemingway was a fascist in spite of himself. Such claims stood at the extremes.[24]

One of the editors of *Time* magazine hailed the story of Robert Jordan as the work of a great and sensitive artist who had now safely recovered from the Red rash.[25] In spite of the compliment at the beginning of the sentence, it ended with a statement which still misrepresented Hemingway's position. He had never caught the Marxist measles. His devotion to truth in art was too effective a means of self-immunization. He knew that to propagandize is to lie, and that the complications which accompany lying may turn a simple rash to a fatal disease. He was immunized, so to speak, by esthetic principle, even if he had not been immunized by lengthy study of the European scene.

He had long since declared against the writer's making a career of politics. But to describe the effect of political forces on the individual life was quite another matter. Where the finger or the fist of power brings pressure on the human being, the artist may

[24] For Mr. Wilson's reference to Hemingway's "Stalinism" see McCaffery, *Ernest Hemingway: The Man and His Work,* p. 256. Hemingway has, it is alleged, "largely sloughed off his Stalinism" and reverted "to seeing events in terms of individuals pitted against specific odds." Hemingway denied the implication, EH to CB, 4/1/51. Burgum's essay is in McCaffery, pp. 308–328, and is generally inaccurate. Among the pejorative judgments on *FWBT* is Alfred Kazin's. He calls this novel "among the least of Hemingway's works." McCaffery, p. 202. Maxwell Geismar said of *FWBT* that it "remains inchoate in its comprehension of the central social issues of our time." McCaffery, p. 186. Malcolm Cowley, on the other hand, agrees with the judgment of the present writer that *FWBT* is Hemingway's best novel.

[25] *Time* 36 (October 21, 1940), p. 95.

legitimately move to his work. This was the situation with the old man at a bridge across the Ebro on Easter Sunday 1938. In his lone retreat from San Carlos, this old Spaniard had been obliged to abandon a cat, two goats, and eight pigeons. He was concerned for their welfare.

"What politics have you?" asked Hemingway.

"I am without politics," said the Spaniard. "I am seventy-six years old. I have come twelve kilometres now and I think I can go no further."

Because of the weather, the fascist air force was neither bombing nor strafing that day. This fact, together with the probability that the abandoned cat, at least, could look out for itself, was the grand total of the old man's Easter luck.[26]

One displaced person in the spring of 1938 helped to dramatize for Hemingway the artist the predicament of the Spanish people. About the middle of March 1939 he began to write his great novel on the predicament of the Spanish people during their Civil War. He chose as his focal point a group of Republican partisans, drawn from many parts of Spain, and living under very primitive conditions in a cave on the high forested slopes of the Sierra de Guadarramas sixty miles northwest of besieged Madrid and behind the fascist lines. The time he chose was the sixty-eight-hour period between Saturday afternoon and Tuesday noon of the last week of May 1937. He worked on the book steadily for a period of eighteen months, rewriting it every day and doing the final revisions on galley proof. When his labors were over he had written the great book about the Spanish Civil War. One could not call it a book "without politics." Yet it was important to point out that the politics had been dramatically embodied in a work of fiction whose moral values transcended political affiliations.[27]

---

[26] First 49, p. 177. Mr. Kazin suggests, quite rightly, that "it was in something of this spirit" (i.e. of "Old Man at the Bridge") that Hemingway wrote FWBT.

[27] Hemingway's progress with his novel may be summarized for the record. By March 25, 1939, he had done about 15,000 words. On May 10, he was still going well, averaging 700–1000 words daily. At this time he reiterated to Perkins that the thing to do with a novel was to finish it, as the thing to do with a war was to win it. By July 10, his MS stood at 56,000 words (14 chapters); and by July 26, 64,000. He spent the summer in the west, working steadily, and by October 27 had 90,000 words. He

The driving emotion behind *For Whom the Bell Tolls* is Hemingway's sense of the betrayal of the Spanish people. Not only were they "killed in vast numbers, starved out, deprived of weapon's" but they were also "betrayed." [28] Worst of all was the betrayal. In a decade of notable betrayals the events in Spain between 1936 and 1939 dwarfed the betrayals of the Abyssinians and the Czechs. The nature of the betrayal of the Spanish people was complex in the extreme. What had chiefly caused it—internal cancer or rape by international hoodlums? The intervention of foreign powers was clearly an important factor in the prolongation of the war and the ultimate fascist victory. The wanton destruction of Guernica—an excellent example of betrayal—was evidently undertaken as a test of German bombing equipment. Hemingway's *Spanish Earth* commentary was quite possibly correct in maintaining that the Army insurrection which opened the war could have been put down in six weeks if German and Italian aid had not been made available to Franco's professionals.

Hemingway's own perspective on the fascist-communist struggle, which had been going on sporadically throughout Europe since the close of World War I, might have indicated a kind of

now told Perkins that the book was designed to contain what people with party affiliations could never write, or even perhaps know, or (if they knew) allow themselves to think. He was then on the point of writing a "part about Madrid" (possibly the present Chapter 18, where Madrid material is inserted as a flashback).

Chapter 23 was finished on January 18, 1940, in Havana. About this time he told Perkins that while under arms he was faithful and loyal to his side, but that, once a war was over, he was a writer—not a Catholic writer or a Party writer or anything but a writer. February 18 found him in the midst of the El Sordo story (Chapter 27). By April 6 he was well into Chapter 33, and thought briefly of *The Undiscovered Country* as a title. By April 22, however, he had settled on *For Whom the Bell Tolls* (Donne's devotion, located in *The Oxford Book of English Prose*, p. 171).

Late in May the end was in sight. He finished Chapter 40 on May 21 and ten days later was in the midst of Chapter 42. Between early June and July 12 he finished Chapter 43 (the last) and worked through his manuscript. For the next two weeks, as copy began to go to the printer, he continued reworking, chapter by chapter. The book was in galley proof by August 13. On September 10, he air-mailed the final 18 galleys from Sun Valley, Idaho, to New York. The total time for writing and revision was thus almost exactly eighteen months.

[28] Hemingway's preface to Regler, *Great Crusade*, p. vii.

tragic inevitability to foreign intervention in Spain's internal troubles. Yet these troubles had been serious before the foreign powers moved in, as Hemingway had duly noted in 1933. The outbreak of the war did not suddenly make an efficient machine from a somewhat inefficient and internally divided republican bureaucracy. Nor was it likely that the native Spanish conservatives would reject the advances of their foreign allies. Any genuinely true picture of the Spanish struggle would need somehow to embody all of these considerations, and to bring them to dramatic focus in the lives of a group of people whose backgrounds and present mode of behavior would fairly represent the total betrayal of Spain.

As he worked through the complexities of his task, Hemingway was sustained by a belief he had long held to: the job of the artist is not to judge but to understand. No matter how hard it may be to believe it in our political age, there is such a thing as the artistic "neutrality" of one who puts humanity above politics and art above propaganda. What Melville said of Captain Vere, the hero of *Billy Budd*, is applicable to the artist Hemingway. "There had got to be established in him some positive convictions which . . . would abide in him essentially unmodified so long as his intelligent part remained unimpaired. . . . His settled convictions were as a dyke against those invading waters of novel opinion, social, political, or otherwise, which carried away as in a torrent no few minds in those days." [29] Hemingway's "dyke" is a belief in the artist's obligation to truth and to art, and to humanity in its extra-political dimension.

For Whom the Bell Tolls offers many examples of the author's determination to maintain that balance without which art may degenerate into propaganda. One of the most conspicuous is Pilar's account of the massacre of the leading citizens of a town near Avila by Pablo and his mob. Pilar has the artist's observational and almost clinical interest in how each of the fascists will die. Deeper than this interest runs her sense of the humanity of the killed and the strange furious mixture of bestiality and humanity among the killers. She watches the spectacle with a cold fascination. But her humanity is revealed in the sick disgust which

[29] Melville, *Billy Budd, Foretopman,* Chapter 6.

assails her from time to time, as it troubles some of the individuals in the mob itself. One finds explicit recognition of how far out of the line of right human action this mob-murder is. But there is also a strong implicit suggestion of the criminal neglect, the inhuman apathy which has allowed the social situation in the villages of Spain to deteriorate so far that such mob action is now the sole recourse of the underdogs. After the massacre, says Pilar, "I went back inside the room and I sat there and I did not wish to think, for that was the worst day of my life until one other day." The "other day" was the day of reckoning. It came seventy-two hours later when the Fascists took the town.[30]

Pilar has led a hard life and is as tough as an old eagle. Yet the heart still beats for humankind even when the head coldly admits the need for violent activity against the enemy. Pilar's sentiments find many echoes among the more sympathetic characters of the novel. When they are put together, they show clearly that, unlike Picasso's "Guernica," *For Whom the Bell Tolls* is not a study in black and white. It is a study of the betrayal of the Spanish people—both by what lay within them and what had been thrust upon them—and it is presented with that special combination of sympathetic involvement and hard-headed detachment which is the mark of the genuine artist. One could not rightly call the novel bipartisan. Yet it is partisan in a larger way than the modern use of the term ordinarily suggests. Its partisanship is in the cause of humanity.

The artist behind his dyke of conviction must likewise be able to understand the nature of these minds which the torrent of opinion carries along in its sweep. Hemingway's grasp of the motivations which strengthened and united, but also split, the extreme leftists is well illustrated in Jordan's contrast between the two communisms of Madrid.[31] One was symbolized in Velázquez 63, the palace which served as headquarters for the International Brigades. Here was the almost puritanical, religious-crusader's side of party feeling. It gave its adherents something like "the feeling you expected to have and did not have when you made your

---

[30] Pilar's account of the massacre occurs on pp. 99–129.
[31] *FWBT*, pp. 234–235. Cf. Jordan's view (p. 230): "He liked to know how it really was, not how it was supposed to be."

first communion. . . . It gave you a part in something that you could believe in wholly and completely and in which you felt an absolute brotherhood with the others who were engaged in it." The religious reference emphasizes how far this secular substitute for religion—a substitute with its own propaganda-built hagiology and its own liturgy—had been able to go in capturing the devotions of foreign idealists.

Six months of the fighting effectively dissipated such devotions for any who kept their eyes and ears open. The idealist involved was shortly aware of the other symbol—the hotel called Gaylord's where the Russian directors of the Republican movement had congregated. Gaylord's symbolized the cold, practical, hard-headed, cynical ruthlessness of the Comintern mind, completely unsentimental and in no way deceived by the propaganda which it daily originated and disseminated. A part of the struggle in Spain lay in the attempt of the idealist to keep his devoutness whole in the face of the actualistic education he got at Gaylord's.

Another of the tensions at work under the surface of Spain's tragedy is dramatized through the boy Joaquín, one of the republican partisans on El Sordo's chancre-like hilltop. This is the conflict between the Catholic faith and the secular pseudo-religion of the communists. At eighteen, Joaquín is just old enough in 1937 to have been raised under the wing of the Church, and just young enough to have suffered irreparably when the fascists shot his parents in Valladolid. Joaquín is imbued now with party doctrine. He especially reverences La Pasionaria, the secularist Joan of Arc in Marxist Spain.

While El Sordo's men prepare their hilltop position, Joaquín admiringly quotes La Pasionaria's slogan: *Resistir y fortificar es vencer*—to hold out and to fortify is to win. The boy is obliged to endure some good-natured raillery from those of his companions to whom such propagandist watchwords are a dirty joke. Yet through the early stages of the fight on the hilltop La Pasionaria sustains him well. Then the planes come. Joaquín has not considered the vulnerability of even Pasionaria-built fortifications to attack from the air. While the drone of the fascist bombers grows in intensity, Joaquín, heavy with dread, begins to invoke

La Pasionaria once again. This time her words stick in his dry throat.

Then he shifted suddenly into "Hail Mary, full of grace, the Lord is with thee; Blessed art thou among women and Blessed is the fruit of thy womb, Jesus. Holy Mary, Mother of God, pray for us sinners now and at the hour of our death. Amen, Holy Mary, Mother of God," he started, then he remembered quick as the roar came now unbearably and started an act of contrition racing in it, "Oh my God, I am heartily sorry for having offended thee who art worthy of all my love. . . ."

When the explosions of the fascist bombs roll under the boy at the very moment of his losing consciousness, he is still repeating the petitional phrase, "Now and at the hour of our death." La Pasionaria is for other times.[32]

La Pasionaria is for bringing passionately inspired news of Marxist victories. She is the occasion for a fine travesty on sentimental propagandists like the *Izvestia* correspondent at Gaylord's hotel.

"She was here with the news and was in such a state of radiant exultation as I have never seen. The truth of the news shone from her face. That great face . . ." says the correspondent happily. . . . "It was one of the greatest moments of the war to me when I heard the report in that great voice where pity, compassion and truth are blended. Goodness and truth shine from her as from a true saint of the people. Not for nothing is she called La Pasionaria."

"Not for nothing," says the other correspondent in a dull voice. "You better write it for *Izvestia* now, before you forget that last beautiful lead." [33]

In the welter of opposed hatreds and in the company of sentimental mystics, the artist must keep his human and moral values unimpaired. Of the native Spaniards in the book, none better exemplifies the right human norm than Anselmo, Jordan's sixty-eight-year-old guide and friend. Other members of Pablo's band show the range of political and moral attitudes across the popular

[32] *FWBT*, p. 134.
[33] *FWBT*, pp. 357–358.

front. At one extreme is the blood-thirst of Pablo, not unlike that of the moonfaced Cuban revolutionist in *To Have and Have Not*. Near him, though at a higher level, stands the brave, relentless, fanatical hater, Agustín, who fiercely says that he would like to swim ten leagues in a broth made from the *cojones* of all the fascists.[34] At the opposite extreme stands, or rather lolls, the irresponsible paganism of the gypsy Rafael. But Anselmo willingly endures discomfort out of loyalty to Jordan's trust, as Rafael would obviously never do. And unlike Pablo or Agustín, Anselmo, with the wisdom of his years, still hates killing even while he admits that it is necessary.

Anselmo's important function is to serve as a yardstick of human values, as Kent does in *King Lear*. "That we should win the war and shoot nobody," he fiercely cries. "That we should govern justly and that all should participate in the benefits according as they have striven for them. And that those who have fought against us should be educated to see their error." The Republic must win and Anselmo will fight for the Republic. Yet much that he must do cuts cruelly across the absolute Christian grain of this admirable old man. With Anselmo as a norm, the tragedy of Spain shows all the darker.[35]

Like Anselmo, Robert Jordan is capable of working for a cause without allowing its heretical errors to eat their way like acid into his deeper convictions. Knowing the inside of both Velázquez 63 and the hotel called Gaylord's, Jordan can qualify as the educated man who is in no way "sucked in." Working efficiently as a dynamiter with the Republican guerrillas, loving Spain, hating fascism, sympathizing with the people who have been and are being betrayed, Jordan still manages to be temperate without being at all tepid. His brain is neither dominated nor deceived by the propagandistic. He remains the free man, the man not taken in, the man doing the necessary job but also making the necessary mental reservations.

Jordan's soliloquy—as he listens from below to the hilltop bat-

<hr />

[34] *FWBT*, p. 286.

[35] *FWBT*, p. 285. Cf. Jordan's comment (p. 287) that Anselmo is "a Christian. Something very rare in Catholic countries." And see the excellent Chapter 15 (pp. 191–201), containing Anselmo's soliloquy on the sin of killing.

tle in which El Sordo's partisans die—is a key passage in this connection. He reflects that he is in love with Maria, even though "there isn't supposed to be any such thing as love in a purely materialistic conception of society." Then he catches himself. Since when did he really entertain any such conception?

"Never. And you never could have. You're not a real Marxist and you know it. You believe in Liberty, Equality, and Fraternity. You believe in Life, Liberty, and the Pursuit of Happiness. Don't ever kid yourself with too much dialectics. They are for some but they are not for you. You have to know them in order not to be a sucker. You have put many things in abeyance to win a war. If this war is lost all of those things are lost. But afterwards you can discard what you do not believe in. There is plenty you do not believe in and plenty that you do believe in." [36]

Robert Jordan is with, but not of, the communists. For the duration of the war he is under communist discipline because they offer "the best discipline and the soundest and sanest for the prosecution of the [Spanish] war." [37] This is simple common sense, just as (though Robert Jordan did not live to see it) it was probably common sense for the Allies to fight side by side with the Russians in the second World War—in order to win it. But where the communist dialectic runs contrary to the older dialectics of the French and the American Revolutions, Jordan will remain as an essential nonconformist, a free man not taken in, though doing his part in the perennial attempts which free men must make if the concept of freedom is to last.

IV. THE EPIC GENRE

The structural form of *For Whom the Bell Tolls* has been conceived with care and executed with the utmost brilliance. The form is that of a series of concentric circles with the all-important bridge in the middle. The great concentration which Hemingway achieves is partly dependent on his skill in keeping attention

[36] *FWBT,* p. 305. With this compare Willard Thorp's remark: "Where does the democratic faith live and speak if not in the pages of *For Whom the Bell Tolls?*" See Margaret Denny and William H. Gilman, eds., *The American Writer and the European Tradition,* Minneapolis, 1950, p. 100.

[37] *FWBT,* p. 163.

focussed on the bridge while projecting the reader imaginatively far beyond that center of operations. Chapter One immediately establishes the vital strategic importance of the bridge in the coming action. Frequent allusions to the bridge keep it in view through the second chapter, and in Chapter Three Jordan goes with Anselmo to make a preliminary inspection. From that time onwards until its climactic destruction, the bridge continues to stand unforgettably as the focal point in the middle of an ever widening series of circles.

The brilliance of execution becomes apparent when the reader stands in imagination on the flooring of the bridge and looks in any direction. He will see his horizons lifting by degrees towards a circumference far beyond the Guadarrama mountains. For the guerrillas' central task, the blowing of the bridge, is only one phase of a larger operation which Hemingway once called "the greatest holding action in history." Since the battle strategy which requires the bridge to be destroyed is early made available to the reader, he has no difficulty in seeing its relation to the next circle outside, where a republican division under General Golz prepares for an attack. The general's attack, in turn, is enough to suggest the outlines of the whole civil war, while the Heinkel bombers and Fiat pursuit planes which cut across the circle —foreign shadows over the Spanish earth—extend our grasp one more circle outwards to the trans-European aspect of the struggle. The outermost ring of the circle is nothing less than the great globe itself. Once the Spanish holding operation is over, the wheel of fire will encompass the earth. The bridge, therefore —such is the structural achievement of this novel—becomes the hub on which the "future of the human race can turn." [38] Wherever the reader moves along the circumferences of the various circles, all radial roads lead to and from this bridge.

If the reader of *For Whom the Bell Tolls* is hardly cramped for space, he is also free to range in time. Jordan's action, particularized though it is, has also a significance *sub specie aeterni-*

---

[38] *FWBT,* p. 43. Cf. Sinclair Lewis's view that *FWBT* crystallizes "the world revolution that began long ago . . . and that will not cease till the human world has either been civilized or destroyed." Lewis, introd., Limited Editions Club reprint of *FWBT,* Princeton University Press, 1942, p. ix.

tatis. The timelessness of the central event invites the reader to compare it with all those other small and local holding actions which are stuck like gems in the web of history and tend to assume an importance out of all proportion to their size. One civil war easily suggests another, as in Jordan's memories of his grandfather who bore arms in America's war of the rebellion. Behind that, in the long perspective, is the bridge where the republican (and anti-monarchist) "peasants" of Concord fired the shot heard round the world. On a bridge across the Tiber young Horatius delayed briefly the advance of a superior force. Still farther back is the action of Leonidas against the Persian host at the hot gates of Thermopylae. The terrain and the odds were not, after all, far different from those of Robert Jordan. There is even the prediction, comparable to Pilar's, that Leonidas will die, and there is a lone Persian cavalryman who comes, like the fascist horseman in Hemingway, to reconnoitre the mountain pass. Jordan could never complain with Eliot's Gerontion that he had not fought at "the hot gates." His bridge is at the center of the history of holding actions; and although his problem is small in scale, it is so conceived and projected as to suggest a struggle of epical dimensions.

In making such a claim for Hemingway's novel, one must reckon with his own assertion that "all bad writers are in love with the epic." Even a few gifted writers have fallen into the error of attempting too much or going about it in the wrong way. The conscious striving for an epic magnitude, as in some of Whitman's poetry and much of Wolfe's prose, may reduce the writing to rhetoric and enlarge the people to set-piece characters whose resemblance to human beings is merely coincidental. There is also the danger that the struggle for the cosmic may backslide into the comic. The grand manner too easily inflates to the grandiose; good sense may be sacrificed to size; quantity may be mistaken for quality; and what was meant to be great will become simply gross.

As a prose epic of the Spanish people, *For Whom the Bell Tolls* commits none of these errors. Indeed the novel is a living example of how, in modern times, the epic quality must probably be projected. The failure of certain modern practitioners of the epic manner rests perhaps primarily upon ignorance of the uses of synecdoche, the device by which a part can be made to function for the whole, and the fact to gain an emblematic power without the loss of its native particularity. Hemingway's war novel, rich as it is in symbolic extensions, is somewhere near a synecdochist's triumph.

What elements of the epic manner may be successfully adapted to modern needs? Despite the obvious gap between Spain and Ilium, the student of the epic may find part of his answer in considering the Homeric parallel. A primitive setting, simple food and wine, the care and use of weapons, the sense of imminent danger, the emphasis on masculine prowess, the presence of varying degrees of courage and cowardice, the rude barbarisms on both sides, the operation of certain religious and magical superstitions, the warrior codes—these, surely, are common ties between the two sets of protagonists. Jordan is not to be scorned as the type of Achilles, and one can recognize in Pablo the rude outlines of a debased and sulking Ajax. Pilar the gypsy, though she reads the lifeline in Jordan's palm instead of consulting the shape and color of animal entrails, makes the consciousness of the supernatural an operative factor.

Nor should the technical comparisons be overlooked. One of the most interesting of these is the intentionally heightened language. Mr. Edward Fenimore has published a valuable essay on the subject. He remarks, for instance, on "the Elizabethan tone" of a number of phrases and sentences.

"That such a tone should haunt Hemingway's pages is [he goes on] inevitable. His tale has much of the epic in its breadth, in the plain fact that his characters mean more than themselves alone, the action they are engaged upon [being] unmistakably a culminating point pushed up by profound national or . . . universal forces. In the Elizabethan, the English possesses an epic language, and it is into the forms of this language that Hemingway, through the very nature of the world he is creating . . . constantly passes." [39]

[39] "English and Spanish in *For Whom the Bell Tolls*," McCaffery, pp. 205–220. See especially pp. 212 and 217. In spite of his criticism of Melville (*GHOA*, p. 20) for the over-use of rhetoric as a substitute for ob-

Yet, as Fenimore observes, this language is carefully tempered. A purely colloquial modern English and an English which belongs in its essence to the King James version of the Bible are brought together to mutual advantage. One example is a brief interchange between the rough-spoken Agustín and the supremely dignified Fernando—who is, incidentally, one of Hemingway's best-drawn minor characters.

"Where the hell are you going?" Agustín asked the grave little man as he came up.

"To my duty," Fernando said with dignity.

"Thy duty," said Agustín mockingly. "I besmirch the milk of thy duty. . . ." [40]

Several of Hemingway's short stories had made a similar collocation of the old and dignified with the new and crass. In "The Gambler, The Nun, and The Radio," for example, the contrast is used to underscore the humor of character. Now, however, with his temperamental sensitivity to the tone of language, and an intuitive feel for what would constitute the proper blend of ancient and modern idiom in the conduct of key scenes, whether they were comic or not, Hemingway developed a language suitable to his epic purposes. The masculine vigor in the march of the narrative comes about, not alone from the author's skill in the unfolding of events but also through his responsiveness to language values.

Outside the technical aspects of language one finds an over-all seriousness of conception which, though high enough to meet even Arnold's stringent requirements, does not preclude rough humor and soldierly badinage. As a means of giving depth to his characterizations, Homer knew and used (if indeed he did not invent) the device of the flashback. As for synecdoche, Homer

---

servation, Hemingway had now reached the point where an admixture of Marlovian and Shakespearean language served him in the elevation of language tone towards the epic level. Yet *FWBT* never falls into rhetoric in the expository passages, as happens frequently in *Moby-Dick*. The Elizabethan-Jacobean tone in *FWBT* is communicated exclusively through dialogue, and even there is carefully "corrected" towards modernity by the intermixture of the contemporary *lingua communis* with the slang removed. Hemingway had been speaking Spanish for 15 years, and his ear was awake to its tempos and its delicate or indelicate formalities.

[40] *FWBT*, p. 92.

was very far from limiting his range of significance by carefully centering his attention on the action before Troy. All bad writers may love the epic. A few good ones, working somewhat after the fashion of Hemingway, can succeed in keeping the epic genre in a state of good health by adapting transferable elements to the needs and expectations of the modern reader.

The principle of characterization-in-depth is strong in *For Whom the Bell Tolls*—more so than in any of Hemingway's previous work. If touch-and-go is the mark of the apprentice and the journeyman, stay-and-see may well be one of the attributes of the master. Even though the qualities which distinguished the younger writer still serve Hemingway at forty, he is now ready to move beyond them. Without, for example, sacrificing the value of *suggestion* (where the reader is required to supply his own imaginative clothing for an idea nakedly projected), Hemingway has come round to an appreciation of the value of *ingestion*. This signifies a bearing within, a willingness to put in, and to allow to operate within the substance of a piece of writing, much that formerly would have been excluded in favor of suggestion.

The result of this willingness is a notable gain in richness and depth without sacrifice of the values inherent in the principle of suggestiveness. What Hemingway allows us to know of Pilar's past, for example, enriches, activates, and deepens our sense of her vital performance in the present. The willingness, even the eagerness, to invent that past, to stay and see how it informs the present, is a mark of the transition achieved by the fully mature artist in Hemingway. The will to report has given place to the willingness to invent, though the values of the will to report have not been sacrificed in the process. There were formerly only limited vistas back through time. Now the full panoply of time past is at work in time present. This mode of operation is likewise habitual to the epic genre.

V. THE PATTERN OF TRAGEDY

If *For Whom the Bell Tolls* is a kind of epic, it is above all a tragic epic. Like the *Iliad*, it may be seen as a study in doom. Madrid, like Troy, was fated to fall. Seventeen months of hind-

sight on the Spanish war helped to mature in Hemingway a feeling that the republican defeat had been virtually inevitable.

"The Spanish civil war was really lost, of course, [he wrote
in 1940] when the Fascists took Irun in the late summer of 1936.
But in a war you can never admit, even to yourself, that it is
lost. Because when you admit it is lost you are beaten." [41]

Hemingway's choice of the early summer of 1937 as the time
of Jordan's action thus takes on special importance. He wanted
a period deep enough into the war so that the possibility of republican defeat could be a meaningful psychological force. But
the time must also be far enough removed from the end of the
war so that some of his people could still believe in a republican
victory. The struggle could not seem to be hopeless. Yet, as a
study in doom, the novel must early isolate and dramatize those
adverse powers and power-failures which would ultimately combine to defeat the Spanish republic.

Robert Jordan's first sight of Pablo gives him an insight into
the nature of one power-failure. No republican, at the beginning
of the movement, was more in command of himself or the situation than Pablo. Now the guerrilla leader is so far gone in defeat-
ist "sadness" and moral cowardice as almost to doom in advance
any undertaking in which he is to play a part.

"I don't like that sadness [Robert Jordan thought]. That sadness is bad. That's the sadness they get before they quit or before they betray. That is the sadness that comes before the sell-
out." [42]

Pablo is a specific Judas, as his stealing of the detonator will
later show. But he is also a recognizable symbol for the general
canker of defeatism, gnawing the tissues of republican morale
from within, and leading to the larger betrayal.

A second internal danger is the inefficiency of the Republican
bureaucracy. A third is an aspect of the Spanish temperament.
One gets the impression that a radical inefficiency stretches all the
way from the higher echelons in Madrid down to the gypsy
Rafael, who is so irresponsible that he runs off to shoot rabbits
when he should be standing guard near Pablo's cave. The Rus-

[41] Hemingway's preface to Regler, *Great Crusade,* p. vii.
[42] *FWBT,* p. 12.

sian General Golz, only half-believing that his attack will not be doomed to failure before it even starts, points up the larger difficulties.

"They are never my attacks [says Golz]. I make them. But they are not mine. The artillery is not mine. I must put in for it. I have never been given what I ask for even when they have it to give. That is the least of it. There are other things. You know how those people are. It is not necessary to go into all of it. Always there is something. Always some one will interfere." [43]

Tangled in red tape like Laocoon in serpents, Golz is not free enough to prosecute a war successfully. The Rafaels of the republican side are too free, and too irresponsible. Bureaucracy and temperament, two more internal foes of the republic, help to fix the doom.

But the most awesome symbol of doom is the air-power of the foreign enemy. All the Spaniards hate it, as they hate the foreigners for interfering in their civil war. When the fascist planes roar over the mountain hide-out, it is always in threes, like the weird sisters, or in those multiples of three with which practitioners of black magic used to conjure.

"The three passed and then came nine more, flying much higher in the minute, pointed formations of threes and threes and threes . . . He could still hear the receding drone. . . . By now they're well beyond the pass with Castile all yellow and tawny beneath them now in the morning . . . and the shadows of the Heinkels moving over the land as the shadows of sharks pass over a sandy floor of the ocean." [44]

When the planes return, Jordan revises his simile into something even more sinister. They have the shape but not the motion of sharks. "They move like no thing that has ever been. They move like mechanized doom." [45] It is by three such planes that

[43] *FWBT*, p. 5. Compare Golz's almost elegiac acceptance of reality, as he speaks over the telephone to Duval at the other end of the novel, when it is known that the plan of the bridge will not work: *"Nous sommes foutus. Oui. Comme toujours. Oui. C'est dommage. Oui. . . .* No. *Rien à faire. Rien. Faut pas penser. Faut accepter. . . . Bon. Nous ferons notre petit possible." FWBT*, pp. 428–430.

[44] *FWBT*, pp. 74–76.

[45] *FWBT*, p. 87.

El Sordo's band will be wiped out at three o'clock of the following Monday afternoon.

Hemingway's linking of the modern bombers with the ancient magic-symbol of number three greatly enhances the emotional effectiveness of the plane-passage. The old epics and the great dramatic tragedies could employ supernatural agents in the full expectation that they would intensify the emotions of pity and terror in the spectator. The rise of naturalism, and the partial decay of superstition, denied the tragic artist direct access to one of his most evocative instruments. Yet within the shadowy subconscious, the perennial human capacity for fear and awe remained to be touched by any artist who could empower new symbols with old terrors.

The book touches the edge of the supernatural also by a considered use of premonition. The primary human agent is the gypsy Pilar, who is both a woman and a kind of witch, though a witch very naturalistically portrayed and very womanly in her witchhood. Her function in part is to sharpen the reader's foreboding and thus to deepen his sense of impending tragedy. Having watched Pablo's degeneration through fear, she is both too wise and too fond of Jordan to reveal that she has seen his coming death in the lines of his hand. (Like the Circean "witch" of *The Sun Also Rises,* she is a good judge of quality.) But the reader's knowledge of Jordan's coming death gives special point to the passage in which Pilar describes, with naturalistic precision, the three blended odors of the smell of death to come.

The woman-witch dialectic is marked often in the book. In this instance, the woman withholds what the witch has gloomily discovered. Her certainty that Jordan will die has motivated her in bringing the lovers together. This is done both for the therapeutic effect of a healthy love affair on Maria, and in order to give Jordan, through Maria, as much of life as three days will hold. This, one might guess, is the tender side of Pilar. But in the passage on the smell of death to come, she adopts the very tone which will arouse Jordan's doubts as to the truth of what she is saying. He doubts and he argues, and the doubting arguments divert his thoughts at least from the probability, if not from the possibility, of death. The rough railing humor of her presentation is meant to save him from a fear which might undo his resolution, or, at any rate, spoil the closing hours of his short, happy life.[46]

This entire aspect of the novel may well remind some readers of the problem which Henry James set himself in *The Wings of the Dove*—though, as always, there is little or no overt resemblance between the two books. "The idea, reduced to its essence," said James of his own major effort, "is that of a young person conscious of a great capacity for life, but early stricken and doomed, condemned to die under short respite, while also enamoured of the world." [47] A marked "capacity for life," a full acceptance and love of the world, is always a driving motive with the Hemingway hero. It grows even stronger as one moves with Hemingway's work through the nineteen-thirties. Yet Nick Adams has it, Jake Barnes has it, Frederick Henry has it. It is strong in Harry Morgan, though he is not very articulate in expressing what he feels. The love of life—the good life—gives special point to the dying reminiscences of that other Harry, the writer on safari in Africa. Yet the two men called Harry are stricken and doomed, condemned to die under short respite, as is Colonel Richard Cantwell, a lover of life, in *Across the River and Into the Trees*.

There are other premonitions in *For Whom the Bell Tolls* than those we owe to Pilar's supersensory gifts. Jordan, as a partisan soldier, must often consider that he may die at the affair of the bridge. He is compelled to recognize the possibility of death. His life among the Guadarramas may well total three-score hours and ten—seventy hours as a substitute for seventy years.[48] In the meteorological bad luck which brings an unseasonal snowfall, in Pablo's defection, and in the bombing of El Sordo, there is a discernible "pattern of tragedy" which he is too sensible to ignore. But he has also a special soldier's talent "not to ignore but to despise whatever bad endings there could be." [49] From the point of view of the reader, therefore, Jordan's predicament is some-

---

[46] *FWBT*, pp. 250–257.
[47] *Works*, New York edition, vol. 19, preface, p. v.
[48] See Jordan's soliloquy, *FWBT*, p. 166.
[49] *FWBT*, p. 393.

thing like that of the torero who knows that he may be killed but despises death and enters the ring in spite of the possibility. The knowledge, derived through Pilar, that Jordan not only *may* but *will* die gives every incident in Jordan's seventy-hour span of life the special poignancy that would be felt by a spectator who knew in advance that he was watching the last fight of a torero. Through this double perspective, Hemingway gets into his novel the very "feeling of life and death" which he was seeking when he first went to watch the Spanish bullfights.

But the idea that a sane consciousness of death will give added depth and meaning to the events of life is only one of the familiar Hemingway themes in *For Whom the Bell Tolls*. Sparing but effective use is also made of the men-without-women, the father-and-son, and the home-versus-war themes. Jordan, for example, shows a kind of spiritual relationship to Pilar in that he can be, by turns, both tender and tough-minded. In one of his aspects, he can love human beings and allow himself to become involved with them, as in his good companionship with Anselmo or his love for Maria. At the other extreme, he must be the cold-minded and detached commander, reserving part of himself in all human relationships so that the necessary job can be done. It is in this detachment that he coldly judges his companions, estimating their relative dependability and expendability, and perfecting his battle-plan in accordance with these estimates. He cannot often expand warmly; as soldier he must contract coldly within himself. "I cannot have a woman, doing what I do," he tells Maria. "But thou art my woman now." After one of their encounters, Maria observes that he is now thinking of something else than love. "Yes," Jordan says, shortly. "My work." On another occasion, talking with Pilar, the men-without-women idea emerges very clearly. "You are a very cold boy," says Pilar. Jordan disagrees. "No," says Pilar. "In the head you are very cold." Jordan replies that he is preoccupied with his work. "But you do not like the things of life?" asks Pilar. "Yes. Very much. But not to interfere with my work." It is not now a liking for hardy masculine comradeship in hunting or fishing or skiing which motivates the Hemingway hero, but a preoccupation with the work a man must do, where women have no place and may even be in the way. The morning

Jordan kills the fascist cavalryman, Maria is still beside him in the sleeping-bag. As he quickly and coldly issues orders to Anselmo and Primitivo, he is aware of Maria behind him, dressing herself under the robe. "She had no place in his life now." At the end of the book, both elements are still visible. He is the republican soldier coolly drawing a bead on the fascist Lieutenant Berrendo, and the husband covering his wife's escape.[50]

The closing scene also rounds off the father-and-son theme which has been introduced in Jordan's soliloquies at various earlier times. Jordan's grandfather fought bravely and successfully in the American Civil War. His father, like the father of Nick Adams, died by his own hand. Jordan has long since forgiven his father for the act, but he is still as ashamed of it as he is proud of his grandfather's soldierly bravery. Now, at the end of the line, as Jordan lies nearly fainting under the ballooning pain from his fractured leg, the father-grandfather opposition once more commands his mind. Suicide would be permissible under the circumstances. But the memory of his grandfather, his true spiritual ancestor, helps him to hold onto his courage and to die in combat.[51]

The significance of Maria, when she is seen in the light of such other heroines as Catherine Barkley, Marie Morgan, and even Dorothy Bridges, is finally symbolic. In the lonely alien region of the Guadarramas, she comes to stand as the image of "home." Most of Hemingway's women tend to take on this special symbolic meaning. Dorothy Bridges (a fairly unsympathetic portrait) is explicitly equated with nostalgia, a somewhat untrustworthy reminder of the comforts and the joys which are so rarely possible in a world besieged by the ideology of terror. Catherine Barkley and Marie Morgan, though in different ways, represent normal domesticity vanquished by war and by the economic struggle for survival. Similarly, Maria stands for the normal in the midst of a terrible abnormality. She has been subjected to all sorts of outrages by her fascist captors. The rape is an act of supreme brutality; only the true tenderness of Jordan, as Pilar well knows, can erase the psychological scars the fascists have left. The cut-

[50] *FWBT*, pp. 73, 161, 91, 267.
[51] *FWBT*, especially Chapter 30, pp. 334–340.

ting of Maria's hair is a symbol of her loss of normal womanhood or girlhood, just as its growing-out indicates her gradual return to balance and health.

One might argue, of course, that the normal male-female situation in Hemingway is something like what took place in the Garden of Eden just after the eating of the fruit of the tree, but before the malediction. All these Eves are as pleasurably ductile as the Adams are hirsute and sexually vigorous. Like all travesties, such a characterization would have its element of truth. But it would tend to ignore the real tenderness with which the "good women" in Hemingway are treated. The fate of the heroines is that they are almost never at home; their virtue is that the best of them carry the home-image with them wherever they go.

A fourth well-tried theme handsomely adapted to the uses of the Spanish tragedy is that of *nada*, or nothingness militant. By placing his action among the high slopes of the Sierra de Guadarramas, a clean, well-lighted place where the weather is cold and the air clear, Hemingway has achieved a kind of idyll in the midst of war, an island (like that of Nick Adams in his afternoon grove on the way to the Big Two-Hearted River) surrounded by the sinister. It is there that Maria, raped and venereally infected by fascist soldiery, is restored to health and sanity. This is a mountain fastness like Burguete in *The Sun Also Rises*, or like the priest's homeland of Abruzzi in *A Farewell to Arms*, or like the Alpine sanctuary to which Frederick and Catherine retire for their short happy life together. One sees again the lowland-versus-highland image; on the plain before Madrid the fascists are deployed, but here are high slopes, concealment, and something like the good life, a veritable island in the midst of *nada*. Still, in the words of Donne's devotion, "no man is an island." In this savage war, no mountain can serve as a permanent sanctuary. El Sordo, on his high hilltop position, finds no good life. Fascist cavalry surround it, and three fascist planes destroy it from above. Similarly, when the bridge is blown, Pablo's mountain cave becomes untenable as a refuge. The partisans plan to retreat across the war-swept lowlands to another mountain fastness in the Sierra de Gredos. But the planes of the enemy, in sinister "threes and threes and threes," can presumably come there, too. "I am tired of the

mountains," says Pilar in a moment of despondency. "In mountains there are only two directions. Down and up, and down leads
only to the road and the towns of the Fascists." And up, one might
add, leads to the foreign bombers, assaulting even the highest
and loneliest peaks.[52]

Hemingway's sense of fascism's betrayal of the Spanish people
has in fact much of the nightmare quality of Picasso's allegorical
painting. The mountain-sanctuary, an essentially private symbol
in Hemingway's earlier books, is now shown to be open to invasion
and destruction by fascist bombers, which the artist carefully
establishes as symbols of the power of evil. If one follows Picasso's
pictorial allegories through the order of composition from the
"Minotauromachy" through the "Sueño y Mentira de Franco" up
to the "Guernica," he will see how an essentially private set of
symbols is made to take on political significance. In the "Minotauromachy" of 1935, Picasso employs motifs from the bullfight
to express symbolically a struggle no doubt personal to himself
as artist and Spaniard. The "Guernica" of 1937, occasioned by
the bombing of an open Spanish city by foreign planes, regrouped
the symbols of the bull and the horse and broke the calm human
figures of the *Minotauromachy* into fragments of anguish and
fear. In one postwar interview, Picasso refused to identify the
bull-figure of the "Guernica" with fascism, though he did give
it the generic meaning of "brutality and darkness"—something
like Goya's "Nada." The horse, transfixed by a spear which has
fallen from above, is however for Picasso a specific symbol for
the Spanish people. In somewhat the same way, the destruction
of El Sordo's band on the hilltop, like the roar of Heinkel bombers above Jordan's high sanctuary, suggests the horror of brutality and darkness unleashed against a betrayed people.[53]

Among those whom fascism will betray are the artists. Robert
Jordan is not only a teacher of Spanish and a lover of Spain; he
is also a writer. As an artist he is fully aware of the threat of
fascist domination. If fascism were the kind of force which fed
upon itself, remaining relatively limited in its dimensions, Jor-

[52] *FWBT*, p. 97.
[53] See Alfred H. Barr, Jr., *Picasso: Fifty Years of His Art*, New York,
1946, p. 202.

dan's manifest duty would belong to the development of his art—
a task so huge that it takes a lifetime to accomplish. During the
years of peace, Jordan wrote one book on Spain and the Spanish people.[54] Presumably he would not be averse to doing another.
But this is not the time.

In the deeper meaning of *For Whom the Bell Tolls,* the invasion
of the high sanctuary *from above* marks a transition in the affairs
of the artist. Unless the force is stopped, it can mean the death of
art as it can mean the death of everything else the artist values
and needs. Fascism has become militant, imperialistic, and international. The artist, devoted though he must be to the development of his art, can no more ignore it than he could ignore a storm
blowing in at his study window and scattering the pages of his
work in progress. His move must be to shut the window against
the storm. Still it will not leave him alone. The lightning strikes
his house, and it is his obvious duty to save his manuscript and
put out the fire. The *blitz* is not what he asked for or what he
wanted. Since it has come, he must take arms against it, and end
it as soon as possible by opposing it. Then he can go back to his
work, if he survives.

VI. THE GREAT WHEEL

In his account of how he went about writing *The Awkward
Age,* James says that he "drew on a sheet of paper . . . the
neat figure of a circle consisting of a number of small rounds disposed at equal distances about a central object." [55] This central
object was his "situation." The small rounds disposed about it
were like a series of small searchlights centering on the situation,
and seeking to illuminate it from all sides. As often in James, the
problem of the artist was to draw, by a geometry of his own,
the limited circle in which his demonstration would transpire. If
he drew his circle well and directed his searchlights with a sufficient intensity, the human relations on which he concentrated
would "stop nowhere." [56]

[54] *FWBT,* p. 248.
[55] Henry James, *Works,* New York edition, vol. 9, preface, p. xvi.
[56] *ibid.,* vol. 1, p. vii.

The central organizing image of *For Whom the Bell Tolls* is also geometrical. We have, of course, in the chief characters, a series of smaller rounds disposed at equal distances about the central object or situation. But beyond these, and spreading out to the edge of the world, we have a whole series of concentric circles. The human relations of the war in Spain "stop nowhere,"—any more than the tragic implications of the art of the bullfight stay confined within the two hours' traffic of a particular afternoon. In fact Hemingway's novel follows an architectural plan comparable to that of a Spanish bullring, which is constructed in a series of concentric circles, so arranged that from any point one can watch the action taking place at the center.

Remembering that Picasso and Hemingway have as artists a common interest in the bullfight, and noting that their separate reactions to the Spanish Civil War produced so remarkable a set of symbolic parallels, one might expect to find Hemingway making use of symbolism derived from the bullfight. That is, one might find both the geometrical *and* the pictorial use of images. To a limited extent this happens, and as usual the pictorial images are fully justified by the psychological situation. All the native Spaniards in the book are of course well acquainted with the terminology of their national sport, as a similar group of Americans might be with that of baseball or football. A few even know the sport from the inside. Before the war began, Pablo worked around bullrings. The boy Joaquín planned a career as torero. And by her own boast, Pilar lived for "nine years with three of the worst-paid matadors" in the business.

One of the most striking and memorable parts of the novel is organized in terms of a pictorial metaphor of the bullfight.[57] This is Pilar's account of the murder of the fascists in the village square at the hands of Pablo's lynch-mob. The natural resemblance between the square and an arena has been furthered by piling carts before the several street-entrances to the square. This is the usual custom in preparation for a *capea,* or amateur bull-baiting show, at the time of a fiesta. The resemblance to a feast-day celebration is emphasized by the fact that some of the peasants, just in from the country, are dressed in their Sunday clothes. The

[57] *FWBT,* pp. 109–129. See also p. 55.

caretaker of the plaza hoses down the dust as would be done for a *capea,* and when the dust has settled a peasant shouts, "When do we get the first fascist? When does the first one come out of the box?"

The eyes of the whole company are fixed on the doorway of the *Ayuntiamento,* where the fascists have been herded, as if by sweating workers at a bullring. The concentration is comparable to that with which a *capea* crowd would watch the cage-door through which a bull was to be released. Once the crowd has tasted blood through the murder of the first fascist, Mayor Don Benito Garcia, it is as though they waited tensely and impatiently for the second bull. Howling in a great voice, a drunkard summarizes the sentiments of a considerable part of the crowd. *"Qué salga el toro! Let the bull out!"*

But this is one of those almost unendurable "bullfights." It will produce no sense of tragic catharsis, no genuine purgation of the emotions. Pilar says that after it was over she felt sick, hollow, ashamed, and oppressed. There was no experience, as happens in a good bullfight, of anything "profound as any religious ecstasy." The total effect was as nasty as that of a jungle grove through which a tribe of baboons have just passed.

Even though, as such affairs often will, this *capea* produced some isolated instances of courage, *pundonor,* and the allied virtues—instances which Pilar describes along with the rest—these are not enough to redeem the total performance. Pilar's feeling is itself a fitting symbol for the reaction of many a reluctant observer to the tragedy of the Spanish war, the international bullfight with a poorly armed matador arrayed against the "brutality and darkness" of Pan-European fascism. If one at this instant remembers "Guernica," he sees that the artists Picasso and Hemingway, drawn as by a magnetic attraction to the pictorial imagery of the bullfight, move along lines precisely parallel. The major difference is that Hemingway, working with a different and more extendable medium, can take care to paint both sides of the picture. He has, to return to the Jamesian metaphor, an opportunity to draw more circles, more wheels of fire.

Within the scope of man's world, turning like a great wheel through empty space, there are in fact many small and large wheels turning for ever. In the quiet of his last Sunday evening inside the cave of Pablo, while Jordan draws his circles and makes his mathematical computations for the dynamiting of the bridge, the simile of a wheel comes into his mind.

"It is like a merry-go-round, Robert Jordan thought. Not a merry-go-round that travels fast, and with a calliope for music, and the children ride on cows with gilded horns, and there are rings to catch with sticks, and there is the blue gas-flare-lit early dark of the Avenue du Maine, with fried fish sold from the next stall, and a wheel of fortune turning with the leather flaps slapping against the posts of the numbered compartments, and the packages of lump sugar piled in pyramids for prizes. No, it is not that kind of a merry-go-round; although the people are waiting, like the men in caps and the women in knitted sweaters, their heads bare in the gaslight and their hair shining, who stand in front of the wheel of fortune as it spins. Yes, those are the people."

Those are the people, French or Spanish or any other, watching the two revolving circles—the temporal merry-go-round and the wheel of fortune. But Jordan has in his mind yet another wheel.

"This [he reflects] is like a wheel that goes up and around. It has been around twice now. It is a vast wheel, set at an angle, and each time it goes around and then is back to where it starts.

"One side is higher than the other and the sweep it makes lifts you back and down to where you started. There are no prizes either, he thought, and no one would choose to ride this wheel. You ride it each time and make the turn with no intention ever to have mounted.

"There is only one turn; one large, elliptical rising and falling turn and you are back where you have started. We are back again now, he thought, and nothing is settled." [58]

Call it the wheel of human conflict. For Jordan, as for all men, the turn of the wheel shows tragic implications. When it has completed its revolution, the rider is back where he started, as on the little wheel of Jordan's relations with Pablo. He has been twice now on *that* wheel, "and twice it has gone around and come back to where it started." Jordan wants no more rides with Pablo, though he will have them before his day is done. In the giant

[58] *FWBT*, pp. 225–226.

clockwork of human relations, the turning wheels may be as small as the arguments with Pablo, or as vast as the elliptical rise and fall in the action of a year of war.

In either of these instances, in three days or three years, you come back to where you began—"and nothing is settled." This is the wheel-like turn of Spain's tragedy, indeed, that after all the agony and all the blood, nothing should be settled, and that Spain should be back where it began, in a medieval situation.

XI · The River and the Trees

> "To be poised against fatality, to meet adverse conditions gracefully, is more than simple endurance; it is an act of aggression, a positive triumph."—Thomas Mann, *Death in Venice*

I. THROUGH THE IRON GATES

Ten years after the publication of his tragic epic on the Spanish civil war came Hemingway's *Across the River and Into the Trees*. It was his fifth novel, and some readers were prepared to rank it fifth in the order of his prose-fiction work of the period 1925–1950. It was clearly less effective in the conversion of readers to a special point of view than *A Farewell to Arms* and *For Whom the Bell Tolls*. It lacked some of the vernal freshness of *The Sun Also Rises*. Its almost elegiac mood prevented it from achieving the dramatic intensity of some of the Morgan stories in *To Have and Have Not,* though the novel of Venice, as a work of art and artifice, was generally superior to the novel of Key West. For those, however, who were prepared to take it seriously, and to read it often enough to grasp its full intention, the book was a genuine contribution to the Hemingway canon. Its intrinsic form was that of a prose poem, with a remarkably complex emotional structure, on the theme of the three ages of man.

It was important to notice that much of the book was composed in Europe. Hemingway began composition early in 1949 among the mountains in the valley of Cortina d'Ampezzo, one of his more ancient haunts, and therefore a kind of proper seat for reminiscence. In 1918 he had often stopped at Bellagio on Como during week-ends from Milan, and he once told Ernest Walsh that he had always liked Stresa (which appears in *A Farewell to Arms*), as well as Sermione and Pallanza. But Cortina had for years been a favored spot, psychologically right for the kind of work on which he was then engaged.

Composition continued in Cortina and afterwards in Cuba, where Hemingway had been living for ten years at Finca Vigia, the large breeze-swept farmhouse at San Francisco de Paula in the hills outside Havana. As in the writing of *The Sun Also Rises* nearly a quarter century earlier, the long first draft was finished in Paris towards the end of the year. On location in Venice during the winter of 1949–1950, he completed the revision, chiefly by means of extensive cutting. After serialization in *Cosmopolitan*, beginning in February and ending in June, the novel was published in book form on September 7, 1950.[1]

In order to complete *Across the River and Into the Trees*, he had interrupted work on a novel of considerably greater size and scope. Its subject, as he told curious inquirers, was the Land, the Sea, and the Air, and he characteristically hoped that the inquirers would not think his subject too ambitious for his talents. Although the book would by no means confine itself to the second world war, his experiences in that war must inevitably affect, in various ways, the development of this major work. As always, it would deal with what Hemingway knew. He knew something about the Land War, having accompanied elements of the First Army through France and into Germany during the summer, fall, and winter of 1944–1945 after the St. Lô break-through. He had also been extremely active in the Sea war from the summer of 1942 to the spring of 1944, having offered his own services, as well as those of his launch, the *Pilar,* to help maintain the anti-submarine cordon in American and Cuban coastal waters under the direction of Naval Intelligence. In the Air war, he had flown a number of missions over Festung Europa with British and American aviation immediately before and after the invasion of Normandy in the late spring of 1944. It was evident that he knew a representative portion of the war as a novelist must know it—from the inside.[2]

[1] EH to Ernest Walsh (fall 1925), and EH to CB, 4/1/51. The reader may note Malcolm Cowley's footnote, McCaffery, p. 35, which briefly refers to Hemingway's serious illness at this time. It was a bad infection in one eye (Hemingway has had consistently bad luck with his eyes from boyhood) resulting from a piece of gunshot wadding.

[2] See Malcolm Cowley, *Life* 26 (January 10, 1949), pp. 86–101. Reprinted, with a few changes, in McCaffery. For some brief accounts of

It was the third war in which he had been actively engaged within the span of thirty-three years. An experience of such magnitude and of such bitter intensity was not immediately adaptable to the purposes of fiction. Even as late as 1949, when he turned aside from his major task to work on his novel of Venice, the traumatic effects of his life in the second world war still rankled in his mind. The story of Colonel Cantwell emerged as a way of exorcising what for Hemingway still had the aspect, and the terrorizing atmosphere, of a recent nightmare. *Across the River and Into the Trees* was a necessary first step in the process of objectifying not only World War II, but also the other wars and the periods of armed truce between the wars which Hemingway had personally known.

The life-story of Colonel Cantwell contains a rubric of the course of time. First is the youth who thinks that life will be better than it is. Then comes the man of experience who finds that it is sometimes—or often—worse than he had anticipated. Finally there is the man who reaches the age and status when death may come at any time through causes that are generally called natural. As he looks back along the closing circle of his days (for the structure of *Across the River,* like that of *For Whom the Bell Tolls,* is that of the closed circle), he is ready to concede that since it might have been worse, it was on the whole good enough, and he is glad (though with certain reservations) to have had it.

Mourir, à Venice, c'est être bien mort was an adage with Henry James [3] who, like Thomas Mann, had given some thought to the subject. Hemingway's version of "death in Venice" could not have been more completely the opposite of Mann's in tone and manner if he had set himself at every turn to contradict the older story. Mann's story is set in the languid dog-days when the foreign vacation-trade is in full and decaying bloom, the bathhouses along the Lido are busy, and the growing threat of the plague must be concealed in order to drive no one away. Hemingway chooses Venice in winter. The cold, gray, sharp air (which

---

Hemingway at war, see Alan Moorehead, *Eclipse,* New York, 1945, p. 164, and Robert Capa, *Slightly Out of Focus,* New York, 1947, pp. 137–138 and 166–171.

[3] James, *Works,* New York edition, vol. 1, preface, p. vi.

for him has often been associated with physical and moral courage) drives steadily across the northern mountains and down the Grand Canal. Mann's hero is a famous writer, Hemingway's a professional soldier. Mann's writer sits and dreams. Hemingway's Colonel acts and remembers.[4]

But the themes of the two stories have much in common. Both ring with the overtones, though they do not accept the didactic limitations, of parables. They have in common the subject of youth contemplated by age, the emotional sense of innocence looking to and longing for experience (this is more marked in Hemingway than in Mann), and the object of exploring the nature and power of imaginative illusion. In Mann, the protagonist interests himself in studying, always from a little distance, a young child of almost angelic beauty. Cantwell spends roughly half the waking hours of his last week-end in the company of a young Italian countess. She is named, of all names, Renata. In her character, as in that of the child in Mann, may be found bloom and beauty and innocence, but also a strong suggestion of old-worldly wisdom. Renata is both as credible and as incredible as the child, and for the same reasons. Though both achieve a degree of actuality within the respective parables, Renata and the boy are both symbolic figures.

The mirror in both stories is held up chiefly to the face of experience. Mann's aged and tiring writer carries the weight of a successful career on his shoulders. Twenty years of fighting in the professional army of the United States have marked the Colonel with the almost innumerable scars he bears. Each of the men is of the indomitable type of Saint Sebastian (well known to the iconology of Venice). Mann calls this saint "the most beautiful figure, if not of art as a whole, at least of the art of literature." He is thinking of Sebastian also when he says that "to be poised against fatality, to meet adverse conditions gracefully, is more than simple endurance; it is an act of aggression, a positive triumph." Cantwell's aggressiveness is not enough to overcome in any but a moral way the eventual triumph of death. But when he comes to rest in the shade of the willows beside the road, he has crossed all his

[4] The Mann comparison is suggested in Northrop Frye's judicious review of the novel in *Hudson Review* 3 (Winter 1951), pp. 611–612.

rivers and met all adverse conditions with as much poise and grace as Mann could wish.

The reader of the *Meditations* of Marcus Aurelius should be able to recognize under Cantwell's profanely rugged exterior the type of the Roman stoic. The Colonel has the further distinction of a sense of humor. He is full enough of wounds, indeed, to have earned the right to jest at scars, though he respects them. They mark, in a way, the stations of his progress, and are the signs of the present state of his maturity. One could call them the stigmata of all that he has met of adversity, and all that he has so far overcome of fatality. One of them will not heal. The right hand, the hand of the non-dreamer, the hand of hard experience, is deformed and split. It has been twice shot through, like the hand and arm of Stonewall Jackson, from whose dying words the title of the novel is taken. Like General Jackson, ex-General Cantwell dies of an inward disease, a smothering paroxysm which he can not confront with his wild-boar truculence, or he might have a chance of facing it down.

He finds himself at fifty with high blood-pressure, occluding coronary arteries, a pocketful of nitroglycerine pills, and the extreme probability that his death may be waiting round any corner of Venice he happens to turn. His problem is not unlike Robert Jordan's—to roll his soldier's universe into a ball and squeeze it as rapidly as possible through the iron gates of life. Renata helps him to immerse himself as strenuously and wholeheartedly in the present as his coronary arteries will allow.

II. THE RAZOR'S EDGE

At the center of the Colonel's character, as possibly also at the center of this time, is a tense Manichean opposition between the tough and the tender, between the brutal and the delicate, between the rude and the remorseful. When W. B. Yeats undertook a somewhat similar character analysis, he used the terms Hic and Ille.[5] They are of use in understanding Colonel Cantwell.

[5] "Ego Dominus Tuus" in *The Collected Poems of W. B. Yeats,* New York, 1940, pp. 183–185. See *FWBT,* p. 304.

Ille is that whole aspect of the Colonel's nature which partakes of the nature of love. This side is shown not only in his relations with Renata, but also in his friendships with bartenders and waiters, motor-boatmen and gondolieri, or with various members of the Venetian nobility. Nobility in the Colonel's Venice is a nonrestricted term. It includes both the modest bearers of inherited titles, like the Barone Alvarito, and those who belong, like the Gran Maestro at the Gritti, to the natural *aristoi*. The Colonel's heart beats for all of these.

Ille has also a capacity for pity. It is the side of Cantwell which makes him love best those who have fought or been mutilated. "Other people were fine," he reflects, "and you liked them and were good friends; but you only felt true tenderness and love for those who had been there and received the castigation that every one receives who goes there long enough." The Colonel's summarizing expression is as tough as the emotion is tender. "I'm a sucker for crips," says he. "And any son of a bitch who has been hit solidly, as every man will be if he stays, then I love him." One of the arrows of outrageous fortune has lost the hotel-waiter Arnaldo his left eye, and he belongs accordingly in the category of the "cripples." [6] Nothing could be more thoughtful than the treatment of Arnaldo by the Colonel, or of Cantwell by Arnaldo. For the Colonel has known the castigation, and though he can draw Inferno-circles and populate them with his enemies as unjustly as Dante did, there is still room for love.

The side that Yeats called Hic is uppermost in the battle with the drunken sailors. Though these are certainly "hit solidly" by the Colonel—so solidly that his wounded hand nearly splits open again—they are anything but loved. They have whistled at Renata, and the chivalric impulses of Ille rise at once to meet the implied insult. But Hic loves to fight, and uses his fists with effectiveness and enjoyment, playing only to win as the true fighter sometimes must. In the end, he walks away without any contrition, or even a backward glance at the fallen sailors. "Let's walk," he tells Renata, "so we make even the backs of our legs look dangerous." [7]

[6] *ARIT*, p. 67.
[7] *ARIT*, pp. 283–285.

The wild-boar attitude is visible, too, in his treatment of the occasional Venetian fascists. There is one in particular, a back-stairs servant at the Gritti Palace Hotel, whom the Colonel once caught in the act of going through his luggage. When this citizen slides the morning paper under the door, Cantwell likes to startle him by taking it before the servant has let go of the other end. It is the Colonel's pleasure and custom not to be caught napping by the always-present opposition.[8]

The soldierly vigilance which never lets him sit down without having both flanks covered is apparent also when he encounters the two ex-fascists during his morning walk to the market. As they come up behind him, the Colonel hears them talking about him on the supposition that he does not understand their language.

"They are making it pretty personal now. It isn't just Americans, it is also me, myself, my gray hair, the slightly crooked way I walk, the combat boots (those, of that stripe, disliked the practicability of combat boots. They liked boots that rang on the flag stones and took a high black polish)."

After turning the next corner and waiting for the former fascists to come up in order to face them down, the Colonel reflects that it was hardly intelligent of them "to think old Infantrymen would not fight this early in the morning against the simple odds of two to one."

"I'd hate to fight in this town where I love the people. I would avoid it. But couldn't those badly educated youths realize what sort of animal they were dealing with? Don't they know how you get to walk that way? Nor any of the other signs that combat people show as surely as a fisherman's hands tell you if he is a fisherman from the creases from the cord cuts." [9]

It was a pity that they were not ten to one instead of only two, the Colonel says to himself. They might have fought then, like the murderers of Matteotti back in the most high and palmy state of Rome, long before their leader was strung up in a filling station.

The love of fighting is part of what the Colonel sums up as the *sale métier* of his profession. Yet this side of him does continuous

[8] *ARIT*, p. 115.
[9] *ARIT*, pp. 186–188.

Manichean battle with what, thinking of Hamlet, one might call the fighting of love. "Sir, in my heart there was a kind of fighting that would not let me sleep." [10] But the Colonel is himself, not a latter-day Hamlet. Though his fifty-year-old modern world is out of joint, he never imagines that he was born to set it right. He has only contrived to do his best along the way. The best, as the rule runs, was none too good, and he knows all about the bitterness of remorse. "It is the mistakes," he says, "that are no good to sleep with. . . . They can certainly crawl into a sack sometimes. They can crawl in and stay in there with you." [11] Even when the horrors come, however, the Colonel is very far from wishing that his beat-up and sullied flesh would melt. He is glad to occupy it as long as luck allows. He accepts without protest the Almighty's edict against self-slaughter. He is content to prepare stoically for "the best way to be over-run," but he is in no hurry.[12] There is always the fighting of love.

One of his deepest affections is for his old comrade-at-arms, the Gran Maestro, who resembles the Colonel in carrying his afflictions gracefully, and in contriving to be happy despite his ulcers and the "small cardiac condition." The two men are "brothers in their membership in the human race, the only club that either one paid dues to, and brothers, too, in their love of an old country, much fought over, and always triumphant in defeat, which they had both defended in their youth." As a badge of the brotherhood, they have invented a fictitious order with the resounding Spanish title, *El Ordine Militar, Nobile y Espirituoso de los Caballeros de Brusadelli*. The knights of Brusadelli pay ironic homage to their "leader" and patron, a notorious Milanese profiteer who once accused his young wife, through due process of law and in public, "of having deprived him of his judgment through her extraordinary sexual demands." [13]

The Order of the Caballeros is, however, much more than a joke on its patron. Its regular members are admitted only on unimpeachable evidence that they have received (and gracefully

---

[10] Act V, scene ii.
[11] *ARIT*, p. 188.
[12] *ARIT*, p. 104.
[13] *ARIT*, pp. 55–57. This organization parodies that of the Carbonari.

survived thus far) the castigation that flesh is heir to. They are the uncomplaining fardel-bearers, who understand the whips and scorns as part of time's earthly business. They are the occupants of the inner circle which always stands at the center of masculine relationships in Hemingway; they have been "hit solidly, as every man will be if he stays." And the Knights of Brusadelli are among those who have stayed.

The admission of Renata is a revealing act of the Order. One way of describing the extended conversations between the countess and the Colonel is to say that they represent the indoctrination of youth by grizzled experience.

"What would you like to know, Daughter?" asks the Colonel at one point in the story.

"Everything," says Renata.

"All right," says the Colonel. "Here goes." [14]

What he has to tell her, as the type of the non-initiate, are some of the more recent events in his "sad trade" of war-making. She hears of the Normandy break-through, the bombing of American troops by their own air support, the serio-comic *opera* of the taking of Paris, and the destruction of an infantry regiment in the forest at Hurtgen. After she has been properly indoctrinated into the intricate ironies by means of the Colonel's recital, it is significant that Renata should be admitted to the Order. "You are a member now," says the Gran Maestro. *"Por merito di guerra."* But it is only an honorary membership. The countess is too young. She still wears the bloom. She cannot show, like Cantwell and the Gran Maestro, "the ever happy face of the old soldier who is still alive and appreciates it." The experience is not really available, in short, except to those who have been there, and had it, and managed to survive without being ruined by it. [15]

Henry James interested himself in the "whimsical theory of two distinct and alternate presences . . . in two quite distinct and 'water-tight' compartments." [16] In Hemingway's portrait of the Colonel we move slightly beyond the area of whimsy, and the compartments of the character are neither wholly distinct nor

[14] *ARIT,* p. 220.
[15] *ARIT,* p. 270.
[16] *Works,* vol. 17, preface, pp. xii–xiii.

water-tight. In fact one keeps breaking in on the other. Among the questions implicit in this complex character is, "How much of all that is good here can survive the onslaughts of evil without being spoiled?" The answer, supplied by the Colonel, is that very much can survive—courage, love, a chivalric code, generosity, the sense of beauty and the sense of the ridiculous, and the capacity for soundly based belief. The distinct and alternate presences of the Colonel's character agree, though not without obstinate questionings, on the necessity for such qualities as these. They constitute the unwritten by-laws of the *Ordine Militar, Nobile y Espirituoso de los Caballeros de Brusadelli.*

Of utmost importance is the capacity for soundly based belief, for what might well be called the desirability of informed illusion. "Every day is a disillusion," says the very young Countess. "No," says the Colonel, flatly. "Every day is a new and fine illusion. But you can cut out everything phony about the illusion as though you would cut it out with a straight-edge razor." [17]

The illusion must be informed, evaluated, tested for the truth it bears. "My Colonel," says the night porter at the Gritti, "I have so little political development that I believe all honorable men are honorable." "Oh you'll get over that," the Colonel assures him. "Don't worry, boy." [18] Cantwell is employing, of course, his usual rough brand of jocularity, but he is making, at the same time, an important point about informed illusion. He well knows that the necessary thing to retain, after the loss of any illusion, is the capacity for belief which made the original illusion possible. It may be that all honorable men are not honorable. It is even very likely. This does not, however, add up to anything like permanent disillusionment with mankind. One gets out the straight-edge razor and performs a delicate operation. Afterwards, if the operation has been well done, the patient will recover.

The Colonel's remark to Renata probably brings the reader somewhere near the center of his complex character as it is presented in the novel. He has the marked ability to combine a mature intellectual toughness and resilience with a deeply felt love for the world extant. He faces with courage and equanimity the

[17] *ARIT,* p. 232.
[18] *ARIT,* p. 182.

evils that surround him and are even inside him. During the heart attack in the lobby of the Gritti, he will not even sit down, though he is gray-faced and sweating. Afterwards he rests "lightly and without illusion," as a hawk might rest, against a corner of the concierge's desk. When he feels well enough to move, he walks carefully and at the proper speed through the streets of Venice to join his girl—the complex image for nearly all that he really loves in the past of his life.[19]

To embody these and other facets of the Colonel's character in a book which carries the exposition almost entirely through dialogue and monologues would have been a sufficient task for an ordinary artist. In a year of hard work, Hemingway not only did this job; he likewise developed, with a craft subtler than one at first suspected, the symbolic pattern in which the Colonel moves.

III. PAST AND PRESENT

As the reader of the novel immerses himself beneath its surface ebb and flow, he soon finds that much more is required of him than a quick and cursory tourist-gondola ride among the urban canals of Venice. He needs to be prepared for the probability that any scene actually carries at least twice the significance he had at first supposed. Having accepted that probability, and having placed himself on the watch for it, he will discover that in Colonel Cantwell's mind nearly all the every-day aspects of Venice operate quite as fully at the level of symbolic meaning as they do in their outward-seeming and easily recognizable selves. In its deeper reaches, *Across the River and Into the Trees* is meant as a symbolic study of a complex state of mind, embodied in a carefully ordered prose poem. It represents the recollection of things past in a state of imaginative hypertension almost the equivalent of a spell.

Hegel once wrote that the necessary precondition for the best lyric poetry was the "poet's ability to absorb the real content absolutely, converting it thereby into his own possession," and grasping certain "relations in the light of his poetic individual-

[19] *ARIT,* p. 196.

ity." [20] This is precisely what has happened with the author, and therefore with the protagonist, of this lyric-poetical novel. In Colonel Cantwell's hypersensitive state of mind, there is special connotative meaning to all the tides and rivers and canals, all the boats and gondolas and gondolieri, all the bridges and mooring-stakes in this lovely "town." The north wind and the far snow-capped mountains, the Countess Renata and her portrait and her heirloom emeralds, the bars and the hotels and the old associates of Venice all mean more to the Colonel than Hemingway will say. But for those who can take a hint, the novel shows an almost absolute absorption of the "real" content into the poet's, and hence the sympathetic reader's, own possession.

Even the most cursory reader of the book knows that every event in Colonel Cantwell's last week-end in Venice has for him a special savor. He is in an intense state of awareness, like the hero of Mann's story. One agent of intensification is the near, consciously accepted, morally scorned, but never ignorable approach of death. Before his departure from Trieste the Colonel has dosed himself heavily with one of the common medications for high blood-pressure, technically known as hypertension. The technical term is almost a metaphor for the Colonel's state of mind. As with Robert Jordan in *For Whom the Bell Tolls* and the dying writer of "The Snows of Kilimanjaro," the emotional hyper-tension of the recognized approach of death gives every observed detail of remaining life a special sharpened value.

The other factor which illuminates his Friday, his Saturday, and his Sunday is not the end but the beginning: his constant, joyous awareness of the way it was for him in the country round Venice in the days of his youth. This is not a mere sentimental height-ening of the good parts of the past. For Cantwell, like his inventor, refuses to cry over departed youth. (Everybody loses all the bloom, Hemingway once told Fitzgerald.[21] A gun or a saddle or a person are all better when they are worn and the bloom is off them. You may lose everything that is fresh and everything that is easy. But you have more *métier* and you know more and when you get flashes of the old juice you get more results with them.)

[20] Hegel, *Philosophy of Fine Art*, London, 1920, vol. 4, p. 201.
[21] EH to FSF, 9/13/29.

But this is not to say that the past is to be rejected. Its value consists in its holding a light behind the present. To be conscious of it in and through the present is to sharpen the meaning of every present incident, and to define in profile the nature of illusion.

For some time before he wrote the Venice novel, Hemingway had shown a marked interest in the effects which may be gained by the collocation of two widely separated periods of time. Such an effect enters very movingly into the short story, "Fathers and Sons." The dying writer of "The Snows of Kilimanjaro" places his two lives side by side—the old free one and the more recent life that has been bought and sold so thoroughly and completely that, shopworn, it can never serve as anything but a sorry contrast to the fine, fresh life of the old days. Harry the writer, dying of gangrene with his work undone, has cause for regret. And there are certain regrets, including a half-buried remorse, which Cantwell feels in bringing together, as in a kind of spell, the time of his youth and the time of his death, in and around the ancient city of the Adriatic.

But Venice for the Colonel is a city of happy spells. His weekly visits, on leave from his command post at Trieste, have always a force like a magical incantation. Driving in from the north-east through the city's ugly suburbs near Mestre he feels again, this Friday, the old exultation. "We are coming into my town," he says silently. "Christ, what a lovely town." His love for the city is nothing new. As a young lieutenant, fighting in the Italian army through a whole wet winter to head off a series of Austrian assaults against the high-road to Venice, he went back to Noghera one clear cold day to have a "gift-wound" dressed. Although he did not enter it at that time, he then first saw the city in the sea, far off like a vision. "It is my city," he now reflects, "because I fought for it when I was a boy, and now that I am half-a-hundred years old, they know I fought for it and am a part owner and they treat me well."

Part of the spell lies in his hospitable acceptance as a Venetian by the Venetians. Though cynics might suppose so, it has nothing to do with his being "a chicken colonel on the winning side." "We all love Venice," says the Barone Alvarito after the duck-shooting expedition. "Perhaps you do the best of all." It is this love which deeply informs the Colonel's Venetian relationships. The anarchist bartender near the *imbarcadero* is an example. He might hate the Colonel as a foreign intruder (like the "over-liberated" boatman in the Veneto). But his real hatred, which the Colonel shares, is for the still recognizable *fascisti,* or for fat, sleek *pescecani* like the postwar rich from Milan who are down for a week-end of gambling on the Lido. The bartender's salute (and it has many echoes) is "My Colonel," a phrase in which the practiced ear might catch the slightest loving stress on the possessive pronoun. There is, indeed, a pride of possession on both sides. The Venetians recognize him as "part owner," even though all of them do not know that he took out a mortgage on a piece of Venice in 1918, depositing his blood and his right knee-cap like permanent collateral at the bank of the Basso Piave near Fossalta.[22]

As a loving man of property, the Colonel reflects that Venice would be a good place to retire to; he might even be buried somewhere near the great villas of the Brenta. In retirement he could do with a simple room in a house where he could look out and watch the boats going by on the canals. "I could read in the mornings and walk around the town before lunch and go every day to see the Tintorettos at the Accademia and to the Scuola San Rocco and eat in good cheap joints behind the market." Venice offers more than a banquet of the senses for a soldier as well educated as Cantwell.

Later, when his spare body fails him finally, he can be "part of the ground where the children play in the evenings, and in the mornings, maybe, they would still be training jumping horses and their hoofs would make a thudding on the turf, and trout would rise in the pool when there was a hatch of fly." As he thinks of it in connection with his departed youth and his approaching death, Venice and the country round it mean very much to him, "more than he could or would ever tell anyone." They mean, in fact, something like the circular entwinement of alpha and omega, the rounding out of a life. For the life of Cantwell has properly begun

[22] *Cantwell's love of Venice:* Cf. *ARIT,* pp. 26, 34, 45, 301.

where it will fittingly end, beside the rivers which drain into the Adriatic and mingle with the tides which ebb and flow among the stones of Venice.[23]

For one in so intense a state of awareness, Venice is full of symbolic reminders. A noteworthy instance is the two mooring-stakes on the canal which leads into the Rio Nuovo.

"They went under the white bridge and under the unfinished wood bridge. Then they left the red bridge on the right and passed under the first high-flying white bridge. Then there was the black iron fretwork bridge on the canal leading into the Rio Nuovo and they passed the two stakes chained together but not touching: like us the Colonel thought. He watched the tide pull at them and he saw how the chains had worn the wood since he first had seen them. That's us, he thought. That's our monument. And how many monuments are there to us in the canals of this town?" [24]

The "us" of this emblem-packed passage would be Lieutenant Cantwell of 1918 and Colonel Cantwell of 1950, chained together by the fact that they are the same person, but separated by the thirty-odd years that have come between. The Colonel is careful to notice that the emblematic stakes are "not touching." In another sense they are very touching indeed. For in the symbolic language of the passage, if one is awake to it and sympathetic with it, is the sum of a lifetime. The tide (take it doubly) pulls at the stakes. The chains (take them doubly) have worn the wood. The stakes (take them doubly, too) are as good a monument as a man could ask.

There are also the bridges, structures of wood and metal arching over Venetian canals and wrenching the Colonel's laboring heart whenever he climbs them to cross. But they are more than obstacles. Because the Colonel is in the state of recollection, they serve him as symbolic reminders of certain milestones in his youthful experience. He never identifies them precisely, merely noting them as they pass, but one might guess that the first white bridge is childhood, the unfinished wooden bridge interrupted adolescence, the red bridge the first far-off war, and the high-flying white bridge an aspect of youthful ambition. At the end of

[23] *Retirement and burial in Venice:* Cf. *ARIT,* pp. 33, 35, 45.
[24] *ARIT,* p. 46.

all these comes the black iron bridge. It is no symbolic accident that this crosses the canal which leads into the Rio Nuovo—the New River. Across the river is where the Colonel will be going before the week-end is out. And here, by this black iron bridge, like a wordless summary of the whole, are the two stakes chained together but not touching.

IV. THE CRAFT AND THE ARMOR

The Colonel's disorder is mechanical, a heart that may go at any time but is kept in action until that time by the kind of tinkering that nitro-glycerine pills can provide. He ought, says his doctor, to drag a chain like a high-octane gasoline truck. The mechanical parallel is not inept. In postwar Venice the Colonel finds any number of similar mechanical disorders. As one who has schooled himself to appreciate all nice ironies, whether comic or tragic, he is prepared to accept each disorder tacitly, bitter-humorously, as an emblem of his own. One, for example, is the elevator in the Gritti-Palace Hotel. It halts, after one ascent, with a "slight hydraulic inaccuracy at the top floor." "Can't you run an elevator properly?" asks the Colonel. "No, my Colonel," the boy said. "The current is not stable." Neither is the Colonel's, as every bridge he crosses in Venice stabbingly shows him.[25]

The most memorable parallel is the old motor in the launch which carries the Colonel to his hotel when he arrives in Venice. Although it resembles a speed boat, being "radiantly varnished and lovingly kept," it derives its power from a tiny, reconditioned Fiat engine, bought from an automobile graveyard and sounding like a stricken tank except that its noises are minute in comparison. As they move through the familiar canals, the Colonel watches the valiant prow of the "delicately brass-striped" craft. He has formerly been striped with brass himself as a general officer, and is both as neatly kept and as "beat-up" as the boat in which he is riding. Therefore he listens to the "metallic agony" of the laboring engine with a specially conditioned sympathy. Even though the Colonel makes no obvious comparisons between the boat and himself, Hemingway's ironic intention is clear:

[25] *ARIT,* p. 66.

"The motor boat came gallantly up beside the piling of the dock. Every move she makes, the Colonel thought, is a triumph of the gallantry of the aging machine. We do not have war horses now like old Traveller, or Marbot's Lysette who fought, personally, at Eylau. We have the gallantry of worn-through rods that refuse to break; the cylinder head that does not blow though it has every right to, and the rest of it." [26]

There is quite a lot to the rest of it. For we have the gallantry also of Old Traveller Cantwell, who has fought, personally, in many places, and can feel, accordingly, a kind of fraternal sympathy with the agony of the vital engine and the still-proud forward motion of the beat-up boat. Again silently, but like a delayed-action corroboration, we have Renata's reaction when she bids the Colonel goodbye two hundred pages later. As they stand on the *imbarcadero,* the Colonel suggests that she return in a faster launch than this "old displaced-engine boat" which has brought them across the river. "I'd rather," says the countess, "take the displaced engine boat if you don't mind." The Colonel does not mind. He knows her choice for what it is—a tacit compliment, a loving gesture, to the gallantry of that cylinder head in his own chest which does not blow, though it has every right to do so. "It's just a muscle," the Colonel has remarked the day before. "Only it is the main muscle. It works as perfectly as a Rolex Oyster Perpetual. The trouble is you cannot send it to the Rolex representative when it goes wrong. When it stops, you just do not know the time. You're dead."

Death is symbolized also in a far more ancient image than a blown cylinder head or a chronometer. *"Fa brutto tempo,"* says the night porter as Cantwell leaves for his early morning game of *solitaire ambulante. "Bruttissimo,"* answers the Colonel, stepping into the wind. And *bruttissimo* is precisely the word for it, since the wind of winter, which plays like a dark undersong throughout the surface gaiety of this last week-end, is also the wind of death. "It's from the high mountains," says Renata as the north wind lashes at the gondola and helps to raise the tide. "Yes," says Ricardo. "And beyond there it's from somewhere else." It is, in-

[26] *ARIT,* pp. 45–52. Cf. the Countess's remark, p. 277, and the Colonel on the Rolex Oyster Perpetual, p. 138.

deed, whether we interpret the remark as simple meteorology or as a form of religious symbolism.[27]

The wind is blowing hard from the mountains on the Friday afternoon of the Colonel's drive by way of Latisana to Venice. It sharpens all the outlines of the buildings on Torcello, Burano, and Murano so that they look "geometrically clear," as the consciousness of approaching death might clarify the vision of a dying man. When the Colonel asks the waiter to open all the windows of his hotel room, the waiter protests that the wind is too strong. But the Colonel will have them open and the wind enters the room as if it were implacably defying the soldier's implacable defiance.

Sometimes, for those who are paying attention, the wind almost identifies itself. When the Colonel and Renata ascend the first bridge of their walk together, the wind lashes at them. Immediately the answering twinge is felt in the Colonel's laboring heart. All through his days in Venice, the wind does its work of buffeting the soldier. He goes about his business and his pleasure, not as if the wind did not exist as an adversary, but as if he scorned it.

His attitude is much the same with respect to the high tides. Like the wind, these have a double meaning for the Colonel. Twice during the gondola ride with Renata, where he comports himself in a manner better becoming his manhood than the state of his health and blood-pressure, he checks the height of the underside of the bridges through which they pass. The first time, while the wind rips wildly under the edges of the blanket, the strain on the Colonel's heart has been such that the gondola is only "inches free" of snagging its bowsprit against the bridge-girders. A little later, when they have turned and are going "with the wind" and have been quiet for a considerable time, he checks "on the bridge that [is] coming up" and notes with relief that there is "clearance." As happens subtly all the time in this novel, the reader may safely assume a symbolic intention behind both passages.[28]

The wind and the tide, the motor-boats and the gondolas, the canals and the bridges and the mooring-stakes, the far mountains and the spreading plain, the hotel-room home, the elevator, the unstable electric current, and perhaps especially the sea-city itself,

[27] *ARIT,* pp. 25, 28 (and cf. 48), 68, 105, 152, 183.
[28] *ARIT,* pp. 155 and 159.

are all of them for the Colonel in his state of heightened awareness, signs and symbols of more than themselves. Each of them in its smaller way (like the city in its total way) is one of his monuments.

As always in Hemingway, death has its opposite numbers—the images of home and the presence of love. Cantwell walks the streets of Venice with his "same old stride" and even breathes deeply as he faces the wind. But he is glad of the welcoming door of Harry's bar. "He had made it again and was at home." Equally welcome is the main entrance at the hotel, where one comes "out of the wind and the cold . . . into the light and warmth of the lobby." Even in the dark of the gondola the home-feeling is re-created. Outside, unremittingly, the wind lashes at the waves. Under the blanket there is no wind. "We are in our home and I love you," says the Countess Renata.[29]

The love is important. Once, in a natural emblem, it is called the island in the great river with the high steep banks. At another time it is presented in the more complex mechanical image of an armored tank. "Don't you feel better to be loved?" asks the girl. "Yes," says the Colonel. In a soldierly metaphor he compares the feeling to that of being within range of enemy fire on a hill "where it was too rocky to dig, and the rocks all solid, but with nothing jutting, and no bulges, and all of a sudden instead of being there naked, I was armoured. Armoured, and the eighty-eights not there. . . ."[30]

This bare and rocky hill, with never a foxhole or a possibility of digging one, and with the enemy all round the base, is a special nightmare of the Colonel's, as it was one of El Sordo's in *For Whom the Bell Tolls*. But he knows the armor that will clothe his nakedness, just as he knows the clean, well-lighted bars and hotels of Venice where a man can be at home even while the north wind blows. In his familiar room at the Gritti—"really home, if a hotel room may be so described"—Richard Cantwell might well echo the feelings of Nick Adams, bedded down in his shelter-half on the bank of the Big Two-Hearted River. "It had been a hard trip. He was very tired. . . . He had made his camp. He was settled.

[29] *ARIT*, pp. 78–79, 106, 151–152.
[30] *ARIT*, pp. 129 and 153.

Nothing could touch him. . . . He was there, in the good place. He was in his home where he had made it." The Colonel, thirty years nearer death than the young Nick Adams, is otherwise in no different a state of happiness. With a decanter of Valpolicella, a portrait of his girl, and a sports column by Red Smith, he is merely a little more comfortable, as is fitting.[31]

V. OPERATION COMPLETED

"You are making the discovery," says the Countess Renata once, politely, to her lover. "I am only the unknown country." [32] The lady might be addressing the reader over the Colonel's shoulder. The discovery to be made about Renata is that, like so many other people and things in the book, she is a symbolic figure. Her portrait and her square-cut emeralds, both of which she lends to the Colonel, are extensions of her symbolic meaning.

Renata exists, of course, merely as a young woman of Venice in love with an aging soldier. Lewis Gannett was thinking of this phase of her existence when he called her "the dream-girl who is a dream of all fair women and never more than a dream." [33] But the real point about Renata is that she is more than a dream.

The Countess is more than Nostalgia, though the sense of the past is one of the gifts she brings to the Colonel. To his imagination, she is like a presiding genius of Venice. One clue to her identity is the translation of her name. She is the figurative image of the Colonel's past youth, still living in the vision-city he once saw from a distance when he fought for Italy on the plains of the Veneto long ago.

A second important clue to her symbolic identity is Renata's age. She is "nearly nineteen," which is precisely the age of the young Cantwell when he got his big wound—the wound that still makes him walk crookedly—at Fossalta in 1918. Her youth, her freshness, and her bravery, like the seemingly inborn wisdom she sometimes displays, are qualities which evidently belonged to young Lieutenant Cantwell in that winter of his rapid growing-up.

[31] *ARIT*, p. 164. Cf. *First 49*, p. 313.
[32] *ARIT*, p. 155.
[33] *New York Herald Tribune*, September 7, 1950.

Renata carries the bloom which he, likewise, owned before the *sale métier* of war-making substituted the scarred, leathery, and battle-smoked patina he now shows.

In Renata's presence (the psychological situation is common), Cantwell is able to return imaginatively to the freshness of his youth. This is the meaning of what at first seems to be a mere passing incident in the Colonel's room at the Gritti-Palace Hotel. The couple have come to wash up before dinner. The Colonel examines his woeful countenance, very critically and in passing, before the bathroom mirror. It looks, he tells himself, like something "cut out of wood by an indifferent craftsman." All of it is covered with ridges, welts, and the thin lines of plastic operations after head-wounds. The Colonel is a *gueule cassée* in spite of all the doctors could do. If the *gueule* is that of experience, and therefore respectable, it does not fit the Colonel's mood of that special moment. "The hell with you," he says to the mirrored image. "You beat-up, miserable. Should we rejoin the ladies?" When he reenters the room where Renata waits, he is "as young as at his first attack,"—*fraîche et rose comme au jour de la bataille.*[34]

The man-woman relationship between the Colonel and his girl is clear, and as simple as these things can ever be. The symbolic relationship is not so clear, though it is revealed by a sufficient number of hints and allusions to make the guessing game a fair one. "I want to be like me, only much, much better and I want to have you love me," says the Colonel's youthful image to the Colonel's aged image during dinner. "Also," she says ("suddenly and unmaskingly"), "I want to be like you. Can I be like you a little while tonight?" The request could be read as a way of phrasing the longing youth feels for experience. The "unmasking" should be noticed because it reveals the process by which the symbolic relationship is to be grasped by the reader.

[34] The incident is in *ARIT*, pp. 111–112. The phrase, "as young as at his first attack," is a rough translation of Edgar Quinet's "fraîche et rose comme au jour de la bataille." When Hemingway was in Paris on the way to Africa in the fall of 1933, James and Norah Joyce came to dinner the last night before the hunters entrained for Marseilles. They ate a roast pheasant and a quarter of the chevreuil which Hemingway had shot in the Sologne. The Quinet line was running in Joyce's head that night. See *GHOA*, pp. 71 and 195. Cf. *ARIT*, p. 272.

In Venice, the city of spells for the Colonel's intensified imagination, it is possible for youth and age to come together, though always only briefly because the realities of this day keep breaking in. The evanescent feeling of union with the past is underscored again in the gondola. "Please hold me very tightly so we can be part of each other for a little while" is the double-edged request of the Countess. The Colonel's answer is likewise doubled-edged, and one of the edges is tipped with irony. "We can try," says Cantwell. In the special, magical atmosphere and mood of Venice, a degree of success is possible.[35]

When the Colonel and his image walk home afterwards across the cold and windswept square in the winter night, they hold together "close and hard in their sorrow and their happiness." If the happiness is in the nature of an illusion, the sorrow is the straight-edge razor that will cut out the false parts. The sorrow originates in the Colonel's awareness of the errors he has made in the course of his hard-bitten life—the women and the soldiers and the countries he has lost, through cruelty and faulty judgment and bad luck, since the days when the bloom was on him and he was starting out. He readily agrees to Renata's suggestion on the following morning: "Please hold me very close and let's not talk, or think, about how things might have been different." The suggestion is sound. The Colonel has already told himself the same thing in the gay and bitter version of Villon: "Où sont les neiges d'antan? Où sont les neiges d'autrefois? Dans le pissoir toute la chose comme ça." Yet the sorrow and the remorse cannot be disposed of so easily. Cantwell must purge himself by confession.[36]

Even when one fully accepts the idea of the Venetian spell, it would be possible to accuse the Colonel of a sentimental romanticization of the days of his youth. This matter is handled by means of Renata's symbolic portrait.[37] "While it is not truly me," says the Countess, "it is the way you like to think of me." The Colonel also assists in the identification of the meaning of the portrait. "Portrait," he says once—"Boy or daughter or my one true love

[35] *Renata's symbolic identity: ARIT,* pp. 82, 91, 96, 142, 156, 160, 210.
[36] *ARIT,* pp. 94, 242, 294, and 112. I owe the confession-idea to Malcolm Cowley.
[37] *ARIT,* pp. 97, 114, 147, 170, 173, 178, 180, 196, 209.

or whatever it is." The picture is interwoven, for him, with the happiness he feels if he looks far enough backward—skipping the *sale métier* of the intervening years. "I'll be damned if I'll turn that in," says he. "I keep that." But at the close of the book, since he cannot take it with him, the Colonel gives back the portrait.

Even while he has it, however, he is quite clear in his mind that it is no substitute for the real thing. There is even a kind of commentary on the relation between life and art in what the Colonel says of the portrait. "The portrait is lovely to have," says he in one of his boar-like moments. But in comparison with the real thing, the living Renata, "it is like skinning a dead horse." He recognizes in the painting a "static" quality which makes it an inadequate substitute for the moving thing. He reflects, evidently, that one can lose himself so far and so long in the past that he gets out of touch with the salutary present. Looking at his own scarred face in the mirror, the Colonel draws the contrast: "Portrait was a thing of the past. Mirror was actuality and of this day."

In a very womanly fashion, knowing the answer in advance, the Countess puts the crucial question about her portrait. "Do you love her more than me?" This is another way of asking the Colonel if he prefers the art to the actual. "I'm not abnormal yet," says the Colonel. "But she's lovely." Later he adds (and the remark is still double-edged): "There's no comparison of course. I don't mean likeness. The likeness is excellent." All art, the argument would run, can be valued because it provides fresh insights into the conglomerate of good and bad which the actual offers to us. Yet all art needs the corrective which can be supplied only by a direct and often-renewed attention to the actual. The Colonel prefers the actual, but he cherishes the art.

Renata's square emeralds have likewise a double function.[38] These are the stones of Venice, cut long ago by master craftsmen. They embody in a lasting art form something, at least, of the deep past of the city. As heirlooms, handed down from mother to daughter through the generations, they represent a history familiar to the Colonel. Being part owner of the city, it is proper that he should be part owner of the emeralds, and the Countess insists on lending the stones to her lover. They are to be kept in his pocket

[38] *ARIT,* pp. 103, 105, 108, 117, 166, 181, 195–197.

like a lucky piece. They are something durable given him by his youth and something tangible for one in the imminent presence of death. "Put your hand in your right-hand pocket and feel very rich," says Renata. "I am rich," says the lover of Venice. The Gran Maestro, sensing that this is a private joke between them (as it is also between the author and the reader), silently departs.

Yet it is a serious kind of joke. Later on, and the action is symbolic, the Colonel transfers the emeralds, "whatever they are," from his right-hand pocket to the inside left pocket of his tunic, beside the old chronometer of his heart. But in the end, having no further use for them where he is going, he gives them back. Like the surrender of his youth and age, as death over-runs his position, the turning-back of the stones is a gesture. It signifies, perhaps, the complete independence of the Colonel's inner self (a Stoic doctrine), and the final aloneness of his being. Like the portrait, the stones have only been lent—as Venice has been lent, as the life itself has been lent. Cantwell is very careful to pay his debts in full and in kind. He knows that after the squaring-up will come the rounding-off. The circle of his days will be closed and completed, and he can die, as he dies, under perfect control and without impediment, in what Mann called a "positive triumph."

Across the River and Into the Trees is not one of Hemingway's major novels. It was not meant to be, any more than Eclogue X was meant to match the *Aeneid,* or *Paradise Regained* to duplicate *Paradise Lost*. One might construct a rough table of correspondences in order to place the book in its relations to the best of his earlier work in long fiction. If *A Farewell to Arms* was his *Romeo and Juliet,* and *For Whom the Bell Tolls* his *King Lear,* this midcentury novel could perhaps be called a lesser kind of *Winter's Tale* or *Tempest*. Its tone is elegiac. It moves like a love-lyric. The round within which its forces are deployed is the rough shape of a life.

The country a novelist knows, said Hemingway, is the country in his heart. Another Venetian, Robert Browning, remarked that if you opened his heart you would "see graved inside of it—Italy." Though the lion-like Colonel with his wild-boar's irascibility would make a surly joke about letting anyone tinker with his own untinkerable chronometer, he shares the love that Browning felt.

De gustibus. For the opening of one's heart, as for its closing, Italy is as good a place as any. To the north, where the cold wind comes from, are the mountains. All around Venice stretches the plain where the young lieutenant lost his feeling of immortality at the age of eighteen, and where the Colonel at fifty completes the operation with a death.

XII · Truth and Poetry

> "Every thing possible to be believed is an image of truth."—William Blake [1]

Goethe called his autobiography *Dichtung und Wahrheit*, Poetry and Truth. The reverse of Goethe's title, as a strategy of emphasis, admirably fits the collected works of Hemingway. From the first he has been dedicated as a writer to the rendering of Wahrheit, the precise and at least partly naturalistic rendering of things as they are and were. Yet under all his brilliant surfaces lies the controlling Dichtung, the symbolic underpainting which gives so remarkable a sense of depth and vitality to what otherwise might be flat two-dimensional portraiture.

The literary histories commonly credit Hemingway with being the "archpriest of naturalists." This has now become a rather tiresome designation. It is also an essentially superficial judgment, at least in the sense that it apparently ignores what is taking place down under. That Hemingway the technician achieves effects simply impossible to his naturalistic forebears or current imitators has sometimes been noticed. The cause behind the majority of these effects, the deep inner Dichtung which runs through all his work, has neither been fully recognized, nor systematically explored. To undertake such an exploration has been one of the tasks of this book.*

---

[1] *The Marriage of Heaven and Hell.*

* Hemingway's most recent publication, the novelette called *The Old Man and the Sea,* bears directly on the point. This remarkable study in stoic endurance, with its underlying use of Christian symbolism, and its prose structure defined by the waves of the sea, is an excellent example of Hemingway's skill in joining art and nature, the truth of things and the poetry of things, a skill of which the present critical study has tried to take the measure.

The idea for the story had been in Hemingway's mind for a dozen years before he felt that he was able to undertake it in writing. On February 7, 1939, he spoke to Maxwell Perkins of two subjects by which he was then very much stirred. One was concerned with the taking of Teruel during

Hemingway's conception of the meaning of Wahrheit, artistically speaking, has not been static. In the course of the development of his art over the past thirty years, his opinions on this complex matter have steadily broadened and deepened. His earliest conviction, to which he adheres still with one side of his artistic consciousness, is well summed up in a remark of Albert Schweitzer's on the *Naturphilosophie* of Goethe: 'Only that knowledge is true which adds nothing to nature, either by thought or imagination; and which recognizes as valid only what comes from a research that is free from prejudices and preconceptions, from a firm and pure determination to find the truth, from a meditation which goes deeply into the heart of nature." [2]

As a partial summary of Hemingway's esthetic (and moral) position, Schweitzer's statement would have to be qualified only by adding "human nature" to the rest of nature. Hemingway has never, in fact, been interested in the phenomenology of the visible universe unless it could help his art to the apprehension of nature's most complex phenomenon, the human mind. A meditation which goes deeply enough into the heart of nature will often end, where it ends in Hemingway, with a meditation which goes deeply into the heart of man.

If a kind of *Naturphilosophie* stands unshaken at one end of Hemingway's moral and artistic scale of values, the other end is very well exemplified in the thought which underlies *Across the River and Into the Trees*. If that novel is read rightly, it is possible

---

the Spanish Civil War, just at this time coming to its sorry conclusion. The second was the story of an ancient mariner who lived in Casablanca on the eastern or windward side of Havana harbor where (until the area burned) commercial fishermen made their headquarters. But Hemingway did not return to this subject until after two more novels had been published and one more war had been fought.

By the end of April 1951 the story at last stood complete in first-draft typescript. Although it had been written, in Hemingway's opinion, "very cleanly," he revised it rigorously during the spring of 1952. *The Old Man and the Sea* was in galley-proof by the middle of May, and in page-proof early in the summer. Following a "one-shot" serialization in *Life* magazine for September 1, the novelette was published in book form on September 8, 1952. Hemingway's characteristic union of Dichtung and Wahrheit is nowhere better exemplified than in this newest of his stories.

[2] Schweitzer, *Goethe: Four Studies,* tr. by Charles Joy, Boston, 1949, pp. 70–71.

to infer from it a definition of "reality" which complements and completes the *Naturphilosophie.* The novel of Venice, both esthetically and philosophically speaking, understands the true nature of reality as a complex inter-action between a salt and an acid. The salt, if one accepts for the moment a chemical analogy, is what may be called an "educated illusion," very carefully purified to eliminate false and spurious elements. The acid is what it has always been in Hemingway—the facts of the matter deliberately faced, fully and courageously accepted.

The "educated illusion" is indispensable, for it is another way of describing the artistic consciousness at work upon its materials. But the facts of the matter, the outward manifestations of the Wahrheit which the artist seeks, are equally important. The facts are always in Hemingway, and they are nearly always faced. Paul Rosenfeld, writing of *In Our Time,* the first book of Hemingway's to be published in the United States, said that it managed to catch the epoch's "feeling of a harsh impersonal force in the universe, permanent, not to be changed, taking both destruction and construction up into itself, and set in motion by their dialectic." [3] It requires no stretch of the esthetic imagination to see Colonel Richard Cantwell as an embodiment of Rosenfeld's dictum. For if the destruction is represented by Cantwell's *sale métier* of warmaking, the construction is visible in his views on the nature and value of illusion. "Every day," says the Colonel's youthful countess, "is a disillusion." But the Colonel flatly denies it. "Every day," says he, "is a new and fine illusion. But you can cut out everything phony about the illusion as though you would cut it out with a straight-edge razor." The sharp cutting edge of the facts of the matter, employed with the proper dexterity and judgment, can bring the illusion into a state of health. The scars of the operation will probably show. But that is no matter. The scars are the evidence of experience, and experience, too, is indispensable. [4]

If Hemingway's mature esthetic is built upon a kind of dialectic, it is a dialectic somewhat to be preferred over the one enunciated by Hegel in his *Philosophy of Fine Art.* "The human spirit," says

---

[3] *New Republic* 45 (November 25, 1925), pp. 22–23.
[4] *ARIT,* p. 232.

Hegel, "descends from the objectivity of the object into its own private domain; it peers into its particular conscious life; it endeavours to satisfy the desire to reproduce the presence and reality of *that* . . . in the experience of heart and reflected idea, and in doing so to unfold the content and activity of the personal life rather than the actual presence of the external fact." [5]

It may be apparent, from what has already been said, how far Hemingway would accept the Hegelian doctrine. In the course of the present study, the reader will have discovered many occasions on which Hemingway has descended from "the objectivity of the object" and into the "private domain" which is the artist's habitual dwelling-place. There he reproduces the reality of the external object in the experience of his heart and in the reflected idea of his artist's mind. Where he reaches beyond Hegel is in his determination to embody the external fact as a constant corrective to the content and activity of the artist's personal life.

Its grasp of reality, its content of Wahrheit, is one guaranty of art's survival power. A second guaranty, not less important, is its use and control of Dichtung. The Dichtung in Hemingway might be provisionally defined as the artist's grasp of the relationship between the temporal and the eternal. That grasp is expressed, in his fiction, through the considered use of imaginative symbols. Most of them come, by way of the artist's imagination, from the visible eternal universe—the mountains and the plains, the rivers and the trees, the weather and the seasons, the land and the sea. To such natural images Hemingway has attached the strong emotional power of his artistic apprehension of them. At the same time, he has always managed to remain faithful to each of the natural phenomena for what, in itself, it really is. As a result of their union with imagination and emotion, the various phenomena rise up as operative symbols in all his art, not less real but more real than they are in themselves because of the way the artist has used them.

Hemingway hinted strongly at this point when he said in 1942 that the writer's "standard of fidelity to the truth should be so

---

[5] Hegel, *Philosophy of Fine Art,* tr. by F. P. B. Osmaston, London, 1920, vol. 4, p. 193.

high that his invention, out of his experience, should produce a truer account than anything factual can be." [6] The *invention* here alluded to could be described in part as that form of symbolic logic which is the artist's own equivalent to the rational logic of the philosophers. Hemingway well knows, with Niebuhr, that "the relation of time and eternity" cannot be expressed in simple rational terms, but "only in symbolic terms." [7] In some writers, the symbols are made over from antecedent literatures. In Hemingway they are derived from the nexus of nature by means of the imaginative apprehension of human experience in nature.

The conjunction of a "naturalistic" Wahrheit with the non-literary symbols of the Dichtung gives Hemingway's best work its special strength and staying power, as well as its special distinction of being the most truly "original" writing in the field of twentieth-century fiction. Alfred Kazin once remarked that "it is hard to think of Hemingway and Faulkner as naturalists, their sensibility is too wide." [8] Hemingway's poetic "sensibility" in fact carries his work far beyond the area of the simple naturalist. Yet the clear seeing and the level-headedness of the undeceivable naturalist is not finally sacrificed to the requirements of the poetic sensibility. The two powers cooperate. One is what nature gives to the artist who has the clairvoyance to recognize it and the patience to select it out from the mass of available impressions. The other is what the artist gives to nature when his sensibility is broad and deep enough to endow natural phenomena with an emotional significance which they do not in themselves possess. Either one, taken by itself, would involve a falsification of experience, a unilateral objectivity or a unilateral subjectivity in the apprehension of what we know. Goethe's title is, however, particularly apposite in that it implies both a distinction and a collaboration. It is through the reciprocal interaction of a natural Wahrheit and a natural Dichtung that Hemingway has been able to offer, as Emilio Cecchi said, "the illusion of having finally hit upon a litera-

[6] Introduction to *Men at War*, New York, 1942, p. xv.

[7] Reinhold Niebuhr, *Beyond Tragedy*, New York, 1938, p. 4.

[8] Alfred Kazin in *The American Writer and the European Tradition*, ed. by Margaret Denny and William H. Gilman, Minneapolis, Minnesota, 1950, p. 121.

ture which has nothing to do with literature, which is not spoiled or weakened by literature." [9] His two-handed grasp on the actual, with the right hand of the head and the left hand of the heart, is the chief of many reasons why his work is likely to last when that of many of his contemporaries in fiction and poetry has been forgotten.

Hemingway's best work is in a happy conspiracy with permanence. The language, the subjects, the underlying symbolic structures all belong to that area of human thought and belief which survives virtually without change from age to age. This area, this continuum, this current flowing unchanged below the surface disturbances, is the true artist's gulf stream. After his return from the green hills of Africa in 1934, he found an image for his point of view among the blue hills of Atlantica.

"When, on the sea, [he wrote] you are alone with it and know that this Gulf Stream you are living with, knowing, learning about, and loving, has moved, as it moves, since before man . . . [then] the things you find out about it, and those that have always lived in it, are permanent and of value because that stream will flow, as it has flowed, after the Indians, after the Spaniards, after the British, after the Americans and after all the Cubans and all the systems of governments, the richness, the poverty, the martyrdom, the sacrifice and the venality and the cruelty are all gone as the high-piled scow of garbage . . . spills off its load into the blue water. . . . The stream, with no visible flow, takes five loads of this a day when things are going well in La Habana and in ten miles along the coast it is as clear and blue and unimpressed as it was ever before the tug hauled out the scow; and the palm fronds of our victories, the worn light bulbs of our great discoveries and the empty condoms of our great loves float with no significance against one single, lasting thing—the stream." [10]

In all things as permanent as this blue river in the sea, the writer who means his work to last must sink his nets, cast his lines, and bring his giants to the gaff. Let the garbage go. It will disappear as all such things have always gone. But the stream will

[9] Emilio Cecchi in *Americana: Raccolta di Narratori,* ed. E. Vittorini, Milan, 1943, introd., p. xvi.
[10] *GHOA,* pp. 149–150.

last. This is the area where Hemingway, the compleat angler, has chosen to fish.

Much of Hemingway's language, like much of his imagery, belongs to the area of the permanent. One of the poets of Genesis said for the land what this modern artist said for the Gulf Stream: "While the earth remaineth, seedtime and harvest, and cold and heat, and summer and winter, and day and night shall not cease." [11] The point of the passage is not alone the images—what the Lord God Jehovah promised not to change—but it is also the language, the permanent *lingua communis* which resists change because it is the expression of those things that do not change. "Some of [Hemingway's] writing has gone bad," said Malcolm Cowley, "but surprisingly little of it." [12] At all times a living language carries a vast burden of the temporary, not only the slang of the current moment, but also faddism, technical jargon, trickery, and the cheap fashionable ornamentation that soon turns green. Under this burden, which vanishes periodically like Havana's garbage in the Gulf Stream, the elder and timeless language moves majestically along, changing very slowly where it changes at all. It is the language of seedtime and harvest, bread and wine, heat and cold, the rising-up and going-down of the sun, and the slow turn of the seasons. Hemingway has it, or at any rate enough of it to carry the content of the impermanent, the temporariness of the contemporary, which even the world's greatest artists, being also men, have been unable to avoid.

Hemingway's services to the permanent have required him to unite what Cyril Connolly once referred to as his "courageous, heart-whole emotional drive" and his "adult and lively intellectual toughness." [13] Both the heart-wholeness and the toughness have been necessary, as Hemingway has realized from the beginning. The first and final thing you have to do in this world, he once told Maxwell Perkins, is to last in it and not be smashed by it, and it is the same way with your work.[14] This is at once a rule for the conduct of life and a rule for the conduct of art: to last,

---

[11] Genesis 8:22.
[12] *The Portable Hemingway,* New York, 1944, introd., p. xxiv.
[13] Introduction, *Horizon,* vols. 93–94, October 1947.
[14] EH to MP, 4/4/32.

and to do work that will last. In line with this conviction, Hemingway has almost literally written his heart out in every major book he has published. He has taken as his ruling idea the determination never to write a false line. Naturally he has written a few; the determined seeker can find lapses of taste, failures in clear communication, instances where the emotional drive overshot esthetic distance and brought the artist too close to his material for the reader's comfort. Pity has sometimes overflowed and irony has sometimes been overplayed. Yet such instances are neither numerous nor, in the end, extremely consequential. Hemingway is very possibly our best meteorologist of emotional climates because he has retained the tough determination to correct his reports for subjective error. As a practical esthetician he has so firmly interwoven in his work the Wahrheit and the Dichtung of the world as he knows it that his art as a whole, if not in all its constituent parts, is likely to stand relatively impervious to the shifting weather of the future.

A conspicuous irony in the present age of iron is the recurrent notion that Hemingway's name belongs on the list of irresponsibles. During the course of his career this accusation has twice erupted, once in the early thirties, and again in 1950. What is meant, of course, is that Hemingway is "socially irresponsible" because he has failed to carry the banner of a particular social group, and to write his novels in terms of a particular social program. To be responsible in this sense he would have had to commit his writing to some form of didacticism, and to hope that history would bear out his interpretation of history. When an artist *as an artist* is not disposed to assume this kind of responsibility, and even goes so far as to imply that those who do are not being faithful to their duty as writers, a degree of unpopularity is probably inevitable for him. This will be true even if, as a man living in society, he does all else that is in his power (by expending money, time, and energy) to ameliorate the evil conditions which other writers may be attempting to overcome through various forms of propaganda-art.

If, on the other hand, one defines the artist's social responsibility as the presentation of the reality of man's experience, no artist of our time has been more responsible than Hemingway, both to his art itself, and to the strong foundation of esthetic and moral conviction on which that art is built. What Mr. Allen Tate has written of the poet's responsibility in our own and other time applies equally to the prose artist of Hemingway's persuasion.

"*To whom* [Mr. Tate asks] is the poet responsible? He is responsible to his *conscience,* in the French sense of the word: the joint action of knowledge and judgment. . . . No crisis, however dire, should be allowed to convince us that the relation of the poet to his permanent reality can ever change. And thus the poet is not responsible to society for a version of what it thinks it is or what it wants. *For what* is the poet responsible? He is responsible for the virtue proper to him as poet, for his special *arête:* for the mastery of a disciplined language which will not shun the full report of the reality conveyed to him by his awareness: he must hold, in Yeats' great phrase, 'reality and justice in a single thought.' " [15]

Between the truth of things and the poetry of things no necessary antagonism exists. The first thirty years of Hemingway's work amply proves and documents this point. His proper virtue as an artist consists in the willing assumption of a responsibility to hold the reality of what is knowably real in steady conjunction with the justice of what is esthetically just. What one might call his art-enlightened empiricism is, however, further strengthened and informed by the consistent operation of a kind of stoic morality. One finds implicit in all his work the half-humorous, half-bitter acceptance of what the act of living brings, though with him merely to endure is never enough. With the endurance and acceptance comes a recognition of the necessity of right action for the soul's sake, the counsel of freedom from perturbation and fear, and the constantly renewed assertion of the complete independence of the inner self.

There is also a visible though unobtrusive natural piety. If it seems non-Christian despite the grave allusions to Our Lord, this is chiefly because Hemingway has carefully refrained from taking doctrinaire sides in all his dramatizations of religious motifs. As one held back by esthetic principle from talking of what he does not know, he offers few speculations on the unknown country

[15] *Hudson Review* 4 (Autumn 1951), p. 333.

at the other side of the grave. But he is neither a moral nor a metaphysical nihilist. The consciousness of God is in his books, and the Book of Common Prayer is seldom far out of his reach. The tragic view of life comes out in his perennial contrast of the permanence of nature and the evanescence of man. But he does not repine. Here is nature and here is man. Here also is something about the nature of manhood.

A Working Check-List

A Working Check-List

Two very useful bibliographical guides to Hemingway have appeared. The first, covering his publications to 1931, is Louis H. Cohn, *A Bibliography of the Works of Ernest Hemingway,* New York, Random House, 1931. This was a limited edition, and is indispensable to serious students of Hemingway. The second is Lee Samuels, *A Hemingway Check List,* New York, Charles Scribner's Sons, 1951, with a valuable prefatory statement by Hemingway. Mr. Samuels brings the list of publications up to 1951, but does not attempt full bibliographical description, nor does he attempt to deal with the many translations into foreign languages of Hemingway's books and short stories. Besides these, there are only a few fugitive bibliographical notes on Hemingway. The following listings have been brought together for the convenience of persons interested in the dates and locations of first appearance of work by Hemingway. They are not meant to be exhaustive, but only to serve any working scholars in the field who may have use for such data. Figures following date of publication in sections I and II indicate the quantity of the first printing.

I. BOOKS

1. *Three Stories and Ten Poems.* Summer [probably July] 1923. 300 copies. Published by Robert McAlmon (Contact Publishing Company), Paris and Dijon. Contains stories: Up in Michigan, Out of Season, My Old Man. Contains poems: Mitragliatrice (P), Oklahoma, Oily Weather (P), Roosevelt (P), Captives, Champs d'Honneur (P), Riparto d'Assolto (P), Montparnasse, Along with Youth, Chapter Heading (P). Note: The six poems labelled (P) had first appearance in *Poetry: A Magazine of Verse* for January 1923. See below, section III.

2. *in our time.* Spring [probably mid-March] 1924. 170 copies. Published by William Bird (Three Mountains Press), Paris. Contains: 1. "Everybody was drunk . . ."; 2. "The first matador got the horn . . ."; 3. "Minarets stuck up in the rain . . ."; 4. "We were in a garden at Mons . . ."; 5. "It was a frightfully hot day . . ."; 6. "They shot the six . . ."; 7. "Nick sat against the wall . . ."; 8. "While the bombardment . . ."; 9. "At two o'clock in the morning . . ."; 10. "One hot evening in Milan . . ."; 11. "In 1919 he was traveling . . ."; 12. "They whack whacked the white horse . . ."; 13. "The crowd shouted all the time . . .";

14. "If it happened right down close . . ."; 15. "I heard the drums coming . . ."; 16. "Maera lay still . . ."; 17. "They hanged Sam Cardinella . . ."; 18. "The king was working. . . ."

Note: This is the uncapitalized or Paris edition of *in our time,* a 32-page book consisting entirely of the miniatures which have since formed the inter-chapters of the American editions of *In Our Time* (1925 and 1930: see below, items 3 and 8), and appear also in the collected edition, *The Fifth Column and the First Forty-nine Stories* (1938). The chapters numbered 1–6 inclusive first appeared in *The Little Review* for April 1, 1923. See below, section III.

3. *In Our Time.* October 5, 1925. 1,335 copies. Published by Boni and Liveright, New York. Contains all the miniatures from *in our time,* though in a slightly different order, together with two of the three stories from *Three Stories and Ten Poems.* Two of the *iot* miniatures have been elevated to the status of short stories (miniature chapter 10 has been titled "A Very Short Story," and miniature chapter 11 has been titled "The Revolutionist"). The untitled miniatures alternate with the titled stories. Besides those already mentioned, there are ten new stories. All but four of these had been printed previously in several of the "little magazines" and in McAlmon's *Contact* anthology (see below, section III). In the following list of contents, the arabic numerals in parentheses represent the *iot* miniatures, and the other stories are represented by their titles.

Contains: (1); Indian Camp; (3); The Doctor and the Doctor's Wife; (4); The End of Something; (5); The Three Day Blow; (6); The Battler; (7); A Very Short Story; (8); Soldier's Home; (9); The Revolutionist; (2); Mr. and Mrs. Elliot; (12); Cat in the Rain; (13); Out of Season; (14); Cross Country Snow; (15); My Old Man; (16); Big Two-Hearted River, Part One; (17); Big Two-Hearted River, Part Two; (18). The stories which appear in this volume for the first time are The End of Something, The Three Day Blow, The Battler, and Cat in the Rain. The order of miniatures and stories followed in this edition was continued in the two later editions.

4. *The Torrents of Spring.* May 28, 1926. 1,250 copies. Published by Charles Scribner's Sons, New York. Note: With this book Hemingway began his long association with Scribner's. Six years later the book was reprinted in Crosby Continental Editions, Paris, 1932. See Caresse Crosby's interesting prefatory epistle.

5. *The Sun Also Rises.* October 22, 1926. 5,090 copies. Published by Scribner's. Note: This was the novel which caused Scribner's to agree to publish *The Torrents of Spring,* which the firm undertook, as Perkins said, "with some misgivings." In a letter to

Perkins dated 4/24/26, Hemingway refers to *SAR* as "the pig that you bought in a poke."

6. *Men Without Women.* October 14, 1927. 7,650 copies. Published, like the rest of Hemingway's work, by Scribner's. Note: By this date Hemingway's reputation as a writer was fairly firmly established. In a letter to Perkins dated 10/1/27, he pointed out that he now had 2 British, 1 Danish, 1 Swedish, 1 French, and 1 German publisher. It is also interesting to recall that in a letter to Perkins of 2/3/30 Hemingway recorded that motion picture interests had paid him $500 for the title, *Men Without Women.* They wanted it to tack on to a picture about men in a disabled submarine, which of course had nothing to do with the contents of Hemingway's short story collection. The order of the stories in *Men Without Women* was the same as that followed in the collected edition of 1938, pp. 331–469. The hitherto unpublished stories in *MWW* were: A Simple Enquiry, Ten Indians, A Pursuit Race, Now I Lay Me. The other ten had appeared before. See below, section III.

7. *A Farewell to Arms.* September 27, 1929. 31,000 copies. Scribner's. Note: This book was Hemingway's first conspicuous success in terms of sales. By 2/14/30, roughly four months after publication, sales stood at 79,251, an average of about 20,000 copies a month.

8. *In Our Time.* October 24, 1930. 3,000 copies. Scribner's. Note: This is a Scribner re-issue of the Boni and Liveright edition of 1925, from which it differs in several particulars, chiefly a new "introduction" by Hemingway, consisting of a miniature later entitled "On the Quai at Smyrna" (see *First 49,* pp. 185–186), and a specially prepared critical essay by Edmund Wilson. For data on minutiae in this connection see Cohn's bibliography, pp. 39–40.

9. *Death in the Afternoon.* September 23, 1932. 10,300 copies. Scribner's. Note: Besides the account of bullfighting, this handbook is diversified with a few short stories, mostly not otherwise "collected." The exception is "A Natural History of the Dead," which was included as a separate story in the *First 49* (1938).

10. *Winner Take Nothing.* October 27, 1933. 20,300 copies. Scribner's. Note: This collection of short stories follows the same order as those on pp. 470–597 of the *First 49.* This was the first appearance of six of the fourteen stories: The Light of the World, A Way You'll Never Be, The Mother of a Queen, One Reader Writes, A Day's Wait, Fathers and Sons. It may also be noted that The Gambler, The Nun, and The Radio was a new title; the story when it first appeared in *Scribner's Magazine* for April, 1933, had been called by the much less apt title: Give Us a Prescription, Doctor.

11. *The Green Hills of Africa.* October 25, 1935. 10,550 copies. Scribner's. Note: Despite serialization in *Scribner's Magazine,* this book went less well than had been anticipated. Perkins wrote Hemingway 2/27/36 that the public had chosen to take *GHOA* as an "interlude." Another factor, which likewise had worked against *DIA* three years earlier, was the Depression.

12. *To Have and Have Not.* October 15, 1937. 10,130 copies. Scribner's. Note: Two of the three stories of Harry Morgan had already appeared as short stories: One Trip Across in *Cosmopolitan* for April 1934 (cf. *THAHN,* pp. 3–64); and The Tradesman's Return in *Esquire* for February 1936 (cf. *THAHN,* pp. 67–87).

13. *The Spanish Earth.* June 15, 1938. 1,000 copies. J. B. Savage Company, Cleveland, Ohio. Note: This book consists of a transcript of the spoken commentary prepared by Hemingway for the Loyalist film of the same title, together with a reprint of the autobiographical essay, "The Heat and the Cold," from the magazine *Verve.* For further information on this book see the footnote on *The Spanish Earth* in the tenth chapter of the present volume.

14. *The Fifth Column and the First Forty-nine Stories.* October 14, 1938. 5,350 copies. Scribner's. Note: This is the collected edition of the short stories, and comprises the contents of *IOT, MWW,* and *WTN.* This is the first printing of the play, and there are four hitherto uncollected stories: The Capital of the World, Old Man at the Bridge, The Short Happy Life of Francis Macomber, The Snows of Kilimanjaro. These had all, however, been printed before in magazines. The Capital of the World is a new title, replacing the title, The Horns of the Bull, which the story had when it first appeared in *Esquire* for June 1936. Old Man at the Bridge, originally a news despatch, had appeared in *Ken* in May 1938.

15. *The Fifth Column.* June 3, 1940. 1,174 copies. Scribner's. Note: This is a separate edition of the play. It was apparently brought out in connection with the production of the play on Broadway in this year.

16. *For Whom the Bell Tolls.* October 21, 1940. 75,000 copies. Scribner's. Note: This was Hemingway's most successful book. By December 28, about nine weeks after publication, sales stood at 189,000 copies. By April 4, 1941, sales had risen to 491,000 copies, and some 565,000 copies were in print.

17. *For Whom the Bell Tolls.* October 1942. 1,500 copies. Printed by Princeton University Press for the Limited Editions Club of New York. Contains a prefatory appreciation by Sinclair Lewis, and decorations by Lynd Ward.

18. *Men at War.* October 22, 1942. Crown Publishers, New York. Edited and with an introduction by Hemingway. Contains the

Caporetto retreat sequence from *FTA* and the El Sordo hilltop episode from *FWBT,* as well as "The Chauffeurs of Madrid," originally an NANA despatch.

19. *A Farewell to Arms.* November 15, 1948. 5,300 copies. Scribner's. Note: This is a new illustrated edition, with a specially prepared short introduction by Hemingway.

20. *Across the River and Into the Trees.* September 7, 1950. 75,000 copies. Scribner's.

21. *The Old Man and the Sea.* September 8, 1952. Scribner's. Note: This long short story first appeared in *Life* for September 1, 1952. It was a dual choice of the Book-of-the-Month Club for September.

II. PAMPHLETS

1. *Today Is Friday.* Summer [probably July] 1926. 300 copies. The As Stable Pamphlets, Englewood, New Jersey. Hemingway's first "play" appeared in *MWW* (and in the *First 49*) as a story.

2. *God Rest You Merry Gentlemen.* 1933. 300 copies. The House of Books, Limited, New York. Note: This is a special limited edition of a short story which was evidently based on Hemingway's experiences as a cub reporter for the *Kansas City Star* in 1917.

III. WORK WHICH FIRST APPEARED IN PERIODICALS OR ANTHOLOGIES

This section includes short stories (ss), poems (p), articles (a), letters (l), and despatches (d). Initials following a number of the entries indicate the book in which the stories were first collected. It should be noted that those stories which first appeared in the various collections are not included here. For a listing of these, see section I, items 2, 3, 6, 8, and 10. Abbreviations used here follow the custom of the present volume: *iot* (*in our time,* Paris, 1924); *IOT* (*In Our Time,* New York, 1925); *MWW* (*Men Without Women*); *WTN* (*Winner Take Nothing*); and *First 49* (*The Fifth Column and the First Forty-nine Stories*).

American Caravan: A Yearbook of American Literature, ed. Van Wyck Brooks, New York, September 1927. Contains (ss) "An Alpine Idyll," pp. 46–51. *MWW.*

Atlantic Monthly:
ss Fifty Grand. Vol. 140, July 1927, pp. 1–15. *MWW.*

The Boulevardier (Paris):
a The Real Spaniard. Vol. 1, October 1927, p. 6.

Collier's:
D Voyage to Victory. Vol. 114, July 22, 1944, pp. 11–13.
D London Fights the Robots. Vol. 114, August 19, 1944, p. 17.
D Battle for Paris. Vol. 114, September 30, 1944, p. 11.
D How We Came to Paris. Vol. 114, October 7, 1944, p. 14.
D The G.I. and the General. Vol. 114, November 4, 1944, p. 11.
D War in the Siegfried Line. Vol. 114, November 18, 1944, p. 18.

Contact Collection of Contemporary Writers, published Paris, 1925.
Contains (ss) "Soldier's Home," pp. 77–86. *IOT.*

Cosmopolitan:
ss After the Storm. Vol. 92, May 1932, pp. 38–41, 155. *WTN.*
ss One Trip Across. Vol. 96, April 1934, pp. 20–23, 108ff. (The
   first section of *THAHN.*)
ss The Short Happy Life of Francis Macomber. Vol. 101, September 1936, pp. 30–33, 166–172. *First 49.*
ss Nobody Ever Dies. Vol. 106, March 1939, pp. 29–31, 74–76.
ss Under the Ridge. Vol. 107, October 1939, pp. 34–35, 102–106.
   (This story turns on the Spanish hatred of foreign interlopers,
   a point very well underlined in *FWBT.*)

Double Dealer (New Orleans):
FABLE A Divine Gesture. Vol. 3, May 1922, pp. 267–268.
P Ultimately. Vol. 3, June 1922, p. 337.

Esquire (This listing prepared by Mr. Stephen Parker):
L Marlin off the Morro. Vol. 1, Autumn 1933, pp. 8, 39, 97.
L The Friend of Spain. Vol. 1, January 1934, pp. 26, 136.
L A Paris Letter. Vol. 1, February 1934, pp. 22, 156.
L a.d. in Africa. Vol. 1, April 1934, pp. 19, 146.
L Shootism vs. Sport. Vol. 2, June 1934, pp. 19, 150.
L Notes on Dangerous Game. Vol. 2, July 1934, pp. 19, 94.
L Out in the Stream. Vol. 2, August 1934, pp. 19, 156, 158.
L Defense of Dirty Words. Vol. 2, September 1934, pp. 19, 158B,
   158D.
L Genio after Josie. Vol. 2, October 1934, pp. 21–22.
L Old Newsman Writes. Vol. 2, December 1934, pp. 25–26.
L Notes on Life and Letters. Vol. 3, January 1935, pp. 21, 159.
L Remembering Shooting Flying. Vol. 3, February 1935, pp. 21,
   152.
L Sailfish off Mombasa. Vol. 3, March 1935, pp. 21, 156.
L The Sights of Whitehead Street. Vol. 3, April 1935, pp. 25, 156.
L a.d. Southern Style. Vol. 3, May 1935, pp. 25, 156.
L On Being Shot Again. Vol. 3, June 1935, pp. 25, 156.
L The President Vanquishes. Vol. 3, July 1935, pp. 23, 167.

L He Who Gets Slap Happy. Vol. 4, August 1935, pp. 19, 182.

L Notes on the Next War. Vol. 4, September 1935, pp. 19, 156.

L Monologue to the Maestro. Vol. 4, October 1935, pp. 21, 174A, 174B.

L The Malady of Power. Vol. 4, November 1935, pp. 31, 198.

L Million Dollar Fright. Vol. 4, December 1935, pp. 35, 190B.

L Wings Always Over Africa. Vol. 5, January 1936, pp. 31, 174–175.

SS The Tradesman's Return. Vol. 5, February 1936, pp. 27, 193–196. (The second section of *THAHN*.)

L On the Blue Water. Vol. 5, April 1936, pp. 31, 184–185.

L There She Breaches. Vol. 5, May 1936, pp. 35, 203–205.

SS The Horns of the Bull. Vol. 5, June 1936, pp. 31, 190–193. (*First 49,* where it was retitled: The Capital of the World.)

SS The Snows of Kilimanjaro. Vol. 6, August 1936, pp. 27, 194–201. *First 49.*

SS The Denunciation. Vol. 10, November 1938, pp. 39, 111–114.

SS The Butterfly and the Tank. Vol. 10, December 1938, pp. 51, 186, 188, 190.

SS Night Before Battle. Vol. 11, February 1939, pp. 27–29, 91–92, 95, 97.

Exile:

P Nothoemist Poem. (Misprint for *Neothomist Poem.*) Vol. 1, Spring 1927.

Fact:

D Hemingway on the Spanish War, March 23, 1937, to May 9, 1938. Published July 15, 1938.

Fortune:

A Bullfighting, Sport and Industry. Vol. 1, March 1930, pp. 83ff.

Free World:

A The Sling and the Pebble. Vol. 11, March 1946, pp. 16–17.

Holiday:

A The Great Blue River. Vol. 6, July 1949, pp. 60ff.

FABLE The Good Lion. Vol. 9, March 1951, pp. 50–51.

FABLE The Faithful Bull. Vol. 9, March 1951, p. 51.

Ken:

A The Time Now, the Place Spain. April 7, 1938.

A Dying, Well or Badly. April 21, 1938.

A The Cardinal Picks a Winner. May 5, 1938.

SS Old Man at the Bridge. May 12, 1938. *First 49.*

A United We Fall upon Ken. June 2, 1938.

A H.M.'s Loyal State Department. June 16, 1938.

A Treachery in Aragon. June 30, 1938.

A Call for Greatness. July 14, 1938.
A My Pal the Gorilla Gargantua. July 28, 1938.
A A Program for U.S. Realism. August 11, 1938.
A Good Generals Hug the Line. August 25, 1938.
A False News to the President. September 8, 1938.
A Fresh Air on an Inside Story. September 22, 1938.
A The Next Outbreak of Peace. January 12, 1939.

Life:
ss The Old Man and the Sea. September 1, 1952.

Little Review:
ss [Six miniatures]. Vol. 9, Spring 1923, pp. 3–5. *iot,* chapters 1–6.
P They All Want Peace. What Is Peace? Vol. 9, Spring 1923, pp. 20–21.
ss Mr. and Mrs. Elliot. Vol. 10, Autumn and Winter 1924–1925, pp. 9–12. *IOT.*
ss Banal Story. Vol. 12, Spring–Summer 1926, pp. 22–23. *MWW.*
P Valentine. Vol. 12, May 1929, p. 42. There is a short covering letter on p. 41.

New Masses:
A Who Murdered the Vets? Vol. 16, September 17, 1935, p. 9.
A On the American Dead in Spain. Vol. 30, February 14, 1939, p. 3.

New Republic:
ss Italy, 1927. Vol. 50, May 18, 1927, pp. 350–353. *MWW,* with the new title, "Che Ti Dice La Patria."
D Hemingway Reports Spain. Vols. 90, May 5, 1937, pp. 376–379; 93, January 12, 1938, pp. 273–276; 94, April 27, 1938, pp. 350–351; and 95, June 8, 1938, pp. 124–126.

New Yorker:
A My Own Life. Vol. 2, February 12, 1927, pp. 23–24.

Poetry: A Magazine of Verse:
P Wanderings [general title for 6 poems]. Vol. 21, January 1923, pp. 193–195. Note: the poem, "They All Want Peace. What Is Peace?" was reprinted in the course of an article in *Poetry,* vol. 37, February 1931. It had originally appeared in *The Little Review* for April 1923.

Querschnitt:
P The Soul of Spain with McAlmon and Bird the Publishers, Part I. Vol. 4, Autumn 1924, pp. 229–230.
P The Earnest Liberal's Lament. Vol. 4, Autumn 1924, p. 231.
P The Soul of Spain with McAlmon and Bird the Publishers, Parts

II–VI. Vol. 4, November 1924, p. 278. Note: Part VI is a miniature on the death of a bull.

P The Lady Poets with Foot Notes. Vol. 4, November 1924, p. 317.

P The Age Demanded. Vol. 5, February 1925, p. 111.

ss The Undefeated. Published in two parts, Vol. 5, Summer 1925 and July 1925, and here entitled "Stierkampf." Appeared also as "L'Invincible" in *Le Navire d'Argent* for March 1926, pp. 624–633. For English version, see below under *This Quarter*.

ss The Man with the Tyrolese Hat. Vol. 16, June 1936, pp. 355–356. Note: This is the extract about Kandisky from *GHOA*.

Scribner's Magazine:

ss The Killers. Vol. 81, March 1927, pp. 227–233. *MWW*.

ss In Another Country. Vol. 81, April 1927, pp. 355–357. *MWW*.

ss A Canary for One. Vol. 81, April 1927, pp. 357–360. *MWW*.

ss Wine of Wyoming. Vol. 88, August 1930, pp. 195–204. *WTN*.

ss A Clean Well-lighted Place. Vol. 93, March 1933, pp. 149–150. *WTN*.

ss Homage to Switzerland. Vol. 93, April 1933, pp. 204–208. *WTN*.

ss Give Us a Prescription, Doctor. Vol. 93, April 1933, pp. 272–278. Note: Retitled in *WTN:* The Gambler, The Nun, and the Radio.

This Quarter:

ss Big Two-Hearted River. Vol. 1, May 1925, pp. 110–128. *IOT*.

A Homage to Ezra [Pound]. Vol. 1, May 1925, pp. 221–225.

ss The Undefeated. Vol. 1, Autumn–Winter 1925–26, pp. 203–232. *MWW*.

ss The Sea Change. Vol. 4, December 1931, pp. 247–251. *WTN*.

transatlantic review:

ss Work in Progress. Vol. 1, April 1924, pp. 230–234. Note: Entitled in *IOT:* Indian Camp.

L And to the United States. The Quarter. Early Spring. Vol. 1, May–June 1924, pp. 355–357. Note: Hemingway here comments that "Dada is dead" and refers to the boxer Criqui (p. 356) "in the contemplation of whose work I experience a certain ecstasy which is not given me by reading the works of my contemporaries."

A And Out of America. Vol. 2, August 1924, pp. 102–103.

L Pamplona Letter. Vol. 2, October 1924, pp. 300–302.

A Conrad. Vol. 2, October 1924, pp. 341–342.

ss The Doctor and the Doctor's Wife. Vol. 2, December 1924, pp. 497–501. *IOT*.

ss Cross Country Snow. Vol. 2, January 1925, pp. 633–638. *IOT*.

transition:

ss Hills Like White Elephants. Vol. 5, August 1927, pp. 9–14. *MWW*.

Verve:

A The Heat and the Cold. Vol. 1, Spring 1938, p. 46. Note: This issue covered the period March–June, and appeared in June. The essay was almost immediately reprinted in the published version of *The Spanish Earth*. Section I, item 13.

Vogue:

A The Clark's Fork Valley, Wyoming. Vol. 93, February 1939, pp. 68, 157.

IV. INTRODUCTIONS, PREFACES, FOREWORDS, CONTRIBUTIONS

Jerome Bahr, *All Good Americans*. New York, 1937. Preface by Hemingway.

James Charters, *This Must Be the Place*. London, 1934. Introduction by Hemingway.

S. K. Farrington, Jr., *Atlantic Game Fishing*. New York, 1939. Introduction by Hemingway.

John Groth, *Studio Europe*. New York, 1945. Introduction by Hemingway.

Henry Hart, ed., *The Writer in a Changing World*. New York, 1937. Contains Hemingway's speech to the Writers' Congress.

Joseph North, *Men in the Ranks*. New York, March 1939. Foreword by Hemingway.

Samuel Putnam, translator, *Kiki's Memoirs*. Paris, 1930. Preface by Hemingway. For interesting bibliographical data see Cohn's Bibliography.

Luis Quintanilla (in collaboration with Elliot Paul and Jay Allen), *All the Brave*. New York, 1939. Preface by Hemingway.

Ben Raeburn, ed., *Treasury for the Free World*. New York, February 1946. Foreword by Hemingway.

Gustav Regler, *The Great Crusade*. New York, 1940. Preface by Hemingway.

Lee Samuels, *A Hemingway Check List*. New York, August 1951. Preface by Hemingway.

Elio Vittorini, *In Sicily*. New York, 1949. Introduction by Hemingway.

V. OBSERVATIONS ON ART AND ARTISTS

Gattorno. Havana, Cuba, April 1935. This publication includes a valuable commentary on the work of Gattorno by Hemingway (pp. 11–

16). The article was later reprinted in *Esquire* 5 (May 1936), pp. 111, 141.

Joan Miro. New York, 1934. Leaflet containing first printing of part of an article on Miro which later appeared in *Cahiers d'Art.*

Waldo Peirce. For some humorous observations by Hemingway on his good friend Peirce, see Harry Salpeter, "Rabelais in a Smock," *Esquire,* Vol. 5, July 1936, pp. 101, 118, 121–122.

Quintanilla. Pierre Matisse Gallery Catalogue, *Exhibition of Drawings and Paintings by Luis Quintanilla.* New York, November 20 to December 4, 1934. Contains appraisal of Quintanilla's work by Hemingway. The article was later reprinted in *Esquire,* Vol. 3, February 1935, pp. 26–27.

See also *Quintanilla: An Exhibition of Drawings of the War in Spain.* Museum of Modern Art, New York, March 1938. Contains a preface by Hemingway.

VI. DESPATCHES FROM THE FAR EAST

The Newspaper *PM.* Between June 10 and June 18, 1941, this newspaper printed six despatches from Hemingway on the situation in the Far East as of six to seven months before Pearl Harbor.

VII. CONTRIBUTIONS TO THE *TORONTO STAR WEEKLY*

The following listing was generously prepared for the author by W. L. McGeary, book editor of the *Toronto Star,* who also, through the kind intercession of the managing editor, provided photostats of certain items. Hemingway has always distinguished sharply between journalism and serious writing, and the following items, though generally of high journalistic calibre, are still journalism. On this point, see Hemingway's opinion as recorded by Captain Cohn in his bibliography, p. 112. The "titles" below are picked up from key words in the headlines.

Circulating library of pictures. February 14, 1920, magazine section, folio 7, unsigned.

Free shaves in Toronto barbers' college. March 6, 1920, magazine, folio 13.

Mayor Church at boxing bouts. March 13, 1920. News section feature page.

Store thieves. April 3, 1920, magazine front.

Tooth-pulling. April 10, 1920, feature page.

Trout season. April 10, 1920, feature page.

Wedding gifts. December 17, 1921, magazine, folio 15. Contains a free-verse poem by Hemingway.

Swiss tourist resorts. February 4, 1922, news section weekly.

Tuna-fishing at Vigo, Spain. February 18, 1922, magazine, folio 15.

Swiss hotels. March 4, 1922, magazine front.

Papal election. March 4, 1922, news section weekly, folio 3.

Majorca. March 11, 1922, news section weekly, folio 13.

Swiss luge. March 18, 1922, magazine, folio 15.

Maran's Goncourt Prize. March 25, 1922, news section weekly, folio 3.

American bohemians in Paris. March 25, 1922, magazine, folio 15.

French politeness. April 25, 1922, magazine front page, second section.

Paris drug scandal. August 12, 1922, news section weekly, folio 11.

European kings. September 15, 1923, magazine front.

Lloyd George. October 6, 1923, news section weekly front page.

Lloyd George in New York. October 6, 1923, news section weekly folio 2.

Bullfights not sport but tragedy. October 20, 1923, magazine front page second section.

Bullfight World Series. October 27, 1923, magazine front page second section.

Shooting game in Europe and Ontario. November 3, 1923, magazine second section, folio 20.

European trout-fishing. November 17, 1923, magazine, folio 11.

General Wolfe's diaries. November 24, 1923, magazine second section, folio 19.

Bank vaults. December 1, 1923, magazine front page second section.

German marks in Toronto. December 8, 1923, magazine, folio 8. Uses byline of John Hadley, name of his son, born in Toronto, October 1923.

War medals. December 8, 1923, magazine second section, folio 21.

Night-life in Europe and Near East. December 15, 1923, magazine second section, folio 21.

Medicated water-supply. December 15, 1923, magazine front page second section.

Christmas in Alps, Milan, Paris. December 22, 1923, magazine, folio 19.

Modern amateur impostors. December 29, 1923, magazine folio 20. One irony here is that Hemingway was later (in the 1930's) to be victimized by one himself.

Betting in Toronto. December 29, 1923, magazine front page.

New Year's Parties. December 29, 1923, magazine, folio 20. Uses John Hadley byline.

Alpine avalanches. January 12, 1924, magazine, folio 20.

Hats in Toronto. January 19, 1924, magazine front page second section.

Chicago visit. January 19, 1924, magazine, folio 19.

Amateur bullfight in Spain. September 13, 1924, magazine feature page.

Index

HEMINGWAY, ERNEST (*cont.*)
Wanderings (summary title for collection in *Poetry: A Magazine of Verse*): 13n, 306
Wedding Gift: 309

FICTIONAL PERSONS

Adams, Helen: 133
Adams, Dr. Henry (father of Nick): 129, 131, 134, 256
Adams, Nick: education of, 127-131; allusions to, 24, 36, 121, 133-134, 136, 254, 256-257, 282-283
Agustín (*FWBT*): 244, 249
Al (in "The Killers"): 122-123
Alice (in "The Light of the World"): 140
Alvarito, The Barone (*ARIT*): 269, 276
Andreson, Ole (in "The Killers"): 122-123
Anselmo (*FWBT*): 133, 243-244, 255
Arnaldo (*ARIT*): 269
Ashley, Lady Brett (*SAR*): 52, 78, 81-93 passim, 110-114, 158, 203, 253
Barkley, Catherine (*FTA*): 98-116 passim; 185, 203, 256-257
Barnes, Jake (*SAR*): 29, 41, 50, 52, 77, 81-93 passim, 114, 132-133, 155-158, 203, 254
Beelips (*THAHN*): 221
Berrendo, Lieutenant (*FWBT*): 254
Braddocks, Mr. and Mrs. (*SAR*): 78
Bradley, Helene (*THAHN*): 213
Brennan, Jack (in "Fifty Grand"): 122
Bridges, Dorothy (*Fifth Column*): 235, 256
Campbell, Mike (*SAR*): 78, 81-83, 190
Campbell, William (in "A Pursuit Race"): 123, 132
Cantwell, Col. Richard (*ARIT*): 3n, 50, 77, 98, 132-133, 154-155, 254, 266-288 passim, 291
Charo (*GHOA*): 172
Coates, Liz (in "Up in Michigan"): 135
Cohn, Robert (*SAR*): 78, 81-93 passim, 114-115, 190
Droopy (*GHOA*): 173
Duval (*FWBT*): 252n

Eddy the "rummy" (*THAHN*): 221
El Sordo (*FWBT*): 50, 242, 245, 253-254, 282
Emilio (*THAHN*): 211
Fernando (*FWBT*): 249
Freddy the bar proprietor (*THAHN*): 216
Garcia, Mayor Don Benito (*FWBT*): 261
Garcia, Manolo (in "The Undefeated"): 122
"Garrick, David" (*GHOA*): 173
Gilmore, Jim (in "Up in Michigan"): 135
Golz, General (*FWBT*): 246, 252, 252n
Gomez (*FWBT*): 182, 204, 210
Gordon, Richard (*THAHN*): 204, 210ff. passim
Gorton, Bill (*SAR*): 29, 50-52, 78, 81-93 passim, 114, 132-133
Gran Maestro (*ARIT*): 133, 269, 271
Greffi, Count (*FTA*): 115
Harrison, Frederick (*THAHN*): 211, 213-214, 217
Harry (in "The Snows of Kilimanjaro"): 187, 191-196 passim, 254, 276
Henry, Lieutenant Frederick (*FTA*): 3n, 98-116 passim, 132, 155, 181, 185, 203, 254, 257
Joaquín (*FWBT*): 242, 260
Johnson, Mr. (in "Homage to Switzerland"): 138-139
Johnson, Yogi (*Torrents of Spring*): 39-40
Jordan, Robert (*FWBT*): 113n, 133, 147, 155, 159, 222, 241-262 passim, 275
Julian (in "The Snows of Kilimanjaro"): 208
Julian (*The Spanish Earth*): 230n
Kamau (*GHOA*): 173
Kandisky (*GHOA*): 31, 118n, 163, 172, 174, 176, 177-178, 180, 307
Karl (*GHOA*): 171-172
Ketchel, Steve (in "The Light of the World"): 140
Krebs, Harold (in "Soldier's Home"): 130, 132
La Pasionaria (*FWBT*): 242-243
Macomber, Francis (in "The Short Happy Life of Francis Macomber"): 187-191, 213